Advance praise for *The Sociology of Social Change*

'In the tradition of Pitirim Sorokin and Robert Nisbet, Piotr Sztompka has written a sweeping, knowledgeable, reflective survey of general ideas about social change from the 19th century to the present. The ideas emphatically include his own provocative synthesis of general models and historical sociology.' *Charles Tilly, New School for Social Research, USA*

'Sztompka has carried out his task heroically and with conspicuous success. This book is the most comprehensive study now available of specifically sociological theories of social change. It is difficult to think of anything he has left out. It will not only be a boon to the senior undergraduates and postgraduates for whom it has been written, but should stimulate sociologists at all levels of the subject.' *Krishan Kumar, University of Kent at Canterbury, UK*

'The most important synthetic survey of social science approaches to social change that has appeared in 25 years. This volume provides a benchmark for theoretical thinking about social change as well as a vital resource for teaching on this much talked about but often badly understood topic.' *Jeff Alexander, UCLA, USA*

'This is an extremely important book on social change. It covers a very wide range of the diverse works which comprise this field – from the beginning of sociology to the contemporary scene. It will be an indispensable book for students, scholars and members of the informed public.' *S. M. Eisenstadt, The Hebrew University of Jerusalem, Israel*

'While providing an outstanding analysis, both historical and critical, of a tremendous amount of theoretical perspectives connected with social change, Sztompka also establishes new foundations for interpreting the transformation processes of contemporary society. There is no doubt that Sztompka's work will be, from now on, a necessary reference for scholars and students dealing with theoretical problems of sociology, political sciences and economics, as well as with empirical research in the same fields.' *Franco Crespi, University of Perugia, Italy*

'I can think of no sociologist with more scope and sense of balance than Piotr Sztompka. *The Sociology of Social Change* gives remarkable evidence of both qualities. It covers the field thoroughly and well; it has to be the authoritative treatment of the subject. Moreover, it balances breadth and depth, objective reporting with critical interpretation, and others' ideas with Sztompka's own.

This volume is simultaneously an original and synthetic contribution to our thinking about social change.' *Neil J. Smelser, University of California, Berkeley, USA*

'Piotr Sztompka's book on social change is at once a masterful textbook, a comprehensive encyclopedia of theoretical approaches and an innovative contribution to the field. Between the Scylla of postmodern scepticism towards progress and the Charybdis of a mere revival of modernization theory, Sztompka finds a way out. His theory is based on a realistic notion of agency, history-making and the contingency of historical events. This book by the prominent Polish sociologist will certainly change sociologists' and historians' view on social change.' *Hans Joas, Free University of Berlin, Germany*

The Sociology of Social Change

Piotr Sztompka

BLACKWELL
Oxford UK & Cambridge USA

Copyright © Piotr Sztompka 1993

The right of Piotr Sztompka to be identified as author of this work has been asserted in accordance with the Copyright, Designs and Patents Act 1988.

First published 1993

First published in USA 1994

Blackwell Publishers
108 Cowley Road
Oxford OX4 1JF
UK

238 Main Street
Cambridge, Massachusetts 02142
USA

British Library Cataloguing in Publication Data

A CIP catalogue record for this book is available from the British Library.

Library of Congress Cataloging-in-Publication Data

Sztompka, Piotr.
    The sociology of social change / Piotr Sztompka.
        p.   cm.
    Includes bibliographical references and index.
    ISBN 0-631-18205-5 (alk. paper). — ISBN 0-631-18206-3 (pbk. : alk. paper)
    1. Social change.   2. Social movements.   3. Sociology—Philosophy.
    I. Title.
    HM101.S9893 1994
    303.4—dc20   93-9824
                                                                            CIP

Typeset in 10½ on 12 pt Garamond by Graphicraft Typesetters Ltd, Hong Kong.

Printed in Great Britain by Hartnolls Ltd, Bodmin, Cornwall

This book is printed on acid-free paper

To my mother

Contents

List of figures

List of tables

Preface

The study of social change is at the very core of sociology. Perhaps all sociology is about change. 'Change is such an evident feature of social reality that any social-scientific theory, whatever its conceptual starting point, must sooner or later address it' (Haferkamp and Smelser 1992a: 1).

This has been true from the origins of sociology. The subject was born in the nineteenth century as an attempt to comprehend the fundamental transition from traditional to modern society, the rise of the urban, industrial, capitalist order. Now, at the close of the twentieth century, we are in the midst of an equally radical transition – from triumphant modernity, gradually spanning the whole globe, to new emerging forms of social life, still nebulous enough to warrant the vague label of 'post-modernity'. The need to understand ongoing social change is again acutely perceived by ordinary people and sociologists alike. It was already clear in the 1970s that 'the most striking feature of contemporary life is the revolutionary pace of social change. Never before have things changed so fast for so much of mankind. Everything is affected: art, science, religion, morality, education, politics, the economy, family life, even the inner aspects of our lives – nothing has escaped' (Lenski and Lenski 1974: 3). It is even more obvious as we move closer to the end of the twentieth century. As it has been put by an insightful observer of the contemporary scene,

> We live today in an era of stunning social change, marked by transformations radically discrepant from those of previous periods. The collapse of Soviet-style socialism, the waning of the bi-polar global distribution of power, the formation of intensified global communication systems, the apparent world-wide triumph of capitalism at a time at which global divisions are becoming acute and ecological problems looming more and more large – all these and other issues confront social science and have to be confronted by social science. (*Giddens 1991: xv*)

The purpose of this book is to take stock of the basic intellectual tools for the analysis, interpretation and understanding of social change, particularly on a macro-sociological or historical scale. Such tools can be searched for in three distinct domains. (1) In common sense, where people have certainly entertained loose ideas, notions and images about social change from the moment they began to think about their own lives. (2) In social and political philosophy, which raised common-sense reflection to the level of an autonomous, specialized, rational pursuit producing complex categories, visions and doctrines. (3) In the social sciences proper, history, economics, political science, social anthropology, sociology, which began to apply methodical, critical, fact-oriented scrutiny to the changing social reality, attaining more rigorous and empirically founded concepts, models and theories. We shall be exclusively concerned with scientific approaches to social change, and even more restrictively, mostly with those proposed within the discipline of sociology. Hence the title *The Sociology of Social Change.*

For almost two centuries sociology has amassed a considerable wealth of concepts, models and theories dealing with social change, all that time sociological approaches to social change have themselves been changing. What parts of that rich heritage should be included in our proposed systematic inventory? Should we focus exclusively on the most recent or most fashionable trends, forgetting all that went before? The answer is an emphatic No. One of the most precious pieces of sociological wisdom is the principle of historism. It says that in order to understand any contemporary phenomenon, we must look back to its origins and the processes that brought it about. The same applies to the realm of ideas; it is impossible to understand contemporary views on social change without recognizing which earlier conceptions they intend to elaborate, and which earlier theories they stand against. We shall follow this principle.

But that does not mean that our goal is an exercise in detailed intellectual genealogy, tracing links, colligations and sequences of all the theories of change that have been proposed since the birth of sociology. It is not a project in the history of ideas, but in systematic sociologal analysis. Hence, with the benefit of hindsight we can afford to be selective, ignoring those conceptions or even whole 'schools' which have proved to be sterile, leading up blind alleys of intellectual development. Instead we shall focus only on those which are still alive and influential. We shall also be systematic rather than chronological in the exposition; less concerned with dating than with logic. And we shall adopt the perspective of a contemporary observer of social change, seeking enlightenment whatever its source and ready to try ideas of every sort from the rich and varied sociological heritage.

As befits a book addressed (although not exclusively) to students, I shall try to be as detached and non-partisan as possible, giving fairly what is due to each of the theories presented. But of course I have beliefs of my own: for example I happen to believe that there is a clear direction in the changes of the theories of change, which evolve away from mechanistic developmental schemes claiming inevitability, necessity and irreversibility for social processes, and towards an emphasis on human agency, the contingency of events and openness of the future. The logic of this intellectual evolution is reflected in the dramaturgy of the book, which starts with classical developmental approaches and leads up to the exposition of the 'theory of social becoming', as both the outcome of earlier theoretical debates and arguably a more adequate approach to current social change. Thus in the course of the exposition I shall try to be 'cold' and objective, but at the conclusion my cards will be put on the table. There is no way to hide it: this is a book with a message and a bias. The author's own point of view will not be kept secret, but rather unravelled openly for scrutiny and critical debate.

For the most part, the book will try to present, elucidate and explicate sociological theories about change. The argument will remain mostly at the level of conceptions and visions. Concrete historical facts will be invoked only in so far as they provide illustrations of specific concepts, models and theories of social change. Hence the reader will be able to learn only indirectly about contemporary or past societies, to find out the facts and data. Our purpose is not to relate what is or was happening, where the social world is moving and how, but rather to provide the lenses through which one can see for oneself, sharper and farther. Or to put it less metaphorically, we wish to supply the language, thought-patterns, moulds for imagination necessary for informed, critical thinking about social change.

Is this goal defensible on practical grounds? What is the use of conceptual and theoretical knowledge of the kind we propose? Here we have to summon another important sociological insight, the principle of reflexivity, which claims that in human society knowledge has direct and immediate practical consequences. What people think about social change is crucially important in moving them to action, and hence it crucially influences the very course and prospects of social change. In this sense, enriching theoretical knowledge about change is by the same token practically relevant for producing change. Ideas about change become a resource for introducing change. The richer such resources are, the wider the variety of available concepts, models and theories, the deeper and more critical their mastery, the more informed and self-aware human actions become, both the everyday actions of common people, and the change-oriented programmes of task-groups, organizations, social movements, governments and other collective actors. The scope and depth of sociological imagination is an important factor in shaping society's fate.

The premises indicated above dictate to some extent the internal construction and logic of the book. Part I will be devoted to the explication of fundamental concepts which, independently of their origins, make up the standard and widely accepted pool of ideas indispensable for the study of change, such as social change itself, social process, development, historical cycle etc. We shall also discuss concepts which are more contested, such as social progress, social time, historical tradition, modernity and globalization. Part II will be devoted to three grand visions of human history which have left the strongest impress on both societal and sociological imagination, providing competing frameworks for the conception and intepretation of social change by ordinary people and sociologists alike. These visions are evolutionism, cyclical theories and historical materialism. They will be discussed both in their orthodox, extreme form, and in later more open versions. It will be shown that, despite numerous critiques, such visions retain a strong influence on contemporary thinking, provide archetypes for common sense and are revived in ever new formulations in sociological discourse. In the long run, however, sociological theory seems to be moving away from grand historical schemes towards more concrete accounts of timed and localized social changes, produced by identifiable actors, individual or collective. This tendency is analysed in part III, which traces the new theoretical movement against developmentalism and towards the brand of theorizing which I propose to label 'the theory of social becoming' (Sztompka 1991b). This is rooted in two influential theoretical trends: theories of agency and historical sociology. These, it is claimed, provide the fourth, alternative approach to social change, gradually superseding the three traditional visions and providing the most adequate tool for interpreting the transformations of contemporary society. In the framework of this approach, the field is open for the study of specific, concrete mechanisms of change, as well as the role of various agencies in fostering change. Those processes which are already well recognized in sociological literature are discussed in part IV, with particular emphasis on the role of intangibles – ideas and norms – as the substance of change, the role of eminent individuals and social movements as agents of change, and the essence of social revolutions as peak manifestations of change.

Acknowledgements

The ideas presented in this book have been tested throughout the years on my students, both at the Jagiellonian University at Cracow and at the University of California at Los Angeles (UCLA). I have learned much from them, as I hope they also have from me; but it was through chance that my lectures have been brought together in one volume. The history of books, like history in general, is highly contingent. I recall one sunny afternoon at UCLA and the lunch we shared with Simon Prosser, the editor at Blackwell's. It was right then, as a result of his editorial magic combined with the spell of the place, that the plan to write this book suddenly appeared both obvious and inevitable.

The bulk of the work was done in the stimulating scholarly environment and personally gratifying milieu of the Swedish Collegium for Advanced Studies in the Social Sciences (SCASSS) at Uppsala in the spring of 1992. My gratitude goes to all other fellows present at that time in the Collegium, as well as to its directors and staff, and particularly to my friends, and formidable competitors in the great game of *les boules*, Jeff Alexander and Björn Wittrock.

Part I

Concepts and Categories

1

Fundamental concepts in the study of change

The organic metaphor: the classic approach to social change

It was at the very birth of sociology that a distinction was conceived which has haunted sociological thinking up to our days and proved to be as misleading as it has been persistent. This was a sort of 'original sin' of our discipline, and the responsibility rests squarely with the father of sociology, Auguste Comte (1798–1857), who divided his system of theory into two separate parts: 'social statics' and 'social dynamics'. Underlying the distinction was an implicit metaphor made fully explicit some time later by Herbert Spencer (1820–1903), the analogy between a society and a biological organism. Social statics was conceived as the study of the anatomy of human society, the composite parts and their arrangement, just like the anatomy of the body (with its organs, skeleton and tissues), whereas social dynamics was assumed to focus on physiology, the processes running inside society, just like bodily functions (respiration, metabolism, circulation of the blood), and producing as their ultimate result the development of society, again comparable to organic growth (from the embryo to maturity). The implication was that there existed something like a steady state of society, which could be perceived and analysed prior to, or independently of, its motion.

Herbert Spencer kept to the same image but altered the terminology. He is the author of another distinction which for more than a century was at the core of sociological language: 'structures' as opposed to 'functions'. The former indicated the internal build-up, shape or form of societal wholes, the latter the modes of their operation or transformation. The same implication, that it was possible to conceive of society as some kind of hard entity or tangible object apart from its operations, or in other words that it was feasible to distil structures from functioning, was confirmed and reinforced.

The methodological legacy of those early ideas was the opposition of two types of procedure, which in the early Comtean formulation was desribed as the search for laws of coexistence (why certain social phenomena invariably appear together) versus the laws of succession (why certain social phenomena invariably precede or follow others). The idea, under various labels, found its way into most textbooks of sociological research: 'synchronic (or cross-sectional) study' was defined as looking at society in a timeless, static perspective, and 'diachronic (or sequential) study', as recognizing the flow of time and focusing on ongoing social changes.

The modern study of change (diachronic research) has been strongly influenced by such views. It has inherited the classic organic metaphor and related distinctions not directly, from Comte, Spencer and other nineteenth-century masters, but via the influential school of twentieth-century sociology known as system theory, functional theory, or structural-functionalism (cf. Sztompka 1974). The system model of society elaborated within that school brought together and generalized all ideas typical for organicism. The whole conceptual apparatus commonly applied to the analysis of change derives primarily from the system model, even when scholars dealing with change do not recognize that, or distance themselves from the systemic and structural-functional theories. It is only recently that the 'system model' has been challenged by an alternative image of society, the processual, or *morphogenetic approach*, and that the concepts applied to social change have been modified accordingly.

The system model: engendering the concept of social change

The idea of a system denotes a complex whole, consisting of multiple elements bound together by various interrelations and separated from the environment by a boundary. Organisms are clearly cases of systems, but so are molecules, buildings, planets, galaxies. Such a generalized notion may be applied to human society at various levels of complexity. At the macro-level, the whole global society (humanity) may be conceived as a system; at the mezzo-level, nation-states and regional political or military alliances could also be seen as systems; at the micro-level, local communities, associations, firms, families or friendship circles may be treated as small systems. Furthermore, qualitatively distinct segments of society like economy, politics and culture may also be grasped in systemic terms. Thus in the hands of system theorists, e.g. Talcott Parsons (1902–79), the notion is not only generalized but found universally applicable.

Social change, accordingly, is conceived as the change occurring within, or embracing the social system. More precisely, it is the difference between various states of the same system succeeding each other in time.

> If we speak of change, we have in mind something that comes into being after some time; that is to say, we are dealing with a difference between what can be observed before that point in time and what we see after that point in time. In order to be able to state differences, the unit of analysis must preserve a minimum of identity – in spite of change over time. (*Strasser and Randall 1981: 16*)

Thus the basic concept of social change involves three ideas: (1) difference, (2) at different temporal moments, (3) between states of the same system. A good example of the standard type of definition runs like this: 'By social change I mean any nonrecurrent alteration of a social system considered as a whole' (Hawley 1978: 787).

Depending on what is seen as changing – what aspects, fragments, dimensions of the system are involved in change – various kinds of change may be distinguished. This is because the overall state of the system is not simple, one-dimensional, but rather emerges as the combined, aggregated result of the state of various components such as:

1 the ultimate elements (e.g. the number and variety of human individuals and their actions)
2 interrelations among elements (e.g. social bonds, loyalties, dependencies, linkages between individuals, interactions, exchanges between actions)
3 the functions of elements in the system as a whole (e.g. the occupational roles played by the individuals, or the necessity of certain actions for the preservation of social order)
4 the boundary (e.g. criteria of inclusion, conditions for acceptance of individuals in the group, recruitment principles in associations, gate-keeping arrangements in organizations etc.)
5 the subsystems (e.g. the number and variety of distinguishable specialized segments, sections, subdivisions)
6 the environment (e.g. natural conditions, or the ambience of other societies, geo-political location).

It is only through their complex interplay that the overall characteristics of the system emerge: equilibrium or disequilibrium, consensus or dissensus, harmony or strife, co-operation or conflict, peace or war, prosperity or crisis etc.

When dissected into its primary components and dimensions the system model implies the following possible changes:

1 change in composition (e.g. migration from one group to another, recruitment to a group, depopulation due to famine, demobilization of a social movement, dispersion of a group)
2 change in structure (e.g. appearance of inequalities, crystallization of power, emergence of friendship-ties, establishing co-operative or competitive relationships)
3 change of functions (e.g. specialization and differentiation of jobs, decay of economic role of the family, assumption of an indoctrinating role by schools or universities)
4 change of boundaries (e.g. merging of groups, relaxing admission criteria and democratization of membership, conquest and incorporation of one group by another)
5 change in the relations of subsystems (e.g. ascendancy of political regime over economic organization, control of the family and the whole private sphere by totalitarian government)

6   change in the environment (e.g. ecological deterioration, earthquake, appearance of the Black Death or HIV virus, obliteration of the bipolar international system).

Sometimes changes are only partial, restricted in scope, without major repercussions for other aspects of the system. The system as a whole remains intact, no overall change of its state occurs, in spite of piecemeal changes going on inside. For example, the strenth of a democratic political system lies in its ability to meet challenges, alleviate grievances and defuse conflicts by partial reforms without jeopardizing the stability and continuity of the state as a whole. This kind of adaptive modification is an illustration of changes *in* the system. But on other occasions change may embrace all (or at least the core) aspects of the system, producing overall mutation and making us treat the new system as fundamentally different from the old one. This is well illustrated by all major social revolutions. This kind of radical transformation deserves to be called a change *of* the system. The borderline between these two cases is somewhat fluid. Changes *in* often accumulate and finally touch the core of the system, turning into changes *of*. Quite often in social systems we observe specific thresholds, beyond which the extensiveness, intensiveness and momentum of fragmentary, piecemeal changes transform the whole identity of the system and lead not only to 'quantitative' but truly 'qualitative' novelty (Granovetter 1978). As all tyrants and dictators learn sooner or later, keeping the lid on public discontent is feasible only up to a certain point, and the slow erosion of their power inevitably opens the door for democracy.

If we look at the sample of definitions of social change to be found in standard textbooks of sociology, we shall see that various authors place the emphasis on different kinds of change, but for most of them structural change in relationships, organization and links among societal components appears to be crucial:

'Social change is the transformation in the organization of society and in patterns of thought and behavior over time' (Macionis 1987: 638).
'Social change is a modification or transformation in the way society is organized' (Persell 1987: 586).
Social change refers to 'variations over time in the relationships among individuals, groups, organizations, cultures, and societies' (Ritzer et al. 1987: 560).
'Social changes are the alterations of behavior patterns, social relationships, institutions, and social structure over time' (Farley 1990: 626).

Perhaps the reason for emphasizing *structural* change is that, more often than other types, it leads to changes *of*, rather than merely changes *in*, society. Social structure makes up a sort of skeleton on which society and its operations are founded. When it changes, all else is apt to change as well.

As we noticed before, the notion of a system may be applied at various levels of societal complexity: macro, mezzo and micro. Accordingly, social change may also be conceived as occurring at the macro-level of international systems, nations, states; at the mezzo-level of corporations, political parties, religious movements, large associations; or at the micro-level of families, communities, occupational groups, cliques, friendship circles. Then the central question becomes how the changes running at those various levels interrelate. On the one hand, sociologists ask what are the macro-effects of micro-events (e.g. how changes in consumer behaviour produce growing inflation, or how shifts in everyday habits transform civilizations and cultures), and on the other hand they ask what are the micro-effects of macro-events (e.g. how revolution changes family life, or how economic crisis influences friendship patterns). 'Social change is mediated through individual actors. Hence theories of structural change must show how macrovariables affect individual motives and choices and how these choices in turn change the macrovariables' (Hernes 1976: 514).

Clusters of changes: raising the complexity of dynamic concepts

The concept of social change comprehends the ultimate, smallest 'atoms' of social dynamics, single shifts in the state of the system or any of its aspects. But single changes are rarely isolated, they are normally linked with others, and sociology has devised more complex concepts to deal with typical forms of such linkages.

The most important is the idea of a 'social process' describing the sequence of interrelated changes. A classical definition is given by Pitirim Sorokin (1889–1968): 'By process is meant any kind of movement, or modification, or transformation, or alteration, or "evolution", in brief any change, of a given logical subject in the course of time, whether it be a change in its place in space or a modification of its quantitative or qualitative aspects' (1937: vol. 1: 153). More precisely the concept denotes: (1) the plurality of changes, (2) referring to the same system (occurring within it, or transforming it as a whole), (3) causally related to each other (in the sense that one change is a causal condition, or at least a partial causal condition, and not merely an accompanying or preceding factor, of the other), and (4) the changes follow each other in a temporal sequence (succeeding each other along the stretch of time). Examples of processes, going from the macro-level toward the micro-level, would include: industrialization, urbanization, globalization, secularization, democratization, escalation of war, mobilization of a social movement, liquidation of a firm, dissolution of a voluntary association, crystallization of a friendship circle, crisis in the family. Again, the crucial theoretical issue is the linkage between microprocesses and macroprocesses.

Among social processes two specific forms have been singled out by sociologists, and for many decades became the focus of their attention. One is 'social development', which describes the process of unfolding of some potentiality inherent in the system. More precisely, the concept signifies a process with three additional characteristics: (1) it is directional, i.e. no state of the system repeats itself at any stage; (2) the state of the system at any later moment represents a higher level of some selected property (e.g. there is growing differentiation of structure, or higher economic output, or the advance of technologies, or enlarged population), or at each later moment the state of the system comes closer to some indicated overall state (e.g. the society approaches the condition of social equality, universal prosperity or democratic representation); and (3) this is stimulated by the immanent (internal, endogenous, auto-dynamic) propensities of the system (e.g. expansion of human population with accompanying growth in density, the resolution of internal contradictions by establishing qualitatively new forms of social life, channelling human inborn creativeness towards significant organizational innovations). The notion of development carries some strong assumptions: the inevitability, necessity and irreversibility of the process it describes. It easily degenerates into a fatalistic and mechanistic view of change, as running independently of human actions, somewhat above human heads, towards a predetermined, ultimate *finale*. We shall soon discuss the large group of theories for which the idea of development has become central, and which can be put together under the label of developmentalism. They include all varieties of evolutionism (from Comte to Parsons) and historical materialism (from Marx to Althusser).

Another form of a social process particularly stressed by sociologists is the 'social cycle'. Here the process is no longer directional, but not haphazard either. It is characterized by two traits: (1) it follows a circular pattern: each state of the system at any given moment is apt to reappear at some moment in the future, and itself is a replica of what had already occurred at some moment in the past; and (2) this repetition is due to some immanent tendency of the system, which by its very nature unfolds in such a specific undulating, or oscillating way. Thus in the short run there are changes, but in the long run there is no change, as the system returns to its initial state. We shall have occasion to present an influential group of theories which interpret human history in terms of social cycles: the cyclical theories of change (from Spengler to Sorokin).

One more concept, perhaps the most debatable, but also most influential in the whole history of human thought (and not only in the history of sociology) is the idea of 'social progress'. It adds axiological, valuational dimension to the more objective and neutral category of social development. Hence it takes us away from strictly scientific, neutral accounts into the normative, prescriptive domain. In principle, by 'progress' we mean: (1) a directional process which (2) steadily brings the system closer to the preferred, beneficial state (or, in other words, to the implementation of certain values selected on ethical grounds, such as happiness, freedom, prosperity, justice, dignity, knowledge etc.), or to the achievement of an ideal society described comprehensively, in its overall shape by numerous social utopias. Most often the idea of progress defines how, according to a given author or the *Weltanschauung* he/she represents, society should look. This clearly falls outside the realm of science, which restricts its interest to what is, rather than what ought to be. But sometimes the idea of progress attains a categorical, descriptive flavour: it carries a claim that, as a matter of empirical fact, some values are necessarily realized in human history, and that in general society inevitably changes for the better (whatever is defined as better by a given author). Such a claim, expressing historiosophical optimism, may already be subjected to test, even though, regrettably, it rarely passes. We shall have much more to say about social progress in chapter 2, about the idea's triumphs, its recent demise and a possible way to salvage it.

The alternative model: the dynamic social field

It is only recently that sociology has put into doubt the validity of organic-systemic models of society, and the very dichotomy of social statics and social dynamics. Two intellectual trends seem to gain in importance: (1) the emphasis on the pervasive dynamic qualities of social reality, i.e. perceiving society in motion ('processual image'), and (2) the avoidance of treating society (group, organization) as an object, i.e. de-reifying social reality ('field image').

The first intimations that the opposition of statics and dynamics may be spurious, and that no changeless objects, entities, structures or wholes can be conceived at all, came from the natural sciences. As Alfred N. Whitehead put it: 'Change is inherent in the very nature of things' (1925: 179). Such a purely dynamic or processual perspective soon turned into the dominant approach, the tendency of modern science to treat events rather than things, processes rather than states, as the ultimate components of reality.

For sociology it meant that society should be conceived not as a steady state but as a process; not as a rigid quasi-object, but as a continuous, unending stream of events. It was recognized that a society (group, community, organization, nation-state) may be said to exist only in so far, and only as long, as something *happens* inside it, some actions are taken, some changes occur, some processes continue to operate. Ontologically speaking, society as a steady state does not and cannot exist. All social reality is pure dynamics, a flow of changes of various speed, intensity, rhythm and tempo. It is not by accident that we often speak of 'social life', perhaps a more fitting metaphor than the old image of a hide-bound, reified super-organism. Because life is nothing else but movement, motion and change, when those stop, there is no more life, but an entirely different condition – nothingness, or as we call it, death.

The methodological consequence of such a dynamic view of social life is the rejection of the validity of purely synchronic studies and the affirmation of a diachronic (historical) perspective. As the leading twentieth-century historian puts it: 'A study of human affairs in movement is certainly more fruitful,

because more realistic, than any attempt to study them in an imaginary condition of rest' (Toynbee 1963: 81).

The image of the object undergoing change is modified accordingly. Society
(group, organization etc.) is no longer viewed as a rigid, 'hard' system, but
rather as a 'soft' field of relationships. Social reality is inter-individual (interpersonal) reality, what exists between or among human individuals, a network of ties, bonds, dependencies, exchanges, loyalties. In other words, it is
a specific social tissue or social fabric binding people together. Such an inter-
individual field is constantly in motion; it expands and contracts (e.g. when
individuals join or leave), strengthens and weakens (when the quality of
their relationships changes, e.g. from acquaintance to friendship), coalesces
and disintegrates (e.g. when leadership appears or dissolves), intermeshes or
separates itself from other segments of the field (e.g. when coalitions or
federations appear or secessions occur). There are specific bundles, knots of
social relationships which we have learned to single out as crucially important
for our life, and we are apt to treat them in reified language: they are what
we call groups, communities, organizations, institutions, nation-states. This
is an illusion that they have an object-like existence. What really exists are
constant processes of grouping and regrouping, rather than stable entities
called groups; there are processes of organizing and reorganizing, rather than
stable organizations; there are processes of 'structuration' (Giddens 1985)
rather than structures; forming rather than forms; fluctuating 'figurations' (Elias
1978) rather than rigid patterns.

When such a perspective is taken, the smallest, fundamental unit of sociological analysis appears to be an 'event'. An event is understood here as any
momentary state of the social field (or any segment thereof). Take as an
example family dinner. It is a moment when certain family members are
gathered together at home, seated at a table, involved in talking and eating.
In precise terms, it is an event. Moments earlier the members of the family
were dispersed, involved in different clusters of relationships: one at the
office, another at school, another in the kitchen, another at the cinema, another
riding in the car; moments later they will be dispersed again: looking at TV,
returning to work for an important after-hours job, driving to a night disco.
What distinguishes this particular bundle of relationships as a family, and
preserves its continuity and identity over time, in spite of constant changes
is: (1) psychological identifications: self-definitions, feelings, attachments,
loyalties; (2) the likelihood of periodical contractions of relationships: getting
together at home, or at least getting in touch from time to time by mail, on
the phone; (3) the particular quality of relationships: their intimacy, diffuseness,
disinterestedness, spontaneity.

The notion of the inter-individual field may be specified. We propose the
following fourfold typology ('INIO scheme', cf. Sztompka 1991b: 124–6) to
distinguish four dimensions or aspects of the field: ideal, normative,
interactional and opportunity. So far, to simplify matters, we have said that
social relationships link human individuals. But what is it that they in fact link

and how? Either the ideas, thoughts, beliefs held by the individuals, which may be similar or different; or the rules guiding their conduct, which may support or contradict each other; or their actual actions, which may be friendly or hostile, co-operative or competitive; or their interests, which may coincide or stand in conflict. There are four kinds of tissue or fabric which emerge in society and bind it together, depending on the kind of entities linked by the networks of relationships: the tissues (1) of ideas, (2) of rules, (3) of actions and (4) of interests. The interlinked networks of ideas (beliefs, convictions, definitions) make up the ideal dimension of the field, its 'social awareness'. The interlinked networks of rules (norms, values, prescriptions, ideals) make up the normative dimension of the field, its 'social institutions'. Both the ideal and normative dimensions add to what has been traditionally referred to as culture. Then the interlinked networks of actions make up the interactional dimension of the field, its 'social organization'. The interlinked networks of interests (life-chances, opportunities, access to resources) make up the opportunity dimension of the field, its 'social hierarchies'. Both the interactional and opportunity dimension add to what may be called the societal fabric in the strict sense. To underline the multidimensionality of the field we shall henceforth use the term 'socio-cultural field'.

At each of the four levels, the socio-cultural field is undergoing perpetual change. We observe (1) the constant articulation, legitimation or reformulation of ideas, the appearance and disappearance of ideologies, creeds, doctrines and theories; (2) the constant institutionalization, reaffirmation or rejection of norms, values, or rules, the emergence and dissolution of ethical codes, legal systems; (3) the constant elaboration, differentiation and reshaping of interactive channels, organizational links, or group ties, the emergence or dissolution of groups, circles and personal networks; (4) the constant crystallization, petrification and redistribution of opportunities, interests, life-chances, the rise and fall, extension and levelling of societal hierarchies.

The true complexity of social life occurring in the socio-cultural field will be grasped if we realize two points. First, that the processes at the four levels do not run independently of each other. Just the reverse: they are interrelated by various cross-dimensional links, for example, the link studied by the sociology of knowledge between the opportunity and ideal dimensions (how life-situations determine beliefs), or the link examined by the sociology of deviance between the normative and interactional dimensions (how norms influence or fail to influence actions). Second, we must realize that the socio-cultural field operates at various levels of complexity: macro, mezzo and micro. It is a notion applicable across all scales of social phenomena. The socio-cultural field of a particular sort manifests itself in families, but also – qualitatively differently – in corporations, political parties, armies, ethnic communities, nation-states, and even the whole global society. Those various manifestations are not isolated; on the contrary, they are interrelated in a most complex manner. The crystallizations and fluctuations of the socio-cultural field, embodied in the social events of the global, regional, local and even most personal sort, significantly co-determine one another. The problem of macro-effects of micro-events, and the opposite problem of micro-effects of macro-events require thorough and extensive study.

Within the model of a fluid socio-cultural field, produced as an alternative vision to the reified social system, the basic concepts of social dynamics introduced earlier retain their validity, but with slightly modified meaning. Thus: (1) social change will mean differences between the states of the social field over time; (2) social process, a sequence of social events (consecutive, different states of the social field); (3) social development, differentiation, expansion, crystallization, articulation of the social field in its various dimensions, resulting from internal, immanent propensities; and (4) social progress, any such developments, provided they are conceived as beneficial relative to some axiological viewpoint.

The main difference from the system model is the conceptualization of changes and processes as truly continuous and never discrete, fragmented or broken. Between two points in time, however close, the movement does not stop. However we narrow down the scale, limiting the time distance between two 'snapshots' of society, this distance is always filled out with changes. The changes flow incessantly, and any two states of the socio-cultural field, whether temporally almost identical or remote, are certainly different. One is reminded of the famous ancient metaphor of the river, into which one cannot step twice, as it will no longer be the same river (Heraclitus 1979). It is only by convention that we conceptually freeze some states important for our practical needs, treating them as single events, and speak of change or process as the sequence of such frozen, 'discrete' points.

Varieties of social processes: a typology

We do not claim exclusive validity for either the systemic or the field model. After all, models are cognitive instruments, and as such must be judged by their effectivenss, fruitfulness and heuristic power. The systemic model has proved extremely influential and underlies most of the theories of social change which are still around. The field model emerges in an attempt to grasp the dynamic nature of society more adequately, but requires a great deal of further conceptual elaboration and empirical corroboration. For the time being it seems wise to take an eclectic stand and to derive our basic conceptual apparatus for the study of social change from both sources. Each throws some light on the extreme variety of dynamic phenomena. Raymond Boudon has a point: 'It is hopeless to try to reduce social change to one unique model' (1981: 133).

To get our bearings in the complex domain of social change, we need to introduce a typology of social processes. It will be based on four major criteria: (1) the form or shape that the process takes; (2) the outcomes or results of the process; (3) the awareness of social processes in the population; (4) the moving force behind the process. We shall also briefly consider (5) the level of social reality where the process operates, and (6) the temporal scope of the process.

The form of social processes

To take the first criterion, if we look at the processes from the distant, external perspective, various forms and shapes can be recognized. Thus, the processes may be directional or non-directional. The directional processes are irreversible and often cummulative. Each consecutive stage is different from any earlier stage and incorporates effects of the earlier stage, while each earlier stage provides prerequisites for the later stage. The idea of irreversibility emphasizes that in human life there are deeds which cannot be un-done, thoughts which cannot be un-thought, feelings which cannot be un-felt, experiences which cannot be un-experienced (Adam 1990: 169). Once they occur, they leave ineradicable traces and inescapably influence the further stages of the process; be it personal career, acquisition of knowledge, falling in love, or surviving war. As examples of directional processes we may indicate the socialization of a child, expansion of a city, technological development of industry, population growth. In this wide sense both individual biography and social history are mostly directional.

But not necessarily in the narrower sense, when specific subtypes of directional processes are taken into account. Some of them may be teleological (or in other words, finalistic), persistently approaching a certain goal or end-state from various starting-points, as if pulled towards it. Examples are provided by so-called theories of convergence, which show how various societies, of utterly diverse traditions, eventually reach similar civilizational or technological achievements, be it in machine production, democratic rule, automobile transportation, telecommunications etc. Other examples of such processes abound in structural-functional literature, which emphasizes the finalistic tendency of the social system to reach a state of equilibrium by means of internal mechanisms which compensate for any disturbances. But there are also directional processes of a different shape. They are developmental, persistently working out, unfolding certain inherent potentialities as if endlessly pushed from within. For example, constant technological expansion is often represented as driven by inherent human innovativeness or creativeness, or territorial conquests as motivated by an inherent acquisitive drive. If the end-state is valued positively, the process is treated as progressive (e.g. elimination of disease and increasing longevity). If it moves away from the positively valued, preferred end-state, we shall call it regressive (e.g. ecological destruction, commercialization of the arts).

Directional processes may be gradual, incremental or, as we sometimes say, linear. When they follow one single trajectory, or pass through similar sequences of necessary stages, they are called unilinear. For example most social evolutionists believe that all human cultures have to go through the same set of stages, some sooner, some later. Those which started earlier or

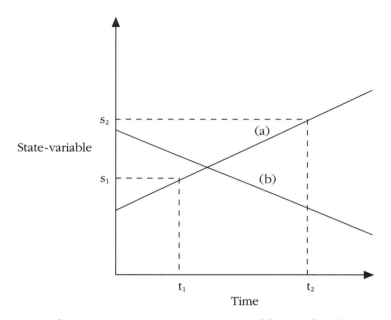

Figure 1.1 Unilinear process or consistent course: (a) ascending (progressive; (b) descending (regressive).

proceeded quicker show the more backward or slow ones how their own future will look; those which are still backward demonstrate to those more advanced how their own past inevitably looked. The unilinear process may be represented as in figure 1.1.

On the other hand, when the processes follow a number of alternative trajectories, skip some stages, substitute others, or add stages not typically found, they are called multilinear. For example when historians describe the origins of capitalism, they indicate various scenarios of the same process in different parts of the world: western, eastern and other patterns. When students of modernization examine Third World countries, they single out various routes they take towards industrial-urban civilization. The schematic representation of the multilinear process can be drawn as in figure 1.2.

The opposites of linear processess are those which proceed by means of qualitative leaps or breakthroughs after prolonged periods of quantitative growth, passing specific thresholds (Granovetter 1978) or effecting certain 'step-functions'. These are non-linear processes. For example, as viewed by Marxists, the sequence of so-called socio-economic formations moves through revolutionary epochs – sudden, fundamental, radical transformations of a whole society after long periods of accumulating contradictions, conflicts, strains and tensions. Such processes can be represented as in figure 1.3.

Non-directional (or fluid) processes may be of two types. Some are purely random, chaotic with no pattern discernible. For example, consider flows of

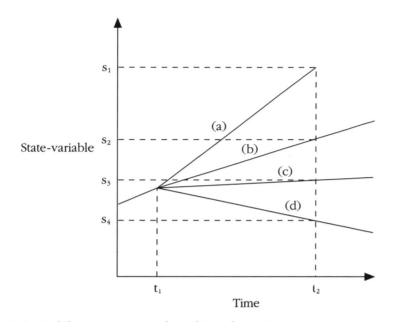

Figure 1.2   Multilinear process or branching alternative courses.

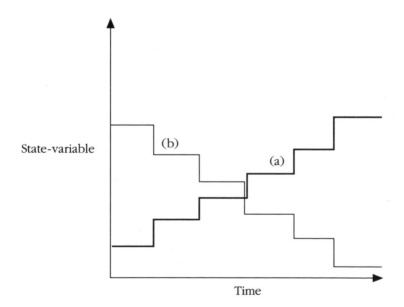

Figure 1.3   Step-functions or quantum leaps: (a) ascending (progressive); (b) descending (regressive).

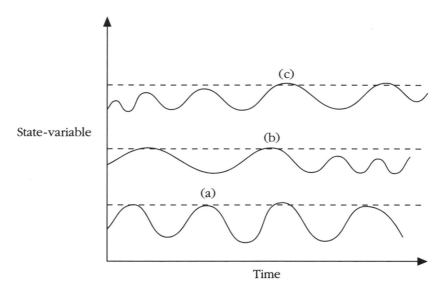

State-variable

(c)

(b)

(a)

Time

Figure 1.4 Cyclical process: (a) regular (equal phases); (b) accelerating (shorter phases); (c) decelerating (longer phases).

excitement in revolutionary crowds, or processes of mobilization and demobilization in social movements, or in children's games. Other processes are oscillatory, following discernible patterns of repetition or at least similarity, when consecutive stages are either identical with, or at least qualitatively resemble, earlier ones. When virtual recurrence is observable, we consider the process as circular, or as a closed cycle. For example, think of the typical working day of a secretary, or the seasonal labour of a farmer, or in a longer time-perspective the routines of a scholar starting to write his/her next book. On the macro-scale, the economic cycles of expansion and recession, boom and stagnation, bull and bear markets, often follow this pattern. The graphic representation will resemble a sinusoid, as in figure 1.4.

When the resemblance is observed, but at a different level of complexity, we consider the process as following the pattern of a spiral, or as an open cycle, for example, the advance of a student through consecutive levels of school or university, with enrolment, terms, breaks, examinations, but each time at a higher educational level; or, on a different scale, economic cycles, but in conditions of overall growth (proverbially two steps forward, one step back); or in the largest time span, the tendency which Arnold Toynbee ascribes to all human history: the gradual perfecting of religion and in general the spiritual life of mankind, through numerous cycles of challenge and response, growth and decay (Toynbee 1934–61); or Karl Marx's vision of the progressive emancipation of humanity through the 'vale of tears', via consecutive cycles of deepening exploitation, alienation, poverty, and their surmounting by revolution (Marx and Engels 1985). If the level achieved after

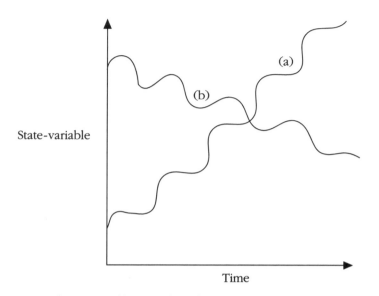

Figure 1.5 Spiral process: (a) ascending (progressive); (b) descending (regressive).

each cycle is higher, as in our examples, we may speak of a developmental (or even progressive) cycle. If on the other hand the level achieved after each reversal is lower on some relevant scale, we shall refer to the process as a regressive cycle, as in figure 1.5.

One limiting case, when the flow of time does not coincide with any changes in the state of the system is known as stagnation (figure 1.6).

Another limiting case, when the changes do not follow any recognizable pattern, may be called a random process (figure 1.7).

The end-results of social processes

The second important consideration and next criterion of our typology has to do with the outcomes produced by the processes. Some processes result in the emergence of completely new social conditions, states of society, social structures etc. These are truly creative and produce fundamental novelty. The term 'morphogenesis' (Buckley 1967: 58–66) may be applied to all processes of this sort. Examples abound: the mobilization of social movements; the establishment of new groups, associations, organizations, parties; the founding of new towns; enacting the constitution of a new state; the spread of a new fashion or lifestyle; the development of a new technological invention, with all its far-reaching consequences. Morphogenetic processes are to be found at the origins of all the civilizational, technological, cultural and social achievements of humankind, from early primitive society up to the modern industrial stage.

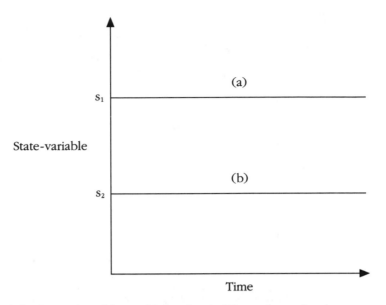

Figure 1.6   Stagnation: (a) at a higher level; (b) at a lower level.

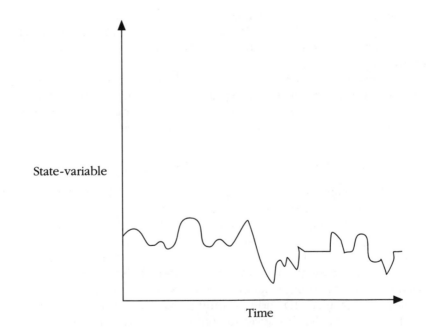

Figure 1.7   Random process.

These must be distinguished from the processes of mere transmutation, which produce less radical results without fundamental novelty. Among these, some do not produce any novelty at all, others result merely in modifying, reforming, reshaping existing social arrangements. The former, known as 'simple reproduction' (or else as compensatory, adaptive, homeostatic, equilibrating or sustaining processes) result in upholding received conditions, preserving the status quo, safeguarding the persistence and continuation of society in an entirely unchanged shape. They are in the focus of attention of the structural-functional school, which is primarily concerned with the prerequisites of stability, social order, harmony, consensus and equilibrium (Parsons 1964). No wonder functionalists have extensively studied a number of simple reproductive processes. One example is socialization, which transmits the cultural heritage of society (values, norms, beliefs, knowledge etc.) from one generation to the next. Others are social control, which eliminates the threat to the stable operation of society brought about by deviance; adaptation and adjustment, which allow stable continuity of social structures in spite of environmental change; unequal distribution of privileges and benefits among social positions, safeguarding smooth recruitment to pre-existent statuses and roles, as in the so-called 'functional theory of stratification' (Davis and Moore 1945). Finally there are constraining and sanctioning systems of etiquette, rules of deference and demeanour etc. as the means for reaffirming traditional status hierarchies.

Whereas simple reproduction keeps everything unchanged, 'extended reproduction' signifies a quantitative enrichment without basic qualitative modification. This occurs, for example, with demographic growth, the spread of suburbs, raising the production of automobiles in a given plant, increasing the recruitment of students to a university, the accumulation of capital by savings. The opposite, quantitative impoverishment, again without qualitative change, may be called 'contracted reproduction', as with the spending of financial reserves without any savings, so-called 'negative growth' of population, the unbridled exploitation of natural resources.

When, apart from quantitative modifications, basic qualitative change occurs we no longer speak of reproduction but rather of 'transformation'. It is not always easy to determine where the borderline is, and which change may count as qualitative. As a rule of thumb, one may require a change of structures, with important modification in the network of relationships obtaining in the social system or the social-cultural field, and/or a change of functions, with important modification in the mode of operation of the system or field. Such changes may be conceived as touching the core of social reality, as their repercussions are usually to be felt in all aspects of social life, transforming its overall quality. For example structural changes occur with the appearance of a leadership and power hierarchy in a group, the bureaucratization of a social movement, the replacement of autocratic rule by democratic government, the levelling of social inequalities by tax reform. Examples of functional change can be seen with the introduction of self-management at an enterprise with the employee council assuming decision-making prerogatives, the adoption of a direct political role by the Church, the shifting of educational functions from the family to schools. 'Transformation' is a synonym for what we earlier called 'changes *of*', whereas 'reproduction' indicates at most 'changes *in*'.

Processes in social consciousness

In all changes occurring in the human world an important consideration is the awareness of change by the people involved, and particularly the awareness of the results that processes bring about (cf. Sztompka 1984b). Introducing the subjective factor into our typology we may distinguish three additional types of changes. Obviously these distinctions cut across earlier ones and may be treated as subcategories of either morphogenesis or reproduction or transformation.

1   The processes may be recognized, anticipated and intended. Paraphrasing the usage proposed by Robert K. Merton (1968: 73) we shall call them 'manifest'. For example, the reform of traffic laws lowers the number of accidents; legalizing currency exchange eliminates the black market; the privatization of retail trade raises the supply of consumer goods.

2   The processes may be unrecognized, unanticipated and unintended. Again, following Merton's lead we shall call them 'latent'. In these cases the change itself and its outcome appear as surprising, and depending on the circumstances may be welcome or the opposite. As an instance, for a long time people were generally unaware of the environmental damage produced by industrialization. So-called ecological consciousness is a relatively recent phenomenon.

3   People may recognize the process, anticipate its course and intend specific effects, but may be entirely wrong on all counts. The process runs against their expectations and produces results different from, or even entirely opposite to, those intended. Applying the term adopted by Merton and Kendall (1944), we shall refer to such a case as a 'boomerang process'. For example, a propaganda campaign may actually strengthen the attitudes it attacks, by mobilizing the defence and provoking a negative reaction; fiscal reform intended to curb inflation may produce recession and higher inflation; or rates of profit may fall as the result of greater competitiveness pushed by the desire to raise profits.

The seat of causality

The next major criterion differentiating between types of social processes has to do with the moving force behind them, the causal factors putting them in motion. The main issue is where such forces or factors originate, whether in the realm undergoing change or outside it. In the former case we speak of an 'endogenous process' (with immanent, or intrinsic causation); in the latter, of an 'exogenous process' (with external, or extrinsic causation). Endogenous processes unfold inherent potentialities, propensities or tendencies enclosed within changing reality. Exogenous processes are reactive, adaptive; they respond to pressures, stimuli, challenges coming from without.

The main problem in distinguishing between endogenous and exogenous processes has to do with the demarcation of what falls within and what falls without the social realm. The seemingly obvious solution is that nature is external to society, and therefore all social processes reacting to natural, environmental stimuli are to be treated as exogenous. Changes of medieval societies in Europe resulting from the Black Death (the epidemic of cholera in the fourteenth century) are exogenous (Topolski 1990: 60–79), as are changes in the patterns and rules of sex in California imposed by the HIV virus, or changes in life-patterns due to climatic shifts, or responses of human communities to natural catastrophes.

But we may narrow down the scale of analysis and draw a borderline no longer between society and nature but between various subsystems, segments or dimensions of society. With this kind of relativization, changes of political regime brought about by economic deficiencies may be treated as exogenous, even though all this clearly happens within society. Similarly the secularization of life imposed by an autocratic political regime will also count as exogenous. Thus, what counts as exogenous and what as endogenous is obviously relative to the level of analysis. But it is also relative to the time-frame in which we view a given process. Let us consider an ecological disaster changing the consumer patterns and everyday life of whole populations. At a given moment in the present, it is clearly the reaction to natural, environmental factors, and hence an exogenous process. In its origin, however, the destruction is itself the product of human actions, and in such a mediated sense the changed lifestyles may be treated as endogenous, brought about indirectly, and of course unintentionally (as a latent process), by the people themselves. Or take another example: a psychopath is killing children, and as a consequence the community mobilizes its defences, schools stop, mothers stay at home. Are these processes exogenous? Yes, to the extent that their cause is ultimately psychological, natural like sickness. But what if the psychopathy is originally caused by faulty socialization or rejection by the community ('stigmatization'), which is after all clearly a social cause? From this perspective the processes occurring in the endangered community will be endogenous, caused by its own earlier neglect of the culprit. Thus, 'Most of the processes can be said to be exogenous-endogenous if one observes them over a long period: while developing they produce results which can affect not only the functioning rules of the system in which they occur, but also the system's environment, causing a reaction to it' (Boudon and Bourricaud 1989: 329). To repeat, the treatment of processes as endogenous or exogenous is always relative to the adopted framework of analysis.

Apart from the formal question of their location relative to the process, the causes of change may be qualitatively, substantively different: natural, demo-graphic, political, economic, technological, cultural, religious and of many other sorts. Sociologists have always had it as their ambition to discover which factors are the most important in inducing change, what are the 'prime movers' of social processes. Among innumerable versions of 'social deter-minisms' indicating various factors as crucial, two main categories of pro-cesses stand out. One category embraces 'materialist processes', brought about by 'hard' technological, economic, environmental, or biological pressures. Others are 'idealistic processes', where the independent causal role of ideology, religion, ethos etc. is recognized. There is a current tendency to abandon such distinctions and treat the causation of processes as concrete and con-tingent, involving the complex interplay of multiple forces or factors, whether material, ideal or any other, in unique permutations. None is treated any longer as *the* ultimate cause of social processes. 'Modern sociology in its scientific forms tends . . . to repudiate the idea according to which there would be a dominant cause of social change' (Boudon and Bourricaud 1989: 326).

Modern sociology not only rejects the absolutization of single, privileged factors of change, it also de-reifies them. It is now widely recognized that speaking of economic, technological or cultural causes of change is a mis-leading shorthand, because behind all these categories the real causally ef-ficient forces are human actions, and exclusively human actions. The problem of *human agency*, central for contemporary sociology, will be discussed in detail later (see chapter 13), but for our present purposes it is important to distinguish two types of processes depending on the location of agency. Some processes emerge as an unintended, and often unrecognized (latent) aggregation of a great multitude of individual actions taken for various private reasons and motives which have nothing to do with the processes they set in motion. Such processes will be called spontaneous (or emerging 'from below'). The standard example is of the innumerable actions taken by consumers and producers, buyers and sellers, employers and employees, which in effect lead to inflation, recession or other macro-economic processes. The opposite case is that of the processes released intentionally, purposefully oriented toward some goals, designed and controlled by an agency equiped with power. We call these *planned*, or imposed 'from above' (cf. Sztompka 1981). Most often they are enacted by means of laws, for example, a rising rate of population growth caused by a pro-nativistic government policy, the elimination of in-efficient industrial plants by a policy of privatization in the aftermath of the anti-communist revolutions of 1989 etc.

Levels of social processes

To close our typology, one important reminder. As we have already indi-cated, and as the examples used so far clearly imply, social processes occur at all three levels of social reality: macro, mezzo and micro. We shall refer to them as macroprocesses, mezzoprocesses and microprocesses respectively.

Macroprocesses run at the most comprehensive level of global society, nation-states, regions, ethnic groups, and their time span is longest, they occur in the *longue durée* (Braudel 1972). The processes of globalization, worldwide recession, environmental destruction, waves of social movements, democratization of political systems, educational advance, uniformization of culture and secularization are examples of macroprocesses. Mezzoprocesses embrace large groups, communities, associations, political parties, armies, bureaucracies. Microprocesses occur in the everyday life-world of human individuals; in small groups, families, schools, occupational settings, friendship circles.

Temporal range of processes

Similarly, there is tremendous variety as to the temporal scope of the processes, their time span. We shall have much more to say about it in chapter 3, but at the moment let us just note that the variety stretches from the processes spending themselves in the extremely short period, fleeting, momentary, all the way to long-range historical tendencies taking centuries and millennia. As we can see, the concept of social process is extremely general and comprehensive, and therefore requires much more precise definition and concretization before it can be usefully applied to historically existing societies.

2

Vicissitudes of the idea of progress

Brief intellectual history

To common sense the idea of progress seems self-evident. It is one of those notions which we normally take for granted because of its widespread use and seemingly clear connotation. In fact, however, it has evolved over the centuries, gradually enriching its content and only slowly acquiring its complex contemporary meaning. Its intellectual origins reach far back in time, and since its birth, deep in antiquity, the notion has become tremendously influential. Christopher Dawson called it 'the working faith of our civilization' (in Lasch 1991: 43), and Robert Nisbet says: 'No single idea has been more important than, perhaps as important as, the idea of progress in Western civilization for nearly three thousand years' (1980: 4).

The explanation of its career is probably to be sought in the fundamental characteristics of the human condition: the perennial gap between realities and aspirations, existence and dreams. Perhaps this permanent tension between what people have and what they would like to have, what they are and what they would like to be, is the key to the success of our never satiated, never satisfied, constantly seeking and striving species. The concept of progress alleviates this existential tension by projecting the hope of a better world into the future, and asserting that its coming is assured, or at least probable. In this way it meets some universal human need, and therefore, in spite of all recent doubts and scepticism, it is perhaps destined to stay with us for a long time to come. As Sidney Pollard has declared, 'The world today believes in progress, because the only possible alternative to the belief in progress would be total despair' (in Lasch 1991: 42).

The first roots of the idea of progress may be found in Greek antiquity. The Greeks perceived the world in the process of growth, as a gradual unfolding of potentialities, passing through fixed stages (epochs) and producing advance and betterment. Plato (427–347 BC) in the *Laws* gives an account of improvements of social organization, stemming from the pristine seeds, and moving towards developed forms. Aristotle (384–322 BC) in his *Politics* traces the development of the political state from the family and tribal organization to the Greek city-state (*polis*), which he conceives as the ideal political arrangement. Protagoras (481–411 BC) provides a detailed reconstruction of progress in culture, from a barbaric state of nature to developed civilization. In all three authors there is a strong assumption of perfectibility of the world, including its social, political and cultural aspects (Nisbet 1980: 10–46).

The second source of the concept is located in the Jewish religious tradition. The biblical emphasis on the prophets and prophecies implies the image of history as sacred, guided by divine will or providence, and therefore predetermined, irreversible and necessary. The design of history embracing all humanity is present from the very beginning and unfolds through the concrete, 'earthly' events, leading to its final culmination in the future 'golden age', 'millennium', paradise. History reveals the course and direction imposed 'from above', and its route is progressive, as it gradually and inexorably approaches the ultimate fulfilment. Exceptionally inspired, charismatically endowed humans – prophets, religious leaders – can read this divine historical design, and predict the course of earthly events.

Both strands of thought, Greek and Jewish, come together in the Judaeo-Christian tradition, which was to permeate western culture for centuries to come. The best exposition of this unique synthesis is to be found in the writings of St Augustine (AD 354–430). 'The idea of progress, according to a widely accepted interpretation, represents a secularized version of the Christian belief in providence' (Lasch 1991: 40).

During the Middle Ages, some new elements were added to the notion of progress. Bernard of Chartres and Roger Bacon (1214–92) applied the concept to the realm of ideas, claimimg that human knowledge undergoes incremental and cumulative growth through the ages, gradually being enriched and perfected. The metaphor of the dwarfs standing on the shoulders of giants, devised by Bernard of Chartres (cf. Merton 1965) and popularized much later by Isaac Newton, depicts the situation of contemporary thinkers who can see better and farther because they use the accumulated wisdom of their predecessors. Even if they are not of gigantic stature themselves, they are stronger with the wisdom of those who came before them. The implication is that knowledge constantly and gradually advances. In the medieval period there also appear the first elaborated social utopias, the idealized, comprehensive images of the earthly paradise, the perfect society to be attained in the future. Depicted by Roger Bacon, Joachim de Fiore and others, they became quite common in later centuries. Social utopias define the direction in which humanity is supposedly moving. They allow for the critique of contemporaneity by contrasting it with the ideal, utopian image, and in this way they provide a rudimentary measure of progress.

An interesting twist to the idea of progress comes with the era of geographical discoveries. It becomes apparent that human societies, cultures, political and economic organizations are not of a piece. The tremendous variety of social arrangements in various parts of the world becomes evident. But to preserve the idea of the unity of mankind and its necessary advancement, the diversity is interpreted in a peculiar way. It is claimed that the variety is due to the different stages of development or progress that different societies have reached. The more primitive are seen as remaining at the earlier stages, showing the more civilized ones an image of their own past; the more civilized represent later stages, offering the more primitive a glimpse of their future. There is the assumption of a common trajectory along which all societies move. To use a metaphor, one may think of a common ladder they all climb, but at various speeds and with unequal success; or a single escalator on which they all stand, though on different steps. At the end of the trajectory, or at the top of the escalator, we shall find the most successful, the most developed and best-civilized societies of the west. This image is a result of an attempt to 'convert perceived heterogeneity into a conceptualized homogeneity: the homogeneity of a single, temporally ordered progression of all peoples in the world from the simplest to the most advanced – which of course, to the people of Western Europe meant themselves' (Nisbet 1980: 149). The long story of ethnocentric bias – western-centrism, or more specifically Euro-centrism, or Americano-centrism – typical for most theories of social change, has already begun at that moment.

The period of the Enlightenment contributes several new emphases to the evolving notion of progress. Jacques Bossuet (1627–1704) introduced the idea of universal history, a common overall pattern underlying the particular histories of various continents, regions or countries. He produced the first developed periodization of universal history, singling out twelve great epochs, which mark the constant betterment of society, and in particlar the constant progress of religion. Condorcet (1743–94) put forward an alternative periodization into ten stages, and suggested a more secular mechanism of progress by means of constant improvements in knowledge and science. Giambattista Vico (1668–1744) hailed the birth of the 'New Science', the search for underlying necessary regularities in human history. Finally Immanuel Kant (1724–1804) provided the suggestive criterion of progress: the meaning and direction of history are set by the growth of individual freedom coupled with the advancement of morality, which curbs the exercise of liberty when it endangers the freedom of others.

Thus we arrive at the nineteenth century, labelled by some as the 'Era of progress', and by others as the 'triumph of the idea of progress' (Nisbet 1980: 170). The idea of progress pervades common sense, becomes universally accepted in philosophy, incorporated in literature, art and science. The spirit of Romantic optimism is accompanied by the belief in reason and human might. Science and technology seem to carry the promise of unlimited expansion and advance. Such an intellectual climate finds its reflection in the new-born field of sociology. All the founding fathers of our discipline profess some version of progress.

Saint-Simon (1760–1825) and Auguste Comte focused on the progress of mind, and envisaged the changes of typical thought-styles as proceeding through three stages: theological, metaphysical and positive. The last is the stage of science: empirical, fact-oriented knowledge able to provide explanations, predictions and practical directives ('Savoir, pour prévoir, pour prévenir', as Comte put it in a famous phrase). 'Positive' science is treated as the crowning achievement of human thought. Herbert Spencer subsumed growth and progress in nature as well as society under the common principle of evolution. He posited the universal principle of structural and functional differentiation (growing complexity of internal organization and operations) as guiding change in both domains. Karl Marx (1818–83) painted the utopia of communist society, and claimed that it is ultimately to be attained by the emancipatory thrust of the exploited classes, utilizing opportunities provided by the growth of productive forces (technologies). The move towards a classless, communist society is to proceed through a series of social revolutions. Max Weber (1864–1920) noticed the pervasive tendency towards the rationalization of social life and social organization (calculation, instrumental considerations, emphasis on efficiency, shunning of emotions and traditions, impersonality of bureaucratic management) and considered this as the main direction in which societies move. Emile Durkheim (1858–1917) pointed to the growing division of labour and concomitant integration of society through 'organic solidarity', born of the mutually beneficial, complementary contributions of societal members.

It is only in the work of Ferdinand Tönnies (1855–1936) that the first doubts about the progressive nature of change, and the first warnings against the side-effects of development are raised (Fletcher 1971, vol. 2: 72). He emphasized the virtues of the earlier traditional *Gemeinschaft*, which was being replaced by modern, industrial and urban *Gesellschaft*. This anticipated the widespread disillusionment with progress, and, among its symptoms, the search for the 'lost community' that was to spread a full century later.

This closes our very general sketch of the origins and evolution of the idea of progress. Gradually the concept became highly complex and multidimensional, and attained its contemporary meaning.

Progress defined

The idea of progress in its original formulation is firmly placed within the model of directional transformation, within some version of developmentalism. It is hard to conceive it either within the organic, structural-functional theories, or in cyclical theories. It is meaningless to speak of societies as progressing, that is improving, becoming better, if they are seen as basically stable, merely reproducing themselves (as in the orthodox structural-functional approach, focused on the equilibrium of the social system), or if they are seen as changing only in closed cycles (returning after a period of time to the point of departure). It is only together with the idea of transformation (change *of*, and not only change *in* a society), that the concept of progress makes any sense. Thus, following Robert Nisbet, progress may be defined as 'the idea that mankind has slowly, gradually and continuously advanced from the original condition of cultural deprivation, ignorance, and insecurity to constantly higher levels of civilization, and that such advancement will, with only occasio-nal setbacks, continue through the present into the future' (Nisbet 1980: 10).

Let us look at this definition, which grasps the original meaning of the concept, a bit more closely. For the sake of analytic precision, the concept of progress may be dissected into several major components. (1) There is the notion of irreversible time, flowing in a linear fashion and providing continu-ity of past, present and future. Progress, by definition, is the positively valued difference between the past and the present (attained progress), or the present and the future (envisaged progress). (2) There is the notion of directional movement, in which no stage repeats itself, and each later stage comes relatively closer to some envisaged final end-state than any earlier stage (an asymptotic approximation to an ultimate fulfilment of professed values). (3) There is the idea of cumulative process, which proceeds either incrementally, step by step, or in a revolutionary way, through periodical qualitative 'jumps'. (4) There is the distiction of typical, 'necessary stages' (phases, epochs) through which the process passes. (5) There is the emphasis on 'endogenous' (internal, immanent) causes of the process, which appears as self-propelled (auto-dynamic) or, in other words, as the unfolding of internal potentialities lying within the society that undergoes change. (6) The process is conceived as inevitable, *necessary*, 'natural'; it cannot be stopped or deflected. (7) There is the notion of *betterment*, advancement (cf. Granovetter 1979), improvement, i.e. the appraisal of each consecutive stage of the process as relatively better than its predecessor, culminating in the final stage that is expected to bring about the complete fulfilment of cherished values such as happiness, abun-dance, freedom, justice, equality etc.

This last point makes us realize that progress is always relative to the values which are taken into account. It is not a purely descriptive, detached, objective concept, but rather a valuational category. The same process may be conceived as progressive or not, depending on the assumed value preferences. These differ widely among individual persons, groups, classes, nations. What con-stitutes progress for some may not be considered progress by others. We must always ask: Progress for whom and in which respect? There is no ab-solute progress. The specification of the values taken as measures or criteria of progress is always necessary.

But does this mean that the choice of such values is a completely subjec-tive, conventional and arbitrary matter? We should not fall into the trap of complete relativism. There are various degrees in which values are relative. At one pole we shall find measures of progress on which most people would probably agree, which may be taken to constitute the closest approximation to the absolute criteria of progress. Take human life itself as the ultimate value. To sceptics and relativists who deny progress in modern society I would address such questions as: Is it not a fact that the average length of life is twice as long in the twentieth century as in the Middle Ages? Can that be due to anything else but medical progress? Clearly it is hard to doubt that the longer life span is something universally desired. Or is not the eradication of many deadly endemic diseases another indication of medical progress? Take efficiency or cost-effectiveness as another non-problematic value. Is it not better to cross the ocean in six hours rather than three months, a feat allowed by technological progress? Is it not preferable to send a fax to waiting weeks for letters to be exchanged, clearly another technological achievement? The third candidate for universal value could be the scope of knowledge. Is it not good that we know much more, and much more deeply, about the mechanisms of nature and society than we did before? Is it not an improvement that hard facts about society, and its history are provided by meticulous, disciplined research, rather than by imagination, fantasy, myths and stereotypes? Can scientific progress be doubted? As Robert Merton puts it:

> today's astronomers may actually have a more solid, more sweeping, and more exacting knowledge of the sun, moon, planets, and stars than did Aristarchos of Samos or even Ptolemy . . . today's demographers just might have a deeper and broader understanding of the dynamics of population change than, say, the 17th-century William Petty or even the early 19th-century Thomas Malthus. (*Merton 1975: 337; 1982*)

On the other hand there are areas where the criteria of progress become highly contestable. In the nineteenth century and well into the twentieth, industrialization, urbanization and modernization were treated as synonymous with progress. Only recently it has turned out that they may have gone too far (overpopulated cities, crowded tourist resorts, cluttered airports, jammed highways, packed beaches, gluts of goods, consumer waste), and also that good things may produce quite vicious side-effects (pollution, depletion of resources, environmental destruction, civilizational diseases). It has also become apparent that progress in one area may often occur only at the cost of regress in another. The current processes of post-communist transition in eastern and central Europe provide a host of illustrations. Democratization, the opening of societies, the emergence of entrepreneurship and a free market are accompanied by rising unemployment and poverty, the loosening of social discipline, with soaring rates of crime and delinquency, factional struggles and ungovernability, and a flood of low-level mass culture. How can the balance of benefits and harms, functions and dysfunctions, be calculated?

For a long stretch of intellectual history, numerous thinkers – from Thomas More to Mao Tse-tung, from Plato to Marx – have believed that it is possible to safeguard progress in all dimensions of society, for all its members at the same time, to attain overall and universal progress. They have drawn the images of perfect societies, social utopias. Such images provided their comprehensive, synthetic criteria of progress. Progress meant coming closer to the perfection of utopia, be it the New Harmony, the millennium, the State of the Sun or communism.

Others, aware of the incompatibilities, ambivalences and incommensurability of various dimensions of progress, proposed more specific criteria. They selected those aspects of social life, which in their view had paramount importance, and defined progress with reference to them. For some, religion was the core domain, and spiritual and moral progress leading to salvation counted most. For others, secular knowledge was crucial, and therefore the progress of knowledge leading to 'positive' science was decisive. Others focused on the domain of everyday life and stressed the importance of social bonds, ties, solidarities, 'ligatures', in a word the presence of 'community' as the most important aspect of progress. Others treated the domain of politics as central, and put forward the criterion of freedom: negative freedom, i.e. freedom *from* constraints, barriers, blocks to individual expression and self-realization, and positive freedom, democratic participation and representation, i.e. freedom *to* influence and shape one's own society. Another version of this criterion was emancipation, i.e. enlarging the scope of those who are full participants, subjects with rights, citizens in a society. In other words progress was measured by a growing inclusiveness and waning exclusiveness in society (expressed by the slogan of *Egalité* in the French Revolution and the following debate on egalitarianism). Other thinkers emphasized technology, considering the growing mastery over nature as the ultimate measure of progress. It was taken to signify the unique might of the human species *vis-à-vis* its environment. Others turned to economy and looked at humanly organized production and equitable distribution as prerequisites of progress, with justice and equality as its basic criteria. Finally, some focused on opportunities, availability of choices and options, occupational, educational, political ideological, recreational etc., as the criterion of progress (Dahrendorf 1979). A narrower variety of this emphasizes consumer options: growing abundance and variety of goods and services available on the market. The criterion of opportunities is often coupled with the notion of equality and inclusiveness, emphasizing equal access to opportunities for the largest segments of society. Not the presence of opportunities and options *per se*, but only the existence of equal and universal life-chances is taken as the measure of progress.

Thus, among the fragmentary, piecemeal criteria of progress (as opposed to the comprehensive utopian images) we find salvation, knowledge, community, freedom (negative and positive), emancipation, mastery over nature, justice, equality, abundance, options, widely accessible life-chances.

The mechanism of progress

There is an equal variety of views about the mechanism of progress. We have in mind three things. First, the moving forces (or agency) of progress: what pushes the social processes in the progressive direction? What are the causal agents activating progress? Second, we have to consider the form or shape that the process takes: What is the trajectory of progress, along what route does it move? And third, we have to examine the mode of operation of a social system resulting in progress: How is progress achieved, by what means is it attained?

Speaking about agency of progress, we may distinguish three consecutive stages in the history of social thought. Early thinkers located the moving force of progress in the supernatural domain. Deities, gods, providence, fate were believed to safeguard the progressive direction of social or historical processes. The sacralization of agency, led to faith in progress as decreed from above, as the endowed bequest, eliciting gratitude as the only feasible form of human reaction. Later thinkers took an alternative view; they located agency in the natural domain. The inherent tendencies and potentialities of society were taken as responsible for the progressive course of social processes (as the tendencies encoded in the genes, embryos, seeds manifest themselves in the growth of organisms). The secularization (naturalization) of agency led to the view of progress as a natural and inexorable unfolding of potentialities, and demanded adaptation or adjustment as the only conceivable human reaction. Finally modern thinkers are inclined to focus on human agents (individual and collective) as producers, constructors of progress. The humanization of agency leads to the view of progress as something to be achieved, constructed, implemented, and therefore requiring creative effort, striving, seeking, as appropriate human attitudes.

Thus as far as agency is concerned, the most fundamental difference divides the notion of automatic, *self-operating* progress (in the sacralized or secular version) from the *activist* notion of progress. The first posits an extra-human agency, the second focuses on people and their actions. The first claims the necessity of progress, the second admits the contingency of progress, which may (but also may not) occur, depending on the actions people take. In the first, progress *happens*, in the second progress *is attained*. The first encourages a passive, wait-and-see, adaptive attitude, the second demands active, creative, constructive commitment.

The form or shape that a process takes is also conceived in many ways. One dimension of the trajectory of progress is its evenness or smoothness. Thus some authors treat progress as a gradual, incremental, piecemeal movement towards better states of society. Take as an example the classical notion of scientific progress: inventions, discoveries, observations, hypotheses slowly accumulate through time, covering an ever larger range of phenomena and reaching deeper into their substance. Knowledge is additive: it grows and expands slowly by small increments. But there is another, alternative image of progress, as an uneven process, working through sudden accelerations and congestions of change, and after a period of quantitative cummulation, undergoing a qualitative move to a higher level. This is the revolutionary (or dialectical) image of progress. Take the same example of science. The modern view advanced by Thomas Kuhn (1970) asserts that scientific progress is achieved through a series of scientific revolutions, radical shifts of a dominant scientific view, rather then merely incremental additions to the same picture of a certain domain. The rejection of an earlier paradigm and adoption of a new one open a period within which normal cummulative work occurs, but only up to a moment when the paradigm is exhausted and impotent in the face of new puzzles. Then, it is inevitably overcome and succeeded by the next paradigm. Quite similarly, in the Marxian view of social and economic progress, social revolutions bring radical, qualitative change of 'socio-economic formations' (slavery into feudalism, feudalism into capitalism, capitalism into socialism and so on). In the long periods between revolutions progress asserts itself in slower, cumulative, purely quantitative fashion (see chapter 11).

The related aspect of what we call the form, or shape of progress has to do with consistency. Is it the process which proceeds linearly, consistently, or just the overall, ultimate tendency which allows temporary regresses, breakdowns, stagnation, detours, and prevails only in the 'last count'? Early evolutionists, e.g. Comte, Spencer and Durkheim, seem to take the first, linear view. Progress of mind or structural differentiation or division of labour are taken to be persistent processes. On the other hand if we take Karl Marx, we see a completely different image. Namely, within each of the socio-economic formations we observe regular, systematic regress – growing exploitation, impoverishment of the masses, mounting grievances and discontents, deeper injustices etc. – which intensify to the degree which makes social revolution inevitable. Revolution means a major progressive leap, but then the same process of internal regress and decay starts again within a new socio-economic formation, at its beginnings highly 'progressive' but then deteriorating and preparing the ground for the next revolution. In the long run, the trajectory of history is progressive; in the short run it incorporates transient phases of regress. It is interesting to note that the Marxian view has some resemblance to the early religious views of progress, e.g to the notion typical of Christianity (as in St Augustine) that salvation and eternal happiness (the City of God) are to be reached only by torment, suffering and deprivations in earthly life. Ultimate well-being is to be earned by earlier unhappy existence.

Finally if we consider the manner of operation of the social system resulting in progress, another pair of opposite images will appear. One image, again typical for early evolutionists. emphasizes the 'peaceful', harmonious unfolding of progressive potentialities. The other focuses on internal tensions, strains, contradictions and conflicts, whose resolution moves the system in the progressive direction. The Manichaean theme of the struggle between the opposing forces of good and evil, positive and negative elements, in which the good eventually prevails, is to be found in various guises in numerous theories of progress. It is already present in St Augustine's dichotomy of the City of Man and the City of God as two polar forces struggling in the world. In the modern period it is characteristic for the dialectics of Hegel and Marx – with the latter's idea of class struggle as the central mechanism of historical progress. We find it in Darwinism, with its notion of the struggle for existence and the survival of the fittest as the secret of natural selection and progressive evolution of the species. It is also present in Freudian psychoanalysis, asserting the permanent tension between the 'id' (biologically rooted drives) and 'superego' (socially imposed constraints) within human personality, and between nature and culture in the extra-personal, outer world.

The demise of the idea of progress

Reigning in social thought for almost three thousand years, the idea of progress seems to have declined in the twentieth century. There are some historical facts which contradict it quite forcefully, and there are some intellectual trends which go againts its deep, fundamental premises (cf. Alexander 1990).

As the twentieth century draws to a close, there are repeated attempts to take stock, and some observers already call it the 'dreadful century'. It is a century which witnessed the Nazi Holocaust and Stalin's Gulags, two world wars, well over 100 million killed in global and local conflicts, widespread unemployment and poverty, famines and epidemics, drug addiction and crime, ecological destruction and depletion of resources, tyrannies and dictatorships of all brands from fascism to communism, and, last but not least, the ever present possibilities of nuclear annihilation and global environmental catastrophe. No wonder there is a widespread disillusionment and disenchantment with the idea of progress (Alexander 1990: 15–38). After all, progress, like most social concepts, is a reflexive notion: it interacts with objective social reality, flourishes in the periods of observable progress, decays in the periods when actual progress becomes questionable. Perhaps the disenchantment is all the more severe as it follows the elevated hopes, widespread optimism, aspirations and promises of the 'era of progress', the period of 'triumphant modernity' in the nineteenth and early twentieth centuries.

Some intellectual trends work in the same direction. Robert Nisbet (1980: 317–351) unravels the major premises of the idea of progress, and claims that all of them come under attack in contemporary thought. Let us mention just some examples. For a long time there has been a conviction of the nobility, even superiority, of western civilization. Recently we observe the 'displacement of the west', the decline of faith in the values and institutions of modern, highly developed societies. Nisbet finds its symptoms first in widespread irrationalism, reborn mysticism, rebellion against reason and science; second, in the subjectivism and egotistic narcissism typical of consumer culture; and third, in reigning pessimism, the dominant image of degeneration, deterioration, decay. Another premise underlying the idea of progress was the affirmation of unrestricted economic and technological growth, the unlimited expansion of human powers. The fashionable idea of 'limits to growth', barriers to expansion (cf. Mishan 1977) clearly counters that. The next premise proclaimed faith in reason and science as the only sources of valid and practically applicable knowledge. Instead we observe both the attack on science, in the name of epistemological relativism, and the attack on reason in the name of emotion, intuition and extra-empirical cognition as well as outright irrationalism. Finally the concept of progress in its modern secular versions was rooted in the 'belief in the intrinsic importance, the ineffaceable worth of life on this earth' (Nisbet 1980: 317). Instead, in modern industrial society, the reigning consumer culture with its emphasis on leisure and hedonistic pleasure, seems to exhaust its gratifying and mobilizing potential, and the 'pall of boredom', the feeling of senselessness, the experience of anomie or alienation have set in.

To Nisbet's list one could add two more premises. First, utopianism, i.e. the articulation of the comprehensive idealized images of the better, desired society. As we have seen, this has been intimately linked to the idea of progress for several centuries. But now we are clearly witnessing an anti-utopian mood. The final blow to utopian thinking has recently been dealt by the fall of the communist system, the last of the failed attempts to realize a utopian vision in the world. What is left is the uncertainty and unpredictability of the future seen as entirely contingent, open to chance and random developments. This undermines the other premise of the idea of progress, orientation towards the future. There is no future-oriented project able to grasp human imagination and mobilize collective action (the role once played so efficiently, e.g by socialist ideas). More specifically, there is no vision of the better world (once provided by the utopia of communism); instead we have either catastrophic prophecies or simple extrapolations of present trends (as e.g.in the.theories of post-industrial society). Furthermore there is no programme of social betterment, there are no guidelines on how to escape contemporary predicaments. No wonder people turn away from the future and take presentist attitudes, focused on immediate gratification, short-time horizons and everyday existence.

As a result of all these historical and intellectual developments, the concept of progress has been replaced by the concept of crisis as the letmotif of the twentieth century. It is true of common consciousness, where pessimistic views of social realities dominate, not only in underdeveloped and poor countries, but also in leading, prosperous ones. People become accustomed to think in terms of recurrent or endemic crisis, economic, political, or cultural. It is also true of social science, where critical accounts of current processes in terms of crisis are abundant. As John Holton puts it: 'Contemporary social thought has become dominated, if not obsessed by the idea of crisis' (Holton 1990: 39). He notes perceptively that we are witnessing a curious 'normalization of crisis'. The concept itself originally derives from drama, or medicine, where it signifies the crossroads, the bifurcation points, moments when the intensification of processes requires some resolution, either of a positive sort (e.g. healing the patient), or of a negative sort (e.g. death). Hence, crisis is temporary, and leads either to improvement or to disaster. In contrast to that meaning, people are apt to conceive social crisis as chronic, endemic, and do not envisage its future elimination.

The demise of the notion of progress, and its replacement by the idea of a chronic crisis, results in the intellectual climate and popular mood where 'social experience is less and less part of an epic, and increasingly part of a soap-opera. . . . One of the most striking symptoms of this epoch of crisis-talk, and crisis normalization is the breakdown of optimistic narratives of social change and historical evolution' (Holton 1990: 43–4). This is clearly an aspect of what 'post-modernists' label as the end of 'grand narratives' (Lyotard 1984).

Does it mean that progess is dead? I doubt it. I would expect that the idea of progress is too important for the human mind, too fundamental to the alleviation of existential tensions and uncertainties, to be eliminated for good. It is suffering temporary breakdown, but sooner or later will regain its hold on human imagination. But to safeguard its continuing viability, it needs to be revised and reformulated, purified of some outdated and misleading premises. One possible direction of such an effort will be suggested next, closing our discussion of progress.

An alternative concept of progress

The recent disenchantment and disillusionment with the idea of progress is closely interwoven with a surge of criticism directed at major varieties of traditional developmentalism. The critique of the 'metaphor of growth', as underlying evolutionism, and the critique of the 'iron laws of history', as proclaimed by dogmatic, orthodox versions of historical materialism, are taken to imply the necessary rejection of the idea of progress (Popper 1950; 1964; Nisbet 1969; 1970; Tilly 1984). But is such a conclusion really warranted? Is it not possible to retain a concept of progress, leaving behind the traditional versions of developmentalism with their unacceptable assumptions of finalism, fatalism or determinism? Is it not possible to rid the idea of its nineteenth-century ballast?

Granted that the idea of progress was originally linked to the image of di-rectional process, there are several questions to be asked about its more spe-cific characteristics. To begin with, at which *phase of the process* is the concept of progress 'anchored', or less metaphorically, which phase of the process is its immediate referent? Three answers are possible. The first, most common in classical sociological theory, refers progress to the final outcome, result, product of the process, defined either as a comprehensive blueprint, a com-plex image of society-to-become (typical for social utopias), or as some speci-fic trait of society and its constituents (e.g. wealth, health, productivity, equality, happiness). One may speak here of 'progress as an ideal'. The second answer locates progress in the overall logic of the process, in which each stage is seen as an improvement over its predecessor, and itself further per-fectible, but without any ultimate end (this would be characteristic for the evo-lutionary notion of gradual differentiation or adaptive upgrading). One may speak here of 'progress as betterment'. Finally, the third answer would relate progress to the originating mechanism of the process, emphasizing the poten-tiality or capacity for progress inherent in human agency. Here, it is not the quality of what actually becomes, but the potentiality for becoming, that becomes the core meaning of progress. Not the achievement but the achieving, not the attainment but striving, not the finding but the quest – these are the marks of progress.

I am going to opt for the last solution. Its rudiments can be found in E. H. Carr's doctrine of 'unlimited progress', as reviewed by Christopher Lasch: 'Without postulating an end to history, he [Carr] argued, men and women could still look forward to improvements "subject to no limits that we can envisage, towards goals which can be defined only as we advance towards them"' (Lasch 1991: 42).

Before elaborating on this position in more detail, I wish to take up another related question, concerning the criteria of progress and their logical status. Some would claim that the criteria or measures of progress are absolute, constant, universal, in a word, unchanging. They supposedly provide us with an external, independent scale with which to appraise the ongoing process. The opposite position is relativistic and historicist. It claims that standards of progress are themselves dynamic, permanently changing, constantly evolving as the process unfolds. The needs, desires, goals, values, or any other measures of progress, are held to be modified with their satisfaction or fulfilment. They are always relative to the concrete phase of the process and never reach an ultimate, final embodiment. What is striven for is changeable and variable, but the striving itself is constant. There is the variability of objects of human desire, but at the same time, the permanence of desiring. Thus the measure of progress is no longer external, but rather immanent to the process itself.

The next question has to do with the deontic status of progress: does it refer to necessities or possibilities? Traditional, developmentalist approaches would treat progress as inevitable, necessary, owing to inexorable laws of evolution or history. More recent, post-developmentalist theories of morphogenesis-structuration (to be discussed in chapter 13) would certainly opt for a different, possibilistic account, where progress is treated as merely contingent, as an open *chance* for betterment which, alas, does not inevitably come about, and may even remain unrecognized by human actors.

Finally one more question has to be asked, about the ontological substratum of progress: What is the substantive nature of this causal, generative force bringing about progress? Four typical answers may be singled out. The doctrine of 'providentialism', encountered in various schools of social philosophy, locates the ultimate, moving force of progress, the agency, in the supernatural order, invokes the divine will, providence, intervention of God. The doctrine of 'heroism' typical for traditional historiography – that elder brother to sociology – locates the agency in the exceptional personal endowment of great men: kings, prophets, leaders, codifiers, revolutionaries, generals etc. This is already an earthly domain, but still extra-social because dependent on the genetic, more or less accidental propensities of individual people. The doctrine of 'organicism' introduces the social component, but in a peculiar way; it treats the causal agency as inherent in the operation of a social organism, its in-built propensity for growth, evolution, development. The origins of progress are social, but, paradoxically, extra-human. People are still absent from the picture, where self-regulating, compensatory, automatic mechanisms seem to reign independently of human efforts. If people appear at all, it is only in the capacity of fully moulded marionettes, unwitting executors, carriers of the preordained verdicts of history; as embodiments of productive forces, technological tendencies, demographic trends, revolutionary *élan*.

It is only in the doctrine of 'constructivism' underlying post-developmentalist theories that the emphasis is turned towards real socialized individuals in their actual social and historical contexts, and the moving force of change, the agency, is located in their normal everyday social activities. Some of the resulting progress may be intended, but mostly it is conceived here as an unintended and often unrecognized result of human efforts, as the product of the 'invisible hand' (Adam Smith), the 'cunning of reason' (Hegel), or 'situational logic' (Karl R. Popper). The agency is finally humanized and socialized at the same time. Common people are brought back into the picture and acquire truly human size, as aware but not omniscient, powerful but not omnipotent, creative but not unconstrained, free but not unlimited. Such an account of the agency is both presupposed and entailed by morphogenesis-structuration theories.

To recapitulate, it is claimed that the new theoretical orientation of post-developmentalism, and particularly of morphogenesis-structuration, suggests a new approach to social progress (1) as a potential capacity, rather than ultimate achievement, (2) as a dynamic, evolving, relative quality of a concrete process, rather than an absolute, universal, external standard, (3) as a historical possibility, opportunity, open option, rather than necessary, inevitable, inexorable tendency, and (4) as a product, often unintended and even unrecognized, of human pluralistic and collective actions, rather than a result of divine will, good intentions of exceptional individuals ('great men') or operation of automatic social mechanisms. This provides a framework for a radically new notion of progress. 'The expectation of indefinite, open-ended improvement, even more than the insistence that improvements can come only through human effort, provides the solution to the puzzle that is otherwise so baffling – the resilience of progressive ideology in the face of discouraging events that have shattered the illusion of utopia' (Lasch 1991: 48).

In the proposed reconstruction, progress is intimately linked with the robust agency. But when may an agency be said to be progressive? From the point of view of progress *any* agency seems certainly better than none. Clearly, in order to have progress, we must have directional change, and if we conceive directional change as produced by human beings, then *some* human agency is an obvious prerequisite of progress. But its operation is only a necessary condition, and by no means a sufficient one for progress to ensue. Do not forget that directional change may also have a backward direction; it may produce regress rather than progress. Thus, it is only a specifically constituted agency, a particular kind of agency which presents the potentiality for progress. What traits of the agency are especially relevant in this connection?

1   First, of course, the characteristics of actors. Here I would emphasize several oppositions which allow of gradations and all intermediate forms. Thus, actors may be creative, innovative, achievement-oriented, or passive, conservative, reconciled with ascribed positions. They may emphasize autonomy, independence, personal integrity, or exhibit conformity, adaptation, dependence. They may have adequate self-awareness of their social situation, or be completely ignorant, trapped in a mythology or false consciousness. Which is the case for the majority of actors, or especially influential kinds of actors, will decisively shape the quality of the agency.

2   The characteristics of structures are equally significant. They may be rich in options, pluralistic, heterogeneous, complex; or just the opposite, they may be poor in options, limited, homogeneous and simple. They may be open, flexible, tolerant, allowing for a large scope of variety; or closed, rigid, dogmatic, effectively eliminating novelty. Again, which kinds of structures surround the majority of actors, or especially influential actors, will be reflected in the quality of the agency.

3   The characteristics of natural environment in which a society is placed exert their impact at two levels: via objective conditions and via subjective attitudes. The natural conditions may be benign, rich in resources, malleable, or harsh, poor and forbidding. And people may attempt to harness, mould, master nature, to adapt it to their needs and aspirations, or they may wish merely to adapt themselves to nature, remain in the state of subjugation and passivity.

4   Keeping in mind the irreducible historical dimension of society, one must emphasize the characteristics of tradition, again at the objective and subjective level. Objectively, it seems to matter whether the tradition is marked by continuity, consistency, long duration, or rather by disruptions, discontinuities, ambiguities. Subjectively, the attitude of pride, respect, rootedness in tradition, may be opposed to presentism and uncritical rejection of the past (so typical for the 'now generation').

5   Finally the characteristics of the expected future may vary significantly too. The attitude of optimism and hope is opposed to pessimism, catastrophism and despair. The belief that the future is contingent, allows of alternative scenarios dependent on human efforts, is opposed to all brands of fatalism and finalism. A long-range image or strategic plan for the future is something quite different from the short-range, immediate expectations or opportunistic, tactical scheming.

If we look again at the full list of variable characteristics of the agency, it will be seen that they fall into two groups. Some determine whether people will want to act towards the transformation of their society; those variables shape action-oriented motivations. Others determine whether people will be able to act; those variables shape action-conducive opportunities. The agency may be thought of as progressive only if it brings together those two pre-requisites – motivations and opportunities; only if people *want to* act, and *can* act accordingly.

I would suppose that such a situation is approximated by the conjunction of conditions at the initial poles of each dichotomy, that is by a combination of: (1) creative, autonomous, and self-aware actors, (2) rich and flexible structures, (3) a benign and actively confronted natural environment, (4) continuous and proudly affirmed tradition, and (5) optimistic, long-range anticipation and planning of the future. This is an ideal type of an 'active society' (to adopt the term of Amitai Etzioni 1968a), generating progress-oriented agency, a society set on the course of progressive self-transformations.

So far we have been characterizing the agency from the external perspective, looking at it from the outside. The properties of the progress-oriented agency were reduced to the nature of conditioning, determining factors impinging upon it from without. Now I wish to take the internal perspective and focus on the operation of the progress-oriented agency, so to speak from within. The question is: what is the *modus operandi* of the agency placed within the set of conditions and influences, structural, personal, natural and historical, comprised by our ideal type?

It will be described by two comprehensive, synthetic notions: freedom and self-transcendence. Thus, the viable, progress-oriented agency is to some extent free. It is free in the sense of negative freedom ('freedom from'), that is to say it commands a certain level of autonomy and independence from constraints; it operates within some open field of options, opportunities, chances; and it is free in the sense of positive freedom ('freedom to'), that is to say it has the capacity to influence, modify, reshape constraints and enhance facilitations; it has some degree of power and control over circumstances.

But its crucial, most important feature is the tendency towards self-transcendence; going beyond itself, overcoming limitations, breaking through constraints, crossing 'frontiers'. To stick with the latter metaphor, self-transcendence occurs at three 'frontiers' of the human condition: transcending nature by harnessing it, controlling, regulating through work; transcending social structures by means of evasions, deviations, reforms and revolutions; and, last but not least, self-transcendence by human actors through learning, training, self-control, achieving, advancing, extending their limited human powers by technology etc.

This propensity may be explained as an ougrowth of two fundamental traits of the human world: the creativity (innovativeness) of actors producing original and novel objects, ideas, institutions; and the cumulative character of constantly expanded and enriched human experience; individually learned in the biographical span, and socially (culturally) transmitted in the historical span. Thus, ultimately, the mainspring of progress is found in the irreducible and essentially unlimited creativity and educability of human beings, able to conceive novelty and to inherit as well as to pass on innovations, permanently enlarging their common pool of knowledge, skills, strategies, techniques etc.

If exercised in conditions described in the ideal type of progress-conducive agency, these human propensities and abilities safeguard self-transcendence and the constant progress of humankind. Let me strongly underline this 'if'. There is no necessity of progress, because it is not preordained that people will be willing and able to exercise their creative capacity. The constraining natural, structural or historical conditions, or the suppressed motivations for activism (e.g. effected by socialization to passivity, by adaptive, defensive mechanisms in the sitiation of constraints, or by vicious lessons, 'scars' from past failures) may prevent creativity from flourishing. Similarly, the process of cumulation, the passing-on of tradition, may be disrupted, both at the biographical and at the historical level (the quality of family, school, church, media and other institutions will be decisive here). In such cases, stagnation or regress rather than progress will be a likely result.

The self-transcendence of society in which the agency participates as an ultimate causal force feeds back on the agency itself, resulting in its own self-transcendence. The actualization of potentialities of the agency via praxis enlarges those very potentialities. Emancipation of the agency through its operation in time results in enlarged freedom and stronger tendencies towards self-transcendence. The ultimate progressiveness of the agency is found in the fact that it not only stimulates progress but actually progresses itself. It is a cumulative historical outcome of its own operation.

3

The temporal dimension of society: social time

Time as the dimension of social life

All social phenomena occur at some moment in time. All social processes stretch over time. In short, social life is lived in time. Time, like space, is a universal context of social life: 'We must grasp the time–space relations inherent in the constitution of all social interaction . . . Any patterns of interaction that exist are situated in time' (Giddens 1979: 3, 202). Time is the indispensable dimension of human reality 'implicated in every aspect of our lives' (Adam 1990: 2). These ontological facts entail epistemological consequences; they are the reason for the 'centrality of time for the subject matter of the social sciences' (Adam 1990: 9), or as Giddens puts it, the 'integrality of time to social theory' (1979: 198).

Obviously, however, time is even more intimately related to social change. The very experience of time and the idea of time derive from the changing nature of reality. It is impossible to conceive of time without reference to some change. And, vice versa, the idea of change apart from time is simply inconceivable. As we remember, time appears in the definition of social change, which usually refers to the difference of two states of the social system *over time* (see chapter 1). Thus, as Pitirim Sorokin puts it with characteristic clarity: 'Any Becoming, Change, Process, Motion, Movement, Dynamic State, in contradistinction to Being, implies time' (1937, vol. 1: 156).

Let us first look at some general properties of time as the dimension of every social phenomenon, and then at some special characteristics of time as an aspect of social change. Every social phenomenon or event is related to other phenomena or events. There are no absolutely single, unique or isolated phenomena or events. One of the forms that such a relation takes is sequential, with precedence and succession linking events in a chain or a process. This is true both of macro-events, mezzo-events and micro-events. War is followed by a peace treaty, elections by the swearing-in of the president, inflation by a declining standard of living, dictatorial policy by oppositional movements. All this happens within the stretch of history. To switch to another dimension, childhood is followed by school education, marriage by bearing children, retirement by death. These events happen within the stretch of biography. Coming even closer to daily realities, breakfast is followed by an underground journey to work. Then lunch-break comes, then a committee meeting, then the return journey home, watching TV, eating dinner, going to bed. These events mark the stretch of everyday life. At all levels, if we take any single event it always has some location in a wider sequence, precedes or succeeds others, happens before or after others. It occurs at some time. Putting it in other words, 'all social acts are temporarily fitted inside of larger social acts. We call this *time embeddedness*' (Lewis and Weigart 1990: 82).

If we look more closely at every social phenomenon or event, we shall see that it is not only related externally to other phenomena but can be internally broken down into components, and that those components are also temporally interrelated. Some internal relations are again sequential, linking earlier and later stages or phases of the phenomenon. We say that each phenomenon or event has some duration, lasts for some time. Take the same examples that we treated before as single events. War, as we know from medieval history, may stretch over 100 years. School education lasts for a decade or more. Breakfast takes half an hour. The scale differs, from macro through mezzo to micro, but the fact that every phenomenon or event takes some time is pretty obvious.

Whenever we think of a phenomenon as momentary, fleeting, instantaneous, it is always a matter of the relative time-framework that we apply. Lightning and thunder may be ostensibly devoid of any duration from our common-sense perspective, but for a physicist they apppear as extremely complex and durable sequences of electric discharges and sound waves. A high jump, a knock-out or a tennis serve may seem extremely swift, but think of all those biological processes occurring in the body of an athlete, each of which has distinct duration. From the point of view of the military strategist, a battle may be just an episode, but not for the soldiers in the trenches. In brief, there are no timeless phenomena or events, either in the sense of location in time or in the sense of extension through time. Sequence and duration are two fundamental aspects of social life, which become reflected as two crucial aspects of time.

Social events and phenomena are also irreversible. Once something has happened, it cannot be undone (Adam 1990: 169). Once you have taken some action it cannot be un-acted; once you have conceived some idea, it cannot be un-thought; once you have learned something, it cannot be un-known; once you have experienced something it cannot be un-experienced. Briefly, life cannot be un-lived. 'Our lives "pass away" in irreversible time with the passing away of the life of the organism' (Giddens 1984: 35).

This is true at all levels of social life. At the macro-level of history, there is no un-waging war, once it has been waged. Of course it can be stopped and a peace treaty signed, but these are already different, succeeding historical events. At the mezzo-level of biography, there is no un-bearing a child once it has been born. Of course one can give a child for adoption, surrender parental authority or simply abandon it, or the child may die young, but these again are different, succeeding biographical events. At the level of everyday life, we know perfectly well that there is no un-fighting of a family fight, even when it is followed by full repentance and accord, just as there is no un-making of the omelette, or un-eating of the heavy dinner, even if one would like to during the sleepless night that follows. All this is comprehended in the metaphorical idea of a flow of time, so that whatever happens next will already be at a different location in the flow. Heraclitus expressed this in antiquity in his famous proposition that one cannot step twice into the same river. In the words of a modern author: 'The action in its repetition can never be the same. Everything involved in it has irrevocably changed in the intervening period' (Adam 1990: 168).

The irreversibility of the time-flow implies the distinction between past, present and future. The distinction, so obvious to us today, is not historically universal; it appeared only at a certain point in the development of human societies, and is intimately related to the invention of writing. Only then did the past stretch back, to be recorded and not only remembered. 'In the strictest sense, history begins with writing' (Goody 1968: 39). The future stretched forward, could be projected and planned, not just loosely imagined. The strongest affirmation of the distinction came only with Judaeo-Christian thought, and from this source it has pervaded the whole of human civilization.

The distinction of time past, time present and time future is also not as sharp as it may seem. Strictly speaking, there is no present, because social processes are continuous, and at every conceivable moment they are incessantly passing from the past to the future; they are already in the past, or no longer in the future. However small the scale we take, there is always the movement, the flow, rather than some frozen state. Even as I am writing these words, every sentence is already in the past before I have completed it. The moment I type it, the word is no longer in the future. The cliché that in the present, the past and the future meet is not devoid of reason. For practical purposes, however, the distinction is of course valid, as long as we remember that what we take as present is conventional, cut off from the continuous flow by means of arbitrary borders. In social life the criterion of demarcation most often has to do with the possibility of human perception and causal influence on the course of events. As Barbara Adam puts it, 'We know past events by records, perceive present ones directly, and know future ones in our imagination only. Past events are determined, present ones are becoming determined, and future ones are yet to be determined . . . The past can no longer be influenced, the present is subject to influence, and the future is only potentially influenceable' (1990: 22).

Time as the aspect of social change

For the study of social change, time is not only a universal dimension, but the core, constitutive factor. In social life change is ubiquitous; strictly speaking, there are no two, temporally distinct states of any social entity (a social action, a group, a community, an institution, a society) that can be identical. Of course, for practical purposes, the needs of our everyday life suggest some magnitudes of differences which can be ignored. Then we speak of stability, as opposed to change. For example, historians may think of some ancient societies as stable, unchanging for centuries or millennia, compared to the accelerated changes typical for the modern period. Social anthropologists may describe some primitive, underdeveloped societies as 'cold', in contra-distinction to the urban-industrial 'hot' societies of the western world. All this, however, is relative. What is treated as stable 'refers mostly to rates of change that are very much slower than those of the observer's frame of reference. Traditional societies are extremely slowly changing when measured and defined against present Western standards' (Adam 1990: 29).

In reality change and time are always there, and the idea of stability is only a handy convention. Even when we use this convention, we cannot escape time, for speaking about stability, we have in mind a relative lack of differences, persistence of traits through relatively prolonged periods of time. 'To speak of social stability cannot involve abstracting from time since stability means continuity over time' (Giddens 1979: 199). Even more so, speaking of stability makes sense only by reference to something else that is changing, other societies, the environment, the membership of groups etc. For example, Eskimo society is stable compared to Canadian, Danish compared to Italian. The American constitutional system is stable compared to American economics or technology. The Catholic Church is stable in spite of the constant turnover of believers, expanding and contracting through centuries.

When related to social changes, time may appear in two guises. First, it may serve as the external framework for the measurement of events and processes, ordering their chaotic flow for the benefit of human orientation or the co-ordination of social actions. This is 'quantitative time', implied by conventional devices like clocks and calendars which allow us to identify the comparative span, speed, intervals, durations of various social occurrences. By the same token they allow us to link or separate in an orderly fashion the innumerable actions taken by individuals and groups in a society. Would an academic lecture be possible if professor and students did not appear in the same room at roughly the same moment, and students from the previous class did not leave before? Would a religious service be performed if the priest and the faithful did not come to the church at the same time? Would a train trip take place if the engine driver, guards and passengers did not arrive at the same platform at the same time? The more complex human society becomes, the greater is the importance of temporal ordering and co-ordination. In modern society no organization would work without the reckoning of time. Imagine a great factory without work shifts, train services or airlines without timetables, restaurants without meal hours. When devices for measuring time are invented and implemented, all social changes – events and phenomena – can be timed, located within that external framework. We may refer here to 'events in time'.

But there is another way in which time blends with social change, no longer as the external, conventional framework, but as an internal, immanent, ontological property of social events and processes. This is 'qualitative time', defined by the nature of social processes. When we consider any actual social processes, they will manifest various temporal qualities:

1   They are typically longer or shorter. For example, compare a battle and a war, legislative reform and long-range moral erosion, revolutionary mobilization and economic growth.

2   They run slower or quicker. For example, compare galloping inflation and the lingering emancipation of women, an instantaneous career in pop art and gradual professional advancement in medicine.

3   They are marked by rhythmic or random intervals. For example, compare waves of economic prosperity and decline, booms and recessions with the disorderly fluctuations of artistic fads and fashions.

4   They are sliced into units of different substantive qualities by means of natural or social circumstances. For example, compare, on the one hand, periods of work and leisure correlated with the natural phenomena of daytime and night-time, or in rural settings, phases of farm labour marked by the equally natural divisions of springtime, summertime, autumn and wintertime, and, on the other hand, socially constructed distinctions of sacred time and secular time, reflected in the difference between national holidays and days of work, periods of mourning and honeymoons, market days and Ramadans, examination sessions and university vacations. In all these cases we encounter 'time in events' rather than simply 'events in time', and this is what we usually mean in sociology by the term 'social time'.

Time reckoning

The measurement of time requires a scale and units. These can be constructed by reference to repetitive events marking intervals and unique events marking the beginning of the scale. Natural events provide the obvious reference points, and the simplest of them is the astronomical cycle, the succession of days and nights, and the succession of the seasons. Some idea of dawn, sunrise, morning, noon, afternoon, evening and sunset is probably universal, imposed by the primordial circumstances of human existence on the earth. Similarly the succession of the seasons, spring, summer, autumn and winter, most often differing in climatic, atmospheric conditions and naturally linked with the cycle of breeding and vegetation, could not be ignored even by the earliest hunting and gathering tribes, and became central for organizing the yearly cycle of activities in horticultural and agricultural societies. Another unit of time, probably universally recognized, is the month, based on the lunar cycle of 29.5 days. In societies basing their economy on fishing and maritime occupations its importance is enhanced by its link with the tides.

Other units of time reflect social rather than natural experiences. This is the case with the week, and its social, hence to some extent conventional, origins are clear in the varied length it takes in various cultures. Eight days in early Rome, seven days in Judaeo-Christian tradition, ten days in China, five or six days in some parts of Africa and Central America. The foundation for the determination of the week was found in the recurrent rhythm of markets and fairs (Goody 1968: 34–35). It also reflected the biological need for rest, allocating one day for leisure or spiritual needs linked with religious faith, allocating a special day for prayer and ritual (Friday in Islam, Saturday in Judaism, Sunday in Christianity). The conventional divisions deriving from religion are also to be found in the yearly scale, e.g. the liturgical year in Christianity, or a daily scale, e.g. the order of daily life in monasteries marked by the hours of prayer (as beautifully described in Umberto Eco's *The Name of the Rose*).

The first technical devices for marking and measuring time, the sundial and the clepsydra, originated in Babylonia and Egypt thousands of years before our era. But there is a long story of numerous inventions before the clock was constructed in Europe in the mid-fourteenth century, the first weight-driven chronometer. Later the spring mechanism was devised, but it was only in the middle of the nineteenth century that the cheap personal watch, available to the mass public and not only to the richest, went on the market in Switzerland and the US, to become the most common and most often used technical instrument of the century to follow.

Clocks and watches made it possible to dissociate time from concrete events, whether natural or social, and to introduce conventional time units, of equal duration, easily countable. The division of the day into twelve hours, based on the system of the zodiac, had already been introduced in ancient Greece. The division of the hour into sixty minutes, and the minute into sixty seconds is a much more recent story, dating from the middle of the fourteenth century.

Time in consciousness and in culture

As a pervasive trait of social life objectively permeating all social events and processes, time has to find its reflection at the subjective level of consciousness. Perception and awareness of time is a universal human experience. Individual people differ to a striking extent in their 'sense of time', e.g. the ability to estimate the duration of events, to identify time moments without clocks (as in guessing the hour), to anticipate the length of the process necessary to achieve some goal (as in setting deadlines), to partition processes into intervals (as in planning the day's work). Some people are obsessively punctual, other notoriously late. The psychology of time is a field which focuses on such and similar phenomena, or, in brief, on the 'inner time' of human individuals.

For sociology, another reflection of the realities of time is more interesting, the socio-psychological or cultural, namely the typical symbols, values, rules and orientations referring to time and shared by groups, communities, classes and other collective, social entities. They become codified, entrenched in social consciousness or culture, acquiring an intersubjective and normative quality, and producing distinct 'temporal profiles' of various societies. The imprint of such common cultural patterns is to be felt in various areas of social life, manifested in specific styles of conduct. If we compare contemporary American culture with, say, Mexican culture, or Germany with Italy, or, in the historical perspective, if we compare early, traditional societies with modern industrial society, we shall discover fundamentally different time orientations. But this is true not only at the macro-level of nations, or ethnic groups. There are some occupations and professions that place a heavy emphasis on the virtues of punctuality, 'saving time' etc., while others treat it much more loosely. Think of business entrepreneurs as contrasted with artists, airline pilots as compared with farmers. Not only occupations and professions, but also social classes, gender and age groups have also been found to be highly differentiated in their time perspectives.

More precisely, when we speak of time orientation or time perspective, the following aspects may be distinguished:

1   The level of awareness of time: this is the most general trait, exemplified at one extreme by an obsessive concern with time, the flow of time, the passing of time, the lack of time etc.(the 'time-is-money syndrome'), and at the opposite extreme marked by indifference, negligence and permissiveness with respect to time (the 'mañana syndrome').

2   The depth of the awareness of time: sometimes only the immediate, nearest time is recognized, and sometimes distant time is also recognized, considered, endowed with importance and meaning. We may speak of a short-distance and a long-distance perspective, irrespective of whether we look forward or backward. The extreme case of the short-distance perspective is sometimes called 'presentism'.

3   The shape or form of time: cyclical or linear. Mircea Eliade (1959) claims that the time conception of 'archaic man' was cyclical, with events unfolding in a recurring rhythm of nature. The linear vision of time begins with Christianity, introducing the concept of future redemption and salvation towards which both world history and all personal biographies consistently approach. But even though the linear view seems to dominate in the modern industrial world, there are important enclaves of cyclical thinking. Michael Young (1988) emphasizes that the cyclical rhythms of social life are intimately related to the rhythmic essence of natural processes. 'Even if it goes against the grain of modern thinking to admit it, I want to draw attention to the crucial survival of the cyclical . . . I am arguing that it would be in accord with the facts of everyday experience, if not with modern stereotypes, to pay more attention to the continued turning of the wheel' (pp. 4, 6). He goes on to present fascinating illustrations of daily cycles of work and leisure, of the

solar year, the religious year, the week, and even the academic and sporting calendar. Similarly, J. David Lewis and Andrew J. Weigart (1990) discuss 'three cycles that in our society are based more or less on three natural sequences defined as meaningful units of time': the daily round, the weekly routine and the yearly seasons.

4   The emphasis on the past or the future: 'The way group members relate themselves to the past and future – i.e. their *time perspective* – is to a large extent dependent upon the group's structure and functions. Time perspective is an integral part of a society's values and individuals orient their actions in the present and toward the future with reference to the groups whose values they share' (Coser and Coser 1990: 191–2). Some societies or groups look backward: they cherish traditions, focus on past achievements, live in history; others look forward, break with traditions, ignore the past, look towards the future. We may speak of retrospective versus prospective orientation. For example, at the most comprehensive level, American society is usually considered as future-oriented, while 'the Chinese use the present as a focal point from which existence flows evenly in both directions' (Coser and Coser 1990: 192). But there is also a lower-level differentiation within every society. Some groups, ethnic, religious, occupational, take time perspectives considerably at variance with others. For example, within American society, some anarchist political factions or religious sects may take a future-oriented, utopian or chiliastic view. Most professions will also be future-oriented, but in a more this-worldly fashion, towards a nearer and more realistically conceived future. The same is true of the American middle class, oriented to achievement, career, and ready to postpone immediate gratification to a future moment. But there may be regions (the Old South) or traditionally oriented families living in their memories of the past. Finally some groups of a marginal sort, outcasts, the homeless, the unemployed, live from day to day, taking a presentist perspective. The same is true of groups placed in unusual, uncertain or dangerous situations, for example troops in battle. The shortening of the time perspective, living in the short run, becomes dominant. One may also predict that 'small children are most present-oriented and older persons are past-oriented' (Lewis and Weigart 1990: 82). In short, 'men are likely to view their present in a different light if they focus on the here and now than if they see the present either as instrumental for the future or as merely a mutilated fragment of a glorious past' (Coser and Coser 1990: 193).

5   The way of conceiving the future: it may be seen as either something to be passively encountered, or rather as something to be actively constructed. The former suggests anticipation and adaptation, the latter, planning and shaping. We may speak of passive or fatalistic orientation (e.g. in religious chiliastic sects) versus active or voluntaristic orientation (e.g in revolutionary social movements). When the latter attitude is coupled with a wide temporal imagination, and embraces not only mundane, everyday affairs but also large-scale historical processes, it is termed 'historicity'. Historicity is 'the conscious knowledge that we are not only historically formed but are forming history;

that history makes us and we make history' (Adam 1990: 146). In the words of another author it is the awareness of the linear elapsing of time and 'the active mobilisation of social forms in the pursuit of their own transformation' (Giddens 1979: 221). Both agree that such an orientation towards the future is itself a historical phenomenon, has arisen only at a certain stage of human civilization, and is particularly salient in the period of modernity.

6 The dominant value-emphasis either on change, novelty and progress, or on recurrence, similarity and order: the former may be called progressive orientation, and opposed to conservative orientation. This ideological pattern refers of course to a much wider area than the awareness of time, but it significantly flavours time orientations as well.

The factor of time may enter the culture of a society, community or social group not only in the general capacity of time orientations, but also in much more specific form of rules (normative expectations) regulating various aspects of human conduct. Such rules will be found both within various institutions, i.e. clusters of norms and values related to important social functions like education, family, economy, politics etc., and within various social roles, i.e. clusters of norms and values linked with specific social positions (statuses) like those of a teacher, manager, worker, student, policeman etc. Briefly, rules dealing with time are structurally embedded in wider networks of rules, in social normative systems.

One important category of such rules has been singled out by Robert K. Merton and called 'socially expected durations' (1982c; 1984). In his view, there are important social norms which constitute the 'prime temporal component of social structures and interpersonal relations' (1968: 365–6). Such norms, embedded in the social structure, regulate the duration of certain acts, the endurance of groups and organizations, the term of offices etc. The point is not only that some forms of social life actually last longer than others, but that there are normative expectations which prescribe how long they should last, and any departure from such norms is socially defined as deviant, provoking social sanctions. Compare marriage, with its expectation of a lifetime bond expressed in a solemn oath, with fleeting acquaintance during holidays abroad. As Merton puts it: 'marriage, which even in these days of growing serial monogamy, is normatively defined as presumptively "permanent or having an indefinitely extended duration" will both generate and tolerate heavier loads of hostility as well as affection than relations, such as acquaintanceship, which are defined as temporary' (1982c: 30). Or compare the family, a group of indeterminate duration, with the task committee nominated for two months. Or again, compare fatherhood, by definition lifelong, with a presidency, limited by the term of office.

Like all social rules, the 'expected durations' strongly influence the thinking and doing of social actors. Usually when the social bond, group membership or status is expected to last long, people take it more seriously, are more committed to it, devote more of their resources (time, energy, money, emotions etc.) to support it, participate more with their entire self, in multiple and varied forms, rather than conducting only narrow, strictly limited tasks. For example, compare the deportment of a mother in the family, with that of a temporary employee in a firm. Even within the occupational domain, there are striking varieties of commitment, depending of the normative definition of duration. Think of Japanese corporations, with their rule of lifelong employment, or universities with tenure for professors, and the effect those norms have on devotion to the job.

If the duration is normatively limited, for example by term of office or the deadline for a task committee, one can observe striking variations of behaviour and commitment between the early period, the middle phases and the time close to termination. The 'lame-duck' pattern at the end of the term, or frantic acceleration of activities before the deadline, are just selected illustrations of such time-dependence.

But the structural rules involving time are not limited to the aspect of duration. There are multiple normative expectations concerning the speed of certain processes (e.g. traffic laws, the prescribed time for graduating from schools or universities, formal or informal norms of proper output in a period of work). There are rules defining proper moments for taking certain statuses (e.g. the age of maturity, the age of military conscription, principles of seniority in occupations, mandatory retirement age). There are norms prescribing rhythms and intervals of processes (e.g. regulating the pattern of meals, daily routine in a hospital, sequence of work-breaks in an office).

It should not be surprising that time, such a pervasive factor of social life, is so pervasively socially regulated.

The functions of social time

There are some universal functions that time serves in every society. And there are also important historical differences between early traditional societies and modern industrial society with respect to the role of time. Wilbert Moore (1963a) suggests triple functions which have to do with three universal aspects of social life: synchronization of simultaneous actions, sequencing of following actions, and determining rate of actions within a temporal unit. Starting from there, we may develop a more extended typology.

1   The first universal requirement of social life which is met by common, accepted systems of reckoning of time is the synchronization of activities. A large part of social life in every society is filled by collective action, things done together by large numbers of people. For collective action to occur, people must find themselves at the same place at the same moment (e.g. come to the football ground to make the audience of a match). Even if their physical presence is not necessary, they have to take certain actions at the same time (e.g. switch on their TV sets and create a 'public' for a certain

show). 'The greater the interdependence of actors, the greater the necessity for temporal synchronisation' (Lewis and Weigart 1990: 96).

2   The next universal requirement is co-ordination. Individual actions do not occur in a vacuum. Large numbers of them are related, leading to a common goal, or adding to the creation of a common product. The division of labour, one of the classical preoccupations of sociology, is the clearest example of that. For individual efforts to be instrumental for the common task they must either occur at the same time, or in some specified time distance or time series. To build a house, the foremen, bricklayers and plumbers must come to work at the same time and organize their day by the clock, so that there will be a logical interrelation of tasks and no mutual interference or obstruction. To win a battle the air force must enter at the precisely right moment together with (or after or before) the infantry, and be joined at the right time by the marines. This is why army strategists pay such attention to 'V-hours', or 'D-hours' as the case may be.

3   A further requirement is 'sequencing'. Social processes run in stages, events follow one another in specific sequences, there is an inherent, necessary 'logic' to most processes. There are many actions which make sense only if they fit into a certain, concrete moment in the process. They cannot be done earlier or later than their proper time. People have to wait, if it is too early for doing something, and they have to rush if the process is moving quickly in order to catch up. Perhaps the best model of this situation is provided by the assembly line in a factory, but the situation is much more universal. The child must enter school at a certain age, the field must be sown at a certain season, and crops taken at another, the enemy must be bombed just before the infantry attack, Christmas cards must be sent in a certain month, and sleeping pills taken at a certain hour of the evening. For all this, time reckoning is indispensable.

4   Another requirement is timing. Some activities can be undertaken only if facilities or resources are available, and they may not be available at all times. There is only some period, on some days of the week when one can go to a bank, a shop, a restaurant or the cinema. Opening hours vary tremendously in various societies, and mastering them is a part of the necessary cultural capacity to act meaningfully and effectively. There are also precise moments when trains, buses, aeroplanes, ships leave and arrive, and no use of transport services would be possible without some acquaintance with the timetables.

5   The next requirement to be mentioned is measuring. The duration of various activities may have decisive social importance, for example determining the length of expected effort (school hours, working hours), the amount of pay (per day, weekly or monthly wages), the excellence of performance (in competitive sports or academic tests), cost of services (of telephone conversations, using electricity, or renting a car), and for many other reasons. Without common, accepted measures, no determination of that sort could be made.

6   The final requirement is differentiating. It is important to break the monotony and routine of living by allocating various periods to various activities. The days devoted to leisure or prayer (even etymologically sanctified as Holy days), the days dominated by sporting events (e.g. Wednesday, so important to football fans in Europe), the periods devoted to holidays, the days or periods for shopping, the seasons for family reunions, carnivals for spontaneous, collective enjoyment, electoral campaigns for intensified political activities – all such extraordinary diversions from work and mundane concerns are cherished by people in all societies, and one of the functions of time is demarcating and isolating proper moments for them.

The significance of all these functions changes with the growing complexity of human society, its institutions and organizations, the tasks and challenges facing its members. Just think of a tribe of hunters and gatherers, as compared to a modern industrial town. In a primitive society, time is the emerging outgrowth of rhythmic activities, repeatable patterns of actions, cycles of seasons, life-cycle, magical or religious observances. People gain some awareness of time *per se*, but it is secondary, derivative from the pressing tasks of everyday existence. In fact, social anthropologists have discovered societies devoid of the category of time. Studying the tribe of Nuers in Sudan, E. E. Evans-Pritchard noticed that they do not possess any idea of time separate from the immediate life-experiences of meteorological or biological phenomena and everyday activities (1963). As Barbara Adam puts it, time is a sort of secondary, dependent variable in the life of early societies. It fulfils exclusively instrumental functions.

If we take the opposite extreme of a modern, industrial society, the situation is reversed. Time becomes the central regulator, co-ordinator, organizer of human activities. Because of that, it acquires a mystifying autonomous quality. It is no longer a tool or instrument but a value in itself. It becomes an independent variable, a primary, determining factor in social life. To use Robert McIver's phrase, there is certain 'despotism of time' in modern civilization; the calendar and the clock become ruling forces. Jack Goody considers the clock as 'the key machine of the modern world, surpassing in importance the steam engine itself' (1968: 33). People become pre-eminently oriented towards dates, hours, deadlines. 'It is the perpetual concern with the passage of time that is characteristic of industrial man' (1968: 40). Time takes the form of a resource which can be spent, saved or allocated, or even of a commodity which may be sold or exchanged. As Benjamin Franklin put it, 'Time is money.' In effect time acquires 'the very specific character . . . in contemporary industrial societies . . . as a resource that may be budgeted, wasted, allocated, sold, or controlled' (Adam 1990: 113). Characterizing modern civilization, Lewis Mumford writes: 'Timed payments; timed contracts; timed work; timed meals; from this period on nothing was quite free from the stamp of the calendar or the clock. Waste of time became for protestant religious preachers . . . one of the most heinous sins' (1964: 2). By the same token, punctuality became one of the great virtues. In an attempt to modernize, in 1983 the Mexican government launched a campaign for the rational use of time, and in the streets of Mexico City one could see huge posters reminding people of Franklin's dictum: 'Tiempo es dinero'. This phenomenon of reification and autonomization of some emergent qualities of social life, which start to live independent existences and to constrain and coerce their very creators, human individuals, is a wider trait of modernity, not restricted to the domain of time.

Major theoretical traditions in the study of time

The classical sociology of time is the achievement of Emile Durkheim (1915), and the members of his 'French school', Marcel Mauss, Henri Hubert, Maurice Halbwachs, Marcel Granet (cf. Banaszczyk 1989). Durkheimians introduced three new emphases, which defined their distinct approach to time, inherited by later sociology: sociological perspective, relational perspective and relativistic perspective.

Common-sense notions of time have treated it as a sort of vague, natural milieu, engulfing all human experiences. Philosophers, and particularly Kant, have considered it as the universal, human way of ordering experience, the form of our sensibility, the a priori 'category of cognition'. It was still natural, but residing in the mind, rather than in reality itself, and imposed upon reality only in the process of acquiring knowledge. Durkheim took the next step, shifting the problem of time to the domain of the social. For him time is the 'social fact', or 'collective representation': the shared reflection or emanation of the collective experiences and social organization of a community or society. As such, it is socially constructed. Like other socially constructed 'social facts', time appears to people as something external, encountered, and exerts some constraining force on their actions. It provides the normative regulation of social life, and in this way feeds back on the society from which it has emanated. It moulds its very creators. Durkheim grasps the dialectics of time: time expresses the rhythm of collective activities, but also, reflexively, regulates such activities.

The social character of time implies that it is not a substance, a specific form of being, but rather a set of relations ordering social events in sequential or rhythmic patterns. One type of relation is simply the before-and-after arrangement. Another is linear time, the directional sequence of unrepeated events (characteristic for 'secular' or 'profane' domains of life). Yet another type is cyclical time, linking events of a repetitive sort (typical for 'sacred' or liturgical time).

The social origins of time imply that it will take distinct forms in the various societies from which it emanates. It is taken to be relative to diverse existential foundations arising in different cultures, or in different epochs. Thus, time is culturally and historically relative.

Later Durkheimians extended such relativism not only to comparisons between societies but to the internal constitution of those societies, their composite parts. Various collectivities (tribes, local communities, cities, occupational groups, age groups, classes) were said to 'live in different times'; various organizations (offices, enterprises, schools) were found to provide specific temporal frameworks for their participants; each type of human activity (political, economic, religious, educational, technical, familial) was seen as conducted in a different time matrix. It was also asserted that there are groups or social categories which are to some extent insulated against the pervasive impact of time, either applying some idiosyncratic time-framework or ignoring time altogether. Examples include children, retired persons, hospital patients, the unemployed, prison inmates, artistic bohemians. We have already learned that there are also rare cases of whole societies which do not recognize time (e.g. the Nuer). This extreme relativism was claimed to hold equally with respect to the objective, real rhythms of social life, to the subjective awareness and perceptions of time, and to the cultural, normative regulation of temporal aspects of society.

Another important contribution to the theory of time comes from Pitirim Sorokin and Robert K. Merton. In their famous article (1937) they analyse what they call 'socio-cultural time', and link it even more closely to the problematics of social change. The emphasis rests on the qualitative and relativistic nature of time. It is never a neutral quantitative scale for measuring changes, but rather it is endowed with a rich content, and it flows differently in various societies. As the authors put it: 'Time systems are varied with social structure' (p. 615). This is due to the fact that the points of reference for reckoning time are selected among socially significant events, and their significance depends on the diverse lifestyles, and dominant problems of different communities and societies. In the earliest societies, they may be determined by hunting seasons; in agricultural societies they may be linked with harvest time, floods, rain periods, tides; later with local markets, festivals and religious holidays and trade fairs; in modern consumer society shopping seasons and vacation seasons are highly characteristic. As a result, dates attain cultural, and not only calendar meaning for particular societies; periods, even if nominally equal, pass with different speeds depending on the concrete culture (for instance, compare the holiday season with the time before Christmas in modern western societies). The flow of time is not neutral, smooth and uniform; there are marked accelerations and vacuums. Sorokin and Merton treat social time as a functional prerequisite of orderly, predictable, co-ordinated and synchronized social life. Being of social origin and endowed with cultural content, it feeds back on society, enhancing end enriching its characteristic rhythms of life.

An important contribution emphasizing the tremendous heterogeneity of qualitative social time comes from Georges Gurvitch (1964). He presents a typology of eight categories of time to be found in a modern society, e.g. the continuous 'enduring-time' of the traditional, kinship-oriented communities, the 'erratic time' of modern technologies, the 'cyclical time' of churches and sects, the 'explosive time' of revolutionary movements (Gurvitch 1990: 71–2). Each society is characterized by a particular configuration of social times, and the choice of time becomes an important aspect of group identity, and consequently inter-group competition and struggles.

An empirically oriented 'sociology of time' is developed, among others, by Eviatar Zerubavel (1981). He believes that 'socio-temporal order' is a fundamental and universal principle of social life. It manifests itself at the objective and subjective level. Societies produce objective, shared 'temporal frames of reference' for its functioning (schedules, timetables, time budgets), and people develop 'standard time orientations' which are indispensable for orienting themselves in the social life of their society. Every social event or social change has its own, proper 'temporal profile', a combination of four temporal characteristics: (1) sequential structure (the pattern of stages specific, for example, for daily routines, religious rituals, occupational career, economic growth etc.), (2) duration (the length of time it lasts), (3) localization in wider sequences ('when' it actually occurs), and (4) repeatedness or uniqueness.

In modern society, an important distinction separates private time and public time. As time turns to a commodity, people sell part of their private time, turning it into working time (Zerubavel 1990: 171). This time is regulated by rigid work schedules (with 'flexitime' being an exception available in some professions, e.g. medical doctors, as distinct from nurses). 'As becomes a bureaucratic age, the modern person's time is rigidly segmented into parts during which he is officially supposed to be accessible in his occupational role, and others during which he is not' (Zerubavel 1990: 172). This is a recent elaboration of the earlier, traditional research focus of the sociology of time, namely the study of 'time-budgets' (Szalai 1972).

These are only some selected examples of the sociological schools or individual scholars taking up the extremely complex problematics of social time, which in recent years has acquired growing salience, and since the 1970s has turned into a separate subdiscipline of sociological studies, with its own journals, conferences and academic associations.

4

Modalities of historical tradition

The processual nature of society

Human societies, at all levels of their internal complexity, are incessantly changing. They change at the macro-level of the economy, polity, and culture; at the mezzo-level of communities, groups, and organizations; and at the micro-level of individual actions and interactions. Society is not an entity, but a multi-level, intermeshed set of processes. As Edward Shils puts it, 'A society is a "trans-temporal" phenomenon. It is not constituted by its existence at a single moment in time. It exists only through time. It is temporally constituted' (1981: 327).

If so, then it is in a constant movement from the past to the future. Its present is just a passing phase between what has occurred and what is coming. In the present state of society, there are both the effects, vestiges, traces of the past, and the seeds, potentialities for the future. The processual nature of society implies that the earlier phases are causally linked with the present phase, and the present phase comprises the causally determining conditions for the next phase.

In this chapter we shall be concerned with the backward link, of the actual state of society with its own earlier history. 'The connection which binds a society to its past can never die out completely; it is inherent in the nature of society . . . A society would not be a society if this bond were not there in some minimal degree' (Shils 1981: 328). This bond of the present with the past is the basis of tradition.

The problem of tradition would not arise if various states of society in the sequence of the process were discrete and not continuous, i.e. if they were terminated completely before new ones were starting. But this is not the case. To quote Shils again: 'A society is in continuous existence' (1981: 168). The past of society does not disappear, or at least not entirely. Fragments of it remain, and provide a sort of environment for succeeding phases, for the continuation of the process. This happens by means of two causal mechanisms. One is material or physical, and the other ideal or psychological – and they mutually enhance themselves.

The material mechanism operates through the survival of objects, artefacts, arrangements produced by the activities of earlier generations, but surrounding the actions taken by the present one. It is rooted in the physical fact of endurance. Houses and bridges, roads and harbours, churches and monuments, tools and machines, smoke in the air and rubbish in the rivers – these make up this inherited material environment in which we live, even though we have not produced it ourselves. This environment, accumulating through the ages, but also eroded and destroyed during the ages, is naturally not a replica of times past, but at most provides some resemblance of how things really were. Its persistence is the *raison d'être* for the scientific discipline of archaeology.

The ideal mechanism operates through the human capacities of memory and communication. The past is preserved because people remember fragments of it. Primarily they remember their own earlier experiences, but the scope of their memory is extended in two ways. First, towards their contemporaries, with whom they may share their memories, and from whom they may learn about past events not personally experienced. In this way, a pool of collective memory is achieved and stored in archives, libraries, museums. Second, the scope of memory is also extended towards predecessors, via historical records of all sorts, in which memories of earlier generations are registered. In this way, a pool of collective memory reaches deep into the past, far beyond the personal recollection of any of the members. Here the importance of writing as one of the fundamental inventions of mankind becomes obvious. 'The development of writing greatly extends the scope of distanciated interaction in space as well as in time' (Giddens 1979: 204). The oral transmission of tradition is incomparably more limited than the written one. It depends on the much smaller circle of people immediately co-present, and it is much more shallow with respect to the time horizon. It is only with the invention of writing that historical consciousness could be born and the study of history could begin in earnest. 'The development of writing underlies the first emergence of the "linear time consciousness" which later, in the West, became the basis of historicity as a feature of social life' (Giddens 1979: 201).

Through the ideal, psychological mechanism people inherit past beliefs, knowledge, symbols, and also norms, values and rules. They are stored, interpreted, used and passed on by various agencies such as families, churches, schools, universities, mass media, armies, firms and political parties. Of course the memory is not infallible, any more than records. What reaches us from the past is preselected, often biased, idealized, distorted by the mediating generations of memorizers and interpreters.

Both mechanisms of transmission material and ideal, interact. The material artefacts surrounding us, and derived from the past, support our memory, provide it with some tangible props in which we may anchor our imagination of earlier society. Some produce such effects as an unintended, latent function (for instance, slum districts, squatter townships and polluted environments remind us of the bleak side of industrialism; weed-covered railtracks in the

American wilderness, reawake the images of the heroic 'frontier' period and the conquest of the west; the Maya pyramids of Yucatan evoke visions of robust early civilizations). Other material objects may be preserved and attended to expressly for this purpose, which then becomes their manifest function. Antique monuments, baroque cathedrals, medieval towns, and in general most objects that we find in museums are intended to illustrate and emphasize the glory and beauty of the past. In exceptional cases they may also serve as dramatic warnings against the wretchedness of the past, as in the case of the Auschwitz Holocaust Museum, or Katyn Forest where thousands of Polish officers were executed by the Soviet secret police.

There is also the reverse influence of inherited beliefs, knowledge, symbols, norms, values and rules, endowing objects with meaning. The Forum Romanum is just a field of ruins if we do not have some knowledge of its original shape and function. The tool or machinery passed to us from an earlier epoch must be accompanied by the memory or an instruction specifying how it should be used. The monument is just a piece of marble if we do not remember or cannot find the inscription telling us whom it represents. The Houses of Parliament are just a stone edifice, if we do not know or cannot find records of electoral laws.

By material and ideal routes, the past, however distorted, enters the present. It may be said to 'exist in the present', in two senses: objectively, when objects from the past are materially preserved, and subjectively, when ideas from the past are remembered and entertained in the consciousness of societal members, to the extent that they become a part of shared culture. In both cases, and in their mutual interaction, the past starts to influence the present, becomes an important co-determinant of the contemporary state of society.

But there is also a third way, through which not a real but a 'contrived' past can also influence the present. The past can be imagined, conceived merely in human fantasy. It may happen unwittingly, as the result of a mistake, an exaggeration, unbriddled ingenuity, or confabulation, but it may also be done on purpose, as a deliberate imaginative construction, pretending to be true. This is the case with 'invented tradition' (Hobsbawm and Ranger 1985). The reasons for such inventions may vary: sometimes it is the need to justify or provide legitimation to actual political actions, sometimes it attempts to mobilize support and participation in current programmes, enhance the image of a leader or strengthen national spirit. Eric Hobsbawm classifies 'invented traditions' into three groups: (1) symbolizing and expressing the social cohesion of communities or nations, (2) legitimizing status, institutions, authority, and (3) socializing into certain values, norms, rules of behaviour (Hobsbawm and Ranger 1985: 9). He claims that 'There is no real sign of weakening in the neo-traditional practices associated either with bodies of men in the public service (armed forces, the law, perhaps even public servants) or in practices associated with the citizens' membership of states' (p. 12). Contrived images of the past, even if entirely untrue, may exert significant causal influence. In this case, as in so many others, the famous 'Thomas Theorem' holds: 'If men define situations as real, they are real in their consequences' (cf. Merton 1968: 475). This is because people take their beliefs into account, act on them, and actions make up what society ultimately is.

These social or psychological mechanisms explain the remarkable fact of continuity, or, to be more precise, the change in continuity and the continuity in change. Thus, on the one hand, social change is never absolute or complete, it occurs against a rich background of sameness. Much of what people 'do and think and aspire to, leaving aside idiosyncratic variations, is an approximate reiteration of what has been done and thought for a long time, long before anyone still alive was born' (Shils 1981: 34). Even revolutionary change, by definition the most comprehensive and radical, leaves multiple aspects of society unchanged. On the other hand, continuity is also never absolute, the heritage is reshaped, distorted, modified or enriched, and every later moment in the life of a society is different from any earlier one.

The concept of tradition

The substance, contents of all that we inherit from the past, all that is transmitted to us in the cummulative, incremental historical process, makes up the heritage of a society. At the macro-level, what a whole society inherits from earlier phases of a historical process makes up the 'historical heritage'; at the mezzo-level, what a community or group inherits from earlier phases of group life makes up the 'group heritage'; at the micro-level, what an individual inherits from earlier phases of his/her biography makes up the 'personal heritage'.

If we keep strictly to the idea that social processes are continuous, and run through long stretches of time, then each phase, including the present, will have to be treated as shaped, influenced by all preceding phases, going back to the very beginning of the process. In this sense, whatever happens in a society of today must be seen as some complex accumulated product of what has been occurring since the origin of mankind, as the result of the whole of human history. To change the level, what a given local community presents now, has crystallized through all events occurring there since its foundation. Who I am now, is the outcome of all my past experiences, of my full biography. It may be argued that such a causal link is to be found in all these cases, systematically weaker but still present when we move back in time. But a causal link is not enough to speak of tradition. The sum of temporarily accumulated causes of the present state of society will not be called tradition, but rather its origins, or genealogy. And the sum of accumulated effects of the past states of society cannot be called tradition either, because it is just what the society is at the present moment, its contemporary state. The concept of tradition becomes meaningless when conceived so widely.

To speak of tradition, the link between the past and the present must be closer, more intimate. It must involve the continued existence of the past in the present, rather than merely indicating the fact that the present originates in the past. This continued existence may take, as we remember, two forms: material and ideal, objective and subjective. By 'tradition' in the first, more comprehensive sense of the term, we shall mean the totality of objects and ideas which derive from the past but are actually to be found in the present, those which have not been destroyed, damaged, abandoned or forgotten. 'Tradition' here means simply the heritage, what really remains from the past. As Shils observes, 'In its barest, most elementary sense, [tradition] means simply a traditum; it is anything which is transmitted or handed down from the past to the present' (1981: 12).

But we may put more restrictive criteria on the concept, narrowing down its scope. By tradition in the second, more narrow sense of the term, we shall mean only specially qualified fragments of the heritage, namely those which not only survive and remain in the present, but retain a strong, intimate link with the present. In the case of objects, they would have to be actually noticed, indicated, endowed with special significance because of their 'pastness'. Royal castles, medieval city walls, ancient ruins, royal carriages, wagons from the prairies and the first Ford T models clearly enter this class, together with innumerable other objects. In the case of ideas (including beliefs, symbols, norms, values, rules, creeds and ideologies), they would have to be actually perceived and followed, would have to influence thinking and conduct, and, again, draw their special significance or legitimacy from their 'pastness'. Ancient notions of democracy, justice, freedom, and also myths of national origins, memories of a country's greatness, techniques of folk medicine and old cooking recipes would be the first examples that come to mind. There may also be objects or ideas of quite recent origin, which are believed to be old and hence are treated with special reverence. This would be the case with contrived or invented traditions. Hugh Trevor-Roper presents an astonishing story of the Scottish Highland tradition, including a complex array of fashion, symbols, badges, melodies – as devised no earlier than the nineteenth century by a pair of bored aristocrats. 'The whole concept of a distinct Highland culture and tradition is a retrospective invention', he claims (1985: 15). Another historian shows how several ceremonial traditions of the British monarchy were purposefully devised. 'New institutions were clothed with the anachronistic allure of archaic but invented spectacle' (Cannadine 1985: 138).

Thus what is crucial in this understanding of tradition is the attitude, the orientation taken by contemporaries towards objects or ideas from the past. This particular attitude or orientation takes a special part from the whole of the historical heritage and elevates it to the category of tradition. The significance, reverence or awe associated with everything that is socially defined as tradition explains the interesting phenomenon of emulating traditions. Houses in the colonial style, furniture *à la* Louis XIV, ancient Persian rugs made in Hong Kong and numerous other objects could be mentioned as illustrations. In brief 'Traditions are not independently self-reproductive or self-elaborating. Only living, knowing, desiring human beings can enact them and reenact them and modify them' (Shils 1981: 14–15) Traditions are created by human beings.

The emergence and change of tradition

Traditions, in the narrow sense defined above, i.e. collections of objects and ideas endowed by people with special meaning because of their origins in the past, are themselves subject to change. They appear at certain moments, when people define certain fragments of the past heritage as tradition; they are modified when people select certain fragments of tradition for special emphasis and ignore others; they endure for some time and they may disappear when objects are abandoned and ideas rejected or forgotten. Traditions may also be revitalized and reappear after long periods of decay. A good example is provided by the revival of ethnic and nationalist traditions in eastern Europe and the former Soviet Union after a period when they were suppressed by communist regimes, as if frozen under the unifying grip of totalitarianism. Active human attitudes towards the remnants of the past, which cut the traditions out of the heterogeneous fabric of our inherited material environment and remembered beliefs and rules, are changing and shifting; and with them, the traditions themselves constantly change.

The birth of tradition may occur in two ways. One genealogy leads 'from below', through the mechanism of emergence. It is a spontaneous, unintended, incremental process and involves large masses of individuals. For some reason or other, certain individuals find some fragments of the historical heritage appealing. This interest, reverence, devotion, awe, disseminates by various routes, embracing the larger population. Their attitudes turn into behaviour – rituals, ceremonies, search for and renovation of old objects, the reinterpretation of old creeds – all of them affirming but also enhancing attitudes. Individual preferences and actions become shared and turn into truly social fact. Thus tradition is born. Paradoxically the process is closely similar to the spread of innovations (to be discussed in chapter 17), though in this case it is rather the discovery or rediscovery of something which already existed in the past.

The second route leads 'from above', through the mechanism of imposition. This is the case when what is to count as tradition is selected, emphasized, brought to public attention and even enforced by individuals commanding power or influence. It may be a king forcing the tradition of his dynasty on his subjects, a dictator drawing on the past glory of the nation, a military commander hailing the stories of great battles, or a famous fashion designer finding inspiration in the past and dictating a 'retro' style.

Notice that the two routes through which traditions appear do not prejudge their content. In particular, this distinction is independent of, and cuts across, another which was discussed earlier, namely the opposition of *authentic* tradition, referring to an actually existing past, and *contrived* tradition, referring to a purely imaginary, devised past. Contrived traditions may be born by emergence, when somebody conceives an attractive vision of the past and is able to infect a sufficient number of other people with the idea. But perhaps more often contrived traditions are devised and imposed by those in power, to serve their political goals. Remember the coronation ceremonies of the Emperor Bokassa, invoking Napoleonic tradition, or those political speeches of not so long ago when one could hear of 'eternal and centuries-long friendship' between the Soviet Union and Libya, or Romania and Mozambique. The decision to rewrite all history textbooks in Russia and former East Germany after the fall of communism in 1989 tells something of the extent to which entire national traditions can be forged or invented.

Once established, traditions undergo various changes. One direction of change is quantitative, a change in the number of followers or supporters. People may be drawn to a certain tradition, which expands and embraces all the population of a nation-state, or even reaches beyond that, acquiring a truly global scale. This is the case of traditions linked with all the great religions, Christianity, Islam and Buddhism. It is also true of some political doctrines and their constitutive traditions: liberal democracy, socialism, conservatism. On the other hand, people may become bored, disenchanted or disappointed with certain traditions, and gradually or suddenly abandon them. The fate of communism and, more generally, leftist traditions at the end of the twentieth century is a very instructive example.

Another direction of change is qualitative, a change in the content of tradition. Some ideas, symbols, values are added, others are dropped; some objects are brought into the scope of the recognized *traditum*, others are discarded. In the area of ideas, symbols and values, it is enough to remind oneself of the impact of the Reformation on the tradition of Christianity, or of the Second Vatican Council on Roman Catholicism. More current examples would include the changes in Labour Party tradition in Britain in recent years, or historical corrections to the idealized, rosy image of the discovery of America coming out on the anniversary of Columbus's voyage, or a wave of 'revisionist' literature on the French Revolution (e.g. Sullivan 1989; Shama 1989), showing it in an entirely new light. In a more tangible area of objects, think of the adding of an Olivetti Lettera typewriter or a Porsche sports car to the collection of the New York Museum of Modern Art, or putting Elvis Presley clothes on auction at Sotheby's, or selling Red Army badges and medals on the streets of Berlin, or bringing antique, dusty furniture from the attics of modern houses.

The crucial question is of course why such changes occur. Part of the answer may be found in the psychological qualities of the human mind, restless and sceptical, striving for novelty and originality, manifesting creativeness and innovativeness, imagination and vision. Nothing can escape the influence of such a tendency, not even tradition. Sooner or later any tradition starts to be questioned, doubted, re-examined, and at the same time new fragments of the past are being discovered and validated as tradition. A special case occurs when tradition is undermined by new facts, when it clashes with realities and is shown up as untrue or useless. It is in the realm of science that this way of superseding tradition by verification, has become institutionalized since the seventeenth century, and turned into the rule of scientific ethos. A less extreme case involves the tradition which, even if not falsified, turns out to be inadequate, dysfunctional, i.e. no longer satisfying any need or requirement when social circumstances have radically changed, and is therefore abandoned.

Another explanation for changes of tradition may be found in the pluralism of traditions and the inevitable clash of any single tradition with competing ones. It may occur between different societies or cultures, or within the same society. The former case (inter-societal clash) has been extensively studied by social anthropologists, especially with reference to colonial conquest, but also in more peaceful forms of cultural contact between entirely different societies, including programmes of forced modernization (see chapter 9). Almost without exception, indigenous traditions are shown to be significantly affected, reshaped or wiped out.

In the latter case (intra-societal pluralism) the clash of traditions may take various forms. Most common is the clash of national or racial traditions in the multi-ethnic or multiracial society. Equally often there is conflict between traditions cherished by different classes or social strata. The suspicion and enmity shown by the less privileged classes towards the traditions of elites are perhaps the most obvious example, erupting as they do in violent forms during social revolutions when royal palaces are burnt, aristocratic mansions ransacked, museums turned into barns or barracks. There may also be varieties of regional traditions, with pronounced mutual animosities. Last but not least, religious traditions have also proved to be seriously divisive.

It would be one-sided, however, to believe that multiple traditions invariably fight amongst themselves. Different traditions may also give each other mutual support. One recent case is the Polish opposition movement Solidarity, which brought together in a peculiar, but as later history proved, explosive and effective mixture, at least three distinct traditions: those of Catholicism, Polish nationalism and spontaneous working-class socialism (the latter of course not identical with the official 'socialist' creed).

The mutual clash, or (more rarely) mutual support of traditions, inevitably influences each of them. Much depends on the relative strength of competing traditions. One common effect in the situation when traditions are markedly unequal in immanent strength (articulation, persuasiveness, scope etc.), or in the amount of support they receive from powerful agents (states, armies, social movements), is the attenuation and erosion of the weaker tradition. Most typically this occurs in the case of colonial conquest, but it is also found in wars, foreign occupations, strongly proselityzing religious campaigns etc. The different effect, when an indigenous tradition is relatively strong or the external tradition not coercively imposed, is the incorporation or cultural borrowing of some elements from the external tradition. Finally, when interacting traditions are relatively equal in strength, the fusion or syncretistic amalgamation of different traditions may occur, preserving core elements of them all, but at the same time noticeably changing each of them. We shall have more to say of these processes in chapter 6.

The functions of tradition

Such are the complex dynamics of traditions. But perhaps an even more fundamental question is not why traditions change, but why they exist at all. Edward Shils makes the strong assertion that 'Human beings cannot survive without traditions even though they are so frequently dissatisfied with their traditions' (1981: 322). If so, what are those universal requirements or needs of individual or social life that are met by traditions? Under what historical circumstances do these needs become more pressing, to result in the eruption and expansion of traditions? This leads us to the problem of the functions of tradition.

1   The first function can be expressed by means of the cliché that tradition is the wisdom of generations. It places within our easy grasp, in our present environment and awareness, the beliefs, norms, values and objects created in the past. It also provides the selection of such fragments of the entire historical heritage, which, for any reason, are found worthwhile. Thus tradition is like a pool of resources, ideal and material, which people may use in their current actions, for building the future out of the past. In particular it may provide blueprints for action (e.g. the tradition of an artistic community, of crafts, of the medical or legal professions), role-models to be emulated (e.g. traditions of heroes, charismatic leaders, saints or prophets), visions of social institutions (e.g. the tradition of monarchy, constitutionalism, parliamentarism), patterns of organizations (e.g. the tradition of the market, democracy or colonialism), images of 'reference societies' (e.g. the tradition of ancient Greece, American or western tradition). People cannot make their social life from scratch, devise everything anew. Tradition provides them with ready building-blocks for shaping their world.

2   A further function is to give legitimation to existing ways of life, institutions, creeds and codes. All of these require some justification to make them binding and win them acceptance. One source of legitimation is found in tradition. Thus it is a common and powerful justification to assert that 'it has always been like that', or that 'people have always believed so', even at the risk of a paradox that some actions will be done only because others did the same in the past, or some beliefs adopted merely becuse they have been adopted before (Shils 1981: 21). Another justification is to invoke the early source or the author of some creed or doctrine ('the Bible says so', or 'Aristotle claimed that', 'Marx condoned such an action'). Another kind of justification claims unbroken continuity of some present institution with the distant past. It was Max Weber who indicated the role of tradition in laying the foundations for authority, i.e. the recognized and accepted power. His example was

the authority of a monarch legitimated by the tradition of a whole earlier dynasty.

3 It is also a function of tradition to provide persuasive symbols of collective identity, strengthen rootedness and reinvigorate primordial loyalties to nations, communities, groups. National traditions, with their anthems, flags, emblems, mythology and public rituals are the prime example. They always reach back into history, using the past for the benefit of current integrative needs. For example, a British historian describes 'the ritual of monarchy as a festival of freedom and celebration of continuity in a worried and distracted age' (Trevor-Roper 1985: 159). Traditions of the regions, cities, local communities have a similar role of binding their citizens or members within a certain space. Traditions of professions and firms, symbolized in badges, logos and legends, evoke dignity and pride in the job. Traditions of universities and schools, expressed in rich ritual, ceremonies, robes etc. help to preserve the autonomy of the scholarly world.

4 Tradition also serves to provide escape from the grievances, dissatisfactions and frustrations of contemporary life. The tradition of a happier past provides a substitute source of pride if society is in crisis. A tradition of earlier sovereignty and independence helps a nation to survive a period of foreign occupation and enslavement. A tradition of lost freedom sooner or later undermines even the most entrenched dictatorship or tyranny. In a poetic metaphor, 'The past is a haven to the spirit which is not at ease in the present' (Shils 1981: 207).

Like all human creations, tradition is not necessarily beneficial to a society or its members, and is marked by functional ambivalence. It may have not only functional but also dysfunctional consequences.

1 First, any tradition, independently of its content, may prevent or restrain creativeness or innovativeness, by providing ready-made solutions to contemporary problems. There may appear a tendency to replace the search for new ways by recourse to old, tested, safe methods. Stagnation will be the likely effect.

2 There may be a tendency to trust traditional ways of life, methods of governing, economic strategies, in spite of a radical change in historical conditions. Sticking to old traditions in changed circumstances is just one manifestation of inertia, typical of many human institutions. The result will be ineffectiveness or complete failure of policies, the disenchantment of citizens, economic or political crisis. A good example is provided by the vicissitudes of post-communist transition in eastern Europe and the former Soviet Union, where the traditions of the nineteenth-century capitalist west, with the idea of a *laissez-faire* economy and the concept of a liberal parliamentary democracy, are treated as iron guidelines of reform. Fetishization of such traditions not only proves to be counterproductive in the entirely different social world already approaching the twenty-first century, but also paralyses the

search for some viable 'third way', between totally rejected socialism and enthusiastically embraced untamed capitalism.

3   Some traditions may be dysfunctional or harmful because of their specific content. Obviously not all that went in the past was good. Human history is full of tragedies and sufferings, destruction, cruelty, exploitation, discrimination, vicious ideologies, irrational creeds, unjust laws, tyrannies and dictatorships. Any of these may be selected as tradition, preserved and cherished by some individuals or groups. Traditions of militarism, imperialism, colonialism, anti-Semitism, Nazizm or Stalinism are just a few illustrations of the phenomenon, constantly existing and periodically intensifying in our modern world. For example, there are worrying signs of a current revival of extreme right traditions in Germany, France and Italy, and of a revival of Stalinism in Russia. The destructive potential of such traditions can hardly be overestimated.

4   Finally there are traditions which are retained not exactly by conscious choice, but rather at the level of 'social subconsciousness', by the sheer force of habit and inertia. They are not particularly cherished or worshipped, but simply accepted as convenient, accustomed ways of living. Students of the former communist countries have devised the term 'homo Sovieticus', to describe a typical mental syndrome generated by the totalitarian system as the trained and adaptive response. It includes such traits as opportunism, passivity and apathy, delegation of responsibility, neglect of work, learned inefficiency, 'disinterested envy', prolonged infantilism (expecting protection and care from the state) and parasitic innovativeness (constant search for loopholes to outwit the system). The survival of such attitudes long after the fall of totalitarianism is a common experience in all societies of the former Soviet bloc. For some people, it is simply the inertia of old ways of life, soon to be broken by the emerging capitalist system, but for others the new work ethos, individual responsibility and competitive spirit imposed by capitalism create challenges hard to accept, and there is nostalgia for the less demanding, strenuous, and uncertain, even if poorer, life of the past. A sort of latent tradition arises, which cannot yet be openly affirmed in the dominant atmosphere of anti-communist victory, but which influences mass actions nevertheless. In the changed circumstances such ingrained habits, and entrenched customs have lost all adaptive value and present formidable obstacles to the transformation of the political and economic system. What is even more dangerous, they may provide a fertile soil for populist demagogues or communist hard-liners.

Traditionalism and anti-traditionalism

A phenomenon as common and as important as tradition inevitably gives rise to meta-evaluations, most general social attitudes towards tradition as such finding expression in ideologies or doctrines about tradition and its role in society. The intrinsic ambivalence of tradition, as we have seen often functional but often also dysfunctional, necessarily leads to diverse judgements.

Articulated ideologies or general climates of opinion favouring tradition may be called 'traditionalism'; those which reject tradition go under the name of 'anti-traditionalism'. It may be hypothetically submitted that periods of dynamic, expansive and successful social development are not conducive to tradition. At such times change and not continuity is the dominant theme. There is a widespread belief that everybody should accept change, seek change, initiate change (Shils 1981: 2). Novelty, originality and difference become highly praised values. People are generally oriented towards the future and not the past. They conceive the image of the future as a direct contradiction of the past. They believe that constructing the future requires active rejection and parting with the past. There is reigning activism, optimism and progressivism, trust in science and technology as instruments for the rational remaking of the world. In such an ideological atmosphere, anti-traditionalism is apt to arise, with a 'now-generation' as its carrier.

Our hypothesis may be corroborated by the example of modernity (to be analyzed in detail in chapter 5). The capitalist-industrial-urban society in its classical nineteenth-century period of rapid expansion and growth was remarkably anti-traditionalist. If it cherished any traditions at all, those were the 'traditions of anti-traditionalism', the fond memories of great revolutions – British, French, American – marking the rejection of the preceding, agricultural, monarchical social order, quite tellingly often labelled as 'traditional'. Much later, in the post-Second World War years of stabilization and prosperity, a similar tendency to shun traditions and celebrate the present and the future could be observed. 'The sanctity and givenness of the past as the major symbolic regulator of social, political, and cultural change and innovation gave way to the acceptance of innovation and an orientation to the future as the basic cultural dimensions' (Eisenstadt 1992a: 424).

In these cases anti-traditionalism takes the form of ignoring tradition rather than fighting against it. It refers to tradition as such, rather than any specific substantive traditions. But it may also take the form of more active critique directed against particular traditions. This happens when their dysfunctional effects become especially salient. Returning to the earlier example, there is a strong campaign against the tradition of 'real socialism' and the syndrome of 'homo Sovieticus', launched by intellectuals in post-communist countries, and aimed at countering the highly detrimental effects of this persistent legacy (Lutynski 1990; Sztompka 1991a). This focused, selective anti-traditionalism does not prevent the afirmation of different traditions, e.g. nationalism, Catholicism, democracy, those of earlier origin and clear functionality for present transformations.

Periods of stagnation, decline or crisis, whether economic, political or cultural, immediately reawake traditions. In difficult times people seek the help of ancestors, an escape from everyday worries, the consolation of a brighter past, and find them in the revival of traditions, older or younger, not least in the tradition of nineteenth-century 'triumphant modernity'. These are the periods of revived traditionalism. At such times traditions appear useful, pre-eminently functional, and their possible dysfunctions are forgotten.

Perhaps the most reasonable ideological posture towards tradition is the 'tradition of critical traditionalism'. It implies an analytic and sceptical attitude, drawing a balance sheet of functions and dysfunctions in each concrete case, taking into account both the content of tradition and the historical circumstances of its affirmation. It avoids the fallacy of blind traditionalism, the uncritical following of traditions informed by the mistaken equivalence of past with good. But it also avoids the opposite fallacy of dogmatic anti-traditionalism, ignoring the beneficial role that tradition as such, and some traditions in particular may play in human society.

5

Modernity and beyond

Modernity defined

As we have emphasized already, sociology was born as an intellectual response to a particular historical period. It arose in the nineteenth century in an attempt to interpret and understand the great transition engulfing the west, from traditional society to a modern, urban, industrial, democratic social order. The bulk of sociological research and theorizing since that time has been focused on modern society. Sociology became a form of scientific self-awareness of modernity, and its most important, classical achievements relate to the experience of triumphant modernity. Even when sociologists ventured in their research beyond the borders of the developed west, most often they looked at other societies as primitive, underdeveloped, pre-modern, taking unashamedly the western-centred perspective and intimating that the emancipation of such societies from Third (or Second) World status can proceed only by emulation of the west (the 'First World'). It is only recently that disenchantment with modernity has set in and sociologists have proclaimed a new era of 'post-modernity' (Lyotard 1984), necessitating new forms of sociological reflection. Even then, the idea of modernity is still central as the reference point; the concept of post-modernity makes sense only by opposition, as a residual, negative notion signifying the rejection of modernity.

There are two ways to define modernity: historically or analytically. The historical concept of modernity refers to a particular time and place; it is dated and localized. It is defined by indicating the exemplum rather than by enumerating characteristics. Two contemporary authors illustrate that approach, even though they differ on precise dating. 'As a first approximation, let us simply say the following: "modernity" refers to modes of social life or organisation which emerged in Europe from about the seventeenth century onwards and which subsequently became more or less worldwide in their influence' (Giddens 1990: 1). 'It took place between the sixteenth and eighteenth centuries; and it began in the countries of northwestern Europe – especially England, the Netherlands, northern France and northern Germany' (Kumar 1988: 5).

Most historians would agree that modernity arose in the aftermath of great revolutions. The American and French revolutions provided the political, institutional framework of modernity: constitutional democracy, the rule of law and the principle of sovereignty of nation-states. The British industrial revolution provided the economic foundation: industrial production by free labour force in urban settings, engendering industralism and urbanism as new modes of life, and capitalism as a new form of appropriation and distribution.

Such historical characterizations, however, even though useful, are clearly not sufficient. Defining the horse by pointing a finger to the animal grazing on the meadow does not pre-empt deeper analytic efforts by zoologists. From the beginning of sociology we encounter repeated attempts to define modernity analytically by discovering its fundamental traits and their unique combination in a specific syndrome.

One of the first accounts was formulated by the founder of sociology himself, Auguste Comte. He indicated several traits of the new social order: (1) concentration of the labour force in urban centres, (2) the organization of work guided by effectiveness and profit, (3) the application of science and technology to production, (4) the appearance of a latent or manifest antagonism between employers and employees, (5) growing social contrasts and inequalities, (6) an economic system based on free enterprise and open competition.

Most sociologists take the negative track, contrasting the image of modernity with traditional, pre-modern society. In effect they produce polar models, dichotomies, contrasting concepts. Their accounts differ markedly, depending on specific theoretical (and sometimes also ideological or ethical) standpoints. A number of polar models were proposed by classical evolutionists: the opposition of 'military' and 'industrial' society by Herbert Spencer, 'Gemeinschaft' and 'Gesellschaft' by Ferdinand Tönnies, and 'mechanical' and 'organic' solidarity by Emile Durkheim. (We shall present all three dichotomies in detail in chapter 7). All of these authors, either in a jubilant mood (Spencer, Durkheim), or with a word of caution (Tönnies), have perceptively located some important features of the emerging social order. An extensive and extremely influential image of the modern capitalist society was drawn by Karl Marx and Friedrich Engels, who gave it a strong ideological and critical flavor. (We shall discuss this in some detail in chapter 11, which is devoted to Marxian 'historical materialism').

Here we wish to present perhaps the most systematic and thorough account of modernity to be found in Max Weber's polar ideal types of 'traditional' versus 'capitalist' society (we follow closely their recent reconstruction by Randall Collins, 1980). Traditional and capitalist society may be contrasted along six dimensions: form of ownership, dominant technology, character of labour-force, means of economic distribution, nature of law, pervasive motivations. This may be represented as in table 5.1.

The Weberian image of capitalism may be summed up in his own words: 'At all events, capitalism is the same as the pursuit of profit by means of continuing rational capitalistic enterprise: that is for the constant renewal of profit, or "profitablity"' (1958: 333), and, what is equally significant, it is characterized by the 'rational organisation of free labour' (p. 338). As Collins sums up that central notion of rational capitalistic enterprise, 'The characteristics of rational capitalism itself are the entrepreneurial organization of capital, rational technology, free labour, unrestricted markets, and calculable law' (1980: 930).

In the post-Second World War period, the most influential conceptual scheme for analysing traditional and modern society was proposed by Talcott Parsons under the label of 'pattern variables' (1951: 76–98, 203–4, 183–9; 1964: 46–51, 58–67). Clearly influenced by Tönnies, Durkheim and Weber, Parsons constructs a sort of multidimensional scale, for comparing different types of social systems. Applying this for our purposes, we can outline two opposed models, with the first, akin to what has been discussed so far as 'traditional society' (table 5.2).

In line with the typical tendency of modern sociology to speak of variables rather than mutually exclusive characteristics of the 'either-or' type, Parsons does not treat these models as depicting real, historical societies, but rather as extreme analytical points on a continuum along which real societies may be placed. Each dimension may also vary in different measure from the others' producing multiple possible profiles of historically unique societies. This implication of Parsons's scheme is put to ingenious use by Marion Levy (1952; 1966).

Aspects of modernity

Apart from the negative definitions of modernity in contrast to traditionalism, there have been numerous attempts to present positive outlines indicating fundamental properties of this specific social type. Such accounts may easily degenerate into *ad hoc* lists of all traits of contemporary societies which come to mind, without any clear hierarchy, order or underlying theoretical rationale. Yet they are indispensable to establishing a deeper and more concrete image of modernity than that provided by the highly general polar models. One of the recent attempts at a more systematic account of modernity is presented by Krishan Kumar (1988). This author follows the strategy of constructing the polar models, but enriches them with concrete empirical observations accumulated in various sociological researches. It seems that this comprehensive catalogue of characteristics typical for modernity comes close to what may be considered as an emerging consensus in the discipline of sociology.

First, following Kumar, we shall enumerate the general features of modernity, and then indicate their repercussions in various, more limited areas of social life: the economy, stratification, politics, culture and everyday life.

1   There are pivotal principles providing the skeleton of modernity. The first principle is individualism. John Naisbitt and Patricia Aburdene (1990) speak of 'the triumph of the individual' as the central among the 'megatrends' characterizing the modern epoch. They mean by that the final ascendancy of

Table 5.1   Weber's opposition of two types of societies

	Traditional-agrarian society	*Capitalist society*
Character of ownership	Tied to hereditary social status (landed aristocracy).	Private appropriation of all the means of production and their concentration under the control of entrepreneurs (land, buildings, machinery, raw materials are all controlled by one agent, and freely exchangeable as private goods on the market).
Mechanization of work	Practically non-existent.	Mechanization of labour as dominant technology, allowing precise calculation and capital accounting. Effectiveness, productivity, rational organization as leading principles of production.
Nature of the labour force	Basically unfree (whether in personal slavery or at least serfdom, i.e. legal attachment to the land).	Labour free to move in response to conditions of demand, from branch to branch or region to region. Immediate producers selling their labour for wages as a commodity on the open market.
The market	Highly limited (by tax barriers, danger of robbery, limited monetary instruments, poor transportation). As a result, either local markets or limited long-distance markets in luxuries.	Trading on the open market not limited by traditional restrictions (class monopolies, limitations of ownership, protectionism etc.). Market as the organizing principle of distribution and consumption.
Prevailing laws	Particularistic, differentially applicable to different social groups. Patrimonial adjudication and enforcement.	Universally applicable, calculable laws allowing for predictability of contracts and enforcement of rights.

Dominant motivations	Centred around satisfacion of needs at accustomed levels. Acceptance of traditional manner of life and rate of profit. As Weber put it: 'The opportunity of earning more was less attractive than that of working less.' (1958: 60).	Unlimited gain (permanently raised profit) as the ultimate motivation of economic behaviour.

Source: Collins 1980, with modifications.

the human individual – instead of community, tribe, group, nation – to the central role in a society (p. 298). An individual is emancipated from irreplaceable, imposed group bonds, free to move among social collectivities, choosing his/her memberships at will, self-determined and responsible for his/her own actions, successes as well as failures.

2   The next principle is differentiation. It is most significant in the sphere of labour, where there appear a great number of specialized, narrowly defined occupations and professions, requiring diverse skills, competences and training. But it is also pronounced in the sphere of consumption, where the staggering variety of options, or 'life-chances' faces every potential consumer (Dahrendorf 1979). Both raise tremendously the scope of choices, in education, occupational career and lifestyle.

3   A further principle is rationality, i.e. calculation and depersonalization in the working of organizations and institutions. This is of course the leitmotif of the Weberian theory of bureaucracy, and bureaucratic organization (in the sense of efficient impersonality of management) is widely considered as one of the central features of modernity. Under this heading one should also place the importance of science as the privileged, most admired and dependable mode of cognition.

4   Next comes economism, by which we mean the domination of all social life by economic activities, economic goals, economic criteria of achievement. Modern society is primarily concerned with goods, their production, distribution and consumption, and of course with money, as a common measure and means of exchange. It pushes into the background alternative possible preoccupations with family and kinship, which pervade early, primitive societies, or politics and warfare, which are typical for traditional, agrarian societies (e.g. in the Middle Ages).

5   The last principle is expansion. Modernity has an inherent tendency to extend its reach, first of all in space, and this is what is meant by the process of globalization (to be discussed in detail in chapter 6). As Anthony Giddens puts it: 'Modernity is inherently globalizing' (1990: 177), i.e. tending to embrace ever larger geographical areas and ultimately to span the whole globe.

Table 5.2   Parsons's 'pattern-variables'

	Traditional society	*Modern society*
Articulation of social structure	Diffuseness, i.e. unarticulated, loose, comprehensive character of roles, groups, social relationships.	Specificity, i.e. advanced specialization of roles and relationships, pronounced division of labour, focused scope of group life.
Bases of status	Ascription, i.e. admission to roles, statuses, groups, relationships based on received factors of birth and heredity.	Achievement, i.e. admission to statuses, roles, groups, relationships based on personal effort and merit.
Criteria of recruitment	Particularism, i.e. selection and treatment of partners in social relationships as well as admission to roles and groups based on unique, personal traits of potential candidates, not necessarily relevant to the job in hand or the nature of groups or relationships.	Universalism, i.e. selection and treatment of partners in social relationships as well as admission to roles and groups based on general, categorial traits, directly relevant to the tasks and nature of groups or relationships.
Focus of appraisal	Collectivism, i.e. evaluation and perception of people focused on their membership in groups, collectives, communities, tribes. Central importance of where they belong rather than who they are.	Individualism, i.e. evaluation and perception of people focused on their individual actions. Central importance of what they do.
Role of emotions	Affectivity, i.e. infusion of emotions into social life.	Neutrality, i.e. prohibition of emotional display, matter-of-fact, rational climate in social life.

Modernity also expands in depth, reaching the most detailed, private and intimate spheres of daily life (e.g. religious convictions, sexual conduct, consumption tastes, patterns of leisure, etc.). 'In both their extensionality and intensionality the transformations involved in modernity are more profound than most sorts of change characteristic of prior periods' (p. 4).

These general organizing principles of modernity are reflected in various sub-domains of social life. Sociologists usually indicate a number of new phenomena emerging in modern societies. Thus, in the area of economy, which is central for the whole system, we observe:

1　unprecedented speed and scope of economic growth, which of course does not preclude occasional or local recessions, but on the whole and in the long run surpasses anything to be found in earlier epochs
2　the shift from agricultural production to industry as the core sector of economy
3　the concentration of economic production in the cities and urban agglomerations
4　the harnessing of inanimate sources of energy to replace human and animal power,
5　pervasive technological innovations embracing all spheres of social life
6　the opening of free competitive labour markets, with a margin of unemployment
7　concentration of labour in factories and huge industrial enterprises
8　the essential role of business entrepreneurs, managers, 'captains of industry' in steering production.

Such an economic system cannot but reshape the whole class structure and hierarchies of stratification, so that:

1　Ownership situation and market position become the main determinants of social status (replacing age, ethnicity, gender, religious allegiance and other traditional factors).
2　Large segments of the population undergo the process of proletarianization and pauperization; they are turned into a propertyless labour force, bound to sell their labour power as a commodity, not participating in the profits it brings about.
3　At the other pole, strong groups of capitalist owners acquire considerable wealth by appropriating and reinvesting profits, and therefore marked social inequalities become ever more salient.
4　In between, a large middle class appears and expands, including various professions, people employed in trade, administration, transportation, education, science and other 'services'.

In the political domain the major changes include:

1　the growing role of the state, which takes up new functions in regulating and co-ordinating production, redistributing wealth, protecting economic sovereignty and stimulating expansion to foreign markets
2　the spread of the rule of law, binding both the state and the citizens
3　growing inclusiveness of citizenship, providing wider social categories with political and civil rights

4   spreading of rational, impersonal bureaucratic organization as the dominant system of management and administration in all areas of social life.

We owe the concept of bureaucratic organization to Max Weber, who constructs its ideal type as consisting of the following traits: (1) specified competences of offices, regulated by law, (2) hierarchy of offices, with differentiated prerogatives and authority, (3) fixed criteria and principles of appointments and promotion, (4) specialized training or sufficient experience as the basis for employment, (5) administrative work as a full-time occupation with fixed salaries, (6) separation of office and changing incumbents who do not own the 'means of administration', (7) written forms of operation guaranteeing accountability and supervision, (8) impersonality of procedure, i.e. 'the exclusion of love, hatred, and every purely personal, especially irrational and incalculable, feeling from the execution of official tasks' (Weber 1954: 351).

In the area of culture, there are four important phenomena:

1   secularization, the diminishing importance of magical and religious beliefs, myths, values and norms, and their replacement by ideas and rules legitimated by 'this-worldly' or 'earthly' arguments and considerations
2   the central role of science, as providing access to true knowledge, which in turn may be utilized in technological or productive practices
3   the democratization of education, embracing large segments of the population at an ever higher level
4   the appearance of mass culture, with aesthetic, literary, artistic products turning into commodities widely available on the market and appealing to unrefined tastes.

Finally, in the area of everyday life, one observes:

1   a notable extension of the domain of work and its separation from family life
2   a growing privatization of the family and its insulation to a larger extent from the social control of the community or wider society
3   the separation of working and leisure time, with expanding scope of the latter
4   the permeating of daily life with the concern for acquisition and consumption of goods, which assume not only a utilitarian but an important symbolic role ('conspicuous consumption', 'shopping' as an activity satisfying in itself independently of the real need for purchases).

This list, long as it is, is certainly incomplete. But it gives us the idea of the quality of society known as modern, and the quality of life that modern people live.

Modern personality

Modern conditions certainly leave their impact on human personalities. There is 'the impact on men, the human costs, if you will, of their exposure to the complex of urbanism, industrialism, mobility, and mass communication' (Inkeles 1976: 321). There are also some personality dispositions which seem to be prerequisites for the full development of modernity. 'The effective functioning of a modern society requires that citizens have certain qualities, attitudes, values, habits, and dispositions' (Inkeles 1976: 321). Thus there is a mutual interaction between the institutional and organizational levels, and the level of personality. Some authors have attempted to unravel the personality syndrome typically linked with modernity: 'modern mentality' (Bellah 1968), or 'a model of the modern man' (Inkeles 1976). The classical research in this area was carried out in the 1970s under the auspices of the Harvard Project on the Social and Cultural Aspects of Development. The comparative study of six developing countries (Argentina, Chile, India, Israel, Nigeria and Pakistan) led the authors to construct the analytic model of modern personality as a set of the following traits:

1 Readiness for new experience and openness to innovation and change. This may take multiple expressions: 'the willingness to adopt a new drug or sanitation method, to accept a new seed or adopt a different fertilizer, to ride on a new means of transportation or turn to a new source of information, to approve a new form of wedding ceremony or new type of schooling for young people' (Inkeles 1976: 327).
2 Readiness to form or hold opinions on a large variety of issues of a wider, public nature, to search for evidence supporting opinions, to recognize the diversity of existing opinions, and even more to value such a diversity in a positive way. 'A modern man is able to acknowledge differences of opinion: he has no need rigidly to deny differences out of the fear that they will upset his own view of the world. He is also less likely to approach opinion in a strictly autocratic or hierarchical way' (Inkeles 1976: 328).
3 Specific orientation toward time: emphasis on the present and the future rather than the past, acceptance of schedules, punctuality.
4 Efficacy, i.e. the 'modern man's confidence in his ability, alone and in concert with other men, to organize his life to master the challenges it presents' (Inkeles 1976: 329). In particular this refers to potential mastery over the natural environment, but also to potential control over problems (political, economic etc.) arising in social life.
5 Planning, i.e. anticipating and organizing future activities aimed towards assumed goals in both the public and the private domain.
6 Trust in the regularity and predictability of social life (economic rules, terms of trade, governmental policies), allowing for calculability of actions.

7   The sense of distributive justice, i.e. 'the belief that rewards should be according to rule rather than whim and that the structure of rewards should, insofar as possible, be in accord with skill and relative contribution' (Inkeles 1976: 330).
8   Interest in, and high value placed on formal education and schooling.
9   Respect for the dignity of others, including those of inferior status or power.

These personality traits are treated not as separate but as interrelated. 'One of the fundamental assumptions of our research', says Inkeles, 'is that these qualities do indeed cohere, that they are a syndrome, that people who have one trait will also manifest others. In other words, we believe that we may speak not only of men who have one or another modern *characteristic*, but of men who may meaningfully be described in their wholeness as modern men' (1976: 333).

Disenchantment with modernity

The nineteenth century is sometimes called the era of triumphant modernity (Alexander 1990). The dominant mood of social theory, reflecting to some extent popular feelings, especially among the rising, successful elites, is highly optimistic. There is a widespread belief in reason, technology, science, an efficient state and productive capitalism as safeguarding permanent progress and the unlimited expansion of humanity. But quite soon it becomes obvious that modernity brings ambivalent effects; not only beneficial but also detrimental, sometimes outright tragic (cf. Aron 1969). In the nineteenth century the critique of capitalist-industrial society is already well under way, and it continues throughout the twentieth.

Perhaps the most persistent theme is brought into the debate by Karl Marx, the idea of 'alienation' (cf. Ollman 1975). Marx believes that human individuals are, by nature, free, creative and sociable. But they abandon these natural propensities when historical conditions arise which do not give opportunities for the exercise of human nature. Such dehumanizing conditions are engendered by all class societies, but particularly by modern capitalism, turning the majority of the people into dependent, exploited and reified pieces of economic machinery. Devoid of control over both his/her labour and its products, the worker becomes alienated, detached from the job, from surrounding groups and finally from him/herself. 'The worker', Marx says, 'does not confirm himself in his work; he denies himself, feels miserable instead of happy, expends no liberal physical and intellectual energy, but mortifies his body and ruins his mind' (Marx and Engels 1960, vol. 1: 553). He no longer participates in free co-operative associations, but instead becomes isolated, estranged from other people and hostile to them, alienated from his fellows. Thus, alienation means the forfeiting of sociocentric impulses (theme of egoism, atomization), lack of creativity (theme of routine, monotony), and in consequence, the abdication of control over actions (theme of passivism), resigning of autonomy (theme of reification, fetishism of commodities which rule over people) and in short the decay of human 'species potentialities'. Human nature becomes inhuman. It can be restored to its full human potentialities only when alienation is healed, and that requires the overthrow of the social conditions that brought it about, the establishing of a classless, socialist society.

Multiple, theoretically pregnant themes comprised by the notion of alienation have been picked up by numerous later scholars and stretched far beyond Marx's original meaning.

1   Alienation was found to obtain not only in the domain of work, but in politics, culture, education, religion, art, leisure, consumption, family and many other areas. The dismal picture of modern society reached its apogee in the work of Erich Fromm, for whom it represented outright 'insanity' (1963; 1966; 1976) and Herbert Marcuse (1964), who treated it as an utterly failed 'project', a blind alley of human history.

2   Another line of critique, based on almost opposite premises, was started by Emile Durkheim with his powerful notion of 'anomie' (cf. Lukes 1985). For Durkheim, people in their natural state are beasts, egoistic, individualistic creatures ready to fight for their interests without any regard for others. It is only when they are bridled by cultural rules, norms and values that the war of all against all can be avoided and harmonious social existence becomes possible. But there are historical circumstances when cultural rules lose their binding force or decay altogether. This is the condition of anomie, normative deregulation or normlessness, when people are left without guidance, feel uprooted and lost. They escape into deviance or suicide, with ensuing anarchy or social chaos. Modern society promotes the condition of anomie, and thereby requires constant attention to the preservation or restoration of strong moral order. The concept of anomie has also had a long and complex career. In the hands of Robert Merton it was applied to a particular case of dissociation in the social structure, between culturally demanded goals and realistically available opportunities for attaining them. When such a dissociation occurs – and Merton believed it was true for major, underprivileged groups in modern American society – various patterned adaptations develop, among them various forms of deviance. In this way Merton's use of the concept initiated an influential trend in the sociology of deviance and criminology (Merton 1938; 1964).

3   A further line of critique runs under the label of 'mass society', or the decay of community. The emphasis is on the socially disintegrative effects of industrialization, urbanization and democratization at both the macro- and micro-level. It follows the hunches already spelled out by Ferdinand Tönnies in his sceptical view of *Gesellschaft* (modern society), as opposed to *Gemeinschaft* (traditional community). These critics claim that in modern

society people have lost their individual identities and started to be treated as anonymous, atomized aggregates of employees, clerks, voters, buyers or spectators. This is due to the scale on which modern society operates, with its extensive markets, audiences, publics, electorates, nation-wide or even supranational organizations. Individual distinctions and unique group attachments have to be blurred or ignored altogether. In effect, interpersonal bonds of common locality, ethnicity, religion and class are severed; individuals become isolated and uprooted. At the personal, psychological level, the loss of community means the deterioration of the quality of life, breeds frustration and suffering. At the political level, it means that people are left at the mercy of impersonal bureaucracies and governments, as an undifferentiated, equalized, dependent mass. Such a mass is vulnerable to manipulation and oppression, and hence the fragmentation of society raises the danger of autocratic or even totalitarian rule. It also facilitates mobilization into all sorts of social movements, as substitutes for missing social bonds. 'These poorly attached and unintegrated people are readily available for activistic modes of intervention in political life and for participation in mass movements that promise them full membership in the national society' (Kornhauser 1968: 60). In this critical tradition, the restoration of community – primary group relationships, bonds of kinship, nation, church, etc. – becomes of major concern.

4   The next critique is of relatively recent origins. We shall put it under the heading of ecology. It could be articulated only when urban-industrial society had accumulated sufficiently salient negative effects from its worldwide operation. Latent dysfunctions and dangers, unintended and unanticipated, turned into manifest grievances when their intensiveness passed a certain threshold. The birth of ecological consciousness among ordinary people was accompanied by varied theoretical contributions. A number of authors focused on the depletion of natural resources, the destruction of the natural environment, genetic repercussions in human population. Some considered the 'limits of growth', and drew catastrophic scenarios for the future of mankind (Mishan 1977). Others, in more positive mood, attempted to specify conditions of 'sustainable growth'. Even though eventually concerned with the fate of society, this kind of critique often rested in the hands of natural scientists, sometimes economists, and only occasionally sociologists themselves.

5   Another critical tradition addresses the global scale and points out the inequalities and imbalances produced by modernity in the international community. Its origins run back to Lenin's theory of imperialism, according to which the logic of the capitalist system with its search for profits, cheap labour and raw materials, as well as extensive markets for its products, leads inevitably to colonial or neo-colonial exploitation of weaker countries or regions of the world by the most developed capitalist centres. In modern sociology it gave rise to the so-called theories of dependency (A. Gunder Frank, E. Cardoso), claiming an inevitable division of the world into core, peripheral and semi-peripheral regions (another version of the First, Second and Third Worlds), with endemic poverty and backwardness in the periphery,

embracing a huge percentage of the human population. More recent interpretation of the same theme suggests a growing cleavage between affluent north and underdeveloped south as the main axis of tensions and conflicts in the future. We shall discuss these views in more detail in chapter 6.

6   The final type of arguments raised against modernity deals with the phenomenon of war. It points out the indisputable fact that the number, scale, viciousness and destructiveness of wars in the modern era is beyond anything known in the past. It is estimated that in the twentieth century alone more than 100 million people have lost their lives in wars. In part this is certainly due to the advanced technology of warfare, itself the result of dramatic technological progress in the period of modernity, but even more importantly it results from major social changes spawned by the industrial-urban system (1) by the divisive consequences of the emphasis on profit, acquisition, appropriation, leading to sharp conflicts of economic interests among nation-states, and (2) by the focus on rational efficiency, calculation and purely instrumental considerations, which have made it possible to degrade people into dispensable objects and suspend all moral considerations that could otherwise have prevented mass carnage. This point is convincingly argued in the recent sociological interpretation of the Holocaust by Zygmunt Bauman (1990). The threat of nuclear war and possibility of total self-destruction of humanity is taken as the ultimate argument against modernity.

Beyond modernity

The ambivalent experience and consequences of modernity, positive and negative, give rise to various theoretical visions concerning the future of human society. One vision is rooted in the optimistic and progressivistic climate of classical sociology and follows the theoretical framework of evolutionism. It claims that the present, mostly beneficial, tendencies will continue in the future, and that modernity will simply evolve in the same direction, reaching more mature, perfected forms. The seeds of the future are to be discovered in the present, in societies of the most advanced type (especially western European and North American), and the image of future society may be projected by the simple extrapolation of observable trends. These are the fundamental assumptions of the theory of post-industrial society as well as of the numerous futurological prophecies from the time before the negative consequences of modernity were so commonly and clearly perceived in the prosperous decades following the Second World War II (for example see Toffler 1970; Naisbitt and Aburdene 1990; Kotkin and Kishimoto 1988).

The classical image of post-industrial society was drawn by Daniel Bell (1974) and Alain Touraine (1974) and inspired a number of followers. It may be summed up by means of five tendencies, which John Naisbitt multiplied and popularized later as 'mega-trends' (Naisbitt and Aburdene 1990).

1   In the economic domain, there is the consecutive shift of dominant sectors: following the move from agricultural to industrial production characteristic of modernity, comes the shift from industry towards services (tertiary sector), embracing a large variety of occupations and professions not involved directly in production: trade, finance, transport, health care, recreation, research, education, administration and government.

2   In class structure and stratificational hierarchy, there is the growing numerical and general societal importance of the service class, and within the service class of professional and technical groups (quarternary sector) employed in the area of science, research and development, and 'human services', i.e. education, health, culture, social welfare, recreation. This aspect is discussed thoroughly by Ralf Dahrendorf in his conception of the 'service class society' (Dahrendorf 1964).

3   In technology, there is the rise of the new 'intellectual technology' (later referred to as 'high-tech') involved in the processing of information rather than raw materials and energy. To refer to this aspect, Zbigniew Brzezinski couched the term: 'technetronic society' (1970).

4   In the dynamics of society, self-sustaining technological growth becomes centrally important.

5   In the value system and pervasive themes of everyday life ('axial principles'), the focus moves to knowledge and its acquisition through various forms of permanent education. Peter Drucker speaks about the 'knowledge society' to stress the importance of this aspect.

As can be seen, all these traits of post-industrialism indicate precisely the intensification of phenomena or processes clearly present in modernity from the very beginning. The authors in this theoretical tradition assume their full unfolding in the future, and, in good evolutionist spirit, try to deduce coming trends from actual kernels.

With the growing awareness of the bleak sides of modernity and the mounting critique of its anti-human consequences, however, comes the idea that modern society should not and cannot continue on its path, but rather must be radically transformed. This alternative vision is rooted in nostalgia for the suddenly rediscovered bright aspects of traditional society. Some authors suggest a return to earlier, traditional forms of social life abandoned or destroyed by the rise of modernity. There are numerous calls to rebuild human communities, reinstall primordial social bonds, revitalize primary groups and relationships. There are equally strong appeals to save and replenish the natural environment of society, and to fight pollution, ecological destruction, and the thoughtless exploitation of natural resources. These and similar ideas provide rallying principles for powerful social movements.

Yet the main thrust of recent social theory is different, premised on the belief in another fundamental, qualitative novelty destined to appear in human history after the epoch of modernity. This is a third vision, and it holds that social transformations cannot be reversed but will move forward towards some qualitatively new type of society to emerge out of the ashes of modernity. It is not yet clear what it will look like, but there are already catchy names for it: 'post-modernity' (Lyotard 1984; Habermas 1987; Bauman 1989b), 'post-history', and 'post-civilization', all of which preserve the forward-looking attitude dear to most people while distancing them from the negative aspects of contemporaneity. No wonder these have attained a considerable vogue even among non-specialists and with the wider public.

The fourth vision is much more restrained in its projections than the theories of post-industrial society, and much less grandiose in its claims than the theories of post-modernity. It limits itself to the detailed analytic dissection of modernity as it appears at the end of the twentieth century in its most ripe forms, without prejudging the direction in which human society will or should move. This is the theory of 'high' or 'late' modernity proposed by Anthony Giddens (1990). It is worth reporting in some detail.

The author submits that it is premature to speak of post-modernity. 'We have not moved beyond modernity but are living precisely through a phase of its radicalisation' (Giddens 1990: 51). 'Rather than entering a period of post-modernity, we are moving into one in which the consequences of modernity are becoming more radicalised and universalised than before' (p. 3). But this is not a simple continuity of earlier trends. Rather, qualitatively new phenomena appear, which basically reshape the contemporary world and 'move us into a new and disturbing universe of experience' (p. 53).

Giddens discusses the traits of 'high modernity' under four headings: trust, risk, opaqueness, and globalization. The crucial importance of trust derives from the pervasive presence in modern life of 'abstract systems', whose principles of operation are not fully transparent to ordinary people, but on whose reliability everyday life depends. Transportation, telecommunications, financial markets, nuclear power plants, military forces, transnational corporations, international organizations and mass media provide examples of those complex, huge, impersonal arrangements which strongly influence social reality. People have to learn to use them and to depend on them. 'With the development of abstract systems, trust in impersonal principles, as well as in anonymous others, becomes indispensable to social existence' (p. 120).

The second major trait of high modernity is the qualitatively new phenomenon of risk. Risk means uncertainty about the consequences of one's own actions, or the undetermined probability of harmful effects occurring independently of individual will. In this sense it is one of the ineradicable predicaments of human life, but in the conditions of high modernity it acquires a new magnitude and pervasiveness. There arises the 'inevitability of living with dangers which are remote from the control not only of individuals, but also of large organisations, including states; and which are of high intensity and life-threatening for millions of human beings and potentially for the whole of humanity' (p. 131).

To be more specific, the 'risk profile' of high modernity is set apart from earlier experiences, both objectively and subjectively; there is both a stronger actual presence of risk, and a stronger perception of risk than ever before. Objectively we observe:

1   The universalization of risk: the new possibility of global catastrophes jeopardizing everybody irrespective of class, ethnic, power positions (e.g. nuclear war, ecological destruction).
2   The globalization of risk: the extension of risk environments over large segments of the human population, touching large masses of people (e.g. financial markets reacting world-wide to political upheavals, military conflicts, price increases of oil, corporate take-overs etc.).
3   The institutionalization of risk: the appearance of organizations having risk as the principle of their operation (e.g. investment markets or stock exchanges, gambling, sports, insurance).
4   The reflexiveness of risk: the emergence or intensification of risk as unintended side-effects or boomerang effects of human actions (e.g. ecological dangers as resulting from industrialization; crime and delinquency as outcomes of faulty socialization; new so-called 'civilizational' diseases produced by work patterns or lifestyles typical of modernity).

Subjectively, there are additional factors making the experience of risk more acute:

1   stronger sensivity to threats and dangers resulting from vanishing magical and religious defences and rationalizations
2   more common awareness of threats through a rising level of education
3   growing recognition of the limitations of expertise and repeated faults in operation of 'abstract systems'.

All these add up to the fourth central trait: 'opaqueness', the uncertain, erratic character of social life in the conditions of high modernity. There are several sources of such uncertainty:

1   Design faults, apt to occur particularly in huge, complex abstract systems.
2   Operator faults, inevitable because of human involvement in the operation and control of abstract systems.
3   The inevitability of unintended and unrecognized (latent) effects. As Giddens puts it: 'No matter how well a system is designed and no matter how efficient its operators, the consequences of its introduction and functioning, in the context of the operation of other systems and of human activity in general, cannot be wholly predicted' (1990: 153).
4   The reflexivity of social knowledge, which, at the very moment that it explains society and makes it seemingly more predictable, may influence the course of social processes in unpredictable ways. 'New

knowledge (concepts, theories, findings) does not simply render the social world more transparent, but alters its nature, spinning it off in novel directions' (pp. 152–3)

5 Extreme differentiation of power, values and interests among members of society and their groupings, which results in rampant relativism and eliminates simple, consensual guidelines for defining and appraising social situations.

The fifth feature of high modernity is continuing globalization (see in detail chapter 6), i.e. the stretching of networks of social relationships, economic, political, cultural, across the whole globe. This results, among other things, in the diminishing role of the nation-state which becomes, as Daniel Bell puts it, 'too small for the big problems of life, and too big for the small problems of life' (in Giddens 1990: 65). More primordial social bonds and group loyalties, for a long time suppressed by nation-states, have a tendency to reappear. 'At the same time as social relations become laterally stretched and as part of the same process, we see the strengthening of pressures for local autonomy and regional cultural identity' (p. 65).

Giddens rounds off his account of high modernity with a discussion of typical reactions that people take to adapt to pervasive uncertainty and risk:

1 Pragmatic acceptance, or the business-as-usual attitude, manifested in the focus on day-to-day tasks and repression of anxiety from consciousness.
2 Sustained optimism, faith that somehow things will turn to the better and dangers will be avoided thanks to providence, science and technology or ultimate human rationality.
3 Cynical pessimism, with a shortened time perspective and a hedonistic tendency to enjoy life here and now, before danger strikes.
4 Radical opposition to the perceived sources of danger, mostly carried out within the framework of social movements. It goes without saying that only this last adaptation is constructive and brings a chance of overcoming some of the threating aspects of modernity.

The idea of 'late modernity' seems to be the most fruitful instrument for the analytic, detached appraisal of the threats, as of the promises, bestowed by the equally frightening and fascinating epoch in which we happen to live.

6

The globalization of human society

From isolation to globalization

One of the historical tendencies particularly salient in the modern era is the move toward globalization. This may be defined as 'the set of processes that yields a single world' (Robertson 1992: 396). Societies become interdependent in all aspects of their lives, political, economic, cultural, and the scope of those interdependencies becomes truly global. 'No country is a self-sufficient island' (Chirot 1977: ix). Humanity is no longer merely a statistical aggregate, or philosophical or ideological category; it turns into a real sociological entity, a social whole of the highest comprehensiveness, embracing all people living on the globe. Today one may speak of a global structure of political, economic and cultural relations, extending beyond any traditional boundaries and binding separate societies into one system. This was not the case even in the relatively recent past. As Peter Worsley puts it, 'until our day human society has never existed' (1984: 1). This ontological change is reflected in the epistemological status of sociology. Today it is mandatory 'to rethink the fundamental assumption, long established in our disciplines, that the primary unit of analysis is the nation, the society, or the culture' (Smelser 1992: 369). A number of sociologists concur with Norbert Elias that sociology is possible only as a sociology of world society (Elias 1986).

The depth of changes may be grasped better if we compare two contrasting, polar cases: one from the historical past and another from the historical present. The past society has witnessed an extremely diversified, pluralistic, heterogeneous mosaic of isolated social units. There were multiple and separate political entities ranging from hordes, tribes, kingdoms, empires, to that relatively recent dominant form – nation-states. There were independent, self-contained autarkic economies, and there were varied indigenous cultures preserving their unique identity, often mutually untranslatable and incommensurable.

Present society shows an entirely different picture. In the political realm we find the supranational units of various scope: political and military blocs (e.g. NATO), imperial spheres of domination (e.g. the former Soviet bloc), coalitions of dominating powers (e.g. the 'Group of Seven'), continental or regional integrative organizations (e.g. the European Community), world-wide international organizations (with the UN and its specialized agencies as the prime example). We also notice rudimentary fragments of an evolving world government, when some authoritative functions are exercised by agencies of supranational competence (e.g. the European Parliament, the International Tribunal of Justice or Interpol), and there is growing political homogenization. With an already completed or an ongoing persistent transition towards democracy in Latin America, southern Europe and post-communist countries, it seems that the system of parliamentary democracy becomes a true 'political universal', a dominant political form across the globe (Fukuyama 1989; 1992).

Turning to the economic domain we observe the growing role of supranational co-ordination and integration (EFTA, EC, OPEC), regional and world-wide economic agreements, the global division of labour and the growing role of multinational and transnational corporations, some of which attain revenues exceeding those of medium-size nation-states. Some of them operate from headquarters in one country (e.g. Nissan or Toyota); others lose definite national roots and operate throughout the world, by means of local subsidiaries, franchises etc. (e.g. Pepsi-Cola, McDonald's, General Motors). They have become new powerful actors on the world economic scene. With the demise of planned, command economies, it seems that the market becomes an 'economic universal', a common economic mechanism embracing the globe. Notice the immediacy with which financial markets across the world react to events in separate countries, even when geographically most distant.

Finally, in the area of culture we see progressing homogenization. Mass media, and particularly TV, turn the entire world into a 'global village' (McLuhan 1964), where the information and images of the most distant events arrive in 'real time', where innumerable millions are exposed to the same cultural experiences (Olympics, rock concerts, *Dynasty*) unifying their tastes, perceptions, preferences. The epitome of this trend is reached with the global news networks (CNN) and newspapers (*Herald Tribune*). The flow of similar consumer products reaches all populations (the 'Coca-Colization phenomenon'). The actual movement of persons – migrations, temporary employment abroad, tourism – provides direct, unmediated acquaintance with foreign patterns. A global language appears, with English taking this role for professional communication in science, technology, business, computers, transportation, and for private communication in travel or tourism. Computer technology enforces another unification: of software, with the same programmes used world-wide as a common pattern of organizing and processing data and information. With the suppression and erosion of local, indigenous cultural traditions it seems that the mass, consumer culture of the western type becomes a 'cultural universal' pervading the globe.

All these multidimensional changes motivate some contemporary historians to launch the project of 'global history' (Schafer 1991). They claim that for the last decades, more or less from the middle of the twentieth century, the globalization tendency has changed the fundamental quality of historical processes. Whatever happens anywhere has global determinants and global repercussions. The national or even regional scale is not enough; national or regional histories do not make sense any more. Instead, all historical events must be studied in the global context. And the emphasis should rest on those historical processes which cross the boundaries of the traditional units of analysis (states, regions, areas) to span the whole globe. Simply speaking, in the globalized world, history runs differently, it has new agents, new mechanisms and new directions, and this cannot be ignored by the historians.

Even before this quite recent theoretical orientation emerged, there had been a long tradition of theoretical efforts to comprehend the globalizing tendencies in their various aspects.

Classical accounts of globalization

There are three theoretical accounts of globalization which may already be treated as clasical: the theory of imperialism, the dependency theory and the world-system theory. All three have a common focus and carry a similar ideological message. They deal mainly with the economic sphere, and they aim at unravelling the mechanisms of exploitation and injustice. Thus they clearly have Marxist roots and take a leftist orientation.

The theory of imperialism is to be found in its rudimentary form as early as J. A. Hobson (1902), and is developed by Vladimir Lenin (1939) and Nikolai Bukharin (1929). Imperialism is taken to be the ultimate stage in the evolution of capitalism, when overproduction and falling rates of profit necessitate defensive measures. Imperial expansion (conquest, colonization, economic control of other countries) is the strategy of capitalism to defend itself against imminent collapse. It serves three crucial economic goals: obtaining a cheap labour force, acquiring cheap raw materials, and opening new markets for the surplus of goods. As a result of imperial domination, the world becomes asymmetrically divided: the image of internal class struggle, with the minority of owners exploiting the majority of disowned, is extrapolated to the external global scene where the limited number of capitalist metropolises are seen as exploiting the vast majority of less developed or underdeveloped societies. As an effect of this inequitable, one-directional flow of resources and profits, the gap between rich and poor countries widens. The rich become richer, and the poor poorer. It is only the world-wide revolution of the exploited which can break this vicious circle (Lenin 1939).

Such an image is elaborated in the mid-twentieth century by the theorists focusing on the relationship between the so-called First and Third Worlds in the post-colonial period, at the time when direct political rule by foreign powers is terminated but economic subjugation remains. The 'theory of de-pendency' finds its origins in Latin America, and reflects mainly on Latin American predicaments. It is based on the assumption that the underdevel-opment of Latin American countries is due not only to internal factors, but in large measure to external constraints. An early forerunner of the theory, Paul Prebisch, claimed a fundamental division of the world economy into a dominating 'centre', made up of highly developed industrial powers, and a 'periphery' of mostly agricultural countries (1950). Following from there, a more sophisticated dependency theory appears, and takes two slightly different versions: one is pessimistic, the other slightly more hopeful. André Gunder Frank (1969) puts forward a pessimistic view of the permanent and irreversible underdevelopment of Latin America, intensification, or at least petrification, of exploitation and backwardness. This is due to several reasons. First, there is a fully assymmetrical relationship between the capitalist metropolises (particularly the US and the multinational corporations dominated by the US) and the dependent 'satellites'. Local resources are exploited, and most of the surplus product is appropriated by foreign capital flowing from the satellites to the metropolises. Second, this kind of lasting economic arrangement engenders particular vested interests of the elites (entrepreneurial, managerial, professional, poltical) of the dependent country. They come to vest their life-chances, investing and purchasing opportunities outside their own country in the dominating metropolises. In this way the local elites are co-opted to the service of foreign capital, becoming ready executors of its plans and schemes. Even though remaining in the country, in their aspirations, loyalties and identifications they are already far away. They turn into the willing or sometimes unwitting guardians of the dependent status of their country.

As a result the 'chain of dependence' emerges. Implicated in the mechanism of external exploitation and admitted to some share of profits, the local elites are not concerned with gaining economic sovereignty. The only social force potentially able to break the chain consists of an underclass, which does not participate in the profits but bears the burden of exploitation. Its relative power *vis-à-vis* the combined forces of the foreign metropolises and their local, loyal servants is usually meagre, and does not warrant change, except for the desperate popular uprising 'from below'.

A slightly more optimistic picture is painted by Fernando Cardoso and E. Faletto in their theory of 'dependent development' (1969). The main problem, they claim, is the lack of an autonomous technology and developed sector of capital goods. 'Dependent capitalism is crippled . . . The accumulation, expansion and self-realization of local capital requires and depends on a dynamic complement outside itself. It must insert itself into the circuit of international capitalism' (Cardoso 1973: 163).

But there is a ray of hope: the condition of dependence produces some unintended side-effects or boomerang effects, slowly undermining its own viability. The inflow of foreign investments creates islands of highly developed, modern enterprises in the sea of backwardness and traditionalism. These serve as exemplars: they educate a skilled working class, train a local managerial elite, open up opportunities for co-operating subsidiary enterprises, produce incentives to imitate their economic success. Entrepreneurial motivations are born and spread, local middle classes slowly arise, the early accumulation of local capital begins. At some stage these incremental, quantitative changes may produce a qualitative leap, the 'take-off' to indigenous growth and economic development, gradually diminishing the dependence. The global economic interconnections appear as the means towards ultimate emancipation rather than an instrument of continuing subjugation. The 'newly industrialized countries' (NICs, e.g. Brazil or Mexico), including the so-called Asian Tigers (Taiwan, South Korea, Singapore, Hong Kong), with similar processes appearing recently in the former communist countries, seem to indicate that this is at least a possible scenario.

The most extensive theoretical project addressing the problem of worldwide economic interdependence was started in the 1970s by Immanuel Wallerstein under the name of 'world-system theory' (1974, 1983). The author distinguishes three major stages in history. The first is the stage of 'minisystems', relatively small, economically self-sufficient units with complete internal division of labour and a single cultural framework. These predominate in the epoch of hunting-and-gathering, and continue towards the epoch of horticultural and agricultural societies.

Then come the 'world-empires': large, much more comprehensive entities, incorporating a considerable number of earlier 'mini-systems'. These are founded on an agricultural economy and provide economic co-ordination by means of strong military and political rule, ruthless administration, rigid taxation and conscription. They are also permanently involved in war and imperial conquest (examples include ancient China, Egypt, Rome). Their continuing viability is undermined by the outgrowth of the bureaucratic apparatus and the complexity of administrative tasks over vast territories.

The epoch of the 'world economy' or 'world system' arises somewhere around the beginning of the sixteenth century. At that time capitalism is born as the dominant economic system. The state steps down as the regulating, co-ordinating agency and is replaced by the market. The sole function of the state remains to safeguard the framework for economic activity, free enterprise and favourable terms of trade.

The capitalist system shows tremendous potential for expansion. Its internal self-propelling dynamics and ability to safeguard the abundance of goods makes it highly attractive to large segments of the population. It also commands political power and military resources which allow it to spread its rule. Developments in transportation, military technology and communications speed its advance across the world. The result is the inequality and hierarchization of the global society. It differentiates into three levels: core societies, peripheral societies and an intermediate type of semi-peripheral societies (this is roughly coextensive with another, more popular division into the First and Third Worlds, with a 'Second World' located midway between the two).

Originating from the core, the leading societies of western Europe, capitalism reaches out toward the semi-peripheries and peripheries. The peripheral, poor societies 'were coerced into the dominant world system run by the core societies, but they remained on the edge of the system, at least in terms of raw power, and also in terms of benefits distributed by the world economy' (Chirot 1977: 9). The 'external arena' of countries not falling into the orbit of the 'world capitalist economy' is shrinking. The transition towards a capitalist market economy that we observe after the collapse of command economies in former communist countries wipes out the vast lacunae of non-capitalist development and seems to corroborate this observation with recent evidence. Thus in the twentieth century the whole globe is gradually incorporated into a single economic system of interdependencies, even though it preserves the uneven pace of development, and therefore retains the asymmetric, highly inegalitarian constitution of the system, with highly developed, less developed and relatively underdeveloped parts. The theory of Immanuel Wallerstein remains the most radical statement of the idea of economic globalization.

Wallerstein's vision was certainly a significant contribution to the theory of change. 'World system theories and researchers have clearly accomplished something of significance in emphasizing the idea that the world is a systemic phenomenon and that much of what has been traditionally analyzed by social scientists in societal, or more broadly, civilizational terms can and should be relativized and discussed along global-systemic lines' (Robertson 1992: 400). The major shortcomings of the theory were its strong economistic bias and the mechanical extrapolation of the idea of class inequalities to the international scene – both undoubtedly the reflection of its Marxist roots. Thus world-system theory soon turned out to be insufficient for understanding the complexity of the global society. Another important dimension, global culture, had to be brought in.

Recent focus: globalization of culture

The origins of the interest in cultural globalization are to be found in the work of social anthropologists, e.g. B. Malinowski (1884–1942) and A. R. Radcliffe Brown (1881–1955), who in their field research came to be confronted with the phenomena of cultural contact, cultural clash or cultural conflict. These were particularly salient when western civilization was penetrating indigenous cultures in the colonially dominated societies. As Daniel Chirot observes, even at the beginning of the twentieth century 'there were very few "traditional" societies left in the world. Virtually all people, aside from the few isolated groups in the most remote parts of the Amazon, in a few parts of Africa, and in certain inaccessible parts of Asia, have already experienced prolonged and extremely unsettling contact with the highly modernized, industrialized, and politically dominant Western world' (1977: 7). Local lifeways, norms and values, customs and mores, religious creeds, patterns of family life, modes of production and consumption, seemed to wither away under the impact of modern, western institutions.

This was the occasion for two opposing ideological responses. Some anthropologists, embracing 'cultural relativism', treated it as a case of 'cultural

imperialism', leading to catastrophic consequences: the elimination of indigenous cultures, the loss of cultural autonomy of dependent societies, general
cultural impoverishment. The others, more in line with the claims of the
colonizing powers, professed 'ethnocentrism', praising the civilizational mission of the west, fighting barbarism and paganism, eradicating savage customs and crushing primitive institutions.

In contemporary society the same reactions are evoked by growing cultural
westernization (or even Americanization). Both in lay thinking and in articulated
ideologies we find the complaint that 'the impressive variety of the world's
cultural systems is waning due to a process of "cultural synchronization" that
is without historical precedent' (Hamelink 1983: 3). The commercialization,
commodification and massification of culture is believed to diminish the quality
of products to the lowest common denominator, and thus result in 'non-
culture' or 'new savagery'. But there is also the opposite orientation. Closely
linked with the vision of modernization and the aspiration to catch up with
the most developed societies, there is the readiness to embrace western patterns
as the means or prerequisites for general societal emancipation, or at least as
the symbols of civilizational advancement. This has always been a typical
attitude of educated, political and economic elites in colonial countries. In recent years a similar perspective has gained wide currency in post-communist
societies. Their extreme pro-western cultural bias (an uncritical 'fetishization' of the west), is bred by the attempt to 'join Europe' and to 'escape
from Asia' (i.e. from backwardness, autocracy, Soviet imperial domination).

In the recent period the unification and homogenization of culture on the
global scale has come about mostly through mass media, with TV as its most
potent carrier. 'Media imperialism' turns the world more and more into a
'global village' where the scope of cultural experiences and products is basically the same. A similar effect is brought about by the unprecedented
intensiveness of travel and tourism, which spreads the patterns of these societies
from which most travellers and tourists are recruited, i.e. again the developed,
industrial societies of the west.

These important processes engender theoretical reflection. One recent
example is the evolving theory of 'global ecumene' proposed by Ulf Hannerz
(1987; 1989a; 1989b). He defines the concept of 'ecumene', as a region of
persistent cultural interaction, interpenetration and exchange. The gradual
expansion of the ecumene achieves in our times truly global dimensions.
Traditional cultures emerge in bounded communities; they are anchored to
a certain space and locality, and are produced, exhibited and reproduced
in direct, face-to-face interactions coextensive in time. By contrast, modern
cultures cross any concrete spatial and temporal location; through modern
technologies of communication and transportation they 'unbind space and
time'.

The cultural flows within the global ecumene are not symmetrical or
recipocal. Instead, most of them are unidirectional, with a clear distinction
between the centre, where cultural messages originate, and the peripheries,

where they are merely adopted. The cultural transfers from the periphery to the centre are highly limited. Some recent but rare examples would include reggae music, Latin American novels and African rock.

Hannerz claims that such an asymmetric structure of the centre-and-periphery type is not a single system, covering all dimensions of culture and all geographical regions of the world. Instead, it is a pluralistic conglomerate with various specialized centres, depending on the kind of cultural traits they promote, and various regional centres, retaining overall cultural domination in specific geographical areas. Furthermore those centres are themselves historically changeable; they shift in time (cf. Tiryakian 1985a). At present, the examples of specialized centres would include: USA in the area of science, technology, and popular culture; France in the domain of up-market food and fashions; Japan in the field of corporate culture and organization. The examples of regional centres would include: Mexico in Latin America, Egypt in the Arab world, the Vatican for Catholic countries, the holy cities of Qum or Mecca for the Islamic community.

Looking towards the future, Hannerz draws four possible scenarios of cultural unification. The first, the 'global homogenization scenario', envisages complete domination by western culture, with the whole world becoming a more or less successful replica of western lifestyles, consumer patterns, values and norms, ideas and beliefs. The same goods in the shops, the same plays in the theatres, the same cars in the streets, the same menus in the restaurants, the same films in the cinemas, the same best-sellers in the bookshops, the same news in the papers, the same soap operas on TV, the same hits in the discos – this is an extreme, exaggerated image of what is already occurring in some parts of the world. Any indigenous specificity disappears under the overwhelming pressure of the homogenizing civilizational impact of the west.

A special version of this process is labelled the 'saturation scenario'. This emphasizes the dimension of time: the periphery slowly, gradually absorbs the cultural patterns of the centre, becomes saturated with them, and in the long run, over several generations, local meanings, cultural forms and sensibilities are eliminated. This is a homogenization with a historical dimension.

The third, the 'peripheral corruption scenario', signifies a decay and distortion of western culture in the course of adoption. The clash with the periphery distorts and corrupts higher values. The first mechanism filters out more sophisticated 'highbrow' achievements, leaving space only for 'lowbrow', lowest-level cultural products. Pornography rather than literary criticism, spy thrillers rather than Nobel prizewinners, *Dynasty* rather than Shakespeare, rap music rather than Beethoven. There are two reasons for this: on the receiving side, the lack of cultural preparedness and more sophisticated tastes; on the sending side, the tendency of 'cultural dumping', i.e. selling the surplus of the worst products on the peripheral markets. The second mechanism is the distortion and corruption of received values in order to adjust them to customary local ways of life. For example, in a traditionally autocratic country, democratic values will easily degenerate into despotism, equality into nepotism, freedom of speech into ugly public squabbles, freedom of association into factionalism, the battlefield of innumerable coteries and cliques.

The fourth scenario, clearly the one closest to Hannerz's personal preferences, is called the 'maturation scenario'. It implies more equal dialogue and exchange, rather than one-sided, blind reception. There is partial, selective reshaping of metropolitan culture by the periphery, enriching it with some local values, giving local interpretation to received ideas, and so on. In effect, there appears a unique fusion or amalgamation of indigenous and imported elements. Global culture plays a stimulating and challenging role in developing indigenous cultural values. In the process it undergoes specification for local conditions. The diversity of cultures remains, but all are revitalized and upgraded by the impact of the centre. Important agents mediating in this process are local cultural entrepreneurs, who select and reshape imported products in line with their own local cultural competence and sensibility and the needs of the local market as they perceive them. An equally important role is played by ordinary people, representing deep structures of the local cultural heritage, embedded in their everyday life-world. They attach their own meanings to the transnational cultural flow, and modify it considerably in the process. One of the mechanisms through which it may proceed is the decomposition of the inflowing cultural items into their content and form. The unpacking of form, style, technique, medium, or, to put it metaphorically, 'cultural language' from the concrete substance of meaning, plot, story, or in other words what the language tells and what it tells about – this allows for raised creativeness, filling the global form with local content. Local cultural values may expand and enrich themselves within this new framework.

The ultimate result is what Hannerz calls 'creolization' (hybridization) of culture. All over the world cultures display mixed origins, present complex syntheses, lose purity and homogeneity. This is brought about by ongoing, historically cumulative interrelatedness between the centre and the peripheries, the multidirectional flow between the transnational and the indigenous. As the author puts it, instead of incorporation into a single global culture, 'a conversation among cultures goes on'.

Strong corroboration of the 'maturation' and 'hybridization' scenario is given by Shmuel Eisenstadt. Summarizing his extensive studies of ancient and modern civilizations, he draws a picture similar to Hannerz's:

> When historical civilizations expand, they challenge the symbolic and institutional premises of the societies that are incorporated into them. This challenge calls for responses from within these societies, which has the effect of opening up new options and possibilities. [Modern societies] share many common characteristics but also evince great differences among themselves. These differences crystallized out of selective incorporation – hence also the transformation – of the major symbolic premises and institutional formations of the original Western civilization as well as of their own civilizations. (*Eisenstadt 1992a: 423*)

The responses of peripheral societies to the expansion of the western core depend, according to Eisenstadt, on several combined factors. (1) The 'point of entry' of a given society into the global order, which decides what aspects of earlier culture are undermined, and which new options are opened (in other words, from where the influence of the core flows). (2) The modes of technology and economic organization, pre-existing in a given society (in other words, in which condition the periphery faces the external pressures). (3) The basic ontological premises concerning the cosmic, social and cultural orders in their mutual interrelations, as well as the composition and strength of the elites which articulate and sanction these ontological visions. (4) The accustomed responses to the conditions of change, which have developed in a given society during its history (e.g. adaptational, or constructive responses) (Eisenstadt 1992a: 427). In sum, the author considers the resulting combination of variety and uniformity as a significant dynamizing potential: 'The relationship of these aspects of the different heterodoxies to the respective orthodoxies of their civilizations greatly influences the direction and the transformative capacities of different civilizations, their responses to change and their innovative directives' (p. 427).

Images of the globalized world and the ideologies of globalism

'Globality is a virtually unavoidable problem of contemporary life' (Robertson 1992: 409). It brings both dangers and hopes. As such, it must be consciously entertained by the people. The processes of globalization embracing, as we have seen, all aspects of contemporary social life, economic, political, cultural, become reflected in the social consciousness. The manner in which people conceive of the world, both their local world and the world as a whole, undergoes considerable change. Various new images of the world appear; some of them remain at the level of common sense, and some become articulated in specific ideologies of globalism or anti-globalism. All of them acquire reflexive causal importance, become independent causal variables co-shaping actual globalizing tendencies. Appearing themselves as responses to globality, they turn into determinants of globality.

Roland Robertson has recently presented an insightful typology of the 'images of world order' (1992: 404–9). He distinguishes four of them. The first, 'Global Gemeinschaft I', conceives of the world as a mosaic of closed, bounded communities, either equal and unique in their institutional and cultural arrangements, or hierarchical, with some leading communities at the top. This image is a kind of negative reaction to globalization, and may result in the ideology of 'anti-globalism'. Its egalitarian version was represented by classical social anthropology with its claim of cultural relativism. The hierarchical version was already present in the conception of China as the Middle Kingdom at the centre of the world, as well as in some doctrines of Islam. Recently it has been rejuvenated in the fundamentalist movements which 'advocate the restoration of their own societal communities to a pristine condition, with the rest of the world being left as a series of closed communities posing no threat to the "best" community' (Robertson 1992: 407).

The second image, 'Global Gemeinschaft II', emphasizes the unity of the human species and advocates the emergence of a fully global community, or the 'global village' in the literal sense, with full globe-wide consensus on values and ideas. This is more of a prescriptive rather than descriptive vision, present already in the ancient idea of the Kingdom of God on earth, and recently reappearing in various ecumenical movements, primarily in the Roman Catholic Church expressly addressing the whole of humanity with a new drive towards 'evangelization', but also in east Asian, particularly Japanese, religious orientations. The secular examples of such a view are to be found in the world peace movement or the ecological movement. Another interesting arena where a similar image seems to appear is international security. Neil Smelser observes the 'evolution of understandings and symbolic meanings of, for example, what international lines may not be crossed without threatening to precipitate international nuclear destruction, what actions are available to back down in confrontations without losing face' (Smelser 1992: 369–94).

The third image, 'Global Gesellschaft I', sees the world as a mosaic of sovereign nation-states, mutually open and involved in intensive economic, political and cultural exchanges. The egalitarian version considers the multiple partners as politically equal and involved in mutually beneficial collaboration. The hierarchical version emphasizes the importance of leading, hegemonic societies (great powers) safeguarding the stability of the world.

Finally the fourth image, 'Global Gesellschaft II', envisages the unification of nation-states under some form of world government, either within a supranational polity or as a close-knit federation. Advocated before now by liberals as well as Marxists, it is again at the centre of political debate, particularly with respect to the transformation of the EC from economic towards more political forms of integration.

The controversies and competition among these images and ideologies make up a significant part of contemporary intellectual debate.

Part II

Three Grand Visions of History

7

Classical evolutionism

The first metaphor: organism and growth

Sociology was born in response to a pressing intellectual and practical demand. It strove to understand and to control the immense social transformations occurring in Europe in the wake of great revolutions: the rise of modern, industrial, urban, capitalist society and the erosion of the traditional, agricultural, communal order. Faced with the new, complex and elusive reality, the nineteenth-century philosophers-turned-sociologists searched for heuristic analogies or metaphorical models in better-known areas. Thus the first metaphor to represent society and its changes was hit upon. It came from biology, and it was the metaphor of an organism and organic growth.

In the hands of its founders, the organic analogy was treated only as a heuristic device, a helpful intellectual tool. They claimed some general similarities between an organism and society, but were equally aware of differences and disparities. It was only much later that the metaphor was taken literally, and societies became reified, treated as real, huge, superindividual organisms. That abuse of the analogy, typical of the school of 'organicism' at the close of the nineteenth century (Martindale 1960: 78–81), turned out to be a sterile blind alley of sociological studies, whereas the limited, heuristic use has proved to have considerable fruitfulness and resilience (cf. Back 1971).

The organic analogy referred primarily to the anatomy, the internal constitution of society. Both organisms and societies were found to consist of discernible elements (cells, individuals) clustered in more complex units (organs, institutions), and bound together, or integrated by a determinate network of relationships (organic anatomy, social bonds). Briefly, they were seen as endowed with structure. But there was a clear recognition that the type of structural integration differed: strong and tight in the case of an organism, no part of which could conceivably exist apart from the whole, and much more loose in the case of society, where both individuals and institutions were seen as retaining some degree of autonomy and self-sufficiency. The organic analogy was also applied to the physiology, the internal operation of society. The organic and social elements and more complex components were seen as performing specific roles, or fulfilling definite functions within their respective wholes, and in that manner contributing to their preservation and continuation (organic or social life). Briefly, the focus was on the similarity of functions. But again, the differences were clearly perceived: the highly specialized, one-function components, or organs in the case of an organism, and multi-functional mutually substitutable elements or subsystems in the case of society.

With respect to the dynamic transformations, in both cases there was a visible interplay of continuity and change. In spite of the constant turnover of elements (cells, tissues in the case of an organism; persons, groups in the case of society), there is considerable persistence of the wholes, which last longer than their parts. In both cases the life span of the organism as well as the history of a society are marked by growth. This is the crucial notion for comprehending change; it provides the first image of social transformations, which was to root itself firmly in sociological theory as well as in common sense, and to remain popular until our own day.

'Growth' means enlargement, expansion, complication and differentiation. It assumes a process which (1) consists in the unfolding of certain immanent potentialities present from the beginning in the object under study (unravelling and displaying what is already encoded in the seed or an embryo), (2) proceeds in one direction and is irreversible (there is no way back from maturity to youth), (3) persists inexorably and cannot be stopped (there is no way to remain young for ever), (4) proceeds gradually, incrementally, step-by-step, and (5) passes discernible stages or phases (e.g. youth, maturity, senility).

The concept of growth provides the core of the sociological idea of evolution, foundational for an influential theoretical school in the study of social change, known as sociological evolutionism. It is necessary to emphasize that this orientation in sociology preceded in time and significantly differed from biological evolutionism (Darwinism). First, it was a theory of ontogenesis referring to a single, unique whole (human society), whereas Darwinism was a theory of phylogenesis, referring to the origins of a species or population. Second, sociologists posited the mechanism of unfolding of immanent potentialities, whereas Darwinists focused on random mutations within the species, the struggle for existence, the survival of the fittest and natural selection of the best-adapted segments of the population. In the former case the process was seen as smooth and the factors responsible for change were construed as endogenous, immanent, whereas in the latter case, the process was accompanied by strains, and the stimulus for change was located in exogenous, environmental pressures. Third, sociological evolutionism was strictly deterministic, postulating an unwaveringly necessary process, whereas biological evolutionism was only probabilistic, and pointed to a likely stochastic trend. Both brands of evolutionism stayed apart. For most of its long career, evolutionism in sociology has ignored or neglected the developments in evolutionary biology. It is only recently that some authors have begun to seek inspiration in biological evolutionism, and to propose an 'evolutionary' (rather than 'evolutionist') theory of social or cultural change, applying selected results of modern biology (Langton 1979; Lopreato 1984; Burns and Dietz 1991; 1992).

The founders of sociological evolutionism

Let us begin at the beginning, and illustrate the classical formulation of sociological evolutionism with the work of six representatives: Comte, Spencer, Morgan, Durkheim, Tonnies and Ward.

Auguste Comte and the idealist concept of evolution

The founder of sociology assumes that in order to understand the period of emerging modernity, it is necessary to put it in the wider historical context, to treat it as just a phase in the long course of human history. Industrial-urban-capitalist society is not an accident, but a natural, necessary outcome of preceding processes. It is impossible to provide adequate explanations, predictions and practical directives applicable to contemporary phenomena without reconstructing the pattern and mechanism of all preceding history.

This he professes to do by means of the famous 'law of three stages'. The driving force of historical change is found in the domain of the mind or spirit: in the ways in which people approach and comprehend reality, the assumptions and methods they apply in the effort to explain, predict and control the world. The quality and quantity of knowledge mastered by a society persistently grow. This central trait of society influences or determines all other aspects of social life, economic, political, military. The human race goes through three stages: theological, metaphysical and positive. In the first stage, people invoke supernatural entities and powers as responsible for earthly events. They refer to spirits or souls embedded in objects, plants, animals (fetishism, animism), then to a multitude of gods responsible for various phases of life (polytheism), and finally to a single omnipotent god (monotheism). This period is characterized by the domination of military life and the widespread institution of slavery. The second, metaphysical stage comes when people replace gods with abstract causes and essences, fundamental principles of reality as conceived by reason. The ideas of sovereignty, rule of law and legal government dominate in political life. The third, positive stage is reached when people invoke laws based on empirical evidence, observation, comparison and experiment. This is the age of science and industrialism. Once the positive stage is reached, the development becomes open-ended, as science is eternally moving forward, approximating reality to a larger and larger degree, but never attaining complete and final truth. The pool of human knowledge is constantly, incrementally enlarged. The quantitative, cumulative growth becomes dominant, once the ultimate approach to reality, the highest qualitative type of positive science, is finally attained. 'Thus, history is the story of changes in mind and society which match and mirror each other' (Mazlish 1966: 197). Evolution is primarily the evolution of the methods of acquiring knowledge and of the resulting pool of knowledge.

Herbert Spencer and the naturalist concept of evolution

Spencer conceives of evolution as the underlying, common principle of all reality, natural and social alike. This commonality is due to the fact that all reality is basically material, consisting of matter, energy and movement. 'Evolution is definable as a change from an incoherent homogeneity to a coherent heterogeneity, accompanying the dissipation of motion and integration of matter' (Spencer 1972: 71). The model of this process is provided by organic growth.

> In its primary stage, every germ consists of a substance that is uniform through-out, both in texture and chemical composition. The first step is the appearance of a difference between two parts of this substance; or, as the phenomenon is called in physiological language, a differentiation. Each of these differentiated divisions presently begins itself to exhibit some contrast of parts; and by and by these secondary differentiations become as definite as the original one . . . By endless such differentiations there is finally produced that complex combination of tissues and organs constituting the adult animal or plant. This is the history of all organisms whatever. (*Spencer 1972: 39*)

In brief, evolution proceeds by means of structural and functional differentiation: (1) from simplicity to complexity, (2) from amorphousness to articulation of parts, (3) from uniformity, homogeneity, to specialization, heterogeneity, and (4) from fluidity to stablility. Such a process is universal: 'Whether it be in the development of the Earth, in the development of Life upon its surface, in the development of Society, of Government, of Manufactures, of Commerce, of Language, Literature, Science, Art, this same evolution of the simple into the complex, through successive differentiations, holds throughout' (Spencer 1972: 40).

In the history of human society, the general law of evolution finds specific implementation. The mechanism of social evolution is based on three regularities. First, there is the inherent instability of uniform, homogeneous populations. Human individuals are fundamentally unequal with respect to hereditary endowment, individual experiences, the environmental conditions in which they live, the accidental opportunities and deprivations which they encounter. Therefore they cannot persist in a homogeneous mass without an emerging differentiation of roles, functions, power, prestige and property. Second, there is the tendency to amplify inequalities, the specialization of roles deepens, disparities of power and wealth grow. In effect, initial differentiations are gradually and cumulatively extended. Third, as people of similar positions (roles, functions, prestige, wealth) tend to cohere, a society becomes divided into factions, classes and groups along class, national and

Table 7.1   Military versus industrial society

Trait	Military society	Industrial society
Dominating activity	Defence and conquest of territory	Peaceful production and exchange of goods and services
Integrating principle	Coercion, rigid sanctions	Voluntary co-operation, contracts
Relation of individuals and the state	State domination, restriction of freedom	State serving individual needs, freedom
Relation of the state and other organizations	Monopoly and domination of the state	Autonomy of private organizations
Political structure	Centralization, autocracy	Decentralization, democracy
Stratification	Ascription, low mobility, closed society	Achievemnt, high mobility, open society
Economic activity	Autarky, protectionism, self-sufficiency	Economic interdependence, free trade
Dominant values	Courage, discipline, obedience, loyalty, patriotism	Initiative, inventiveness, independence, truthfulness

occupational differences. Once the boundaries guarding these identities are raised, the segregation of a population is strengthened and the return to homogeneity is no longer possible.

This mechanism produces the sequence of distinguishable stages in human history, from simple societies (mutually isolated, permeated with identical or similar activities of all members, devoid of political organization), through complex societies (where division of labour among individuals, and division of functions between segments of society appear, with hierarchical political organization attaining central importance), then doubly complex societies (possessing common territory, a permanent constitution and system of laws), up to civilizations (most complex social wholes, nation-states, federations of states or large empires).

To underline the direction in which this evolutionary process moves Spencer introduces the first polar, dichotomous typology of societies. Analytically drawn opposite ideal types are treated as marking the starting- and end-points of a chronological sequence. This strategy of specifying the course of evolutionary process was to become popular, and we shall find it also in the work of later evolutionists. In the Spencerian version, it is the opposition of military society and industrial society. The typology may be summarized in a schematic form (table 7.1), which is a slight modification of the account given by Neil J. Smelser (1968: 246).

Lewis Morgan (1818–81) and the materialist concept of evolution

The American anthropologist Lewis Morgan introduced a variant of the evolutionary idea focused on the domain of technology. He was the first in the long line of technological determinists who located the ultimate moving forces of social change in the area of inventions and discoveries, gradually transforming the entire way of life of human populations. Morgan believed that the uniformity and continuity of evolution derive from the underlying universality and persistence of human material needs. Such needs, typical for the human species (e.g. for food, shelter, comfort, security etc.), provide the stimuli for the incessant search for means to satisfy them. Thus the push for technological innovations originates in natural, material needs experienced by human beings. Once new technologies are attained, they change the whole character of society, influencing the forms of family life and kinship organization, the patterns of economy and politics, cultural values and everyday life.

The history of mankind follows three distinct phases: savagery, barbarism and civilization, delimited by significant technological breakthroughs. Thus in the period of 'lower savagery' we observe simple subsistence, based on the gathering of fruits and nuts. 'Middle savagery' witnesses the discovery of fire and fishing methods. In 'upper savagery', the invention of bow and arrow highly facilitates hunting. In 'lower barbarism' the production of pottery is a significant technological advance. In 'middle barbarism', we observe the domestication of animals and irrigation as new agricultural techniques. In 'upper barbarism', the production of iron and iron tools becomes of revolutionary significance. Finally the birth of 'civilization' is marked by the invention of the phonetic alphabet and the art of writing (Harris 1968: 181).

This type of monocausal, technological explanation became influential. It reappeared in the Marxist school, and the intellectual conduit was provided by Friedrich Engels, who utilized Morgan's ideas in his own book *On the Origins of the Family, Private Property and the State* (1884). It was also picked up much later by representatives of neo-evolutionism: e.g. Leslie White and Gerhard Lenski (see chapter 8).

Emile Durkheim and the sociologistic concept of evolution

The French classic of sociological thought was emphatically anti-reductionistic; he refused to search for the causes of social phenomena anywhere else than the domain of specific social reality (*sui generis* 'social facts'). Such an orientation is clearly reflected in his view of social evolution put forward in

Table 7.2 Mechanical versus organic solidarity

Trait	Mechanical solidarity	Organic solidarity
Character of activities Main social bond	Similar, uniform Moral and religious consensus	Highly differentiated Complementarity and mutual dependence
The position of an individual	Collectivism, focus on a group, community	Individualism, focus on autonomous individuals
Economic structure	Isolated, autarkic, self-sufficient groups	Division of labour, mutual dependence of groups, exchange
Social control	Repressive laws punishing offences (criminal law)	Restitutive law, safeguarding contracts (civil law)

his early book *De la division du travail social* (1893). The main direction of evolution is seen in the growing division of labour, differentiation of tasks, duties and occupational roles as society moves forward in time. This tendency is related to demographic factors: growing population results in growing demographic density and brings about growing 'moral density', meaning the intensiveness of interactions, complexity of social relationships or, briefly, the quality of the social bond. Following Spencer's strategy, Durkheim proposes another dichotomous typology of societies based on the different quality of social bonds: 'mechanical solidarity' is rooted in similarity of undifferentiated functions and tasks; 'organic solidarity' is rooted in the complementarity, co-operation and mutual indispensability of highly diversified roles and occupations. The typology is treated as a chronological scheme, depicting the initial point and the end-point of social evolution: history moves from 'mechanical solidarity' to 'organic solidarity'. The polar types may be summarized in a schematic form (table 7.2).

Ferdinand Tönnies and evolution without progress

A similar typology of societies may be found in a famous treatise by Tönnies titled *Gemeinschaft und Gesellschaft* (1887). The personal, intimate, primary, autotelic social ties characterizing the 'community' turn into impersonal, mediated, secondary and purely instrumental contacts in modern 'society'. More specifically, the direction of evolution may be represented in a scheme (table 7.3).

The uniqueness of Tönnies's approach is shown by his critical attitude

Table 7.3 *Gemeinschaft* versus *Gesellschaft*

Trait	Gemeinschaft	Gesellschaft
Social relationships	Kinship	Economic exchange
Typical institutions	Family	State and economy
Image of an individual	Self	Person, citizen
Form of wealth	Land	Money
Type of law	Family law	Law of contracts
Central institutions	Village	City
Social control	Folkways, mores, religion	Law and public opinion

towards modern society, and particularly his nostalgia for the lost community. He is a rare example of an evolutionist who does not treat evolution as synonymous with progress. In his view, evolution runs counter to human needs, leading to deterioration rather than the improvement of human condition.

Lester Ward (1841–1913) and the evolution of evolution

A very interesting idea is added to the theory of evolution, by an American classic of the field, Lester Ward, in his *Dynamic Sociology* (1883). Ward claims that the mechanism of evolution is not constant but itself changes in time. In its wide sweep, evolution embraces also the very mechanism of evolution. The most important borderline divides the period of spontaneous, natural evolution ('genesis') from the relatively recent period of human, goal-oriented evolution ('telesis'). The latter is unique in being guided by the awareness and purposefulness of human actors. To be more specific, evolution starts as 'cosmogenesis', embracing the entire universe. At some moment the phenomenon of life appears, and a new evolutionary mechanism of 'biogenesis' emerges and supplements the continuing cosmogenesis. At some later moment human beings appear, and another evolutionary mechanism rooted in mind and consciousness (known as 'anthropogenesis') starts to operate together with the former two, supplementing the cosmo- and biogenesis. Finally, human beings attain a new form of organization, society, and since that time the new mechanism of social evolution (labelled 'sociogenesis') adds itself to all earlier ones. In effect, four mechanisms operate together, controlling the superimposed layers of processes of various origins: cosmogenesis, biogenesis, anthropogenesis and sociogenesis. With the last two phases, evolution takes a new turn. Planning, anticipating, constructing the future provide entirely new possibilities of social change. Evolution runs on ever new, higher levels, and in the process becomes more multidimensional and humanized (cf. Gella 1966).

The common core of evolutionist theory

In the work of the classical evolutionists the specific image of social and historical change gradually took shape. In spite of differences between authors, all seemed to accept a number of common assumptions which provide the core of evolutionist theory.

1   All evolutionists assume that the whole of human history has a unique form, pattern, 'logic' or meaning underlying the multitude of seemingly haphazard and unconnected events (Berlin 1966; Addis 1968). This pattern can be discovered; it is knowable, and the goal of evolutionary theory is to reconstruct it. Such a reconstruction will provide understanding of past history and open the way to predicting future history.

2   The object undergoing change is taken to be the whole of human society, humanity, mankind. It is treated as a single, most comprehensive whole. Even if some authors focus on the evolution of some selected fragment or aspect of society, say religion (Benjamin Kidd) or morals (Edward Westermarck) or technology (Lewis Morgan), it is understood that it evolves together with the whole of society, that it is just a symptom of total social evolution.

3   This whole is conceived in organic terms, by application of the *organic analogy*, as a tightly integrated system of components and subsystems, all of them, singly and together, contributing to the maintenance and continuation of the whole.

4   The focus is on the changes of such an organic whole, of the social system. If the changes *in* elements, components or subsystems are considered, it is only from the persective of their contribution to the overall evolution of society.

5   The change of society is treated as ubiquitous, as a natural, necessary and inescapable trait of social reality. If stability or stagnation are observed, they are interpreted as blocked, arrested change, and treated as exeptions.

6   Because it applies to a single entity, society as a whole evolutionary change is treated as a single, all-encompassing process, which may be perceived and studied as a totality, at its own highest level of abstraction.

7   The change of society is seen as directional, moving from primitive to developed forms, from simple to complex states, from dispersion to aggregation, from homogeneity to heterogeneity, from chaos to organization. This movement is consistent and irreversible; no earlier state of society repeats itself, and each later state is higher on the scale of complexity and differentiation.

8   The evolutionary change is conceived as unilinear, following a single, pre-established pattern or trajectory. Obvious differences among various fragmentary societies or cultures within human society as a whole are due to the slower or quicker pace of the same evolutionary process in various parts

of the world. More primitive or backward societies are simply delayed in the process, but will inevitably move along the same path, following the more developed ones, and in particular the most mature societies of the west. 'The fundamental criterion of the series is an equation between modernity, as revealed in Western societies, and maturity; conversely, traditionalism suggests immaturity and lack of development' (Smith 1976: 37). Contemporary primitive societies show us what our western society looked like in the past. Western society shows to more primitive societies what they will look like in the future. The analytical scale of differentiation is coextensive with the chronological scale of development. To put it metaphorically, there is only one moving escalator, on which various societies or cultures occupy higher or lower steps.

9   This common evolutionary trajectory is divided into distinct stages, phases or periods, which follow a constant sequence, and none of which can be skipped.

10   Evolutionary change is perceived as gradual, continuous, incremental and cumulative. The overall movement of evolution is smooth and involves no radical discontinuities, breakdowns or accelerations. Even if fragmentary societies, cultures or civilizations experience crises, backlashes or eruptions, that does not impair the overall gradualness of change.

11   It is claimed that evolution has a universal and uniform causal mechanism; at all stages there are the same processes involved, and the same causes moving the process forward. (A notable exception is Lester Ward with his notion of a sequence of various evolutionary mechanisms, but even in his theory the ultimate underlying evolutionary 'logic' is the same.) Most authors take the monocausal stand, positing a single, unique cause as the ultimate determinant of the evolutionary process.

12   The innate impulse towards change is located within the very 'nature' of human society, deriving from its basic need for self-realization and self-transformation. Thus the ultimate causes of evolutionary change are conceived as immanent, endogenous. Evolution is an unfolding of intra-social potentialities, from the embryonic to the mature forms.

13   Evolutionary change is seen as spontaneous. It proceeds in unintended and mostly unrecognized ways, and produces latent results which are aggregated and accumulated composite effects of processes of which the members of society are not aware. (Again, we must note the exceptional position of Lester Ward, who in his notion of 'telesis', recognized the possibility of goal-oriented, planned change.)

14   Evolutionary change is taken to be tantamount with progress; it results in the constant improvement of society, the betterment of human life. Most classical evolutionists subscribe to the belief, typical for the optimistic climate of their epoch, that 'civilization has moved, is moving, and will move in a desirable direction' (Bock 1978: 40). A notable exception is Ferdinand Tönnies, who raised the first warning agasignt blind belief in the benefits of change.

Weaknesses of classical evolutionism

All the assumptions listed above are highly contestable. They may be criticized and rejected on many grounds: theoretical, when they lead to implausible implications, or require untenable premises; empirical, when they are not borne out by the facts of social life and clash with historical evidence; moral, when they violate or undermine widely accepted values. In fact, all these lines of criticism were followed, and brought about a breakdown and temporary demise of evolutionist theory in the first half of the twentieth century, until it re-emerged in the revised form known as neo-evolutionism around the 1950s.

1   The assumption of overall historical pattern or logic has been questioned by numerous professional historians, whose detailed, concrete, fact-oriented approach inclined them to take an opposite, 'eventist' or 'ideographic' stand, emphasizing the contingency and randomness of historical occurrences. Even those who took a 'nomothetic' perspective, allowing for the existence of regularities and patterns in history, gave them limited scope – an epoch, period, region, nation-state – and refused to apply them to all humanity. They were ready to formulate 'laws concerning history' (concrete history of this or that country, or this or that era), but not the 'laws of history' (considered globally) (Mandelbaum 1957). The thorough philosophical and logical critique of the assumption came later, with the work of Karl R. Popper (1964), to be discussed in chapter 12.

2   The assumption of all human society as the entity undergoing evolutionary change was put in doubt by the growing evidence of tremendous plurality, variety, heterogeneity of human populations: tribes, local communities, nation-states, civilizations. Their strong individual idenity, relative autonomy and isolation led several social anthropologists to treat them separately and to trace their separate evolutionary paths.

3   The over-integrated, organic image of society was undermined by the common observation of conflicts, strains and tensions, the notorious dysfunctionality of some social institutions or patterns and the relative functional autonomy of some segments or aspects of society. It was found that the components of society were not necessarily beneficial for the persistence of the whole, but often became detrimental and disruptive. The new conflict model of society did not lend itself to the evolutionist interpretation of change.

4   It was noticed that the overwhelming proportion of social changes are limited in scope and have the character of changes *in*, occurring within the same social type, rather than between different social types. Therefore the focus on the much more rare fundamental changes *of* the whole social system was found to be unwarranted. It was also emphasized that only a fraction of changes *in* could be immediately related to changes *of* as their prerequisites or co-determinants. Most of the changes *in* are either neutral with respect to the whole system, or safeguard its reproduction rather than transformation.

5   The absolutization of change was linked with the bias of the modern epoch, where change appears as taken for granted, and, even more so, as a highly desirable quality of social life. Quickly accumulating anthropological and historical evidence had a debunking role. It indicated prolonged periods of stability, stagnation and conservation of traditional patterns as typical for earlier history. Continuity had to be treated as at least equally 'natural' with change.

6   It was observed that the single, unique process of change is only an abstract concept, without any ontological foundation. It has only nominal but not real existence. What really exists is a multitude of fragmentary processes which are either mutually independent, parallel, cross-cutting, overlapping, amplifying or contradictory. What we perceive and can document historically are several processes such as urbanization, industralization, migrations, proletarianization, secularization or democratization etc., but not 'social change' as such.

7   The uniform directionality of evolution was challenged by massive cases of reversals, backlashes, breakdowns, crises and even total collapses of states or civilizations. When such regressive processes occur in core regions of human society, it is hard to dismiss them as irrelevant. In fact they produce a temporary reversal of historical processes on a much larger scale. Think of the collapse of Greek or Roman or Maya civilizations and the impact it had on the entire world of their period. De-differentiation, homogenization, dispersion and disorganization on a large scale are common historical facts which do not fit into the mould of evolutionist thought (Tiryakian 1985c: 118–34; 1992: 78–96).

8   The idea of unilinear evolution supposedly following one single path is countered with three kinds of arguments. Some refer to the qualitative variety of human societies and the impossibility of ranking all of them along a common scale of differentiation, maturity or advancement. Some non-western societies, or at least some of their institutions, must be treated as simply different rather than backward. The possibility of local, peculiar evolutionary trajectories of various regions, civilizations and cultures must be admitted on empirical grounds. The 'horizontal view of history' (Smith 1976: 40), assuming that what comes later is simply different, seems more adequate than the 'vertical view', which ranks everything which comes later as higher on the scale. Other arguments turn against the ethnocentric bias and belief in the ultimate value of western institutions or ways of life as the peak of the evolutionary scale. The opposite standpoint of cultural relativism is taken to be morally preferable. Still other arguments invoke the theoretical idea of diffusion. If, as evolutionists claim, societies at various levels of evolutionary development coexist at the same historical period, than there is no reason to assume that their future development, following isolated, mutually independent paths, will simply replicate the overall evolutionary scenario. Just the reverse: societies become mutually interdependent, there is the reciprocal exchange and borrowing of organizational forms, cultural rules, lifestyles etc. This complex

flow of inter-societal influences may significantly reshape the develomental route taken by each society.

9   The same diffusionist argument counters the idea of inexorable stages. Some stages may be omitted and some processes accelerated precisely because of the use made of the experiences of other societies, or through outright intrusion by other societies (conquest, colonization, domination). Diffusionism provides 'valuable correctives, particularly to the notion of developmental stages whether for every society or for the whole of humanity. The most important was that migration and demonstration effects (i.e. the movement of men and ideas) were constantly altering existing patterns and units' (Smith 1976: 43).

10   The gradual, incremental vision of change does not fit the extremely pervasive experience of discontinuities, ruptures, mutations, thresholds, qualitative steps or cataclysmic breaks in human history.

11   The historical evidence speaks against simplistic monocausality. It points to the role of multiple causes, direct and indirect, immediate and distant in complex permutations. Historical events and changes turn out most often to be combined effects of unique sets of causes, none of which can be taken as exclusive or even universally prior. Perhaps if priority may be assigned to some type of causes, it is itself temporary and historically relative. The fact that modern society seems to be shaped by economic factors, does not preclude the possibility that in earlier empires the political factor could be predominant, or that in early primitive society the domain of family and kinship exerted the strongest causal impact in social life. It is also clearly the case (as L. Ward hinted with considerable insight) that in modern society a much larger scope of changes is produced and controlled in intended, planned fashion, which basically transforms the evolutionary mechanism.

12   The neglect of exogenous causation of social change manifest in such phenomena as conquest, colonization, diffusion, cultural contact, demonstration effect, environmental changes, natural disasters and calamities etc. is perhaps the most serious weakness of classical evolutionism. 'It can safely be claimed that a large part of historical record would be incomprehensible without explanations in terms of transunit influences' (Smith 1976: 133). Of course, it may be an equally serious mistake to move from the exclusive 'endogenist' to the exclusive 'exogenist' perspective. The emphasis or balanced treatment of both types of causation must be decided, depending on the concrete historical case.

13   As has already been indicated, the full spontaneity of evolution cannot be upheld if we recognize the importance of human efforts in shaping and reshaping human societies, from ancient reforms or codifications of laws and mores to the revolutionary political projects of the modern era, with all varieties of human initiatives, plans and policies in between. Some part of change has always been intended and recognized, and the share of such changes seems to be growing as societies advance. Some authors speak of 'humanistic history' as opposed to 'natural history', meaning the period when

purposeful construction of social institutions acquires widespread importance (Topolski 1978).

14   The link of evolutionism with progressivism makes the notion of evolution particularly suspicious to those critics of contemporary civilization who are disillusioned with progress. The implication that evolution brings improvement and betterment of human life seems to be countered by the tragic experience of the twentieth century and the frightening prospects of further, unbridled development of industry, technology, warfare, and urbanism. Times when crisis becomes the leitmotif of common sense and sociological theory alike cannot be receptive to the idea of evolution.

Under the concentrated fire of all those and similar arguments, classical evolutionism lost its focal place in the theory of social change. But its career was not yet over. It was to reappear in a highly revised form more than a century after its birth, under the label of neo-evolutionism.

8

Neo-evolutionism

The rebirth of evolutionism

After a period of critique, rejection and abandonement, sociological evolutionism returned to the forefront of academic debate in the 1950s. However, it turned to new intellectual sources and accordingly took new directions. In this new, revised form it has continued as an influential school of the theory of change up to the present.

Neo-evolutionism seeks new foundations for its claims. Instead of philosophical or historiosophical inspirations, it attempts to draw on the results of concrete, empirical disciplines dealing with social changes, and particularly palaeontology, archaeology, cultural anthropology, ethnology and historiography. Those disciplines have flourished in the twentieth century, and neo-evolutionists want to use their results. One implication of the accumulated evidence is clear, they claim, namely the general support for the idea of directional, linear transformations, moving towards growing differentiation of societies. As Gerhard Lenski puts it,

> The basic outlines of human history from the Lower Paleolithic through the Bronze Age are now clear. They can be described only in developmental terms: evidence of increasing numbers in the human population, evidence of human residence in more diverse habitats, evidence of increasingly complex technology, and evidence of increasing production of durable goods and accumulating capital. Historians pick up the story where archeologists leave off, and their findings both reinforce and extend the picture provided by those of the archeologists: continuing growth in population; continuing advances in technology, in production, and in capital accumulation; and, in addition, social systems that generally become more complex, more differentiated, more urban, and more powerful as time goes on. (*Lenski 1976: 551*)

Similarly, Talcott Parsons claims that 'Developments in biological theory and in the social sciences have created firm grounds for accepting the fundamental continuity of society and culture as part of a more general theory of the evolution of living systems' (1971: 2). Thus evolution is not a myth – the neo-evolutionists claim – but a confirmed reality. Only it must be studied in scientific rather than speculative fashion, taking into account all valid criticisms raised against classical evolutionism and all later achievements of the social scientific disciplines, including sociology itself.

This persuasion leads neo-evolutionism to depart markedly from classical evolutionism. (1) The focus is moved from the evolution of the global human society as a whole towards processes appearing in more limited social entities: civilizations, cultures, separate societies (tribes, nation-states etc.). (2) The main concern is with the causal mechanisms of evolution, rather than with the sequence of necessary stages. In other words explanations rather than typological schemes are most strongly sought. (3) The accounts of evolution are formulated in categorical, descriptive terms, avoiding valuations and intimations of progress. 'For contemporary evolutionists, sociocultural evolution has a much more restricted meaning, one with no implicit moral judgments' (Lenski and Lenski 1974: 79). (4) The propositions are phrased in a probabilistic, stochastic fashion rather than a straightforward deterministic manner. (5) There is a gradual incorporation of insights from the other branch of evolutionism, Darwinian, biological evolutionism, which has developed extensively and independently, producing rich results in the biological sciences.

Neo-evolutionism in cultural anthropology

The career of neo-evolutionism begins in cultural anthropology. The work of several authors leads to the gradual liberalization, and even complete removal, of rigid assumptions typical of classical evolutionism. In this way neo-evolutionism acknowledges and adapts itself to the earlier extensive critique. We shall outline some selected work in this area.

Leslie White and the move towards technological determinism

In two influential books: *Science of Culture* (1949) and *Evolution of Culture* (1959), the American ethnologist Leslie White draws the image of culture as the adaptive device by which the human species accommodates itself to nature, mainly by means of harnessing free energy and putting it to work for the satisfaction of human needs.

All parts of culture are interrelated but 'the primary role is played by technological system', with political organization, normative structure, knowledge systems and ideologies as derivative or secondary. Culture develops and advances through the increase of the type of energy, the amount of energy harnessed per capita per year, and the efficiency with which the energy is utilized. This factor determines growing human mastery over nature, which White sees as the fundamental evolutionary tendency.

There is a regular evolutionary sequence of energy utilization: at the outset, people utilize bodily, physical energy; then with the domestication of animals, animal energy is harnessed for human use; then with the agricultural revolution the energy of the soil becomes most important; then the discovery of fuels opens vast new resources of energy; finally the energy of nuclear fission is controlled and the atomic era begins.

The development of culture has biological origins and roots in the natural human endowment. But once born, human culture acquires partial autonomy; it has a life and momentum of its own and evolves according to its own specific mechanisms and regularities. Thus the development of culture is mostly endogenous; the last major dramatic changes in the external, natural environment took place at least 20,000–25,000 years ago. The later dynamism of a culture cannot be explained as a response to exogenous challenges, but must be tackled on its own, specific cultural level. The key to the evolution of a culture is to be found in the culture itself.

Julian Steward and the concept of multilinear evolution

Another American anthropologist, Julian Steward, in a book on the *Theory of Culture Change* (1955), took an even more decisive step away from evolutionist orthodoxy. He abandons grand historiosophy for the search for 'middle-range' regularities of historical change. This leads him to the study of multiple and diversified cultures (in the plural), rather than a single, comprehensive culture of all humanity (in the singular). 'Twentieth-century research has accumulated a mass of evidence which overwhelmingly supports the contention that particular cultures diverge significantly from one another and do not pass through unilinear stages' (Steward 1979: 28).

Cultures are viewed as discrete entities located in various ecological niches, and as acquiring varied shape through adaptation to different conditions. The focus shifts to the differences between cultures, discoverable by comparative research in distant and separated geographical areas, as well as to the internal diversification of cultural components or dimensions. Cultures differ from other cultures, and aspects of each culture differ from other aspects of the same culture.

Evolution embraces all such concrete cultural entities, whether separate cultures or separate cultural fields, but in each of them runs differently and follows specific mechanisms. Hence evolution must be treated as multilinear, and this in two senses. First, in the inter-societal sense: evolution runs along different paths in various societies, because of the unique conditions in which they find themselves. Second, in the intra-societal sense: the evolution of various social fields (culture, economy, politics, art, law etc.) follows different courses and employs different mechanisms. Multilinear evolution is 'interested in particular cultures, but instead of finding local variations and diversity troublesome facts which force the frame of reference from the particular to the general, it deals only with those limited parallels of form, function, and sequence which have empirical validity. What is lost in universality will be gained in concreteness and specificity' (Steward 1979: 19).

The determination and analysis of parallels is an objective of multilinear evolution.

In spite of those varietes, there is some more general causal principle behind evolutionary changes: the preponderance of 'techno-economic' factors, which play a strategic role in every human society. But this does not imply strict technological determinism. Rather the domination of techno-economic among other causal factors is treated as probabilistic distribution. The core of society, causally shaping its changes, consists primarily of technological and economic institutions, but may also comprise, with diminishing probability, some aspects of socio-political organization, and most rarely of ideology.

The cultural core is defined as

> the constellation of features which are most closely related to subsistence activities and economic arrangements. The core includes such social, political, and religious patterns as are empirically determined to be closely connected with these arrangements. Innumerable other features may have great potential variability because they are less strongly tied to the core. These latter, or secondary features, are determined to a greater extent by purely cultural-historical factors – by random innovations or by diffusion – and they give the appearance of outward distinctiveness to cultures with similar cores. (*Steward 1979: 37*)

Techno-economics is most often decisive, and rarely acquires peripheral causal status; politics much more often occupies the periphery, and ideology is most likely to be only a secondary, derivative force in the hierarchy of social causation. It is only when he techno-economic core is transformed that the major evolutionary shifts can be noticed and new cultural types appear. 'Over the millennia cultures in different environments have changed tremendously, and these changes are basically traceable to new adaptations required by changing technology and productive arrangements' (Steward 1979: 37). In history, the dominant direction of evolution is marked by the increased structural complexity ('socio-cultural integration') of the units engaged in collective action: from families at the earliest stage, through tribes, to states in the modern period. This is represented in figure 8.1.

An interesting critique and elaboration of Steward's theory is put forward by Anthony Smith. First, he notices that cultural variety among societies is in fact greater than the variety of their natural environmental conditions (ecological niches), which means that at least some 'surplus variety' is unexplainable by reference to the mechanism of adaptation and must be referred to some autonomous intra-cultural mechanisms of development. Second, the strength of determination by ecological or techno-economic factors depends on the phase of evolution: predominant in the early phases, it allows much more political or ideological determination at the later stages. Forms of governement, religion and art my acquire a more autonomous role. The more developed a society, the greater is the degree to which 'the environment tends to set limits to cultural variation and change, rather than propel the unit

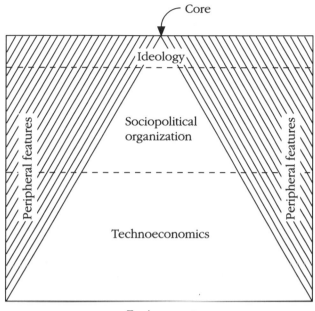

Figure 8.1 Steward's image of the social system (*source*: Kaplan and Manners 1972: 47). Reproduced by permission of Prentice Hall, Inc.

towards change' (Smith 1976: 48). Steward's scheme is thus put into motion and endowed with a time dimension.

Marshall Sahlins and E. Service: the distinction of general and specific evolution

In their *Evolution and Culture* (1960), Sahlins and Service attempt to revindicate one of the main themes of classical evolutionism, and reconcile it with the findings of new evolutionary theory. 'General evolution' may be validly studied at the highest level of abstraction, as the overall direction of humanity, in which new cultural types constantly emerge. It follows the scale of growing adaptability, systemic complexity and higher organization. In contrast to that, 'specific evolution' comprises the concrete ways in which the new cultural types adapt themselves to specific environments. Here societies exhibit considerable creativity, which results in a great diversity of cultures. As the authors say, 'well adapted culture is biased. Its design has been refined in a special direction, its environment narrowly specified, how it shall operate definitively stated.' This provides it with an identity, uniqueness and strength, but also may engender some potential weakness. Namely, 'general evolution' and 'specific evolution' may run into conflict. Specific evolution implies perfect adjustment to a concrete environment, whereas general evolution implies increasing autonomy and mastery over an environment as the prerequisite for future adaptability. Thus 'the society or culture may become so adapted through specialization to its environment, so well adjusted in its ecological niche, that it is no longer adaptable, no longer able to innovate for a leap forward to higher levels of technological and social organisation' (Smith 1976: 47). Stagnation rather than change will be a likely result.

Neo-evolutionism in sociology

Neo-evolutionism took hold in sociology as the reaction to the orthodox versions of the structural-functional approach, the school dominating sociological theory in the 1950s, but coming under attack for its presumed static bias. The revised evolutionary theory was either proposed as the alternative to functionalism by the outsiders to the functionalist school, or as the modification and extension of functionalism destined to save it, by the leading functionalists themselves. We shall discuss two most influential examples of sociological neo-evolutionism.

Gerhard and Jean Lenski: the ecological-evolutionary approach

The authors define their main perspective with reference to biological sciences:

> it shares with the evolutionary approach in biology an intense interest in the process of change – especially basic, long-term, developmental, and adaptive change – and in the related processes of competition and conflict. With the ecological approach in biology, it shares an interest in the ties of interdependence within and among populations and in the relations between populations and their environments. (*Lenski and Lenski 1974: 23*)

Thus it is emphasized that human history is not just a sequence of 'one damn thing after another . . . a tangled web of events without any meaningful patterns or trends' (p. 76). On the contrary: 'the presence of long-term trends is clearly evident' (Lenski 1976: 554).

The most significant trend is technological advance. In spite of occasional cases of 'technostasis' and regression, this is a prevailing direction of change. Socio-cultural evolution is defined simply as 'technological advance and its consequences' (Lenski and Lenski 1974: 79). The essence of technological advance comes down to the changing scope and quality of information relevant for controlling the environment. 'I am inclined to believe that underlying all, or most, of these trends is a single master trend that explains the others. This is the growth in the store of information available to humans – especially information relevant to the manipulation of the material world, that is, technology' (Lenski 1976: 555).

The emancipation of the human species from the animal world was itself due to the advancement in learning and sharing of information. The basic form of information is purely genetic, the higher form is individual learning; then comes communication by signs (sharing information with others immediately co-present) and finally communication by means of symbols, coding information, preserving it and sharing with others not necessarily co-present, not even necessarily coterminous in time (passing and accumulating information from one generation to another). 'Symbol systems have provided mankind with a radically new way of relating and adapting to the biophysical world . . . Symbol systems are the functional analogue of genetic systems' (Lenski and Lenski 1974: 18). It is likely that in the future the amount and quality of information available to the human species will allow it to put its own evolution under conscious and purposeful control. This will crown the process of 'evolution of evolution', the constant advancement of evolutionary mechanisms themselves.

All other aspects of social life are strongly linked with the character of technology. 'A society's solutions to its technological problems function as a set of conditions that determines the range of solutions the society can apply to other problems' (Lenski and Lenski 1974: 80). The dominant course of determination follows the sequence: 'technology – economy – polity – distributive system' (Lenski 1966: 436). But the authors are emphatic about treating technological determination as merely probabilistic, and they allow feedbacks from other aspects of society to technology. But in general, 'Technological advance is the chief determinant of that constellation of global trends – in population, language, social structure, and ideology – which defines the basic outlines of human history' (Lenski and Lenski 1974: 110).

Thus technology provides the main criterion for the periodization of human societies into stages or evolutionary phases: (1) hunting and gathering, to 7000 BC, (2) horticultural, from 7000 to 3000 BC (3) agrarian, from 3000 BC to AD 1800 and (4) industrial, from AD 1800. Depending on local ecological conditions, there may be alternative, multiple lines of evolution branching from the maincourse, and therefore distinct variants of the main types. Some societies may develop equivalent but different technologies at the same overall level of efficiency, measurable as 'the value of society's gross product divided by the human energy expended in its production' (Lenski 1966: 93). The resulting typology of societies is presented in figure 8.2.

Talcott Parsons and the extended theory of differentiation

At the close of his long and prolific career Talcott Parsons came to grips with the problem of long-range historical change. In two volumes, *Societies: Evolutionary and Comparative Perspectives* (1966), and *The System of Modern Societies* (1971) he put his earlier structural-functional concepts to use for interpreting the evolutionary transformations of human society.

Parsons distinguishes two kinds of processes occurring in any social

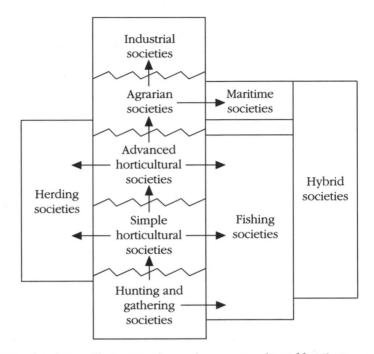

Figure 8.2   Lenski's evolutionist scheme (*source*: Lenski 1966: 92). Reproduced by permission of McGraw Hill, Publishers.

system. Integrative and control processes have compensatory effects: they restore equilibrium after disturbances, and safeguard the continuity and re-production of society. But there are also processes of structural change touching the core system of values and norms. 'Structural change is a change in values controlling relationships between system units' (Lackey 1987: 85).

Structural changes follow the evolutionary pattern. Every next phase in the process is distinguished by growing complexity with an increase in the number and variety of specialized units within a system, with the consequent necessity for new forms of co-operation, co-ordination and organization. 'Socio-cultural evolution, like organic evolution, has proceeded by variation and differentiation from simple to progressively more complex forms' (Parsons 1966: 2). In other words, 'the directional factor is an increase in generalized adaptive capacity' (p. 26). But this is only an overall trend which does not preclude diversity of specific evolutionary trajectories. Evolution is not unilinear but multilinear: 'Contrary to some early conceptions in the field, however, it has not proceeded in a single neatly definable line, but at every level has included a rather wide variety of different forms and types' (p. 2).

There are four basic mechanisms of evolution: differentiation, adaptive upgrading, inclusion and value generalization (Parsons 1966: 22–3; 1971:

26–8). (1) First is the mechanism of differentiation, i.e. formation of new structurally and functionally specific units. 'Differentiation is the division of a unit or structure in a social system into two or more units or structures that differ in their characteristics and functional significance for the system' (Parsons 1971: 26). As an example there is the split of the peasant family household into the modern family household and modern employing organization. (2) Next is the mechanism of adaptive upgrading, i.e. the rise of efficiency of each of new units, their more specialized and effective performance compared to earlier more uniform wholes. 'Adaptive upgrading is the process by which a wider range of resources is made available to social units, so that their functioning can be freed from some of the restrictions on its predecessors' (1971: 27). For instance, a modern factory makes more products, more varied products, and does it more effectively than the peasant household. (3) Then comes the mechanism of inclusion, i.e. the integration of new units into the society, safeguarding their harmonious operation in a new context. 'These problems can be met only by the inclusion of the new units, structures and mechanisms within the normative framework of the societal community' (1971: 27), among others the generation of new norms, values and rules. (4) There is the mechanism of value generalization, i.e. formulating the normative standards at a sufficiently general level to embrace the new, diversified units and provide them with support and legitimation. 'When the network of socially structured situations becomes more complex, the value pattern itself must be couched at a higher level of generality in order to ensure social stability' (1971: 27). Those four mechanisms operate together. 'The state of any given society and, still more, of a system of related societies . . . is a complex resultant of progressive cycles involving these (and other) processes of change' (1966: 23).

The evolution follows discernible stages: (1) primitive, (2) advanced primitive, (3) intermediate and (4) modern. The primitive society is highly uniform and homogeneous. It is not differentiated into specialized subsystems. The core social bonds are provided by kinship and religion. Participation in society is defined by ascriptive statuses and particularistic criteria. An advanced primitive stage is reached when the division into subsystems appears: political functions (goal-attainment) emancipate themselves from religion (pattern-maintenance), and within the latter subsystem, sacred and secular values become further differentiated. Participation in society becomes stratified, and more emphasis is given to the criterion of achievement rather than ascription. Intermediate societies are marked by the development of writing, which allows for the accumulation of information, distanced communication and transmission of tradition. Developed social stratification appears, dominated by universalistic principles. Values become generalized and legitimated in secular ways. Finally 'the modern type of society has emerged in a single evolutionary arena, the West which is essentially the area of Europe that fell heir to the western half of the Roman Empire north of the Mediterranean. The society of Western Christendom, then, provided the base from which what we shall call the "system" of modern societies "took off"' (Parsons 1971: 1). The crucial traits of modernity are: (1) the complete differentiation of the four subsystems in a society: adaptational, goal-attaining, integrative and pattern-maintaining, (2) the dominant role of economy, characterized by mass production, bureaucratic organization, the pervasiveness of market and money as a generalized arena and medium of exchange respectively, (3) the development of the legal system as the main mechanism of social co-ordination and control, (4) stratification based on universalistic criteria of achievement, (5) the extension of impersonal, mediated, complex networks of social relationships.

Parsons's image of evolution was criticized for its pro-western bias.

> He can only envisage a single main stem of evolutionary advance, namely the 'Western' from Israel and Greece through Rome to the modern West. All the rest, it is clear, have proved evolutionary failures, however well adapted to their environment they may be. Such a cladogenetic scheme is plainly ethnocentric. Its series is derived from a selective reading of Western history, in terms of attributes which have proved significant and valuable in the social experience of industrial Western states, notably America. (*Smith 1976: 52*).

This bias appears strongest when Parsons closes his discussion of evolution with a conclusion: in our times there has appeared a 'lead society', culminating the evolutionary process, and this society is the United States. 'The United States, the "first new nation", has come to play a role approximately comparable to that of England in the seventeenth century' (Parsons 1971: 87). That is primarily because

> it synthesizes to a high degree the equality of opportunity stressed in socialism. It presupposes a market system, a strong legal order relatively independent of government, and a 'nation-state' emancipated from specific religious and ethnic control. The educational revolution has been considered as a crucial innovation, especially with regard to the emphasis on the associational pattern, as well as on openness of opportunity. Above all, American society has gone farther than any comparable large-scale society in its dissociation from the older ascriptive inequalities and the institutionalization of a basically egalitarian pattern. (*Parsons 1971: 114*)

This depiction is too idealistic, and departs from some more harsh realities of American life. It reads strangely in the 1990s when recently released official data show that one in every seven US citizens lives below the level of poverty, the unemployment rate comes close to 10 per cent, racial and ethnic tensions break out with new force, economic recession persists and American economic leadership in the world is contested by both the Far East and a uniting Europe. But Parsons's remarks must be put in a historical context. When those words were written the US was going through a period of prosperity, abundance and optimism. His work reflected that mood, and so at times came close to apologetics and ideology. 'Talcott Parsons, writing in the United States in the 1950s and 1960s, felt that he was living at the apex of human civilization, just as Auguste Comte in the 1830s believed that his own France showed the face of the future to less modern societies of his time' (Collins 1988: 39).

Neo-functionalism and the debate about differentiation

In the 1980s there began an important theoretical debate focused around one of the basic claims of evolutionism: that social evolution proceeds in the direction of growing structural and functional differentiation. The idea was already present in Herbert Spencer's account of the general 'law of evolution' (see chapter 7). But it was fully articulated and elaborated only by Emile Durkheim in his first major book, *De la division du travail social* (1893). Picking out one aspect of differentiation, the division of labour, Durkheim asserts a general regularity: 'If one takes away the various forms the division of labor assumes according to conditions of time and place, there remains the fact that it advances regularly in history' (1964: 233). The polar typology of 'mechanical solidarity' and 'organic solidarity' (see table 7.2) is just an elaboration on that idea. Durkheim's formulation has become most influential for later debate. 'Although the notion that society changes through a process of institutional specialization can be traced back to earlier times, the modern theory of social change as differentiation may be seen as beginning with Durkheim' (Alexander 1988a: 51).

The concept of the division of labour refers primarily to the domain of work, and to the specialization of occupations or professions. The concept of differentiation is a generalization of that. As defined by Neil J. Smelser, 'Structural differentiation is a process whereby one social role or organization . . . differentiates into two or more roles or organizations . . . The new social units are structurally distinct from each other, but taken together are functionally equivalent to the original unit' (1959: 2). The division of labour is just a sub-case of differentation. Dietrich Rueschemeyer explicates the distinction:

> Structural differentiation encompasses division of labour, but it goes in two respects beyond the older concept. While division of labour pertains to work roles, and in complex societies primarily to full-time jobs and occupations, the concept of differentiation is not confined to the economic sphere and includes political, cultural, and other social roles as well. Furthermore, differentation refers to the specialization of organizations and institutions as well as of roles. (*Rueschemeyer 1986: 141*)

It is obvious that the idea of differentiation includes quite adequately the 'general contours of world history' (Alexander 1988a: 49), as well as general traits of the modern epoch, when the phenomenon reaches unprecedented scope. But there are two respects in which the idea is deficient: it does not provide the causal mechanism explaining the pervasive tendency towards differentiation (what Durkheim proposed by means of demographic pressure, or 'moral density' is hardly satisfactory), and it does not provide concrete, historically rooted, 'phase-specific' analyses of the diverse consequences, side-effects, strains and tensions engendered by differentation in various epochs, as well as quite common cases of reversals, structural fusions, de-differentiations and devolutions. The tension between the level of general tendency, causal mechanism and contingent historical developments is labelled by Alexander as 'Durkheim's problem'. It motivates later attempts to extend the theory of differentiation 'downward', towards unravelling the underlying causal process and acknowledging historical realities.

These attempts were already undertaken by the first generation of structural-functionalists: Talcott Parsons (1966; 1971, see above), Neil Smelser (1959), Shmuel Eisenstadt (1963). Later, in the 1980s the thread was picked up by the so-called 'neo-functionalist' school (e.g. Alexander 1985; Rueschemeyer 1986; Alexander 1988a; Alexander and Colomy 1988; Tiryakian 1992). 'These revisions proceed from the common assumption that differentiation does, indeed, provide an intuitively meaningful framework for understanding the nature of the modern world. But an effort to interrelate this general model to institutions, processes, and phase-specific strains preoccupies most differentiation theorists in the present day' (Alexander 1988a: 69).

As an illustration of what may be called the neo-differentiation theory, I will take Dietrich Rueschemeyer's book on *Power and the Division of Labour* (1986). The author attempts to meet both challenges raised by Durkheim's omisions: he tries to supplant causal mechanism, and to anchor the tendency in contingent facts, allowing for exceptions and reversals of the overall trend. Assuming with Durkheim that 'Division of labour and social differentiation are the social processes that underlie shifts toward more complex social structures' (Rueschemeyer 1986: 1), he focuses on one significant factor that causally contributes to differentiation, namely power. The factors of greater efficiency, productivity or adaptability put forward by earlier functionalists only beg the question. The real issues are: Efficiency for whom (by whose criteria)? Productivity for whom (according to whose 'preference structures')? Adaptability for whom (satisfying whose needs)? He argues that the powerful are always able to impose division of labour consistently with their particular interests, or to block differentiation if it happens to be contrary to their interests. The amply documented thesis of the book is that 'It is the most powerful interests that most determine which efficiency criteria will select among different forms of division of labour and thus shape the particular forms of social production and reproduction' (p. 171). Turning the argument to concrete historical circumstances, Rueschemeyer boldly faces Durkheim's second challenge: not to ignore the exceptions from the tendency. Several examples of de-differentiation, defined as 'reversals of specialization and the fusions of functions' (p. 141) prove that the tendency is highly contingent. (1) There are examples of stagnation typical for numerous agricultural societies, so pervasive in the world for large stretches of history. (2) There are famous cases of decline after advances in the division of labour: the fall of the Roman Empire, the Byzantine Empire, devolutionary periods in Egypt or Persia are just selected cases. (3) There are counter-tendencies at different levels of social structures: e.g. with centralization and deepened division of labour at the governmental level, local units (village, city, region) often undergo devolutionary processes; similarly with growing specialization of jobs at the level of the national economy, locally there may be 'incentives to return to much simpler and poorer ways of making a living' (p. 150). (4) In modern society there arise particularly interesting cases of de-differentation: the general, unifying role of the citizen, cutting across all other social divisions, as well as moral and religious individualism (e.g in the Protestant religion), taking away a crucial part of religious concerns from the specialized institutions of the Church or priesthood. The invoking of power differentials and contesting group interests as causal factors arresting, blocking or reversing differentiation proves its explanatory strength also with respect to these exceptional deviations from the general tendency.

Rueschemeyer's contribution is just a recent example of how 'Durkhcim's problem' and the related research programme informs the ongoing theoretical debate which has now lasted for almost a century.

The turn towards biological evolutionism

As we remember, the sociological evolutionism of Comte or Spencer predated the formulation of evolutionary theory in biology, and in particular its most influential statement by Charles Darwin (1809–82) in his fundamental treatise *On the Origin of Species* (1859). Both classical evolutionism in sociology and most neo-evolutionist schools have followed the Spencerian image of organic growth rather than the Darwinian image of natural selection. It is only recently that sociology has turned seriously to the Darwinian roots. In place of earlier theories labelled 'developmental' or 'ontogenetic' (Burns and Dietz 1992: 3), as 'stage theories' or 'organic differentiation theories' (Collins 1988: 13), some neo-evolutionists propose 'natural selection theories' (Collins 1988: 29), or theories of 'sociocultural variation and selective retention' (Lopreato 1984: 236). They share the belief that 'the Darwinian model reveals fundamental analytical similarities between the biological and sociocultural processes of evolution' (Langton 1979: 306), and 'attempt to describe the mechanisms that produce sociocultural evolution by analogy to the Darwinian model of random variation and selection' (Lopreato 1984: 264).

In effect, the basic metaphors or models underlying evolutionary theorizing are entirely rephrased. Randall Collins gives an apt summary of the distinction: the classical theory

> takes embryology as the model and represents society as growing like an organism, becoming not only larger but differentiating into specialized organs and

> functions . . . A second biological analogy is to the Darwinian theory of how
> species evolve through the variation and natural selection of those forms best
> adapted to their environments . . . Differentiation sees societies as analogous to
> single organisms, growing during their lifetime; natural selection sees societies
> as analogous to the variety of species (populations of organisms), some of
> which are selected as favorable adaptations, and some of which are not. (*Collins
> 1988: 13*)

This change of perspective stimulates a new wave of theorizing. Once again,
'in the last decade, evolutionary thinking has moved from the periphery of
social theory to the core' (Burns and Dietz 1992: 3).

The basic mechanism of evolution was defined by Darwin as 'the preservation of favourable variations and the rejection of injurious variations'
(1964: 81). There are three principles which make up the logic of the
process. First, the principle of variation (random mutations) in the population. Second the principle of selection (struggle for existence) among differentially endowed individuals. Third the principle of the survival of the fittest
(reproductive success), resulting in the reproduction of traits carried by
selected individuals ('inheritable' characteristics) in future populations.

In evolutionary biology one of the main issues already had to do with the
character of the components singled out in the population. From an early
and naive view, which treated concrete fully-fledged individuals as competitors among whom the struggle for survival and natural selection occur,
the discoveries of Johann G. Mendel (1822–84) led to the highly abstract notion of genes and a genetic pool as the terrain of evolutionary selection. A
parallel intellectual development is noticeable in the sociological or 'socio-
cultural' theory of evolution. It is no longer populations of persons which
are conceived as evolving, but rather sets of abstract social relations, or, in
the most recent version, sets of rules, articulated in 'rule systems' (Burns and
Dietz 1992: 261; See also Dietz and Burns 1992). Parallelism of reasoning,
and even of the language used, to the biological conception are unmistak-
able. 'Our approach', Burns and Dietz proclaim, 'focuses on the processes
by which social rules are generated, selected, and transmitted or reproduced . . . Evolutionary forces act on variability in the population. Transmission and selection processes favor some rules and lead to their increased
prevalence. This is reproductive success, or cultural fitness' (1992: 263).

Another riddle shared by biological and sociological theory has to do with
the sources of initial variability. Why are the elements of the population so
heterogeneous and diversified? Some authors admit: 'like Darwin, contemporary
social scientists are profoundly ignorant of the laws governing the production
of variations' (Langton 1979: 292). At most they venture to refer to innovations,
discoveries, aberrations, behavioural accidents, idiosyncrasies and similar
random and unpredictable factors. Another position claims that in human
society variation may not necessarily be blind and random, but also result
from purposeful design, be 'wilful in the sense that human beings are goal-
oriented and constantly engaged in the search for strategies or behaviors that

are in some sense superior to old ones' (Lopreato 1984: 247). This fact makes the emergence of variation less indeterminate than it might otherwise have been. An even deeper probe into the secret of variations is available to the authors focusing on the evolution of rule systems. Tom Burns and Thomas Dietz suggest that the variability of rules may stem from six circumstances. (1) There is the necessary verbalization of rules during their social transmission (by teachers), and this opens the door for idiosyncratic formulations. (2) Any implementation of rules, which are general by definition, requires interpretation, and this is another opportunity for idiosyncrasies. (3) People make mistakes and errors in the articulation and implementation of rules. (4) People actively search for and experiment with rules, particularly if they are dissatisfied with those which are binding. (5) People engage in playful or even perverse activities, which may generate new rules extending to the serious domains of life. (6) There is always an infiltration of alien rules, either by personal contact or vicarious encounter (through the mass media) (Burns and Dietz 1992: 264).

The third riddle refers to the crucial mechanism of selection, i.e. 'differential reproduction of modes of action and thought within societies' (Langton 1979: 302). Why are some elements inherited and others abandoned? 'How are certain combinations, among the plethora produced every moment in any given population, singled out by the selectors for retention and institutionalization?' (Lopreato 1984: 251). This question in fact embraces three distinct queries: Who, or what serves as an agent conducting selection? What are the criteria applied in the process of selection? How is the selection effected?

As to the agents, Burns and Dietz distingush 'p-selection' carried out consciously by power-holders, reformers, leaders, who set the rules for others; 's-selection' produced by unwitting constraints or facilitations engendered by established structures; and 'm-selection' working through the natural, objective limits of the material environment. For instance, 'human agents cannot enact rules which violate the laws of physics and biology' (1992: 266–7). The authors emphasize the importance of self-conscious, purposeful human agency, neglected or totally ignored in more mechanistic versions of evolutionism. 'Agency provides a mechanism for generating change in rule systems that is far more powerful than error or migration, one that matches the dynamic, inventive and often playful character of human life' (p. 275).

As far as the criteria of selection are concerned, it is an established tradition to mention adaptability or reproductive success, i.e. the functional value of a certain institution, rule, way of life, for survival and ability to reproduce. Some authors go further than that, pointing out that sheer survival or fitness is rarely the sole consideration, and that in human society an important selector may be the 'enhancement of satisfaction or creature comforts' (Lopreato 1984: 256). Finally, one could suggest as an ultimate criterion the enhancement of society's agential capacities: the potential of self-transformation (see chapter 15).

Similarly, the mode in which the selection is effected is perceived in ever more complex ways, from the simple Darwinian 'struggle for survival', through the 'struggle for reinforcements', i.e. 'efforts to obtain the things which will fulfill needs and wants' (Langton 1979: 297), to the 'struggle for satisfaction', i.e. 'favorable balance of pleasure over pain' (Lopreato 1984: 257). I would suggest one more, perhaps an ultimate mode of selection: the 'struggle for agency', i.e. for emancipation from negative constraints and the enhancement of positive freedom to transform one's own society (see chapter 15).

As its proponents frankly admit, the neo-evolutionist theory of socio-cultural selection is still 'in a very early stage of development in the social sciences' (Burns and Dietz 1992: 275). But already it looks much more promising than classical evolutionism, as well as some non-Darwinian brands of neo-evolutionism discussed earlier. Its basic novelty includes the rejection of determinism, finalism, fatalism, linearity and gradualness. In their place there are strong new emphases on chance, randomness, contingency, open-endedness of the process, qualitative thresholds, and the crucial role of human agency. The research programme it implies is highly ambitious: 'Success may require a theoretical synthesis of evolutionary biology and social science as well as richer and more systematic knowledge of the environmental, including cultural, conditions and historical vicissitudes of Homo Sapiens and his society' (Lopreato 1984: 236).

9

Theories of modernization, old and new

The last embodiments of evolutionism

There are three senses in which one may speak of the idea of modernization. One is most general, synonymous with all kinds of progressive social change, when society moves ahead along some accepted scale of improvement. This usage is fully relativistic in a historical sense and can apply to all historical periods. Getting out of caves and building the first shelters was clearly a case of modernization, just as abandoning horse carts for automobiles and typewriters for word processors, to mention more recent instances. This meaning of the term will not interest us here, as it is not specific enough, and there are other good terms to be used instead.The second meaning is more historically specific. It invokes the idea of 'modernity', a rich complex of social, political, economic, cultural, and mental transformations occurring in the west from the sixteenth century onward, and reaching its apogee in the nineteenth and twentieth centuries. It involves processes of industrialization, urbanization, rationalization, bureaucratization, democratization, the ascendancy of capitalism, the spread of individualism and achievement motivation, the affirmation of reason and science, and many other processes discussed in detail in chapter 5. 'Modernization' in this sense means attaining modernity, coming closer to that specific, historically located institutional, organizational and attitudinal syndrome: 'the process, through which a traditional or pretechnological society passes as it is transformed into a society characterized by machine technology, rational and secular attitudes, and highly differentiated social structures' (O'Connell 1976: 13). In this sense most classical work in sociology is about modernization: Comte and Spencer, Marx and Weber, Durkheim and Tönnies produce accounts of this process crucial for the history of Europe and the US in their time.

Finally, there is the most specific meaning of the term: 'modernization' referring only to backward or underdeveloped societies and describing their efforts to catch up with the leading, most developed countries coexisting with them at the same historical period within the global society. In other words, it describes the movement from the peripheries to the core of modern society. A group of specific approaches to social change running under the name of modernization, neo-modernization and convergence theories adopts this narrow meaning of 'modernization'. They will be our main focus in this chapter.

Theories of modernization and convergence are the product of the post-Second World War era. Both have been formulated in response to the new emerging division of human society into three distinct 'worlds': the First World of the developed industrial societies, including western Europe and the US, but soon to be joined by Japan and the 'newly industrialized countries' of the Far East; the Second World of the authoritarian 'socialist' societies dominated by the Soviet Union, moving at a huge social cost along the path of enforced industrialization; and the Third World of the post-colonial societies of the south and the east, severely underdeveloped and often remaining deep in the pre-industrial era. How to conceptualize and explain social change in such a heterogeneous and clearly unequal global setting, taking into account growing interactions and mutual interdependence of the First, the Second and the Third Worlds? This became the serious challenge for the theorists of change. Classical theories of modernization focused on the contrast between the First and the Third World, whereas theories of convergence, as well as recently emerging theories of post-communist transition, take the cleavage between the First and the Second World as their main theme.

The period of high popularity of both theories in their classical, initial form, falls in the 1950s and mid-1960s. The contributions of Marion Levy (1966), Everett Hagen (1962), Talcott Parsons (1966), Neil Smelser (1959), Daniel Lerner (1958), David Apter (1968) and Shmuel Eisenstadt (1973) to the theory of modernization, and the work of Clark Kerr (Kerr et al. 1960), Samuel Huntington (1968), Walt Rostow (1960) in the field of convergence theory are widely read and acclaimed. Then, in the 1970s and up to mid-1980s strong criticisms were made, resulting in the decline, even the complete demise, of both theories. But, at the end of the 1980s we observe some revival of modernization theory, and its revised versions are proposed under the labels of 'neo-modernization' (Tiryakian 1991) or 'post-modernization' (Alexander 1992). At the beginning of the 1990s, in the aftermath of the collapse of communism, convergence theory also re-entered the mainstream of sociological debate, forming one of the possible accounts of the post-communist transition.

Both modernization and convergence theory may be treated as the last embodiments of the evolutionist orientation. This is particularly true of the early versions of both theories, with the gradual liberalization of strong evolutionist assumptions under the pressure of criticism, and their virtual rejection in neo-modernization and neo-convergence variants. At the beginning, however, in the search for theoretical models useful for interpreting the advance from less developed to more developed 'worlds', both theories turned to evolutionism, at that time still dominant in sociological thinking about change. 'Though their terminology may be somewhat novel, the manner in which modernization theorists tend to approach the study of social change in non-Western societies is deeply rooted in the perspective of developmentalism which was already firmly established in the conventional wisdom of Western social science well before the end of the nineteenth century' (Tipps 1976: 64).

Thus they assumed (1) that changes are unilinear, and hence that less developed societies have to follow the same path that more developed societies have already trodden, retracing the same steps, or standing lower on the same escalator. (2) They believed that changes are irreversible, and move inevitably in the direction of modernity, the common final end of developmental processes, which they identified with the industrialized, capitalist, democratic societies of the west. (3) They considered changes as gradual, incremental, effected in a non-disruptive, peaceful manner. (4) They indicated a regular sequence of stages through which the processes move, none of which could supposedly be skipped, e.g. 'traditional–transitional–modern' (Apter 1968), 'traditional–achieving preconditions for take-off–taking off to sustained growth–maturing–reaching mass consumption level' (Rostow 1960). (5) They put the emphasis on endogenous, immanent causation, and described the driving force of change in terms of structural and functional differentiation, adaptive upgrading and similar notions of evolutionist provenance. (6) They preached progressivism, believing that the processes of modernization bring about universal improvement of social life, a betterment of the human condition. To put it briefly, modernization and convergence were considered necessary, irreversible, endogenous and ultimately beneficial.

Even at that early stage, however, there were already some departures from evolutionist ideas, particularly visible in modernization theory. Apart from the special problematic focus on the Third World (or Second World, in the case of convergence theory), there was a new emphasis on social engineering and planning, and a more specific vision of the final end. Rather than a spontaneous tendency working itself out 'from below', modernization was most often considered as a process initiated and controlled 'from above', by enlightened political elites determined to pull their countries up from backwardness by means of purposeful, planned efforts. Rather than providing vague utopian visions of the better society, modernization theorists were adopting more tangible images, namely the existing, most developed societies of the western, capitalist world. Modernization, therefore, meant something different from spontaneous development in the overall progressive direction. It meant purposeful imitation of western societies, taken as blueprints of modernity. Western industrial democracies served as 'model countries' (Bendix 1964), 'reference societies' or 'pace setters' (Tiryakian 1985a), and the 'follower countries' were seen as chasing or catching up with them. 'Modernization is not a self-sustaining evolutionary process progressing on its own. Rather, it is a process of emulation, of the transplantation of pattern and products from the achievements of other countries to one's own' (Chodak 1973: 257).

The concept of modernization

Modernization, in the specific sense adopted by the modernization theories of the 1950s and 1960s, has been defined in three ways: historical, relativistic and analytical.

In the historical definitions it is synonymous with westernization or Americanization. It is seen as the movement towards historically specific, localized and dated societies. Two examples of such accounts may be quoted. Shmuel Eisenstadt says: 'Historically, modernisation is the process of change towards those types of social, economic and political systems that have developed in Western Europe and North America from the seventeenth century to the nineteenth and have then spread to other European countries and in the nineteenth and twentieth centuries to the South American, Asian, and African continents' (1966b: 1). Wilbert Moore gives a similar depiction: 'Modernization is a "total" transformation of a traditional or pre-modern society into the types of technology and associated social organization that characterize the "advanced", economically prosperous, and relatively politically stable nations of the Western World' (1963b: 89). Approaches of this sort are most vulnerable to the fallacy of ethnocentrism.

This danger is partly avoided by the relativistic definitions which do not invoke specific spatial or temporal parameters but focus on the substance of the process, whenever and wherever it occurs. Again, two examples may be provided. Edward Tiryakian observes: 'Modernity is not hic et nunc contemporaneity. From a world historical process perspective, modernity pertains to state-of-the-art or leading-edge innovations or breakthroughs in cognitive, moral, ethical, technological, and social arrangements that contribute to the enhancement of the human condition' (1985a: 134). A similar account is given by Szymon Chodak: 'Modernization is a special, important instance of the development of societies, an instance where conscientious efforts are made to achieve higher chosen standards' (1973: 256). In the relativistic sense, modernization means purposeful emulation of standards which are considered modern either by the population at large or by its enlightened segments or by ruling elites. But these standards may vary. The 'epicentres' of modernity, i.e. the locations of leading, reference societies in which the achievements perceived as modern are most common, are not fixed once and for all. They are historically changeable. Edward Tiryakian traces such 'moving epicenters of modernity', from the 'seedbed' societies of Greece and Israel, through ancient Rome, north and north-western Europe in the Middle Ages, the ascendancy of the United States, and the present shift towards the Far East, the Pacific Rim, or perhaps in the future back to a united Europe (1985a).

The analytical definitions become more specific than that, trying to delineate the dimensions of a modern society purposefully implanted in pre-modern, traditional settings. Some of them focus on structural aspects. Thus Neil Smelser describes modernization as a complex, multidimensional transition embracing six areas. In the economic realm it means: (1) rooting technologies in scientific knowledge, (2) moving from subsistence farming to commercial agriculture, (3) replacing human and animal power with inanimate energy and machine production, (4) spreading of urban forms of settlement and spatial concentration of the labour force. In the political arena, modernization signifies the transition from tribal authority to systems of suffrage, representation, political parties and democratic rule. In the realm of education, it involves the elimination of illiteracy and growing emphasis on knowledge, trained skills and competences. In the religious sphere, it indicates secularization. In family life, it is marked by a diminished role of kinship ties and greater functional specialization of the family. In the domaim of stratification, modernization means emphasis on mobility and individual achievement rather than on ascription (Smelser 1973: 747–8).

Some other analytic accounts of modernization adopt a psychological rather than a structural perspective. They delineate a specific type of personality, supposedly characteristic for modern societies. 'Modern personality' was described in chapter 5 as the peculiar syndrome made up of the following traits: (1) independence of traditional authorities, anti-dogmatism in thinking, (2) concern with public matters, (3) openness to new experience, (4) belief in science and reason, (5) planning, anticipation, orientation towards the future, ability to defer gratification, (6) high aspirations: educational, cultural and professional (Inkeles 1976; Inkeles and Smith 1974). Modernization in this area means approaching such a typical personality configuration and the suppression of opposite, traditional personality traits. In sum, it involves 'greater ability to adjust to the broadening societal horizons; the development of some ego-flexibility, widening spheres of interest, and growing potential empathy toward other people and situations; a growing appreciation of self-advancement, mobility; and an increasing emphasis on the present as the meaningful temporal dimension of human existence' (Eisenstadt 1983: 226).

The mechanisms of modernization

What is the causal mechanism of the push (or pull) towards modernity so widely encountered in underdeveloped societies? The theorists differ on this issue, and several hypotheses are proposed.

Some authors invoke traditional evolutionist reasoning (of the Spencerian or Durkheimian brand) with its metaphor of growth. Structural and functional differentiation (and more concretely, division of labour) is an inevitable, 'natural' process which can be slowed down or even blocked for a time, but eventually has to prevail. If one takes such a perspective, the main issue becomes the discovery of those factors which halt the differentiation (growth) of underdeveloped societies, and the business of policy is to search for ways to remove those blocks. The underlying assumption is that societies will modernize if only they are not hampered in the process. The push for modernization is believed to be spontaneous, emerging from below. The task for political elites is only to demolish the barriers to modernization, which guard traditional, backward ways of life, institutions and organizational patterns.

Other hypotheses invoke more sophisticated evolutionary reasoning (of the Darwinian brand) with its idea of variety and the survival of the fittest. In the clash or competition among societies (cultures, economies, forms of organization, military systems) modernity provides a competitive edge. It is more adaptive, more efficient, makes it possible to satisfy more needs of larger masses at higher levels. The prerequisite of modernization is the co-existence of various societies, and the necessity of those at lower levels of development is to modernize or perish. The adaptive upgrading may be incremental, again evolving 'from below', but then it is very slow. It may be accelerated when enlightened political elites become aware of the adaptive handicap of their societies and impose modernizing reforms 'from above', coupling them with educational campaigns, spreading the awareness of the benefits of modernity.

Such awareness may also develop spontaneously, among ordinary people through the 'demonstration effect' of more modern societies, with their higher standards of life, affluence and personal freedom. For the citizens of under-developed, backward countries the experience of the benefits of modernity may be actual or vicarious. Opportunities for actual encounters with modern life-ways, institutions and organizations grow with the improvement of communication, growth of tourism, business travel etc. Chances for mediated, vicarious experience of modernity (and especially its 'rosy' sides) arise with mass media and telecommunications, from Hollywood films to satellite TV. When the pull towards modernity embraces the masses, it may often run against the vested interests of the entrenched political elites. Then, the prerequisite for modernization is the ascendancy of new modernizing elites, winning over the conservatives, and able to release the accumulated modernizing potential of a society.

A quite specific mechanism of modernization is put forward by convergence theory. In its classical form (C. Kerr, S. Huntington, W. Rostow and others) it comes close to technological determinism. Thus, it claims that the character of the dominant technology enforces (evokes) specific forms of social organization, political life, cultural patterns, everyday conduct and even beliefs and attitudes. Assuming that technology has its own immanent logic of development driven by the sequence of discoveries and innovations, the ascendancy of modern technologies will sooner or later evoke the whole syndrome of modernity, producing similarity or even uniformity across various societies, and eliminating local differences. This uniformity-engendering 'logic of industrialism' is summarized by John Goldthorpe: 'As industrialism advances and becomes increasingly a world-wide phenomenon . . . the range of viable institutional structures and of viable systems of value and belief is necessarily reduced. All societies, whatever the path by which they entered the industrial world, will tend to approximate, even if asymptotically, the pure industrial form' (1971: 263). Or in the words of another author: 'Modernization is a homogenizing process. Many different types of traditional societies exist; indeed, traditional societies, some argue, have little in common except their lack of modernity. Modern societies, on the other hand, share basic similarities. Modernization produces tendencies toward convergence among societies' (Huntington 1976: 31).

More specific, empirical studies of convergence carried out in the 1970s dealt with several areas where supposedly uniformization was observed. These include: an occupational structure adapted to the needs of industry, a demographic structure with lower birth rates and prolonged life expectation, the change from an extended to a nuclear family system, new forms of mass education, the factory as a common mode of organization of the labour force, an increase in per capita income, the appearance of consumer markets, democratization in political life (Weinberg 1976: 356). Comparative research, however, has also been producing considerable evidence of divergences existing in similarly industrialized countries, especially where the political systems are different. To reconcile the thesis of convergence with such contrary evidence, some authors claim that convergence is confined to the core of an industrial system, leaving wide possibilities of divergence. 'This core would inlude the factory system of production, a stratification system based on a complex and extensive division of labor and hierarchy of skills, an extensive commercialization of goods and services and their transfer through the market, and an educational system capable of filling the various niches in the occupational and stratificational system' (Feldman and Moore 1962: 146).

The critique of the idea of modernization

The idea of modernization came under strong criticism at the end of the 1960s and in the 1970s. It was attacked both on empirical grounds, as contrary to historical evidence, and on theoretical grounds, as based on untenable assumptions. On the empirical side it was claimed that modernizing efforts most often did not produce the results they had promised. In underdeveloped countries poverty was persistent or even increasing, autocratic and dictatorial regimes were widespread, wars and disturbances were common, the sacralization of life and new forms of religious fundamentalism proliferated, ideological fervour continued, new varieties of nationalism, factionalism and regionalism appeared.

There were also numerous pathological side-effects of modernization. Destroying traditional institutions and life-ways often produced social disorganization, chaos and anomie. Deviance and delinquency were on the rise. Disharmony of economic sectors and desynchronization of changes in various subsystems of society resulted in inefficiency and waste. As an informed observer testified: 'in these societies, all these developments did not give rise to the development, especially in the political field, of viable modern institutional systems capable of absorbing continuously changing, diversified problems and demands' (Eisenstadt 1966a: 435).

On the *theoretical* side, the underlying evolutionist assumptions were found unacceptable. The possibility of multilinear developments, following various paths of modernization rather than one single track, was indicated: 'the different starting points of the processes of modernization of these societies have greatly influenced the specific contours of their development and the problems encountered in the course of it' (Eisenstadt 1966b: 2).

The strict opposition of tradition and modernity was found misleading, and the benefits of traditionalism in some areas reaffirmed. 'Not only do modern societies incorporate many traditional elements, but traditional societies often have many universalistic, achievement-oriented, bureaucratic characteristics which are normally thought of as modern' (Huntington 1976: 38). 'One can go further and argue not only that coexistence is possible but that modernization itself may strengthen tradition' (Huntington 1976: 36). 'Traditional symbols and leadership forms can be vital parts of the value bases supporting modernizing frameworks' (Gusfield 1966: 352).

The importance of an external, global context and exogenous causation was emphasized in place of an exclusive endogenous focus. 'Any theoretical framework which fails to incorporate such significant variables as the impact of war, conquest, colonial domination, international political or military relationships, or of international trade and the cross-national flow of capital cannot hope to explain either the origins of these societies or the nature of their struggles for political and economic autonomy' (Tipps 1976: 74).

The regular sequence of stages in modernization was put into doubt: 'The latecomers, it could be argued, can modernize rapidly through revolutionary means and by borrowing the experience and technology of the early modernizers. The entire process can thus be telescoped, and the assumption that there is a well-defined progression of phases – preconditions, take off, drive to maturity, and the like – through which all societies must move is likely to be invalid' (Huntington 1976: 38).

Finally, the ethnocentric, western-oriented conception of the goals of modernization was questioned, as 'many of the new modern and modernizing societies and states did not develop in the direction of European nation-states' (Eisenstadt 1983: 236). This was enough to destroy the appeal of modernization theory, at least for some time.

Similarly, the historical predictions implied by the convergence theory simply turned out to be untrue. 'The fact that great institutional variability exists among different modern and modernizing societies – not only among the transitional but also among the more developed and even the highly industrialized societies – became more and more apparent' (Eisenstadt 1992a: 422). Instead of convergence, growing divergence appeared as a dominant feature of modern societies, and modernization could no longer be seen as the common, ultimate final point of the evolution of all societies.

Neo-modernization and neo-convergence theory

As early as the 1980s we observe some revival of modernization theory (Tiryakian 1985a), and after 1989 it clearly finds a new focus in the effort of post-communist societies to 'enter', or 're-enter' Europe (i.e. the modern, western world). It is realized that modernization theory may be useful for understanding these new historical processes, and therefore 'to dismiss it and the notion of modernity altogether may be as grievous a mistake as having made modernization the core of attention for social change in the 1960s' (Tiryakian 1985a: 132). Calls are heard for 'the reappraisal of the studies of modernization, a reappraisal entailing also a very far-reaching reformulation of the whole vision of modernity and development' (Eisenstadt 1983: 239). In response to this challenge the projects of 'neo-modernization theory' (Tiryakian 1991) or 'post-modernization theory' (Alexander 1992) are put forward. The revived and revised modernization theory takes into account the experience of the post-communist world, and in effect modifies its central assumptions.

The crucial difference between modernizing processes in the Third World and in the post-communist Second World is due to the legacy of 'real socialism'. Whereas in the post-colonial countries, the starting-point was usually the traditional, pre-modern society, preserved in more or less unchanged shape, in the Soviet Union and eastern Europe, both the ruling ideology and the highly politicized, centralized and planned economic system were for many decades involved in the promotion of modernization 'from above'. As a result, what has been achieved is far from genuine modernity. It may be called 'fake modernity'. What I mean by 'fake modernity' is the incoherent, disharmonious, internally contradictory combination of three components: (1) imposed modernity in some domains of social life, coupled with (2) the vestiges of traditional, pre-modern society in many others, and all that dressed up with (3) the symbolic ornamentations pretending to imitate western modernity.

Let us draw a simplified balance sheet of the legacy of so-called 'real socialism' in this area. On the side of modernity, there was: imposed industralization, with an obsessive emphasis on heavy industry; a shift from the agricultural to the industrial sector; extensive proletarianization; chaotic urbanization; highly efficient control of the population by a bureaucratic apparatus of administration, police and army; a strong autocratic state. There also appeared, sometimes in extreme degrees, all the unintended side-effects of modernity, including environmental destruction, pollution, depletion of resources, anomie and apathy in the mass society. What has been missing, and is still absent today is: private ownership; rational, accountable, calculable organization of production; the functioning market; the rule of law; abundance of consumer goods and options; dependable 'abstract systems' like telecommunication, airline systems, road networks, banking infrastructure (Giddens 1990); robust entrepreneurial elites and middle classes; a rooted work ethic and individualism; functioning pluralistic democracy. Somehow these societies seem perversely to have attained all the dreary sides of modernity and have shunned all the bright sides. They have paid the costs without reaping the profits. This strange and schizoid legacy is still around, and is there to stay, probably for a generation or more.

Eastern Europe has not only inherited a fake modernity, in some respects it has also returned to pre-modernity, lingering all those decades under the façade of a unified socialist bloc. Internal autocratic regimes, and external imperial domination have suppressed all primordial divisions, producing fake homogeneity and consensus (the atrophy of 'civil society'). Ethnic, regional, religious diversity disappeared for the time being. With the fall of the external empire and ongoing internal liberalization, well-suppressed but never out-grown pre-modern loyalties, solidarities and attachments were bound to re-appear. The bloc as a whole and each country internally emerged more divided and internally split than anybody could have predicted, as if frozen in the pre-modern era, in all the old national, ethnic, regional conflicts and resentments. The unifying effects of capitalism, the market and democracy did not operate, and once the artificial blockades were lifted, the pre-modern, ugly face of Soviet and eastern European societies appeared in full clarity.

Finally there is this strange area of symbolic embellishments, which baffled and sometimes also misled western observers: the constitutions, the parlia-ments, the elections, referendums, the local self-government etc. Insiders know perfectly well to what extent it was all sham and what a purely instrumental role it played. 'Both the constitutions and the elections attested to the fact that these totalitarian regimes, in their mode of legitimation, in their relations between the center and the periphery, but also in their overall cultural and political program, were modern regimes' (Eisenstadt 1992b: 32). Yet even in this distorted form of ideological façade, the ideas of constitutionalism, de-mocracy, representation etc. entered social consciousness and could turn into battle cries of the opposition in the new historical situation. 'This specific political socialization could easily, under appropriate conditions, intensify their awareness of the contradictions between the promises of the regimes and their performance' (Eisenstadt 1992b: 34).

All this requires serious rethinking of the concept of modernity and the theories of modernization. Such an effort is already under way, and its di-rections can be grasped by means of ten points.

1   The agency, the driving force of modernization, is no longer seen as restricted to governments or political elites acting 'from above'. Rather, the mass mobilization 'from below' for the sake of modernization, most often contesting inert or conservative governments, becomes the focus of attention. Spontaneous social movements and emerging charismatic leaders are consid-ered as the main modernizing agencies.

2   Modernization is no longer seen as a solution devised and accepted by enlightened elites and imposed upon resistant, traditionally oriented populations, as was most often the case in the Third World countries. Rather it reflects commonly held, spontaneous aspirations of the population, in-flamed by the demonstration effect of western affluence, liberty and modern life styles (*'Dynasty* syndrome') as perceived through the widely available mass media or personal contacts.

3   Instead of the emphasis on endogenous, immanent forces of modernization, the role of exogenous factors is recognized, including the world geo-
political balance, the availability of external economic and financial support,
the openness of the international markets, and, last but not least, the availability of convincing ideological resources: political or social doctrines or
theories encouraging modernizing efforts by affirming the values of modernity (e.g. individualism, discipline, work ethic, self-reliance, responsibility,
reason, science, progress, freedom).

4   In place of the single, unique model of modernity to be emulated by
backward societies (in classical theory, most often the model of the US), the
idea of 'moving epicentres of modernity' is introduced, and its corollary, the
notion of alternative 'reference societies' (Tiryakian 1985a). It is claimed that
the American model may not necessarily be relevant for post-communist
societies, and that in general the western pattern of modernization is not necessarily superior, exportable and applicable everywhere. The suggestions
for serious consideration of Japan or 'Asian Tigers' (NICs) as more relevant
examples appear more often.

5   In place of a uniform process of modernization, a more diversified
image is proposed. It is indicated that in various areas of social life modernization has a different tempo, rhythm and sequences, and in effect a desynchronization of modernizing efforts is apt to recur. Ralf Dahrendorf warns
against the 'dilemma of three clocks' facing post-communist societies, and
argues that while in the area of legal constitutional reform, six months may
be enough, in the economic domain six years may be too little. At the level
of deep-lying life-ways, attitudes, values making up modern 'civil society', its
renewal may take generations (Dahrendorf 1990).

6   A less optimistic picture of modernization is drawn, avoiding the naive
voluntarism of some early theories. The experience of post-communist societies clearly shows that not all is possible and attainable, and not all depends
on sheer political will. Much more emphasis is put on blockades, barriers,
'friction' (Etzioni 1991; Sztompka 1992), and also the inevitable reversals,
backlashes and breakdowns of modernization.

7   Instead of an almost exclusive concern with economic growth, much
more attention is directed towards human values, attitudes, symbolic meanings, and cultural codes, briefly the 'intangibles and imponderables' (Sztompka
1991a), as prerequisites of successful modernization. The classical notion of
'modern personality' is revived, but given a different role; it is no longer
treated as the desired outcome of modernizing processes, but rather as a
necessary precondition for economic take-off.

8   The anti-traditionalist bias of early theory is corrected by pointing out
that indigenous traditions may hide important pro-modernization themes.
Instead of rejecting tradition, which may be counterproductive by provoking
strong resistance, it is rather proposed to exploit tradition, by discovering
'traditions of modernization', and treating them as the legitimation for current
modernizing efforts. This may be particularly relevant in the case of former

socialist societies, which before the long episode of 'fake modernity', actually freezing them in the pre-modern state, usually had experienced some periods of capitalist growth or democratic evolution (e.g. Czechoslovakia or Poland between the world wars).

9   The internally split character of post-communist societies, with some enclaves of modernity resulting from imposed industrialization and urbanization and extensive areas of pre-modernity (in widespread attitudes, life-ways, political institutions, class composition etc.) opens up a central issue of strategy: what to do with those tangible vestiges of 'real socialism', e.g. huge state-owned, and most often technologically outdated industrial enterprises. The main debate evolves between the proponents of the 'Big Bang' approach (Sachs, Åslund, Balcerowicz), advocating complete deconstruction of the economic, political and cultural remnants of socialism, and starting modernization from scratch, and 'gradualists' who would like to salvage the existing heritage, even at the cost of a slower advance towards modernity. As the arguments of both sides are strong, the resolution of this issue remains open.

10   The last factor which makes the present modernizing efforts of post-communist societies certainly different, and perhaps more difficult than the modernization of Third World countries after the Second World War, is the ideological climate prevailing in the 'model societies' of the developed west. At the end of the twentieth century the era of 'triumphant modernity', with its prosperity, optimism and expansionist drive seems to be over. The crisis rather than progress becomes the leitmotif of social consciousness (Holton 1990). Acute awareness of the side-effects and unintended 'boomerang effects' of modernity produces disenchantment, disillusionment and outright rejection. At the theoretical level, 'post-modernism' becomes the fashion of the day. It seems as if western societies were ready to jump off the train of modernity, bored with the journey, just at the moment when the post-communist east frantically is trying to get on board. In this situation, it is harder to find unambiguous ideological support for modernizing efforts, running under the aegis of liberal democracy and market economy – the only conceivable direction, if we discount the fascist alternative, and some misty and mysterious 'Third Way'. The generalized account of this peculiar predicament has to find its place within a revised modernization theory.

The neo-modernization theory is thus purged of all evolutionist or developmentalist overtones; it does not assume any necessary, unique goal nor an irreversible course of historical change. Instead, modernization is seen as a historically contingent process of constructing, spreading and legitimating the institutions and values of modernity: democracy, market, education, rational administration, self-discipline, work ethos etc. Becoming modern (or escaping 'fake modernity') is still a vital challenge for post-communist societies. Hence revised modernization theory defends its continuing viability.

If we now turn to the theory of convergence, the analytic job will be much easier, because most of the discussion above directly applies. But there are peculiarities, too, which require brief comment. As we remember, the theory of convergence dealt expressly with the divide between the First and the Second World (developed industrial societies, and industrializing socialist countries), and it claimed that the underlying, technological 'logic of industrialism', will inevitably produce a mutual affinity of their economic, political and cultural spheres. Because of this focus, recent historical events are even more immediately relevant than in the case of the theory of modernization.

There are at least three lessons to be drawn from the fall of communism which put in doubt some tenets of convergence theory. First, the idea of mutuality or reciprocity simply turned out not to be true. Instead of mutual rapprochement between the two systems, each drawing something from its counterpart, resulting in some emerging 'third form' of a new socio-political regime, we are witnessing in fact the totally one-directional flow, with western patterns invariably dominating and finally totally victorious. Second, convergence theory implied a peaceful, gradual intermeshing of components from both systems rather than the sudden disintegration and ultimate breakdown of the communist world. It envisaged a slow evolution of 'real socialism' embracing western patterns, rather than rapid and radical revolution. Third, it turned out that the most powerful factor leading to the revolution was not the permeating of socialist societies with high technology. It was still far from that. Instead, the psychological factor of aspirations, awakened by 'demonstration effects' of western patterns, seemed to be crucial. Among those aspirations were also, though not pre-eminently modern, developed technologies. Thus it was not the push of western technologies, as theory predicted, but the pull of aspirations towards such technologies in the deepening conditions of technological backwardness. It is not that socialist countries became technologically modernized, but rather that at some point their underdeveloped technologies became unbearable for the people in the conditions of globalized competition and windows opened on the world (through the flow of information, people, images and ideas).

The example of modernization theory and convergence theory demonstrates how historical events may provide powerful stimuli for rethinking, reworking and fundamentally revising those sociological theories of change which have direct empirical (historical) relevance. Both the modernization theory and convergence theory acquire new vitality in the new historical circumstances, serving as useful explanatory or interpretative devices for the phenomena of post-communist transition.

10

Theories of historical cycles

The logic of cyclical theories

The theory of cycles takes a different view of historical process from those of the theories originating in evolutionism. It represents the alternative image of history. Instead of persistent direction, it sees recurrence; instead of constant novelty, it sees repetition; instead of an unlimited unfolding of potentialities, it sees the periodical exhaustion of potentialities and temporary return to the beginning of the process. Social and historical change does not move along a line, but rather in a circle.

Like all theories of history, this one also is rooted in analogies or metaphors deriving from common sense. It abandons the evolutionist metaphor of organic growth, and instead turns to the experience widely encountered in everyday life of repetitions, recurrences or undulations. (1) There are obvious astronomical cycles and their repercussions: day and night (work and sleep), phases of the moon (tides), seasons of the year (regular periods of vegetation, rhythm of agricultural labour, patterns of holidays in modern society). (2) There are biological cycles, with important consequences for social life: birth, childhood, adolescence, maturity, old age, death (the rise and fall of active participation in social life marked by such thresholds as going to school, getting a first job, establishing a family, bringing up children, retiring). (3) There are clearly perceived political, economic and social cycles on the macro-scale: governments come and go, recessions follow booms, periods of prosperity alternate with times of crisis, international tensions are followed by periods of thaw or *détente*, social turmoil turns into long stretches of stability. (4) There are also obvious cycles on the micro-scale of everyday life: the daily rhythm of family events, the weekly rhythm of working days and weekends, the yearly rhythm of holidays and festivities. In the poetic idiom of Pitirim Sorokin: 'The great symphony of social life is "scored" for a countless number of separate processes, each proceeding in a wavelike manner and recurring in space, in time, in both space and time, periodically or nonperiodically, after short or long intervals' (1937, vol. 1: 170).

The pervasiveness of such cyclical phenomena has suggested the extension of the underlying image to the level of history. Its meaning, shape, form or logic came to be interpreted in terms of cycles. The idea that there is such

an overall shape or logic of historical process under the surface of innumerable historical events was clearly retained. But it was interpreted in strikingly
different ways.

Before turning our attention to actual examples of cyclical theories, let us
explicate the concept of a cycle in a more precise and formal manner. Whereas,
in the directional process, each consecutive phase is different from any phase
preceding it in time, in the cyclical process the state of the changing system
at some later time will be the same as (or fundamentally similar to) the state
of the system at some earlier time. This general characterization allows for a
large variety of cyclical processes, depending on the more concrete features:
the scope of similarity between repeated states of the system, the span of time
separating repeated occurrences, the number of repetitions in the whole cycle.

Pitirim Sorokin suggests distinguishing complete cycles from relative cycles:

> In the completely cyclical process the last phase of a given recurrence returns
> to its first phase, and the cycle begins again, traversing the same route through
> which it has passed before. In the relatively cyclical process, on the other hand,
> the direction of the recurring process does not coincide completely with that of
> the series of previous recurrences. There is some deviation from cycle to cycle.
> (*1937, vol. 1: 184–5*)

To put it in other words, the process may run in circles when the consecutive
states of the system, after some period of time, recur exactly as before (for
example, the sunset). Or the process may follow a spiral, when the consecutive states are fundamentally similar but not identical (morning congestion on
the roads, growing from year to year). An ascending spiral will signify repetition at a quantitatively higher level (cyclical progress), a descending one
will signify repetition at a quantitatively lower level (cyclical regress).

The duration of a cycle may be long or short. This of course cannot be
measured in an absolute way, but only relatively to the kind of processes
considered. In biology, the life-cycle of a butterfly will be short compared to
that of a whale. In sociology, the daily cycle of family life will be short, and
the cycle of an occupational career long. In economics, the production cycle
of a car will be short, and of a ship long, or the investment and profit cycle
in retail trade will be short, and in heavy industry much longer. In politics,
the cycle of parliamentary sessions (the parliamentary calendar) will be short,
the election cycle long.

It is also important whether the cycle follows a rhythmic or non-rhythmic
pattern. In the first case, there is an equal interval between the phases of the
cycle; In the second, the interval is unequal. If it is entirely random, we have
a random cycle. But there may be some regularity underlying a non-rhythmic
pattern. If the intervals become consistently shorter, we have an accelerated
(quickening) cycle (for example, scientific discoveries or technological innovations in the modern era). If the intervals become consistently longer we
encounter a decelerated cycle (slowing down).

Finally cycles may differ in the number of phases they go through. If there are only two phases distinguished in the cycle, it is a dichotomous cycle (for example, day and night, work and rest, war and peace, boom and recession). If there are three phases, we have a triadic cycle (for example, emergence–maturity–decline, original sin–redemption–salvation). If more phases are distinguished, we may speak of a multiple cycle (for example, childhood–youth–maturity–old age–death in an individual life-course, mobilization–recruitment–leadership formation-bureaucratization–demobilization–dispersion, in the 'career' of a social movement).

Forerunners of the cyclical image

It is quite likely that the cyclical image of processes imposed itself on common thinking even earlier than the more complex image of growth. Certainly it must have been present in human perception of the world long before it entered more systematic theories. In philosophical thought, as so many other ideas, it originated in ancient Greece. Aristotle says: 'That which has been is that which shall be; and that which has been done is that which shall be done: and there is no new thing under the sun' (quoted in Sorokin 1937, vol. 1: 170). In the writings of Herodotus (fifth century BC) we find the first full exposition of the cycle of political regimes: monarchy–tyranny–oligarchy–democracy–mob rule. In the work of Polybius (200–118 BC) there is a similar claim, namely that all political units (polities) pass through the inexorable cycle of growth, zenith and decay.

Comparable ideas occurred in the Middle Ages to that perceptive observer of social life Ibn Khaldun (1332–1406). He too is credited with the cliché, 'there is nothing new under the sun'. In history we encounter constant repetitions. More specifically, he sees a regular life-cycle of civilizations, quite like the cycle of living organisms: growth–maturity–senility. There is a similar cycle of political regimes, which have an approximate span of 100 years, or three generations. There is a cycle of changing social bonds or solidarities typical for everyday life in human groups. It proceeds through three stages: (1) There are strongly developed feelings of solidarity brought about by the hard conditions of nomadic life in the desert. (2) With the appearance of sedentary, localized cultures and growing abundance, group ties deteriorate and solidarity is weakened. (3) This leads to the complete collapse of social bonds and dispersion of groups, followed again by their crystallization on the basis of new, emerging social ties.

In the epoch of the Enlightenment, the cyclical image is finally extended to the entire span of human history by Giambattista Vico. He is perhaps the first to suggest (in his famous *New Science*, 1725) that social life and history can be studied in a scientific manner and their regularities discovered. This is because society and history are ultimately human products, results of human actions, and must therefore be accessible to human cognition, in principle knowable. In his own search for such historical regularities, he comes to the image of an ascending spiral. The typical process occurring both at the overall, general level of mankind and at the concrete level of particular civilizations, cultures or societies, takes the form of recurrences, but not exact repetitions (*corsi* and *ricorsi*). The cycles are replicated at ever higher levels, with some modification. At each turn of the cycle, new phenomena emerge.

More concretely, the characteristic historical cycle follows three stages: (1) anarchy and savagery; (2) order and civilization, accompanied by the rule of reason and peaceful industry; (3) the decay of civilization, with new barbarism setting in. These stages are related to various aspects of social life and form of government (theocracy, aristocracy, republic or monarchy), type of law, characteristic language (hieroglyphics, symbolics, vernacular). There is also some correlation with dominant characterological types: crude, severe, benign, delicate, dissolute. Up to his own time, Vico believes, there had been two cycles: one in antiquity, closed by the fall of Rome; and one started in the revived barbarism of the Middle Ages, and reaching its final phase in his own epoch. He paints a dismal picture of corrupted urban masses, egotistic beasts divided into factions and fighting civil wars. 'Cities are apt to be turned into forests and the forests into dens and lairs of men' (quoted in Mazlish 1966: 41). But his cyclical image suggests some optimism; eventually a new cycle will be started and mankind will be reborn.

Vico seems to suggest that the underlying causal mechanism of this recurrent cycle is psychological and has to do with the dominant motivations and attitudes encoded in human nature. 'Men first feel necessity, then look for utility, next attend to comfort, still later amuse themselves with pleasure, thence grow dissolute in luxury, and finally go mad and waste their substance' (Vico 1961: 37). As Bruce Mazlish comments: 'Historical to his core, Vico welcomed the notion of constant change and flux around a fixed pole of man's nature' (1966: 41).

Historiosophies of the rise and fall of civilizations

As we approach the modern epoch, a number of philosophers take the cyclical metaphor and apply it to the entire span of human history. As a result of regrouping and reinterpreting historical materials, the grand historiosophical theories emerge. We shall pick out three of them: by the Russian Nikolai Danilevsky, the German Oswald Spengler and the Englishman Arnold Toynbee.

Nikolai Danilevsky (1822–85) won wide fame only posthumously through French and German translations of his book *Russia and Europe* (1890 and 1920 respectively). He conceives of human history as articulated in distinct, comprehensive units, 'historico-cultural types' or civilizations. Western or, in other words, Germano-Romanic civilization is only one of many that have flourished in history. The mistake of the historians is to consider this civilization as the highest and to construct a linear chronology of epochs (ancient–medieval–modern) as approaching the culmination in the modern west. In reality there is no common chronology for various civilizations: there is no single event which could reasonably divide the destiny of all of mankind into periods applicable to all humanity, for there never has been and hardly ever will be any event that will synchronously mean the same and be of the same importance to all of humanity' (quoted in Sorokin 1966: 180). Civilizations have their own internal logic of development, each passes its unique life-sequence, and none is the best or perfect. 'Each civilization emerges, develops its own morphological form, its own values, thus enriching the total treasury of human cultural achievement, and then passes away without being continued in its specific and essential form by any other civilization' (quoted in Sorokin 1966: 181).

History is created by people, but their historical role differs. Accordingly there are three types of historical agents: (1) The positive agents of history, i.e. those societies (tribes, peoples) which created great civilizations (separate historico-cultural types): Egyptian, Assyro-Babylonian, Chinese, Hindu, Persian, Hebrew, Greek, Roman, Arabian and Germano-Romanic (European). (2) There are the negative agents of history, i.e. those tribes or peoples who played a destructive role in bringing the final collapse of senile, decaying civilizations (e.g. the Huns, the Mongols, the Turks). (3) On the other hand, there are the peoples and tribes devoid of creative *élan*. These represent only the 'ethnograpic material' used by creative societies for the building of their own civilizations. Sometimes, after the disintegration of the great civilizations, their composite tribes or peoples turn back to the level of 'ethnographic material', passive, dispersed populations.

Civilizations are creative in selective fields, they have specific individual foci or leading themes. For Greek civlization it was beauty, for Semitic civilization religion, for Roman civilization law and administration, for Chinese the practical and the useful, for Indian imagination, fantasy, and mysticism, for Germano-Romanic science and technology.

There is a typical cycle of development observable in the fate or life-course of each of the great civilizations. (1) There is the period of emergence and crystallization, sometimes quite prolonged. This ends when the civilization appears and takes distinct shape and form, establishing its cultural and political independence and common language. (2) Then the blossoming phase comes, when the civilization develops its creative potential to the full along some specialized themes. This period is usually relatively brief (Danilevsky estimates it as 400–600 years) and ends when the fund of the civilization's creative forces is exhausted. (3) Lack of creativeness, petrification and eventual dissolution of the civilization signify the final phase of the cycle. Danilevsky believed that European (Germano-Romanic) civilization had entered the phase of degeneration, which is manifested by several symptoms: growing cynicism, secularization, weakening innovativeness, insatiable lust for power and world domination. On the other hand, the new Russian-Slavic civilization was in the ascendant, and would blossom in the future. Such is the final, slightly ethno-centric message of Danilevsky's historiosophy.

His theory anicipated another, independently attained historiosophical syn-thesis, that of Oswald Spengler (1880–1936). The most influential of Spengler's works, *The Decline of the West*, came out in 1918. There is no linear progress in history, he claims, but rather a set of life-stories of separate, unique, self-contained organic wholes, called 'high cultures', which 'bloom on the soil of an exactly definable landscape, to which plantlike it remains bound' and die when they have 'actualized the full sum of possibilities in the shape of peoples, languages, dogmas, arts, states, sciences' (Spengler 1939: 106). History is the 'collective biography' of such cultures.

Each individual culture follows a life-cycle of childhood, youth, manhood and old age; it emerges, grows and, after fulfilling its destiny, dies. The de-clining phase of culture is labelled 'civilization'. In this phase of petrification and agony, culture exhibits certain characteristic traits: a cosmopolitan instead of local perspective, loose urban relationships replacing blood ties, a scientific and abstract approach in place of natural religious sensibility, mass instead of folk values, money instead of real values, sex instead of motherhood, the politics of brute force supplanting consensus. In such a state of decline or agony a civilization may last long, but eventually it is doomed to disperse and disappear.

Spengler singles out eight 'high cultures', and analyses their fates. They are: Egyptian, Babylonian, Indian, Chinese, Classical (Graeco-Roman), Arabian, Mexican, and western (originating about AD 1000). Each of the great cultures has its dominant theme, or 'prime symbol', which has repercussions in all cultural components, gives particular flavour to the ways of thinking and acting of its members, and determines the character of science and philosophy, art and knowledge, typical mentality, customs and life-patterns. Consequently there is no universal, common knowledge, science or philosophy in various cultures, but rather multiple, particular thought-systems relative to a given culture. For example, the 'prime symbol' of Graeco-Roman culture is the cult of the sensuous, individual body, the Apollonian theme. In Chinese culture, it is 'tao', an indefinable, wandering, multilinear 'way' or direction of life (Sorokin 1966: 191). For western culture, the 'prime symbol' is 'limitless space', and the conception of time is that of a destiny which stretches out into infinity, the Faustian theme. As Bruce Mazlish comments: 'Obviously, what Spengler is seeking is the "spirit" of a culture or a period . . . Naturally, each spirit will be sui generis for each culture, and will pervade all aspects of the culture. Because it pervades and animates all aspects, every fact and happen-ing in the culture serves . . . as a symbol of that culture and spirit' (1966: 328). This was cultural relativism *par excellence*: 'Truths are truths only in relation to a particular mankind' (quoted in Mazlish 1966: 332).

The life-course of 'high cultures' cannot be explained causally. Rather it is a 'destiny cycle'. It is a manifestation of inward necessity or destiny, and can be grasped only by intuition. 'We observe that swift and deep changes assert themselves in the history of great Cultures, without assignable causes, influences or purposes of any kind' (quoted in Sorokin 1966: 192). Similarly, the birth of cultures has no causes. Cultures do not emerge because of particular propensities of certain populations or societies. Rather, the process occurs the other way round, appearing by the verdict of destiny, they select some societies as their carriers or agents.

Spengler's diagnosis and predictions concerning the fate of western culture, which had already entered its degenerating phase of civilization, are very gloomy. At the core of contemporary society he finds the 'megalopolis', the world city surrounded by provinces. 'Within this world-city there is a new sort of nomad, a parasitical city dweller, rootless, traditionless, without a past. The city population is a mass, not a people or race' (Mazlish 1966: 342). No wonder that in the near future 'it will lie in fragments, forgotten, our railways and steamships as dead as the Roman roads and Chinese wall, our giant cities and scyscrapers in ruins like old Memphis and Babylon. The history of the megalopolitan machine technics is fast drawing to its inevitable close. It will be eaten up from within, like the grand form of any and every Culture' (quoted in Sorokin 1966: 194).

The most extensive and historically rooted theory of civilizations and their life-cycles is presented by Arnold Toynbee (1889–1975). In the twelve volumes of his *Study of History*, published over a period of twenty-seven years (1934–61) by the Oxford University Press, he attempts to generalize from a vast range of material covering the whole of recorded history.

He claims that the proper unit of historical study is not mankind as a whole, nor single nation-states, but rather intermediate units which have greater spatial and temporal extension than individual societies but are smaller than humanity, namely civilizations, twenty-one of which can be singled out. The list is similar, although more extensive, than those of Danilevsky or Spengler. Nevertheless the idea of a specific, dominant potentiality in each civilization reappears. For example: it is aesthetics in the Hellenic civilization, religion in the Hindu civilization, science and mechanical technology in western civilization.

Civilizations arise through double, combined factors: the presence of a creative minority and environmental conditions, neither too unfavourable nor too favourable. The mechanism of the birth as well as the continued dynamics of civilizations is embodied in the idea of the challenges and the response. The environment (initially natural, but later also social) is incessantly challenging society, and society, through its creative minority, devises means to deal with it. Once a challenge is responded to, a new challenge follows, and a new response ensues. In the growth phase of a civilization, the responses are successful, people make unprecedented efforts to meet unprecedented challenges, and in this way shatter 'the cake of custom', but in the phase of breakdown, disintegration and dissolution they cease to be creative. Civilizations perish from the inside, by a growing inability to meet new arising challenges. 'The nature of the breakdown of civilizations can be summed up in three points: a failure of creative power in the minority, an answering withdrawal of mimesis on the part of the majority [who refuse blindly to follow and imitate the successful elite], and a consequent loss of social unity in the society as a whole' (quoted in Sorokin 1966: 200). An additional factor is the revolt of the 'external proletariat', i.e. the barbarians who no longer accept being subjugated or incorporated once the civilization starts to crumble. The destiny of most civilizations is always final dissolution, even though they may linger in the petrified state of decline for long periods of time. Among great civilizations, no less than sixteen are now 'dead and buried'.

At the close of his synthesis, without abandoning the idea of cycles within each of the civilizations, Toynbee claims that there is a common underlying pattern or unique logic manifesting itself in the longest run and embracing all of them together. This is the progress of spirituality and religion. Civilizations are the 'handmaids' of religion. 'It is the historical function of civilizations to serve, by their downfalls, as stepping-stones to a progressive process of the revelation of always deeper religious insight, and the gift of ever more grace to act on this insight' (Toynbee 1948: 236)

Sociological theories of cyclical change

The grand cyclical schemes have mostly been proposed by philosophers, historians or philosophers of history rather than sociologists. But in sociology proper, we also find important examples of cyclical thinking. Two of them deserve particular attention.

Vilfredo Pareto: the circulation of elites

The classical account of social cycles operating on a smaller scale within separate societies rather than huge civilizations is given by Vilfredo Pareto (1848–1923) in his monumental *Trattato di sociologia generale* (1916).

Pareto draws an image of society as a social system, which itself, as well as its constitutive segments (politics, economy, ideology), goes through repeated cycles of equilibrium, destabilization, disequilibrium and new equilibrium. There is an overall social cycle, and there are specific segmental cycles: political-miltary, economic-industrial and ideological-religious, all of them following a similar pattern. To understand how the cycles operate, it is necessary to take a glimpse at Pareto's vision of the anatomy of the social system.

It is taken to consist of three types of interrelated abstract components (variables): residues, i.e. immanent human tendencies or propensities; interests, i.e. objective conditions serving human needs; and derivations, i.e. justifications and rationalizations that people devise to legitimate their residues and interests.

Residues are crucial; they provide the primary, determiming factor of social life. Among a variety of residues that people exhibit, two alternative types are of crucial importance, representing two alternative strategies that people apply to reach their goals: cunning or force. The residues of 'combination' ('class I') comprise such personality traits as: innovativeness, entrepreneurial spirit, readiness for risk, activism, expansiveness, craving for novelty and originality. The opposite residues of 'persistence' ('class II') comprise: prudence, cautiousness, traditionalism, valuing safety, opting for stability and continuity, emphasizing loyalty, legalism and patriotism.

Societies manifest the principle of heterogeneity: their populations consist of unequal members. There are always some elites, made of those who excel in particular fields of activity: political (governing) elites, economic elites, ideological (intellectual) elites. The character of an elite depends on the distribution of residues among their members, and in particular on the proportion of 'class I' and 'class II' residues. An elite thinks and acts differently when it is dominated by members with innovative residues of 'combination' from when it is pervaded by conservative residues of 'persistence'.

Social and historical change is conceived as a cyclical replacement of elites: their ascendancy, decay and replacement. As Pareto puts it: 'History is the graveyard of aristocracies' (i.e. elites of all sorts). The underlying mechanism of this process is based on alternating waves of residues gaining and losing dominance within the elites. To be more concrete, let us trace three typical cycles of such changes.

In the political-military cycle, the main actors are strong rulers (the 'lions') and cunning administrators (the 'foxes'). Let us take the rule of the lions as the starting-point of the cycle. Their rule is rooted in conquest, war, territorial expansion, domination over other societies. The military virtues, loyalty, attachment to community and tradition, count most. The governing elite is pervaded by the residues of persistence. Sooner or later, however, such predispositions are not sufficient. In periods of peace, different talents are needed for management, administration, organization, calculation. People representing residues of 'combination' (the foxes) are selected and co-opted, slowly infiltrating the elite and erasing the domination of the lions. They are finally able to outwit the lions and take power. But here the second phase of the cycle begins. The foxes neglect 'foreign policy', endanger the military might of the society, abandon traditional values. This provokes a conservative backlash, when the lions mobilize and overthrow the foxes by force, their most efficient weapon. Eventually, the cycle begins anew. 'Generally, an elite relying on courage, force, violence, is followed by a bourgeois, plutocratic elite, depending on ruse, intrigue, and ideology, and vice versa' (Maier 1964: 51).

In the economic domain we observe a similar story. The economic-industrial cycle involves different actors: the rentiers and speculators. Let us assume that the former dominate the economic elite. They display the residues of persistence, oriented towards secure ownership, minimalization of risk, saving rather than investing profits, stable income. The overall effect of their policies is stagnation or even recession. Social discontent and grievances engender pressure for improvement and reform. Speculators, innovators, entrepreneurs are co-opted to the economic elite, slowly infiltrate it and undermine the domination of the rentiers. Eventually the rentiers lose importance and are deposed from the elite. In the second phase of the cycle, the accelerated change, uncertainty about the future, chaos and the anomie inevitably accompanying reforms provoke a conservative backlash led by the rentiers, whose social significance rises, and whose dominance is finally restored.

In the ideological-religious cycle priests guarding the faith and the critical intellectuals defending reason are the main actors. Let us assume that social consciousness is dominated by faith, dogmatism and traditionalism. Among the ideological elite we shall note the predominant residues of 'persistence'. Sooner or later, however, searching and sceptical human nature asserts itself: heresies appear, new concepts, ideas, images are put forward and gain currency. The ideological monolith is weakened, alternative thinking appears and slowly undermines the rule of faith. Reason and its representatives, critical intellectuals endowed with residues of combination, get to the fore. The epoch of science, technology, instrumental thinking and calculation of effectiveness closes the first phase of the cycle. But then the craving for meaning, ultimate principles and final truth reasserts itself and cannot be satisfied by science and technology. The revival of mythical and magical thinking opens new opportunities for the priests, strong with their residues of persistence. Critical intellectuals are pushed to the margin of society. Fundamentalism and dogmatism return.

Pitirim Sorokin: the rhythms of cultural change

Another sociological theory of cycles is of more modern origins. The focus of the monumental cyclical theory of Pitirim Sorokin, put forward in four volumes titled *Social and Cultural Dynamics* (1937), is culture. He defines culture as 'the sum total of everything which is created or modified by the conscious or unconscious activity of two or more individuals interacting with one another or conditioning one another's behavior' (vol. 1: 3). The tremendous variety of cultural items falling into this category do not constitute a simple 'congery' (loose conglomeration) but rather an integrated system. They represent an 'internal or logico-meaningful unity', the highest form of integration in which 'each part, when set in its designated position, is no longer noticeable as a part, but all the parts together form, as it were, a seamless garment' (vol. 1: 19). Underlying such a unity there is one common 'central principle (the "reason") which permeates all the components, gives sense and significance to each of them, and in this way makes cosmos of a chaos of unintegrated fragments' (p. 32). The central principle of culture is to be sought in the realm of meaning and may be referred to as 'culture mentality'.

On the basis of his extremely thorough analysis of various aspects of human culture–art, knowledge, ethics, law, warfare–over the centuries, Sorokin proposes a distinction of two opposite, mutually irreconcilable types of culture.

Each has its own mentality; its own system of truth and knowledge; its own philosophy and Weltanschauung; its own type of religion and standards of 'holiness'; its own system of right and wrong; its own forms of art and literature; its own mores, laws, code of conduct; its own predominant forms of social relationships; it own economic and political organization; and, finally its own type of human personality, with a peculiar mentality and conduct (*1937, vol. 1:* 67).

Two opposite cultural types are labelled as Ideational and Sensate. They are understood as ideal types, not to be found in their purity in any epoch, with real cultures taking various mixed, intermediate forms, one of which deserves separate designation as Idealistic.

The Ideational culture is characterized by the following premises: (1) The nature of reality is spiritual, immaterial, hidden behind the superficial material and sensuous appearances (e.g. God, Nirvana, Tao, Brahma). It is eternal and unchanging. (2) The needs and ends are mainly spiritual (salvation of the soul, service to God, performance of sacred duty, moral obligations). (3) The means to satisfy those ends focus on the self-improvement of the mind and body, organs, wishes, convictions, the whole personality, in order to liberate it from sensuous temptations and concerns and detaching it from earthly existence. These basic premises have numerous further implications. (4) They entail the notion of truth as attainable by inner experience (revelation, meditation, ecstasy, divine inspiration) and therefore absolute and eternal. (5) They imply the idea of the good rooted in immaterial, inner, spiritual, supersensory values (eternal life, the City of God, union with Brahma), and therefore ultimate and everlasting.

The Sensate culture makes opposite assumptions: (1) The only reality is material, accessible to the senses. It is taken to be transitory, and constantly modified: 'a Becoming, Process, Change, Flux, Evolution, Progress, Transformation' (Sorokin 1937: vol. 1: 73). (2) The needs and ends are purely carnal or sensual (hunger and thirst, sex, shelter, comfort). (3) The method of satisfying them is the modification and exploitation of the external environment. These fundamental premises entail others. (4) The truth is to be found only in sensuous experience, and is treated as temporary and relative. (5) The good is rooted in sensate, empirical, material values (pleasure, enjoyment, happiness, utility), and therefore moral principles are flexible, relativistic, varying according to circumstances and situations.

The intermediate Idealistic culture represents a balanced mixture of Ideational and Sensate elements: (1) Reality is many-sided, both material and supernatural. (2) Needs are both bodily and spiritual. (3) Their satisfaction requires both the improvement of the self and the transformation of the environment. In brief: 'Recognizing the Ideational values as supreme, it does not declare the Sensate world as mere illusion or of negative value; on the contrary, as far as the sensate is in harmony with the Ideational, it possesses positive value' (Sorokin 1937, vol. 1: 75).

The crucial moment comes when Sorokin applies this analytic typology to

Table 10.1   Sorokin's periodization of history

Greece, eight–sixth century BC	Ideational
Greece, fith century BC	Idealist
Rome, fourth century BC–fourth century AD	Sensate
Europe, fourth–sixth century AD	Idealist
Europe, sixth–twelfth century	Ideational
Europe, twelfth–fourteenth century	Idealist
Europe, fourteenth century to the present	Sensate

the flow of historical process. He conceives the main pattern of historical change in cyclical terms. 'Sociocultural fluctuations, i.e. recurrent processes in social and cultural life and in human history–these are the main concern of the present study' (1937, vol. 1: 153). 'The most general pattern of the socio-cultural change is that of incessantly varying recurrent processes' (vol. 4: 73). The processes often reverse their direction and repeat themselves. 'Bricfly or for an extensivc time, in the same or in several social systems, a process moves in a certain quantitative or qualitative or spatial direction, or in all these directions, reaches its "point of saturation", and then often reverses its movements' (vol. 1: 170). Such fluctuations, punctuatcd by the reversal of direction of significant processes, can be observed at the largest scale of history, which appears as divided into epochs, eras or periods. The most important principle of such periodization is the alternation of the dominant types of culture mentality and cultural systems: thc repeated sequence of Ideational, Idealistic and Sensate cultures.

The author reconstructs historical 'waves' and 'fluctuations' primarily within Graeco-Roman or western culture, covering with his investigations a span of more than 2,500 years. It turns out that the cycles do not signify complete repetition, but rather ever new representations and embodiments of the same underlying principles. It also appears that the cycles do not follow any constant rhythm and are not of equal duration. 'History repeats itself, but its themes recur in variations ever new–with changes not only in content but also in rhythms and tempo' (vol. 2: 201–2). In effect, we get the periodization of western history given in table 10.1.

The causal mechanism underlying the 'super-rhythm of ideational–idealis-tic–sensate phases in the Graeco-Roman and Western systems of culture' (Sorokin 1937, vol. 4: 737) is the exhaustion of possibilities, spending of the creative potentialities of each consecutive system. 'When each of these ex-hausts the creative fund of cognitive, moral, aesthetic, political, and other values, and continues to dominate not through its creative grace but mainly by inertia, fraud, coercion, tricks, and pseudo-values, such a system is bound to decline as sterile, often poisonous, and disserviceable to its mem-bers and humanity at large' (Sorokin 1963: 435). The decay of the system opens the opportunities for an alternative system to arise and display its own potentialities, up to a moment when they also become exhausted, and the whole process repeats itself. The unfolding of the potentialities of each system depends primarily on the actions of its members. It is transformed from the inside, by the force of human activity. Sorokin emphasizes the principle of immanent causation. But external factors may also play some role, presenting challenges and speeding up or retarding, facilitating or inhibiting the immanent development of cultural systems.

Sorokin's diagnosis of the western civilization of his time is extremely critical. He believes that the Sensate phase in which it has been engulfed for several centuries has reached ultimate saturation, which produces a number of negative, pathological phenomena and general cultural decline. There are numerous symptoms of that. We have gone all the way from the beauty of medieval church music to the 'cacophony of jazz', from Gothic cathedrals to modern slums, from the sculptures of Michelangelo to pornographic journals, from the poetry of Byron to spy thrillers. In contemporary art, Sorokin despairs 'prostitutes, criminals, street urchins, the insane, hypocrites, rogues and other subsocial types are its favorite "heroes" ' (in Bierstedt 1981: 337). His immediate forecasts are also pesimistic:

1 There will be moral and aesthetic anarchy.
2 People will become reified, treated like mechanisms.
3 Moral and intellectual consensus will be lost, and chaos of opinions and beliefs will prevail.
4 Social order will be kept by coercion alone, and political rule will be legitimated by force.
5 Freedom will degenerate into empty slogans intended to mislead and enslave the masses.
6 The disruption of the family will proceed.
7 The lowest-denominator mass culture will replace higher artistic expression.
8 The quality of life and general standards of living will fall.
9 Social pathology will grow.
10 Apathy, narrow egotism and escape into the private sphere will dominate in political life.

A dismal picture indeed. Nevertheless, in the long run, the logic of the historical process which Sorokin claims to have discovered provides ground for optimism. A new Ideational phase will inevitably follow. 'The possible decline of our present-day Sensate phase does not necessarily mean the end of the Western culture, any more than did the decay of medieval Ideationalism. There was a shift from a withered Ideational to a resplendent Sensate phase, just as there may again be a turn from our superannuated Sensatism to a new and vigorous Ideationalism' (1937: vol. 1: xiii). A cyclical theory may equally feed utter pessimism and extreme optimism, as, according to the logic of the cycle, sooner or later both the highest and the lowest points of human achievement will inevitably reappear.

11

Historical materialism

Evolutionist and Hegelian roots

In this chapter we turn to another vision of history which, in spite of its close link with evolutionism, must be treated as separate. It goes under the name of historical materialism, and is to be found in the work of Karl Marx, Friedrich Engels and their numerous followers.

Marx's theory was deeply rooted in the nineteenth-century intellectual climate. He shared all the fundamental presuppositions of the epoch. With respect to human history, these implied the image of a 'natural' process, in the sense of being regular and knowable. History, like all other domains of reality, should be a subject of nomological science. The scientific approach will make it possible to discover the meaning, patterns, tendencies in historical events, even on the largest world-historical scale, and this in turn will enable the human species to control its destiny. Marx's ultimate goal was to specify the 'iron laws' of human history in order to shape it in a progressive direction. His lifelong credo was stated early in his career, in the eleventh of the *Theses on Feuerbach* (1845): 'The philosophers have only interpreted the world, in various ways; the point however is to change it' (Marx and Engels 1968: 30).

Some of Marx's basic substantive claims concerning history are a simple replication of the evolutionist creed. Thus (1) Marx was a staunch believer in progress as the overall direction of the historical process. He shared the optimism of the evolutionists, emphasizing the constant betterment of society. (2) He looked at history as pushed forward from within, as the unfolding of immanent, endogenous, intra-societal forces. (3) He saw history as moving through the sequence of distinguishable stages, along a uniform path (even though he was aware of some exceptions and deviations from the standard trajectory, e.g. what he called 'Asiatic formation'). (4) He noticed the growing complication and differentiation of societies as the dominant historical trend, putting special emphasis on the division of labour. Hence, some of the work of the founders of Marxism is indistinguishable from classical evolutionism. Just look at Engels's *The Origins of the Family, Private Property and the State* (1884). This is merely an extended commentary and sequel to the evolutionist theory of Lewis Morgan.

The true specificity of historical materialism as compared to evolutionism begins only when Marx embraces the teachings of Georg Wilhelm Friedrich Hegel (1770–1831), and in particular his concept of 'dialectics'. In the extremely intricate interpretation of history, as put forward by Hegel in his *Phenomenology of Spirit* (1807) and the *Lectures on the Philosophy of History* (1832), one may distinguish two aspects. First is the form, pattern or logic of the historical process. This is what is primarily meant by dialectics. The second is the substance, the indication of forces and agents moving history forward. Here we find Hegel's idealistic notion of the *Geist* (i.e. spirit), as the real substratum and agency of history. Marx approached Hegel selectively: he accepted the formal idea of dialectics but rejected the idealistic content of the theory. Following another German philosopher of his time Ludwig Feuerbach (1804–72), he 'set out to develop his own materialistic philosophy as an inversion of Hegelianism . . . turning Hegelian philosophy upside down' (Avineri 1968: 12).

Hegel's idea of a dialectical course (form, pattern) of history included the following assumptions, all of which will also be found in the work of Marx.

1   History manifests directional, ascending, progressive development. 'Hegel is claiming that if we take a world historical perspective, we will see that there is an inner *logos* to the seemingly chaotic multiplicity of events. This *logos* has a teleological form. There is a narrative or "story" to be discovered in history' (Bernstein 1972: 18). This story is optimistic: '*Geist* guides history to its true and final aim – the complete realization of freedom' (p. 18).

2   The historical development is not linear, straight and consistent. Rather it proceeds by means of breakdowns, reversals, backlashes, achieving its overall progressive shape only in the final count. 'The self-realization and self-fulfillment of *Geist* takes place only by self-destruction . . . History is the scenario of perpetual struggle and self-destruction where all finite social institutions are destroyed and *aufgehoben* [constructively overcome]' (Bernstein 1972: 21). The metaphor of a spiral explains the idea: the process moves back and forth, but when it seemingly returns to earlier conditions, this in fact happens already at the higher level. Each revolution of the cycle produces some measure of progress, even if it occurs at the cost of temporary regress.

3   The historical development is also not gradual, smooth and cumulative. Rather it proceeds by means of specific thresholds, when the basic quality of the process radically (and rapidly) changes. Such thresholds or qualitative breaks mark natural stages or phases of history. The metaphor of steps is quite helpful in understanding this peculiar shape of history.

4   The sequence of historical stages is divided into three parts. This triple pattern is applicable to various historical horizons. At the most comprehensive world-historical scale, the story of *Geist* goes through its prehistory of primitive existence, then the history of its dependence and enslavement accompanied by the struggle for emancipation (all of this starting, for Hegel, with the establishment of states), towards the final phase when the *Geist* achieves full freedom, self-realization and self-knowledge. This triple logic resembles a biblical pattern of Eden, earthly condemnation and redemption,

and ultimate salvation in Heaven. But on the more restricted temporal scale, within each of the epochs marking the stages on this epic cycle, three sub-phases can also be distinguished: ascendancy, fulfilment and decay, preparing the ground for the opening of the next cycle, at the higher level.

5   The historical process is moved by immanent, endogenous forces. '*Geist* is the principle of self-activity itself' (Bernstein 1972: 21). In other words, it comprises the causes of its own transformation.

6   Those immanent forces are found in the principle of negativity: contradictions, strains, tensions, and their resolution. The *Geist* is permeated with constant struggle, it is 'at war with itself'. 'The self-realization and self-fulfilment of *Geist* takes place only by self-destruction . . . But the power of negativity does not result in meaningless destruction: it is the means by which the progressive development toward concrete freedom is realized' (Bernstein 1972: 21).

7   The historical process runs at various levels. Actual historical events, and even concrete human conduct, are guided by the 'cunning of reason', which makes them produce unwittingly the overall progressive tendency at the world-historical level of *Geist*. Here the true historical tendency manifests itself as consistent and necessary, in spite of the multitude of concrete historical occurrences.

This was the dialectical framework in which history was placed. In the original Hegelian version it was a framework imposed upon history, where the autonomous story of *Geist*, running at its own metaphysical level, was merely reflected in actual historical facts. Hegel's famous remark about Napoleon at the victorious battlefield of Jena, as 'the *Geist* on horseback' illustrates this perspective quite tellingly. 'When he happens to refer to historical events, he does so only to illustrate a point. The facts of history provide only footnotes to the theme of the *Phenomenology*. Of course, since the process is necessary, it is in fact revealed in World History, but it can be explained, so Hegel believes, without reference to what has actually happened' (Plamenatz 1986, vol. 2: 148).

Marx found this approach unacceptable and undertook a formidable attempt to rephrase it in material terms, i.e. by reference to the world as it objectively exists, including nature, society and human individuals. For him history is not the trajectory of the *Geist* but the sequence of changes of human society. Its moving principle is to be searched for in 'sensous human activity, Praxis' (Marx and Engels 1968: 28). Dialectics have been brought down to earth and adopted as a tool for understanding the real, human world.

The Marxian image of history: three-level reconstruction

The Marxian image of history, like the rest of his legacy, has been considerably transformed by the generations of his interpreters and followers. Marxists after Marx have made various uses of the his reconstruction of the historical process. Numerous versions of historical materialism, making a long spectrum from the 'dogmatic Marxism' of Stalin (1879–1953) to the 'activist interpretation' of Gramsci (1891–1937), always invoke the authority of Marx as their source, even though each is clearly different from the other, mutually inconsistent, and sometimes outright opposite in their claims. As Steven Lukes puts it: 'Marxist tradition is no monolithic unity but a contested terrain' (1985: 2).

Metatheoretical reflection about this puzzling fate of Marx's theory may follow two tracks. Most students (and particularly the critics or enemies) of Marx usually trace it to the alleged internal inconsistency of his theory. The sources of later divergences are sought in the antinomies of Marx's original work (either as the opposition of biographical periods, with 'Mature Marx' negating 'Young Marx', or – even less defensible – as the opposition of themes haunting him all his life, running parallel through all his theories, or as the ambivalence and inconsistency in the selection of ontological levels at which he decided to approach social life and history). This may be called 'the hostile explanation'.

But there is also the alternative, 'sympathetic explanation', which I would like to advocate. As its motto we may take the ironic quip of R. Aron: 'If only there were not so many millions of Marxists, there would be no question at all about what Marx's leading ideas are or what is central to his thought' (1968, vol. 1: 145). The sympathetic interpretation gives Marx the benefit of the doubt. Is it not possible that the divergence of continuations and interpretations results from the fallacies committed by followers and interpreters, rather than the original guilt of Marx? Is it not possible that their one-sided emphases were due to the myopia of pre-synthetic thinking, whereas Marx was a forerunner of the synthetic, multidimensional view of society? Is it not the case that later theorists pick out either 'structuralist' or 'agential' emphases, 'historicist' or 'humanist' themes from Marx's work, because they treat the focus on structures and processes and the focus on individuals and actions as mutually exclusive alternatives, whereas Marx himself treated them as complementary, grasping two sides of the same complex reality? Thus, what the 'hostile explanation' would call incoherence, and treat as Marxian weakness, the 'sympathetic interpretation' calls multidimensionality and treats as his major strength, in fact anticipating a much later evolution of sociological theory towards a synthetic many-sided image of the social world.

The reconstruction of historical materialism that I am going to present in this chapter is inevitably only one among many possible interpretations of Marx. It will be guided by a 'sympathetic perspective' and assume the internal coherence of the Marxian image of history, worked out over the years in a great array of contributions, with diverse logical status, incomparable substantive weight and intended for various audiences.

My main claim is that historical materialism is the multidimensional theory of history elaborated at three distinct levels of discourse: world-historical, social-structural and action-individual. To put it otherwise, there are in fact three interrelated partial theories, constitutive of historical materialism: the theory of socio-economic formations, at the top level; the theory of class-struggle at the intermediate level; and the theory of human individual (or 'species-being', to use Marx's phrase) at the bottom level. They are not only dealing with different subject-matter, not only located in different places of Marx's *oeuvre*, but they are formulated in different languages. Some (e.g. fragments of class theory and theory of individuals) in the concrete-empirical language in which Marx describes phenomena more or less immediately observable; persons, their activities, the groups they form, the products of their labour etc. Good examples of such concrete-empirical discourse may be found in *The Class Struggles in France* (1850), *The Eighteenth Brumaire of Louis Bonaparte* (1852), *The Civil War in France* (1871), and occasionally as illustrations in other works. But obviously Marx's heart is not there, and as soon as he takes up the challenge of explaining, accounting for empirical realities, searching for their mechanisms or 'laws of motion', the empirical language is abandoned and we encounter abstract-theoretical considerations. The bulk of his work (e.g. the theory of socio-economic formation, large fragments of the theory of classes and some parts of the theory of 'species being' and alienation) is taken up by this kind of discourse, where major concepts do not have immediate, direct empirical referents, but are constructs, models, idealizations useful for organizing experience. At this level, there is no more talk of persons or groups, but rather of 'surplus value', 'productive relations', 'economic basis', 'superstructure', 'class consciousness', 'objective class interests', 'class for itself', 'alienation', 'reification' etc. *Capital* (1867), *The German Ideology* (1846), and *Contribution to the Critique of Political Economy* (1859) provide good examples of this entirely different thought-style.

Three theories that we have distinguished make up a coherent, hierarchical edifice. They are linked by the relation of interpretation – from the top towards the bottom, and by the relation of aggregation – from the bottom to the top. Going down the steps, the lower-level theories grasp the mechanisms of processes stipulated at the higher level, they give more concrete empirical interpretation of the claims advanced there. Going up the steps, the upper-level theories, describe the aggregate effects of processes running at the lower levels, generalizing about their combined, often unintended and unrecognized outcomes.

Thus the mechanism of the changes in socio-economic formations is provided by the theory of social classes. For example, the general claim about the inevitable self-destruction of capitalism is filled with empirical flesh by the mechanism of relative pauperization and mobilization of the working class, eventually erupting in anti-capitalist revolution. As Raymond Aron comments: 'The mechanism of the self-destruction of capitalism is a sociological one and operates through the behavior of social groups' (1968, vol. 1: 174). But in turn, the reasons why classes arise at all and struggle with other classes may be found only at the lower level, in the theory of individuals and their actions, which ascribes to human beings certain specific propensities, 'powers' and aspirations, and explains why, facing alienation and deprivation, they readily mobilize for revolutionary action. If we reverse the order from the bottom upwards, three steps will be visible again: the emancipatory efforts of alienated individuals bring them together with those of similar economic interests and result in the emergence of classes. The evolving struggles between classes culminate in social revolution and result in the change of the whole socio-economic formation.

Let us trace the implications of such a triple theoretical construction for all major issues of social dynamics. To begin with, there are clearly three visions of the future towards which societies move, three final states taken as the criteria of progress. At the world-historical level, Marx envisages the emergence of communism, i.e. primarily full abundance of economic goods safeguarded by the explosive development of 'productive forces' (technologies), abolition of private property and the withering away of the state. At the social-structural level he predicts the establishment of a classless society of equals, realizing the principle 'to each according to his needs'. At the action-individual level he hopes for complete disalienation of the societal members, i.e. the achievement of full freedom: negative freedom *from* all structural constraints, and positive freedom *to* shape social organization and institutions according to one's will.

Similarly, there are three courses followed by social change, three guises in which the pattern of a spiral manifests itself in history. At the world-historical level, there is the movement from common ownership and primitive forms of self-rule, through private ownership and political rule, to communist economic and political equality, 'the free association of free producers'. At the social-structural level, there is the movement from pre-class community, through class-divided society to the classless society of the future. At the action-individual level, there is the shift from primitive spontaneity, through alienation and reification, towards disalienation, emancipation and freedom.

There are, likewise, three notions of revolutions, marking the thresholds of qualitative change in the course of history. At the world-historical level, revolutions signify fundamental transformations of the whole socio-economic formation. At the socio-structural level, revolutions involve the replacement of a ruling class by a contending class. At the action-individual level, revolution refers to massive collective actions in which the interests (primarily economic) of some people prevail over the interests of other people.

The notion of interests has three meanings, too. At the world-historical level, systemic vested interests are objective, entailed by location in the socio-economic formation, in the system of production. At the socio-structural level, class-interests become viewed as subjective, and their awareness evolves into class consciousness. At the action-individual level, interests mean intentions, motivations, personal goals (among which economic intentions, motivations and goals are assumed to rank highest).

There are also three permutations of the dialectical mechanism of change, rooted in immanent strains, tensions and their eventual resolution. At the world-historical level, there are objective contradictions among the segments of socio-economic formation, and there is the standard sequence (chain) of their resolution, from the economic basis towards the political and legal superstructure and 'forms of social consciousness'. At the socio-structural level, there is class conflict, evolving from objective class contradictions, through perceived class antagonisms and hostilities to actual class struggle and revolutionary breakthrough. At the action-individual level, there is the creative thrust constrained by natural or social conditions, constant effort directed against those constraints, resulting in growing human control over nature and over the social environment.

Finally, there are three modes of causal determination, operating at different levels. The answer to the basic question whether social change is necessary or contingent, entirely determined or partly voluntaristic, finalistic or open-ended, will take various forms depending on the theoretical level at which it is raised. Thus, at the world-historical level, Marx asserts strong determinism. The overall historical process is seen as irreversible, passing through definite, in principle uniform stages, and inevitably leading to the establishment of communism. At the socio-structural level, much weaker determination reigns. Classes take collective actions ultimately informed by their economic interests and aimed at their affirmation or defence. They may also lack sufficient awareness of their interests, and they may have mistaken, false consciousness of their interests. Sometimes they may be misled and cheated into action by irresponsible leaders, demagogues, *agents provocateurs*. In all these cases classes may act contrary to their economic interests. Their actions will escape economic determination. At the action-individual level, there is the strongest ingredient of voluntarism, free choice, spontanous decisions, contingency and chance. Actions are underdetermined. Each individual person can in principle act against his/her economic interests. Some do so, putting other considerations (e.g. emotional, traditional, ideological) to the fore. On the whole, however, people are rational, and their economic calculations provide the basic premises of their intentions, motivations and purposes. Thus, even though for each person, distributively, there is considerable indeterminism, collectively, in a mass of actions economic determination prevails. Everybody is free to choose, but it is also safe to predict what choices most people will make.

Thus Marx depicts historical change as gradually spreading through all three levels. The actual process of historical changes starts at the lowest level of acting individuals. Here presumably Marx locates the ultimate agency, the causal driving force of all social and historical changes. Each person is a free, deciding agent. But in their actions people have to recognize the received structural conditions within which they are placed. Most often they take structurally entailed economic interests into account. The commonality of economic interests (and the related opposition of interests with respect to others) links them with similarly placed individuals into social classes and sets them against members of other classes. For the defence of their economic interests social classes enter the class struggle with opposite classes. The progressive classes, i.e. those with vested interests in the expansive development of 'productive forces' (modern technologies) prevail, establishing new modes of production. The rest of the socio-economic formation must adapt to this new economic system, completing the fundamental transformation of the whole society, i.e. the social revolution. And then this story repeats itself.

This simplified picture must now be filled out with more details, by reconstructing basic Marxian ideas, referring to each of the three levels in turn.

The action-individual level: the theory of 'species being'

The ultimate components, the basic ontological substratum of society, are human individuals. This is a platitude which Marx certainly accepts, together with most social thinkers, as the point of departure for social theory. 'The premises from which we begin', he says, 'are the real individuals, their activity and the material conditions under which they live, both those they found already existing and those produced by their activity. These premises can thus be verified in a purely empirical way' (in McLellan 1971: 127–8).

Common sense ends here, and the concept of an individual is expressed in a highly original way. First of all it is not substantive but relational (contextual). Human nature is not characterized by means of a constant set of universal properties, but rather by a specifically human relationship to the environment, by ways of relating people to the social and natural context in which they exist. It is a derivative of the network of those relationships to society and to nature in which a human individual is enmeshed. Those exclusively human ways of relating oneself to the environment are universal and constant, but of course they may vary in their concrete forms and produce historical and cultural diversity. Relational aspects of human nature are universal, substantive aspects, historical and idiosyncratic. One of the messages carried by the sixth of Marx's famous *Theses on Feuerbach* is, I presume, immediately relevant here: 'The human essence is no abstraction inherent in each single individual. In its reality it is the ensemble of the social relations'(Marx and Engels 1968: 29). As a contemporary commentator reads this thesis: 'Marx's point, of course, was that human nature is not a property which simply inhabits man, such as the egoism of the "economic man", but rather is a relation between men'(Swingewood 1975: 95). Thus a human individual appears as a nodal point, a knot in the wider network of social relationships. This social location – and the consequent fact of social moulding of individuals, as well as the reciprocal impact of individuals on the context of their social life – is a universal property of the human condition, whereas the typical combinations of relational networks vary historically, and idiosyncratic bundles of such relations vary individually.

There are two kinds of relations by means of which Marx defines human nature. To facilitate further discussion I shall give them the names 'participation' and 'creation'. Characterizing the first, Marx focuses on human relations with other people ('social relations', in the strict sense). But it could be extended, without violating Marxian meaning, to relations with nature, to participation and harmonious belonging to the natural world. Conversely, characterizing the second kind of relations, creation, Marx focuses almost exclusively on human relations with nature. But again it could be extended to attitudes to other people and social objects, meaning for example the urge to change, educate, convince others, or reform social organizations, or construct new groups etc. Thus participation and creation can manifest themselves with respect to both contexts of human life: social (other people) and natural (objects).

Because of Marx's emphasis on the relation of participation, his concept of human nature is not psychological but sociological. It is a common misunderstanding that to focus on an individual inevitably implies a psychological perspective. Agreeing with Tucker, that 'no other major writer has displayed such a lack of curiosity about the psychological dimensions of social life' (Tucker 1980: 22), one should not draw the mistaken conclusion that Marx was neglecting the study of individuals. An individual can be seen from various points of view. For a psychologist, the individual *per se* is the crucial subject-matter, and the focus is on the functioning of the mind or personality in its cognitive, emotional, volitional, motivational, attitudinal or other aspects. For a sociologist, the crucial subject-matter is composed of specific superindividual, or inter-individual objects: interactions, social relations, social collectivities, communities, groups, societies etc.

The sociological perspective applied to *any* phenomenon comes down to perceiving that phenomenon in the context of such specific superindividual or inter-individual wholes, as their element, or at least as related to them in patterned ways. Therefore, the individual is a subject-matter relevant to sociology only in so far as he/she is implicated in some wider social fabric. From the sociological perspective an individual will therefore be seen not as a fully-fledged person (with specific, unique internal psychological make-up), but rather as an abstract, one-dimensional 'slice' of a person: (1) an actor in a social action directed towards other people or oriented by their reactions, (2) a partner in social interaction, (3) a participant in the social relationship, (4) a member of a social collectivity or a group, (5) an incumbent of a social position, (6) a performer of a social role. For sociology, the issue of human nature concerns the characteristics of a person in his partial capacities as actor, partner, participant, member, incumbent or performer, and in those capacities only.

The direct proof that Marx was studying human individuals from a sociological perspective may be found in his numerous declarations that people (capitalists, peasants, proletarians) interest him only as representatives of social classes (members of specifically defined groups) or embodiments of economic categories (occupants of specific positions in the system of production and distribution), or representatives of historical tendencies (carriers of wider historical processes). Marx often emphasizes the equivalence of humanness and social existence. There is no person outside society; each individual is bound to others by innumerable relationships of interdependence, and thus the social bond is constitutive of the human condition and human nature. 'Man', Marx says, 'is in the most literal sense of the word a *zoon politikon*, not only a social animal but an animal that can develop into an individual only in society. Production by isolated individuals outside society . . . is as great an absurdity as the idea of the development of language without individuals living together and talking to one another' (Marx 1971: 17–18).

But even more telling indirect proof of Marx's consistent sociological approach will emerge if we consider the necessary method of characterizing human nature implied by such a perspective, which seems to be close to Marx's approach. If a truly sociological perspective requires looking at people as participants in wider social wholes, then the focus has to move towards human action. This is because people participate in wider wholes by means of activity of various sorts. Some specifically directed or oriented activity makes up social action; mutually oriented and co-ordinated activities make up an interaction; persistent, repeatable and regulated activities *vis-à-vis* one another involve individuals in social relationships; activities creating a bond with some people and a distance (or hostility) to other people make an individual a member of a social group; a unique set of activities defines a social position (e.g. an occupation); and a unique set of expected, prescribed activities delimits a social role. To perform all those activities individuals must possess specific capabilities, abilities, skills, talents. 'An analysis of social action might start with a model and then ask what sort of actors are needed for it' (Hollis 1987). In other words the properties of an acting, participating individual (an actor) are derivable from the properties of a typically human, participative activity (action). This point was clearly grasped by Gramsci: 'one can say that man is essentially "political" since it is through the activity of transforming and constantly directing other men that man realises his "humanity", his "human nature"' (Gramsci 1971: 360).

Turning to the second kind of uniquely human relation to the environment, which we labelled 'creation', it may easily be noticed that it is also constituted by a specific type of activity. In creative activity individuals externalize their 'powers', abilities, talents, by producing objects. In those objects they confirm themselves, find the objectified expression of their individual potential. As Marx puts it, '[Man] duplicates himself not only intellectually, in his mind, but also actively, in reality, and thus can look at his image in a world he has created' (in McLellan 1971: 142). Obviously, to do all that, human individuals have to command certain capacities, abilities, skills, or, as Marx would put it, special 'powers'. Again, the properties of an acting, creative individual (an actor) are derivable from the properties of that typically human, creative activity (action).

Marx clearly conceives the properties of human action to be the key to an understanding of human nature; he 'sees persons as preeminently actors' (Rubinstein 1981: 139). He claims explicitly: 'As individuals express their lives, so they are' (Marx and Engels 1975: 61), echoing almost literally the Hegelian belief that 'Spirit is what it does, and its nature is revealed only in the sum of its activities' (Plamenatz 1975: 64). Marx elaborates this idea: 'The whole character of a species . . . is contained in the character of its life activity, and free, conscious activity is man's species character' (Marx and Engels 1960, vol. 1: 553). And here again he seems to paraphrase Hegel, for whom 'Mind or Spirit is nothing apart from its activities, and its nature is revealed only in them, and exists only as so revealed' (Plamenatz 1975: 63). As a contemporary commentator aptly observes: 'For Marx man manifests himself as a species being through activity of a kind, quality, and pace that could only be done by human beings' (Ollman 1975: 84).

This emphasis on action as a primary, constitutive dimension of human beings is even more pronounced in the 'activist Marxism' after Marx. Gramsci answers the question: 'What is man?' in a most telling way: 'What we mean is: what can man become? That is, can man dominate his own destiny, can he "make himself", can he create his own life? We maintain therefore that man is a process, and, more exactly, the process of his actions' (Gramsci 1971: 351).

Several analytical traits of action, as conceived by Marx, can be listed.

1   Action is seen as conscious and purposeful in terms of a means – ends scheme. As Engels develops this point, 'In the history of society . . . actors are all endowed with consciousness, are men acting with deliberation or passion, working towards definite goals; nothing happens without a conscious purpose, without an intended aim' (Marx and Engels 1968: 622).

2   Action is seen as involving some degree of self-consciousness or critical self-awareness on the part of the actors. It may be called, to use the phrase of Rom Harre, 'reflexive monitoring' of action by human subjects (Harre and Secord, 1972). As Marx puts it, 'Man is a being for himself.' He expands on this point thus: 'The animal is immediately identifiable with its life activity. It does not distinguish itself from it. Man makes his life activity itself the object of his will and consciousness . . . Conscious life activity directly distinguishes man from animal life activity' (Marx and Engels 1960, vol. 1: 553).

3   Action is conceived as preceded by some anticipation or planning. In Marx's picturesque prose, 'What distinguishes the worst of architects from the best of bees is this: that the architect raises his structure in imagination before he erects it in reality. At the end of every labour process, we get a result that already existed in the imagination of the labourer at its commencement' (1954, vol. 1: 174).

4   Action is believed to involve some degree of consistency and persistence in its execution. According to Marx a human being, as opposed to an animal, 'not only effects a change of form in the material on which he works,

but he also realizes a purpose of his own that gives a law to his *modus operandi*, and to which he must subordinate his will' (1954, vol. 1: 174).

5   Action is innovative, i.e. actively facing the environment, oriented towards the world of nature and/or towards other people, in the attempt to modify it, transform it, produce some novelty. For Marx labour is a creative activity *par excellence*.

6   Action is collective, i.e. always related to other people, oriented towards them, dependent on them, co-ordinated with them, clashing with them etc. 'All production', Marx says, 'is the appropriation of nature by the individual within and through a certain form of society' (1955: 230), and this can be extended to all other human activities.

To act in the way described above, an actor must possess a set of capacities, abilities, faculties. Some of them come down to the ability to control action. They are self-awareness, projective consciousness, persistence. Others reduce to the ability to preserve some autonomy of action *vis-à-vis* external, environmental pressures. Here such faculties as innovativeness, sociocentric orientation coupled with personal integrity, some level of indeterminacy and capriciousness – 'the ability to act otherwise' (Giddens 1979) – would count as crucial. All those capacities make up Marx's image of human nature as the inherent potentiality for typically human action.

The actualization of those potentialities in action influences those very potentialities. Creating a 'humanized' world out of a natural environment, and shaping patterns of social organization out of fluid and random human encounters, actors are also reshaping, enriching and perfecting their own selves; their knowledge, abilities, skills, faculties. Creation becomes, in a certain sense, self-creation. John Plamenatz sees Marx as an exponent of the

> idea of man as a self-creative being: that is to say, a being who develops the capacities peculiar to his species as he lives and works with his fellows, and who in the process acquires his ideas of the world and of himself . . . a being, who, unlike all others known to us, in some sense makes himself, so that humanity in him is more an achievement that a natural condition. (*1975: 3, 34*)

This interpretation is well corroborated by Marx's numerous observations, for example: 'By thus acting on the external world and changing it, [an individual] at the same time changes his own nature. He develops his slumbering powers and compels them to act in obedience to his sway' (1954, vol.1: 173).

All those traits of human action and human nature are represented most strongly in the process of labour and in the human capacity for labour. This is the leitmotif for Gyorgy Lukács, who treats labour as 'the model of all social practice, of all human conduct' (1984, vol. 2/1: 67). Marx himself defined labour as a fundamental species activity, a 'life-activity' indispensable for the survival, reproduction and evolution of human society, and directed towards the subjugation and appropration of nature. It is seen as the sum of efforts through which human beings modify, transform, control nature, adapting it to their needs.

> Labor [Marx says] is, in the first place, a process in which both man and Nature participate, and in which man of his own accord starts, regulates and controls the material reactions between himself and Nature. He opposes himself to Nature as one of her own forces, setting in motion arms and legs, head and hands, the natural forces of his body, in order to appropriate Nature's productions in a form adapted to his own wants. (*in McLellan 1971: 148*)

Lukács indicates that labour need not be addressed directly to nature, it may also influence other people (e.g. educating them, organizing them, leading them), with the production of 'use values' becoming only the ultimate, indirect result (1984, vol. 2/1: 67).

But whatever its specific form, it clearly epitomizes two relationships characteristic for the human condition: creativeness and participation. On the one hand, it is the objectification, externalization, actualization of human 'powers' and capacities in products; on the other, it is always conducted in some social context, co-operative, competitive or authoritative. Labour exemplifies all other traits of human action as well. For Lukács its crucial component is the 'teleological assumption', and in complex forms of production, the extended chains of such 'assumptions'. He has in mind the subordination of action, or the sequence of actions, to the goal or project preconceived in advance. This is the ultimate origin of symbols and language, as symbols are the projects of action in compressed form, actualizing specfic potentialities of human orientation to the natural and social environment (transforming, shaping, conquering, ordering etc.). Labour exerts also a reverse influence on the labourer, enhancing his capacities and 'powers' for future labour; it is self-creative conduct. As Plamenatz describes it: 'It is . . . supremely educative activity, the activity which helps to form the agent as well as the things he acts on. It is through his work above all that man comes to understand and control himself, that he acquires his image of himself' (Plamenatz 1975: 118). Or, to put the same thing in more philosophical idiom, 'While the subject, in Marx's view, shapes the object, the reciprocal is also true, as the object shapes the subject' (Rubinstein 1981: 169).

It is not by accident that when Marx provides an account of the pathology of human nature in his theory of alienation, he starts from the alienation of labour, and only later generalizes the picture to all manifestations of human 'species nature'. In a class society 'the worker becomes alien to his own activity and alien to the products he produces. His own activity is no longer perceived as his own, and the products of his work no longer belong to him' (Israel 1971: 43). This condition of labour spreads to all areas of human life. As in a distorting mirror, Marx draws a dehumanized picture of the human being, prevailing under conditions of class society, which from the point of view of human nature are pathological, exceptional, even though in fact still predominant.

This counter-image provides strong corroboration of the foregoing picture of a healthy, 'sane' human nature. Thus alienation is the substantial reversal of the relationships binding people with the natural as well as the social milieu, the severing of the relationships of creativity and participation. Man is no longer creative: 'Species life, productive life . . . turns into a mere means of sustaining the worker's individual existence' (Marx and Engels 1960, vol. 1: 553). Again: 'The worker does not confirm himself in his work; he denies himself, feels miserable instead of happy, expends no liberal physical and intellectual energy, but mortifies his body and ruins his mind' (p. 550). He no longer participates in free co-operative associations, but instead becomes isolated, estranged from other people, and hostile to them – alienated from his fellows. Thus alienation means the forfeiting of sociocentric impulses (theme of egoism, atomization), lack of creativity (theme of monotony), and in consequence, the abdication of control over actions (theme of passivism), resigning of autonomy (theme of reification, fetishism of commodities etc.), and, in short, the decay of human 'species potentialities'. Human nature becomes inhuman. By reading Marx's powerful criticism of the fate of an individual in a class society, the image of human nature from his early philo-sophical writings reappears, but only in a reversed mode.

Having presented an analytic reconstruction of the Marxian idea of human nature, one is tempted to find some synthetic principle of its operation, some generating mechanism making people actualize in action their inherent po-tentialities *qua* actors, and develop those potentialities in the process. We find promising hints in two appraisals of Marx's work. Erich Fromm believes that 'For Marx man is characterized by the "principle of movement" . . . The principle of movement must not be understood mechanically but as a drive, creative vitality, energy; human passion for Marx is the essential power of man striving energetically for its object' (Fromm 1966: 30). J. McMurtry seems to follow the same track:

> What is most striking about Marx's concept of human nature is the inherent generative force it imputes to man. Man is, for Marx, by the very needs of his nature impelled to ever more productive undertakings, which his special intrin-sic capacities are uniquely able to prosecute . . . Hence man is by his very con-stitution continually excited into activity, forever pressed by intrinsic demand into vital material expressiveness whose most truly human form is work in its 'unadulterated' form, or productive activity akin to creative art. (*McMurtry 1978: 35–6*).

I will label this fundamental drive or mechanism 'the human tendency towards transcendence and self-transcendence': overcoming limitations, op-posing constraints, fighting enemies, crossing frontiers, breaking barriers (both external, environmental, and internal, imposed by limited human endowment) by means of intensive activity. This is how human history begins, and this is what keeps it running.

The socio-structural level: the theory of classes

Human actors and their actions do not exist in a vacuum, but rather in a context of wider social wholes. Larger social wholes arise when networks of relationships (social structures) emerge, linking separate individuals. There is clear evidence that Marx conceived of social wholes not in the reified way, but in such a modern relational fashion. In the *Grundrisse* we find an explicit statement: 'Society is not a sum of individuals, but it expresses the totality of those relations and situations, in which the individuals mutually confront each other' (1953: 176). Contemporary commentators consider this as the most characteristic trait of Marxian ontology. For example Bertell Ollman says: 'Every factor which enters into Marx's study of capitalism is a "definite social relationship". The relation is the irreducible minimum for all units in Marx's conception of social reality. This is really the nub of our difficulty in understanding Marxism, whose subject matter is not simply society, but society conceived of "relationally" ' (1975: 14–15). A similar observation is made by Swingewood: 'The stress is on society as a definite structure within which human intentions and actions occur' (1975: 37).

Perceiving the totalities as relational structures is just the other side of perceiving the individuals as structurally implicated (what was referred to earlier as the Marxian 'sociological' approach to human individuals). Marx's consistent structuralism is manifested with reference to both levels of social reality, totalities as well as individualities (Sztompka 1979: 287–323).

Individuals get together and establish collectivities, groups, associations etc. when there is some commonality among them (and accordingly, some difference separating them from other people). Various bases of the social bond are possible. One of particular importance for Marx is the ownership situation, the similar level of possession of goods. Not all goods, though. There is one particular category of goods which are most attractive and sought for by people because of their unique property: they are not lost in consumption but are able to generate more goods, grow, extend, multiply themselves. They are 'the means of production': land, raw materials, buildings, tools, machinery, capital. Possession of them safeguards the satisfaction of other needs of the owners, and makes it possible subsequently to raise the levels of satisfaction. The ownership, or lack of ownership, of the means of production is therefore the most important aspect of the human life-situation, one's position in a society. It determines one's basic objective interests, understood as obtaining a social situation which guarantees the maximum satisfaction of needs. The fact of ownership and the consequent vested interest in the preservation of beneficial social conditions produce a bond among the owners; and the lack of ownership and consequent interest in radically changing social conditions of deprivation produce a bond among the dispossessed. Thus social classes arise – for Marx, as the most important kinds of social groups. Giddens summarizes the almost universal consensus reigning today on the Marxian meaning of a social class: 'Classes are constituted by the relationship of groupings of individuals to the ownership of private property in the means of production' (Giddens 1971: 37).

This peculiar social bond logically entails the division of society into two opposite, polar classes: those who have the means of production, and those who do not, and therefore have to sell their labour (the only marketable commodity they possess) in order to survive. The polar model of society appears, with ownership, wealth and abundance at one pole, and hired labour, poverty and deprivation at the other: the world of 'haves' and 'have-nots', rich and poor, privileged and exploited. 'Master and slave, patrician and plebeian, lord and serf, guildmaster and journeyman, in a word oppressor and oppressed, stood in a constant opposition to one another' (Marx and Engels 1968: 35–6).

This image is endowed with intrinsic dynamism. Marx identifies at least two kinds of permanent transformations occurring in the model. One has to do with the whole polarized structure, the other with the components of this structure, opposite classes. The first is the historical tendency to simplify social distinctions and to eliminate all groupings, or at least, to eliminate the strategic importance of all groupings except those rooted in differentials of ownership. This growing polarization reaches its limit in capitalist society: 'The epoch of the bourgeoisie', Marx says, 'possesses however this distinctive feature: it has simplified the class antagonisms. Society as a whole is more and more splitting up into two great hostile camps, into two great classes directly facing each other: Bourgeoisie and Proletariat' (Marx and Engels 1968: 36).

Alongside the trend towards polarization, there is another one, towards a growing internal crystalization of classes. This is expressed by Marx's distinction between 'class in itself' and 'class for itself'. Commonality of the ownership position among a plurality of individuals is not sufficient for their real operation as a fully-fledged class. Sooner or later they tend to acquire some awareness of the commonality (and a corresponding opposition to other classes), to initiate mutual communication and interaction, to produce some more persistent forms of internal organization (e.g. leadership, political representation), resulting in the emergence of the mature 'class for itself', able to articulate and defend its interests.

The ultimate source, the stimulus for this permanent dynamics of polarization and crystallization, is found again in the immanent contradictions of class structure. The model is auto-dynamic, self-transforming. Marx describes the typical relationships between classes as mutual opposition. At least three types of such opposition are singled out. First, there is the objective contradiction of interests between those who have and those who have not: the larger the scope and extent to which the interests of the owners are realized, or their needs satisfied, the more difficult it becomes for non-owners to realize their interests or to satisfy their needs. This may be labelled 'class contradiction'. Second, the objective contradiction may become subjectively perceived by the members of the respective classes. Then it produces feelings of hostility, distrust, enmity on both sides. This type of relationship may be called 'class antagonism'. Finally, the antagonism may acquire external manifestations in the economic, political, ideological arena; it may become transformed into more or less organized collective behaviour or collective action of class members directed against the members of the opposite class. 'Classes carried on an uninterrupted, now hidden, now open fight, a fight that each time ended either in a revolutionary re-constitution of society at large, or in the common ruin of the contending classes' (Marx and Engels 1968: 36). 'Class struggle' seems a term most appropriate here. It is via class contradictions, antagonisms and struggles, coupled with a permanent pressure towards their resolution, that society exhibits the tendency toward self-transcendence.

The world-historical level: the theory of socio-economic formation

The relational view of social reality, so typical of Marx, is to be found also at the highest level of his theoretical construction, where he treats society in the most abstract way. He is quite explicit: 'The relations of production in their totality constitute what is called the social relations, society, and specifically, a society at a definite stage of historical development, a society with a peculiar, distinctive character' (Marx and Engels 1968: 81).

The foundations of Marx's theory of socio-economic formation, developed most extensively in *Capital* (1867) are laid down in this often quoted passage from the preface to a *Contribution to a Critique of Political Economy* (1859):

> In the social production of their life, men enter into definite relations that are indispensable and independent of their will, relations of production which correspond to a definite stage of development of their material productive forces. The sum total of these relations of production constitutes the economic structure of society, the real foundation on which rises a legal and political superstructure and to which correspond definite forms of social consciousness. (*Marx and Engels 1968: 182*)

This model of a most comprehensive social whole (in contemporary terminology we could say: of the social system) may be represented by means of figure 11.1.

In line with Marx's consistent dynamic orientation, the model was constructed as in constant internal movement; it included incessant changes elicited by specific endogenous forces. There is an inherent dynamic principle in the model. Marx sees it as constantly changing, leading ultimately to complete self-transformation. 'At a certain stage of their development, the material productive forces of society come into conflict with the existing relations of production . . . From forms of development of productive forces these relations turn into their fetters. Then begins the epoch of social revolution. With a

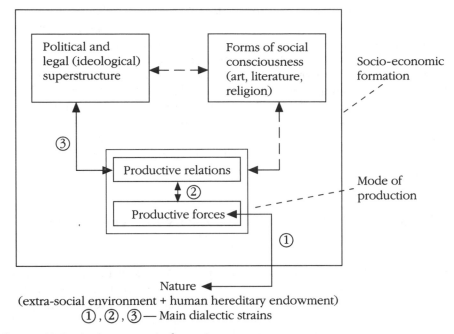

Figure 11.1 Socio-economic formation.

change of economic foundation the whole immense superstructure is more or less rapidly transformed' (Marx and Engels 1968: 183).

The transformations are autodynamic, immanent, endogenous; they are instigated by endemic contradictions, strains and tensions within the structure. These occur at three points: (1) At the border between society and environment (nature), as a constantly reappearing contradiction between any given level of technology and the challenges posed by extra-social conditions as well as human biological constitution. Such a contradiction provides the impetus for the permanent development of productive forces. (2) Another contradiction appears between the achieved level of technology and the existing social organization of productive processes, unfit for the most effective application of available productive forces. Such a contradiction provides the impetus for progressive changes of productive relations. (3) The final contradiction emerges between the newly established type of productive relations and the traditional system of political, legal and ideological institutions (superstructure), no longer instrumental for the economic substructure. This contradiction leads to the transformation of the political regime and the legal organization of society. Owing to internal contradictions and a constant pressure towards their resolution, society manifests a constant tendency towards self-transcendence.

The 'riddle of history' is precisely how single phases in the operation of the model link in a cumulative sequence, producing a series of regular, patterned, directional transformations (cf. Addis 1968; 1969). The problem of 'making history' is how human agency influences not only the actual functioning (operation) of a society but also its long-range development (transformations). It is only here that a truly dynamic perspective is introduced. If we look at the overall pattern of human history as depicted by Marx, we shall see how these internal mechanisms of self-transcendence produce linear, directional, progressive transformations of society, the sequence of socio-economic formations marked by consecutive social revolutions (cf. Habermas 1983).

There are five socio-economic formations: primitive community, slavery, feudalism, capitalism and communism. Or, in a simpler scheme covering the most important divisions, three main epochs in human history: pre-class, unalienated societies (primitive community); class societies permeated with alienation (slavery, feudalism and capitalism); and classless unalienated societies (communism). Marx believes that the most significant moment comes with modern capitalist society and its inevitable transition to communism. This historical threshold signifies the passing from the 'kingdom of necessity' to the 'kingdom of freedom', it ends the 'prehistory' of human society, and opens the epoch of its true, humanistic, free 'history'. The agent of this epochal change is found in the modern proletariat, the class of the exploited and dispossessed, whose objective interests can be satisfied only by the complete abolition of class divisions and class rule. As a result of communist revolution, the 'free association of free producers' will be established, bringing to the close the long period of inequalities, exploitation and human misery. Ultimate progress will be realized at great human cost paid during the whole epoch of class societies. Here we have come full circle, back to the Hegelian dream of the final victory of freedom.

Multidimensional theory of history-making

In the interpetation of Marxian theory provided above, history is seen as produced by the complex interplay of human actions and structural conditions (class divisions and socio-economic formations). This mutual linkage between various levels at which history proceeds is expressed by the category of 'praxis'. Already outlined in the work of Marx, the notion of praxis becomes central for one lineage of Marxism known as the 'humanist' or 'activist' school, and represented, among others by Antonio Gramsci, Gyorgy Lukács (1885–1971) and Erich Fromm.

Marx is clearly aware of the mutual dependence of the various levels. In the most general language he claims: 'Circumstances make men in the same measure that men make circumstances' (in McLellan 1971: 129). The same message is carried by the third of the *Theses on Feuerbach* (1845): 'The materialist doctrine that men are products of circumstances and upbringing, and that, therefore, changed men are products of other circumstances and changed upbringing, forgets that it is men that change circumstances and that the educator himself needs educating' (in McLellan 1971: 204).

In the context of such considerations Marx introduces the notion of praxis, defined as the area where human actions and structural conditions (classes, formations) mutually interpenetrate, as the process whereby they mutually co-determine each other. To quote Marx: 'The coincidence of the changing of circumstances and of human activity or self-changing can be conceived and rationally understood only as revolutionary practice' (in McLellan 1971: 204). In a different place: 'In revolutionary activity, the changing of oneself coincides with the changing of circumstances' (in McLellan 1971: 199).

Some commentators believe that Marx's theory of praxis 'provides the key for understanding his basic outlook from his early speculations to his mature thought' (Bernstein 1972: xi). They claim that it is the exemplar of his efforts to attain a synthetic, multidimensional model of society: 'Marx sought to overcome the extreme one-sidedness of both the idealist and materialist doctrines in a new dialectical synthesis of his own' (Zeitlin 1981: 2). The idea of praxis as bridging the gap between individuals and social totalities was taken up by 'activist Marxists', particularly Gramsci and Lukács. The former referred to the whole of the Marxian opus as 'the philosophy of praxis' (Gramsci 1971), and devoted most of his own work to showing that 'effective human action is the consequence neither of pure will nor of inexorable forces, but of a particular kind of interaction between objective circumstances and the creative spirit of man' (Femia 1987: 121). The latter explicitly refers to praxis as the 'central concept' of his major book (Lukács 1971: xviii), in which the dialectical fusion of subject and object is a leading preoccupation. Drawing from Hegel, he finds the fusion effected in history, and he identifies its embodiment in the proletariat.

What is the ultimate causal force mobilizing social-historical praxis, the complex, multi-level process of history-making? At which level of the theoretical edifice is it to be located? The 'activist interpretation' rejects any fatalist or finalist assumptions or mechanistic models, and focuses on the active role of human agents (masses, classes, social movements, leaders etc.) in making crucial choices influencing the course of history. There is some good textual evidence that the activist image of history is present at least in some of Marx's writings. Consider the following statements: 'The first premise of all human history is, of course, the existence of living human individuals' (in McLellan 1971: 127). Or more specifically: 'The whole of what is called world history is nothing but the creation of man by human labor, and the emergence of nature for man; he therefore has the evident and irrefutable proof of his self-creation, of his own origins' (in Fromm 1966: 26). Or, when Marx quotes Vico in an unmistakably approving context: 'Human history differs from natural history in this, that we have made the former but not the latter' (in Fromm 1966: 15). Thus a general hint as to the creative, constructive nature of the historical process is clearly given by Marx, both in his early, youthful work and in mature analyses.

This is taken up by both the leaders of the 'activist interpretation'. For Gramsci, 'History is the will of men who act on nature in order to change their world, to effect their goals, to satisfy their needs' (in Femia 1987: 64), or 'History is a continuous struggle of individuals and groups to change that which exists in any given moment' (p. 99). He explicitly opts for a reading of Marx which

> postulates as the dominant factor in history not raw economic facts but man, men in societies, men who interact with one another . . . and develop through these contacts (civilization) a collective, social will; men who come to understand economic facts, judge them and adapt them to their will, so that this will becomes the motive force of the economy, the moulder of objective reality. (*in Femia 1987: 90*)

The contemporary commentator has a point: 'The central theme of the notebooks is the re-emphasis on man as the maker of his own history rather than as a reflection of structural determinants' (Femia 1987: 64). In Lukács the same emphasis is obvious:

> History is no longer an enigmatic flux to which men and things are subjected. It is no longer a thing to be explained by the intervention of transcendental powers or made meaningful by reference to transcendental values. History is . . . the product (albeit the unconscious one) of man's own activity . . . It contains nothing that does not lead back ultimately to men and to relations between men. (*Lukács 1971: 186*).

Obviously human actions do not occur in a vacuum, and are neither random nor entirely free. Marx develops the idea of human historical creativeness, specifying two frontiers, parameters delimiting its field. The first limit has to do with the endowment of human actors: what people are, and consequently what they are able to do. One may say that in this way history-making is conditioned 'from below'. Marx and Engels make a famous statement which seems to touch this limitation:

> History does nothing; it does not possess immense riches, it does not fight battles. It is men, real, living men, who do all this, who possess things and fight battles. It is not 'history' which uses men as a means of achieving – as if it were an individual person – its own ends. History is nothing but the activity of men in pursuit of their ends. (*in McLellan 1971: 125*)

The second limit has to do with the circumstances, situation of action, due to the character of structures and the phase of transformation within which actors happen to live and act. One may say that in this way history-making is conditioned 'from above'. As Marx puts it: 'Men make their own history, but they do not make it just as they please; they do not make it under circumstances chosen by themselves, but under circumstances directly encountered, given and transmitted from the past' (Marx and Engels 1968: 97).

But what is the nature of those circumstances? Are they simply given, encountered, provided by providence or fate? Here we reach the crux of Marxian activism. He leaves no doubt about that: the structures limiting present actions are themselves produced by human actors, by their past actions, or by the actions of their predecessors. They are not superhuman, but entirely human creations. Here is Marx's most telling statement referring to the sphere of technological development:

> Men are not free to choose their productive forces – which are the basis of all their history – for every productive force is an acquired force, the product of former activity. The productive forces are therefore the result of practical human energy; but this energy is itself conditioned by the circumstances in which men find themselves, by the productive forces already acquired, by the social form which exists before they do, which they do not create, which is the product of the preceding generation. (*in McLellan 1971: 130*)

There is a cumulative sequence of actions undertaken by actors within existing structures; then production of new structures by those actions; and again acting within limits provided by new structures. In the words of Marx himself: 'History is nothing but the succession of the separate generations, each of which exploits the materials, the forms of capital, the productive forces handed down to it by all preceding ones, and thus on the one hand continues the traditional activity in completely changed circumstances and, on the other, modifies the old circumstances with a completely changed activity' (Fromm 1966: 211).

In effect, the actors' endowment is gradually enriched and structures undergo gradual development. Marx explains

> Because of this simple fact that every succeeding generation finds itself in possession of the productive forces acquired by the previous generation, which serve it as a raw material for new production, a coherence arises in human history, a history of humanity which takes shape is all the more a history of humanity as the productive forces of man and therefore his social relations have been more developed. (*in McLellan 1971: 130*)

To sum it up: each phase of the process reshapes the initial conditions and alters the field of possibilities open for the next phase of history-making. Praxis operates under circumstances left by earlier praxis. But the ultimate causal force putting all this complex sequence in motion is the human agency with its in-built propensity to transcendence and self-transcendence.

Historical materialism was the most complex theory of social and historical change, which attempted to save the evolutionist belief in the overall progressive pattern of human history and to show how this pattern emerges from the operation of society as the complex, accumulated result of human actions. In other words, Marx still believed that there was a historical fate, but saw the fate as shaped not by gods, or *Geist*, or providence, but by people themselves. In this sense, historical materialism provides a bridge between traditional and modern theories of social change. On one leg, Marx stands firmly in the nineteenth century, but on the other he stretches far into the twentieth. Marxian historical materialism anticipated and prepared the conceptual ground under two influential approaches to historical change dominating at the end of the twentieth century: historical sociology and theories of agency. These will be our preoccupation in the following chapters.

Part III

The Alternative Vision:
Making History

12

Against developmentalism: the modern critique

The refutation of 'historicism': Karl R. Popper

We have seen that both evolutionism and Marxian historical materialism share certain fundamental assumptions. They are both forms of developmentalism: an approach postulating irreducible, emergent qualities and regularities of the historical process, endowing it with internal logic, sense and direction. The idea that history runs on its own, along some predetermined course, towards some pre-set goal has raised doubts and criticisms almost since its inception, but it was only in the second half of the twentieth century that elaborate critical accounts of developmentalism were given, which eventually led to the demise of the approach and its slow replacement by an alternative vision of social change and historical process. In this chapter, four such major critiques of developmentalism will be presented in chronological order: those of Karl R. Popper, Robert Nisbet, Charles Tilly and Immanuel Wallerstein. This will prepare the ground for the positive exposition of the post-developmental approach which, we shall submit, provides a more adequate account of social and historical dynamics.

Karl R. Popper formulated his classical critique of what he called 'historicism' in 1957, in a little book entitled *The Poverty of Historicism*, and then in the 'Postscript: after twenty years', to his fundamental *Logic of Scientific Discovery* (1968). By fallacious 'historicism' (as different from valid 'historism') he meant a doctrine or orientation in the social sciences distinguished by a number of claims: ontological, epistemological and methodological. (1) First, it presents an ontological vision of what history is: 'The theory that society will necessarily change but along a predetermined path that cannot change, through stages predetermined by inexorable necessity' (1964: 51). In this account we recognize the typical triad of ontological assumptions, which, in our earlier discussion, has always been found to underlie all evolutionist or historical-materialist accounts: determinism ('predetermined path'), fatalism ('inexorable necessity') and finalism ('predetermined stages' leading to some ultimate stage, 'the end of history'). (2) Popper ascribes to 'historicism' a strong epistemological claim, namely that the laws of history are knowable, can be unravelled by inquiry: 'I mean by "historicism"', he says, 'an approach to the social sciences which assumes that historical prediction is their principal aim, and which assumes that this aim is attainable by discovering the "rhythms" or the "patterns", the "laws" or the "trends" that underlie the evolution of history' (1964: 3). In a different place: 'The belief, more especialy, that it is the task of the social sciences to lay bare the law of evolution of society in order to foretell the future ... might be perhaps described as the central historicist doctrine' (p. 106). (3) There is the accompanying methodological postulate for sociological research: to focus on predictive goals, to provide 'historical prediction', or simply to 'foretell the future', as the ultimate aim of social science.

Popper argues that all these assumptions are mistaken, and have had harmful effects for sociological research as well as social policy. As the central critical claim of the book he puts forward the thesis that 'the belief in historical destiny is sheer superstition, and that there can be no prediction of the course of human history by scientific or any other rational methods' (1964: v). As a consequence 'holistic social engineering', i.e. attempts to use the knowledge of the necessary trends and anticipated future for constructing social institutions (as opposed to 'piecemeal social engineering', i.e. small-scale, melioristic efforts) can only be irrational, utopian and doomed to failure. Historicism engenders a mood of fatalism and passivism, exhorts 'social midwifery', i.e. restricting political intervention to forwarding supposedly inevitable events, and justifies 'moral futurism', i.e. a belief that all is good which fits the demands of future development. This latter statement is clearly the form of the morally doubtful claim that the end justifies the means, and may easily be used to legitimate tyranny, despotism or even totalitarianism.

There are several arguments which Popper puts forward to undermine historicism and substantiate his critical claims. As the foundation for logical and methodological critique, which is his focus, he makes five points concerning human society and its history. (1) That there is no universal history of mankind, but rather disparate and varied histories of various segments of human society. (2) That there is a large amount of contingency and variation in the conditions in which social regularities operate, and that each historical event is 'the resultant of momentary constellations of contesting forces' (1964: 47). A historicist, Popper says, is 'deficient in imagination, for he cannot imagine a change in the conditions of change' (p. 130). (3) That there is a contingent, irrational and erratic personal factor in history. (4) That human history is a unique, non-repeatable process, with no other comparable cases. (5) Perhaps most importantly, that knowledge is a crucial dimension of human society, and its level significantly influences all other dimensions.

The major consequence of these facts about society is that only conditional scientific prediction, recognizing varying local circumstances and specific initial conditions, is valid, whereas historical prophecy concerning universal history running along a predetermined path in constant conditions is in principle impossible. 'This, we may say, is the central mistake of historicism. Its "laws of development" turn out to be absolute trends; trends which like laws do not depend on initial conditions, and which carry us irresistibly in a certain direction into the future. They are the basis of unconditional prophecies, as opposed to conditional scientific predictions' (1964: 128).

Another important consequence is the impossibility of universal laws of an evolutionary sort, and the necessity to restrict social scientific results either to 'piecemeal' conditional laws or accounts of contingent trends. There cannot be a law of evolution because the evolution of societies is a unique historical case (with no available replication).

> We cannot hope to test a universal hypothesis nor to find a natural law accept-able to science if we are for ever confined to the observation of one unique process. Nor can the observation of one unique process help us to foresee its future development. The most careful observation of one developing caterpillar will not help us to predict its transformation into a butterfly. (*1964: 109*)

What we can attain are at most historical trends, giving no grounds for fore-telling the future. 'A statement asserting the existence of a trend at a certain time and place would be a singular historical statement, not a universal law' (p. 115), and trends cannot support predictions.

The same consequences are found to follow from the most crucial obser-vation: that knowledge is an intrinsic part of social reality, causally effective with respect to other dimensions of society. Popper's ultimate, logical refu-tation of historicism goes along the following lines:

> The course of human history is strongly influenced by the growth of hu-man knowledge.
>
> We cannot predict, by rational or scientific methods, the future growth of our scientific knowledge. It is self-contradictory to think that we can antici-pate today what we shall know only tomorrow. To predict future knowl-edge is absurd, because at the moment of prediction it would already be present knowledge. To predict future knowledge cannot be anything dif-ferent from just knowing, here and now.
>
> We cannot, therefore, predict the future course of human history, because we cannot know now what will be known (discovered, invented) in the future.

All these arguments come down to the same ultimate conclusion: we must reject the possibility of theoretical history; there can be no scientific theory of historical development serving as a basis for historical prediction (1964: vi–vii). In place of a refuted 'historicist' vision, Popper puts forward his own creed. It is summarized by a contemporary commentator:

> He is an indeterminist who believes that change is the result of our attempts to solve our problems – and that our attempts to solve our problems involve, among other unpredictables, imagination, choice, and luck. Of these we are responsible for our choices. Insofar as any process of direction is at work, it is

we . . . who move history forward. Any purposes it embodies are our purposes. Any meaning it has is meaning we give it. (*Magee 1973: 97*)

Clearly he anticipated all the core ideas of the post-developmentalist theories of agency, history-making and social becoming, to be discussed in later chapters.

The misleading metaphor of growth: Robert Nisbet

The next compelling critique of developmentalism was presented more than a decade later by Robert Nisbet in his *Social Change and History* (1969) and related articles (Nisbet 1970).

The point of departure for Nisbet is the counterposition of biological and social evolutionism. The legacy of Darwin and Mendel, he stresses, is completely different from the legacy of Spencer or Comte. (1) Biological evolutionism searches for a mechanism of change, and therefore provides explanations and allows predictions. Social evolutionism purports to grasp the course, direction and stages of the historical process, and therefore is only a descriptive account. (2) For biological evolutionists, the subject-matter is the aggregate, population, species, whereas for social evolutionists it is the singular object, a society, a community, a group, a social class, an institution (e.g family, law or religion). (3) The biologists consider the mechanism of changes in the population as stochastic, working out through great numbers of partly accidental individual events, and therefore allowing only for probabilistic generalizations or laws. The sociologists, on the other hand, trace supposedly inexorable, necessary and irreversible tendencies, seeking for deterministic laws about the direction and sequence of change. 'Whereas the biological theory became (very considerably in its Darwinian statement, wholly after it was fused with Mendel's great researches) a population and statistical theory, the theory of social evolution was, and remains to this day, a typological construction' (Nisbet 1969: 162). (4) The substantive explanatory mechanisms are strikingly different. In biology, processes of natural selection (Darwin), genetic variation (Mendel) and survival of the fittest are central. In sociology, the structural and functional differentiation is treated as the core mechanism of evolution.

The secret of this specificity of social evolutionism is discovered in a particular image, which in spite of its biological provenance is entirely foreign to biological evolutionism. Namely, at the core of the sociological idea of evolution or development is the 'metaphor of growth', the model of the natural unfolding of a single individual organism (rather than the species) from the embryonic stage to maturity. 'Such growth is not the model of Darwinian natural selection or of post-Darwinian theory in biology' (1969: 164). It is the invention of the nineteenth-century classics of sociology, and it has shown tremendous vitality, being preserved till our time in various neo-evolutionist, neo-modernization or neo-Marxist variants.

There are numerous implications of the metaphor of growth, defined by Nisbet as 'the analogy of change in society to change in the growth-processes of the individual organism' (1969: 166):

1   Change is natural and normal; it is a typical life-process which cannot be halted as long as the organism lives (or society persists).
2   Change is directional; it goes through the sequence of stages, where the past, the present and the future are connected in one single series.
3   The direction of change is set by the final goal of ultimate maturity, which in the case of society is most often understood as modernity of the western type – industrialization, urbanization, mass culture, democracy etc.
4   Change is immanent, endogenous; it is a function of the system itself, unfolding from within and realizing a pattern of change pre-set already in the embryo ('the present is pregnant with the future', as the saying goes).
5   Change is continuous, gradual, cumulative, follows a step-by-step pattern along constant sequences of stages ('Nature does not make leaps', Leibniz said, and the same applies to society).
6   Change is necessary to the nature of the system, like the inexorable unfolding of potentiality into actuality. 'For all social evolutionists necessity was a cardinal element of what they deemed to be a scientific theory of change' (1969: 181).
7   Change proceeds from uniform causes; the originating forces of change are themselves unchangeable, identical in the past, present and future (e.g. Comte's tendencies of the mind, Hegel's contradictions, Marx's class conflict etc.).

All the foregoing claims can be refuted, and hence the metaphor of growth itself is shown to be untenable. Thus:

1   Fixity, stability and persistence are at least as natural and normal as change. What we quite often observe in human societies is inertia, a conservative bent, reluctance to change accustomed ways of behaviour, the rule of habit and custom.
2   There is no simple, linear directionality in change, nor any ultimate goal of change.
3   Social change is often exogenous, stimulated by occurrences external to the society. Such external causation is crucial for moving the society from inertia, stability and persistence. 'Significant change is overwhelmingly the result of non-developmental factors; that is to says, factors inseparable from external events and intrusions' (1969: 280).
4   Discontinuity of change is most often the case. Change usually involves crisis and continues until some new transient form of adaptation is tentatively reached.

5   There is no necessity or irreversibility of social changes; changes may not come, and there are all sorts of reversals and backlashes in history.
6   The causes of social change are multiple and varied, they are culturally and historically relative.

As a positive alternative to developmentalism, Nisbet submits the serious study of history. In spite of appearances, neither evolutionism nor historical materialism has anything in common with historiography. What they proposed was at most '"abstract history", history divorced from all particularity of the events, actions, personages, places, and periods that was the very substance of what the historians were concerned with' (1969: 165). Developmentalists ignored the historical sources, trying to build their schemes above history. They produced theories imposed upon history, rather than theories of history. 'Their objective . . . was to discern the provisions for change, natural change, that lie within society or culture and that do not depend for their existence upon the myriad random events and actions of the historical record' (p. 234). Then they fell into the trap of misplaced concreteness, treating their rationally devised abstract schemes and interpretations as accounts of historical realities. Even more, they tried to deduce from them concrete historical predictions of historical events.

The antidote to developmentalist temptations is historical concreteness. 'For the student of social change, any effort to deal with the problem of change except in terms of time and particularity courts disaster – or banality' (1969: 252) 'The more concrete, empirical and behavioral our subject matter, the less the applicability to it of the theory of development and its several conceptual elements' (p. 267). The metaphor of growth does not find any place in serious historical research. 'When we look at the actual social behavior of an area, we see not growth but history; history that refuses to be cut to Procrustean beds' (p. 285).

Contingency, concreteness, exogenous causation – these are the emphases of Nisbet's picture of historical change. Again, similar ideas will return in the modern post-developmentalist theories of social change, to be presented in chapters 13, 14 and 15.

'Pernicious postulates': Charles Tilly

Another fifteen years passed before the next major attack against developmentalism was mounted by Charles Tilly in *Big Structures, Large Processes, Huge Comparisons* (1984). The author claims that sociology is trapped in the assumptions deriving from the nineteenth century, and finds this to be particularly obvious in the study of social change. The sociology of change must escape the trap without abandoning the valid problematic agenda set by the great masters. 'We must hold on to the nineteenth-century problems, but let go of the nineteenth-century intellectual apparatus' (Tilly 1984: 59).

There are eight 'pernicious postulates' inherited from the nineteenth century which must be rejected, as 'all eight are mistakes' (1984: 12):

1   Society is a thing apart, has some objective existence as a totality (social organism, social system) and divides itself into smaller wholes, into distinct, separate societies.
2   The explanation of social behaviour must invoke the impact of external, constraining society (social structure) on individual minds (human personality).
3   Social change is a coherent general phenomenon, which can be studied and explained as a whole.
4   There is a succession of stages, each more advanced (progressive) than the previous stage.
5   Differentiation (e.g. division of labour, specialization of organs or functions) is the main logic and dominant trend of the historical process.
6   Social order depends on the balance between differentiation and integration.
7   Social pathology, deviance etc. result from the strain of excessively rapid social change.
8   Illegitimate forms of conflict and coercion stem from change and disorder, whereas legitimate forms serve integration and control.

Historical evidence shows that those postulates are untenable. Thus:

1   Society must not be seen as an entity or a distinguishable whole, but rather as a fluid, complex, overlapping, cross-cutting and superimposed network of 'multiple social relationships, some quite localized, and some worldwide in scale' (1984: 25). Particular congeries, knots in this network are singled out for historical or sociological study, and then attain vicarious existence under the name of nation-states, social organizations, social groups etc.
2   Determining factors in social life are not reified external social wholes, but interactions, relationships among societal members, emerging interpersonal structures.
3   Instead of a single master process of social change, in reality there are numerous fragmentary processes of various levels of complexity, running parrallel, or in opposite directions, separate or overlapping, and 'social change' is only an abstract term for their overall, aggregated and accumulated results.
4   Historical facts do not allow us to postulate any discernible stages in a historical process, and even more clearly put into doubt any ascriptions of progress.
5   Differentiation cannot be regarded as a master-process of social change, as equally often we observe the processes of de-differentiation (disorganization, regression, collapse of structures etc.).

6   Social order is not necessarily due to integrative mechanisms, as various forms of contention, collective violence, protests etc. are under certain circumstances the only rational forms to pursue collective interest and safeguard a more acceptable order.

7   Social change does not necessarily produce generalized structural strain, with social pathology or deviance as its symptoms.

8   Coercion in the service of 'law and order', carried out by the state and its officials, may sometimes be indistinguishable from crime and delinquency, disrupting social order.

As we see, Tilly's prescription against the 'pernicious postulates' of the nineteenth century is similar to Nisbet's: a turn to deep, concrete historical study rooted in evidence. His own prolific work in the area of social movements and revolutions, where he proves his high competence as a historian, testifies eloquently to the fruitfulness of this advice (cf. Tilly and Tilly 1975; Tilly 1978; 1979a).

'Unthinking' the nineteenth century: Immanuel Wallerstein

The author of the 'world-system theory' (discussed above in chapter 6) shares the scepticism of Nisbet and Tilly as regards the validity of the nineteenth-century paradigm. Immanuel Wallerstein is quite radical in his critique, and demands not only revision and modification of the legacy that sociological masters have left to us but rather complete rejection of the assumptions typical of nineteenth-century thought. As he puts it in the title of his book, there is a need for *Unthinking Social Sciences* (1991). His goal is explained as follows:

> in addition to rethinking which is 'normal', I believe we need to 'unthink' nineteenth-century social science, because many of its presumptions – which, in my view, are misleading and constrictive – still have far too strong a hold on our mentalities. These presumptions, once considered liberating of the spirit, serve today as the central intellectual barrier to useful analysis of the social world. (*Wallerstein 1991: 1*)

Among the misleading concepts inherited from the nineteenth century, he singles out 'development' as the greatest villain.

> What seems to me the key, and most questionable, concept of nineteenth-century social science [is] the concept of 'development' . . . Here is an idea which has been eminently influential, highly misleading (precisely because, in its partial correctness, it has seemed so persuasively self-evident), and consequently generative of false expectations (both intellectually and politically). And yet there are very few indeed who are ready truly to unthink this central notion. (*Wallerstein 1991: 2*)

The notion of development is found unacceptable primarily because it is unable to come to terms with the dominant historical trend of the modern world, the process of globalization. There are two aspects of this inadequacy.

1   By its very definition the concept of development refers to immanent, endogenous change, generated from within the society (group, class, community, 'social system') and proceeding by means of the gradual unfolding of inherent potentialities. But, Wallerstein claims, the real social world is different: it exhibits mostly exogenous changes, generated by external sources. It stays stable until moved from the outside. Thus the central role in the historical dynamics is played by international, global factors and influences. The push for change derives from inter-societal contacts, competition, clash, conflict, conquest and similar events, rather than intra-societal embryonic potentialities. This is the first reason why it is futile to think in terms of development.

2   The other aspect has to do with the image of each society (nation-state) as isolated, sovereign, to some extent autonomous or autarkic, and evolving according to its own, specific tendencies and directions. This idea of the fragmentation of human society and its articulation into distinct units, rooted in developmentalist thinking, is clearly untenable in a globalized world. 'It is futile to analyze the processes of the societal development of our multiple (national) "societies" as if they were autonomous, internally evolving structures, when they are and have been in fact primarily structures created by, and taking form in response to, world-scale processes' (Wallerstein 1991: 77).

Wallerstein finds two additional reasons why it is mandatory to get rid of the concept of development.

1   There is its intimate link with the most questionable notion of progress, which, in his view, has several major flaws. (a) It suggests a constant direction of change, whereas in point of historical fact social processes fluctuate, turn about, reverse their course, pause or halt. Their directionality cannot be assumed a priori; it is, at most, a contingent possibility, appearing under specific circumstances. (b) Another flaw is the optimistic assumption of unending betterment produced by developmental processes. It does not require much reflection to note that always in some respect, and often in many respects, the later stages of human history can hardly be defined as improvements compared with earlier stages. Therefore, the valuational issue of progress must also be treated as contingent and historically relative.

> World-system analysis wants to remove the idea of progress from the status of a trajectory and open it up as an analytical variable. There may be better and there may be worse historical systems (and we can debate the criteria by which to judge). It is not at all certain that there has been a linear trend – upward, downward or straightforward. Perhaps the trend line is uneven, or perhaps indeterminate. (*Wallerstein 1991: 254*)

2   The final reason is of a more general nature, it has to do with the internal constitution of social scientific disciplines. Namely, the notion of development belongs among those which perpetuate the nineteenth-century 'original sin' of the social sciences, the artificial and unfounded distinction into three subfields: economic, political and social (cultural). Most often the processes of economic, political and social (or cultural) development are discussed separately, and studied in mutual isolation by different researchers, enhancing the illusion that there are three separate trajectories of change. 'We have been bequeathed a terrible legacy by nineteenth-century social science. It is the assertion that social reality occurs in three different and separate arenas: the political, the economic, and the socio-cultural . . . This is nonsense in terms of how the world really works' (Wallerstein 1991: 264). 'The holy trinity of politics/economics/society-culture has no intellectual heuristic value today' (p. 265). The science of globalized society must become interdisciplinary, and this is the final reason why it should renounce the idea of development.

The persistent critique of developmentalism over the span of several decades has led to the slow erosion and finally the utter demise of this approach. At the close of the twentieth century both of its major versions, evolutionism and historical materialism seem already to belong to the history of social thought. In their place, an alternative, post-developmentalist view of social change is coming to the fore of sociological imagination. This will be the subject of the next three chapters.

13

History as a human product:
the evolving theory of agency

In search of agency

Probably since the dawn of human self-reflection people have been seeking for the ultimate causes of events, the motors of phenomena and processes, the forces responsible for their own fate. Inevitably this became one of the perennial, leading themes of social thought and, much later, of sociological science. Here it was defined as the quest for the underlying, moving springs of social dynamics, the operation and transformation of society. In this long evolution of human thought 'agency' has been gradually secularized, humanized and socialized.

At the beginning it was placed outside the human and social world, in the domain of the supernatural. Whether in the guise of animistic forces, personified deities, singular gods or metaphysical providence, agency was always operating from without, shaping and controlling individual and collective life, human biographies and social histories.

In the next stage the agency was brought down to earth, located in slowly unravelling natural forces of various sorts. Human society, its functioning and change, were believed to be direct products of natural determination, physical, biological, climatic, geographical, even astronomical. Agency became secularized. It was still outside humanity and society but somehow closer.

It took more time before agential powers were ascribed to human beings, but even then not all human beings. Agency was located exclusively in Great Men: prophets, heroes, leaders, commanders, discoverers, inventors, geniuses. They were the movers of society, but their charismatic capacities were not from society; rather they were inborn, genetically inherited and individually developed. The agency became humanized, but not yet socialized. An interesting variant of this theme is to be found in modern structural-functionalism, where responsibility for the changes *of* society (as opposed to changes *in* society) is ascribed to deviants, those who undermine established social ways. But deviance 'occurs for sociologically – and that means structurally – unknown and unknowable reasons. It is the bacillus that attacks the system from the dark depths of the individual psyche or the nebulous reaches of the outside world' (Dahrendorf 1968: 116).

With the birth of sociology, a surprising twist occurred: agency became socialized, but dehumanized again. It was located squarely within society, but society itself was conceived in organismic terms, as the self-regulating and self-transforming whole. The metaphor of an organism used to describe the functioning of society and the metaphor of growth applied to its development had the same implication: agency was treated as an inherent power of the social organism, its specific, but unanalysed, taken-for-granted *élan vital*, necessarily manifesting itself in social life and in directional, irreversible social change. This 'sociological fallacy' (Nisbet 1970: 203), an original sin of our discipline, haunted sociology for a long time. It underlay all varieties of evolutionism and developmentalism, with their visions of history occurring somewhere above human heads; it became one of the most obvious weaknesses of orthodox functionalism or mechanistic system theory, presenting us with strange models of society without people. Critics demanded: 'Let us get men back in, and let us put some blood in them' (Homans 1971: 113). In due time those calls were heeded, and agency finally found its proper place: in the actions of social agents. It became humanized and socialized at the same time.

Great Men (and, as the times changed, also Great Women) returned as agents, but their exceptional powers were treated as an emanation of society rather than an inborn quality. They were seen as embodiments, crystallizers of structural tensions, social moods, historical traditions. They were the leaders but, paradoxically, only because they knew how to follow those they led. Their conduct took the form of 'representative activities': 'carried out on behalf of people, in order to keep futures open for them' (Dahrendorf 1980: 18), or – to put it in different terminology – the exercise of 'meta-power', that is shaping the social contexts for others: 'power to structure social relationships, to alter the "type of game" the actors play, or to manipulate or change the distribution of resources or the conditions governing interaction or exchanges among the actors involved' (Baumgartner et al. 1976: 225).

The next step came in sociological thinking about agency. The seat of it moved from personal endowment to social roles, and particularly those roles which have inherent agential prerogatives to introduce and even enforce changes. The problem of legitimacy of offices and their incumbents came to the fore.

Perhaps the most crucial step was taken when the idea of agency was extended downwards, to all people and not only the elect few, to all social roles and not only powerful offices. It was recognized that obviously each individual has only a minuscule say in social change, but at the same time social change must be treated as a composite result of what all individuals do. Distributively each has a minor, practically invisible agential power, but collectively they are all-powerful. Two neighbouring disciplines lend a hand to sociology at this theoretical juncture. The metaphor of the market, borrowed from economics, helped in understanding how the 'invisible hand' emerges out of multiple and dispersed decisions taken by innumerable producers, consumers, buyers and sellers; and a metaphor borrowed from linguistics helped to understand how in everyday practices people create, recreate and change their own society, just as in everyday speech they produce, reproduce and modify their language. The notion of unintended, latent effects of human action (Merton 1976) became crucial, as social change was seen as the aggregated and historically accumulated result of what all societal members do for their own private reasons and egotistic purposes.

At least in modern society, however, it has to be recognized that not all social change is unintended, and not all people act in isolation. The notion of intended, planned change and the concept of collective, group action supplement the image of spontanous change brought about by individuals. With this, agency finds its final embodiment in collective, or corporate agents. Some are seen as acting from above, through enactment. These are governments, legislatures, corporations, administrative bodies etc. Others act from below, incrementally inducing changes. These are associations, pressure groups, lobbies, social movements. Their complex interplay makes up the political stage of contemporary societies, and their intended outcomes cross with the dispersed everyday activities of individual actors, performed on the stage of everyday life. Thus, individuals and collectivities together shape the twisting course of human history.

We have retraced the odyssey of the idea of agency through the labyrinth of social and sociological thought. At the entrance it was entirely superhuman and extrasocial. At the exit it appeared as fully human and fully social in the two guises of individual actors and collective agents. Recent sociological theory focuses on both, attempting to unravel the secrets of their operation and the mechanisms through which they produce and reproduce social reality. Let us follow this route in more detail.

Modern theories of agency

Walter Buckley and the concept of morphogenesis

The genealogy of the modern theory of agency can be traced back to 1967 and Walter Buckley's *Sociology and Modern Systems Theory*. Coming from the traditions of structural-functionalism and general systems theory, Walter Buckley wanted to revise them by incorporating the insights of other theoretical orientations: exchange theory, symbolic interactionism, theory of games, models of collective behaviour. The basis for this integration was still the system model. He believed that 'the system model has the potential to synthesize the interaction models into a coherent conceptual scheme – a basic theory – of the sociocultural process' (1967: 81). To the structural-functional model of self-regulating, homeostatic (or, as he called it, 'morphostatic') system pervaded with negative, compensatory feedbacks, he counterposed the model of a 'morphogenetic system' with positive, amplifying feedbacks, in which the structures were constantly being built and transformed. 'The model assumes an ongoing system of interacting components with an internal source of tension, the whole engaged in continuous transaction with its varying external and internal environment, such that the latter tend to become selectively "mapped" into its structure in some way' (p. 128). He defined the central, strategic notion thus: 'Morphogenesis will refer to those processes which tend to elaborate or change a system's given form, structure or state' (p. 58). The emphasis on the active, constructive side of social functioning was a significant breakthrough in theoretical perspective, even though Buckley still remained trapped in some premises of the framework he purportedly rejected, the organismic and mechanistic models. His morphogenetic system 'emerges', 'comes to be built up', 'generates, elaborates, and restructures itself'. There is some automatism in all this, as well as some reified, hard quality in the system itself. Agency is not yet liberated from its systemic cage.

Amitai Etzioni and the active society

A year later Amitai Etzioni came out with his seminal account of 'active society' (Etzioni 1968a), labelled later as the 'theory of self-guidance' (Breed 1971). At the heart of this there is the notion of 'mobilization' or 'societal activation':

> The theory of societal guidance differs most from other theories in contemporary social science in that it sees the mobilization drives of collectivities and societies as a major source of their own transformations and of the transformations of their relations to other societal units. As a societal unit mobilizes . . . it tends to change its own structure and boundaries and the structure of the supra-unit of which it is a member. (*Etzioni 1968a: 393*)

Human society is seen as a 'macroscopic and permanent social movement' engaged in an 'intensive and perpetual self-transformation' (1968a: viii). The ultimate motor of this is found in the 'self-triggered transformability' (p. 121), and 'creative responsiveness' (p. 504) of the people; the locus of such capacities is the collectivities, groups and social organizations; and the mechanism is identified as collective action, mostly in the framework of a political process.

> A theory of guidance asks how a given actor [understood as a collectivity] guides a process and how he changes a unit's structure or boundaries . . . The theory of societal guidance asks, in addition, how a given structure was modelled, how it is maintained, how it can be altered, where the seats of power are, who commands knowledge, and who has the capacity to commit. (*p. 78*)

Even though Etzioni also derived his ideas from system theory or cybernetics, he was able to avoid reification or automatism by finding the true agents of social self-transformation in various kinds of collectivities. The hunt for elusive agency was made much more concrete.

Alain Touraine, Michel Crozier and Erhard Friedberg:
some French contributions

In the second part of the 1970s some French contributions to the theory of agency have to be noticed. Since that time 'the rapid break-up of a reifying vision of society', so typical of a particular French version of structuralism, has begun (Chazel 1988: 197). Perhaps the most important representative of this trend is Alain Touraine. From the time he outlined the image of the 'self-producing society' (Touraine 1977) his prolific work has had a strong critical edge. It was directed against both developmentalism and structuralism, and the main charge was that they 'subordinate the sense of collective action to immutable laws or requirements of historical reality' (1985: 81), and in consequence eliminate the actor (the subject) from the sociological perspective, treating him/her as an epiphenomenon, a sheer emanation of the system:

> The evolutionist or historist conception appeals to comparative history or even to philosophy of history. It tries to show that societies are ordered in a march towards progress, rationality and the reinforcement of the nation-state. It is irrelevant to the study of social actors themselves: it is sufficient to analyse their acts as the expression either of positive tendencies or of the internal contradictions of a given system. (*1985: 91*)

'The return of the actor' is necessary (Touraine 1984); 'we must reaffirm the need to return to the idea that men make their own history' (1985: 88). This is possible only within an image of society as a contingent, fluid product of human efforts: 'society is nothing but the unstable and rather incoherent result of social relations and social conflicts' (p. 85).

The making of society and history is carried out by collective action, and its principal agents for Touraine are social movements (Touraine 1985). This crucial embodiment of agency is understood, rather idiosyncratically, as those forms of collective mobilization which directly attack the cultural foundations of society, its specific mode of 'historicity'. 'The social movement . . . is first of all an actor, since historical reality is built through the conflicts and negotiations of social movements that give a specific social form to cultural orientations' (1985: 87). The rejection of evolutionism and the ascent of social movements to the role of core actors are linked by Touraine with the emergence of the 'post-industrial society', where the 'capacity for self-action' is dramatically increased, the scope of options and possibilities enlarged, and therefore 'these societies see themselves as the products of their own actions, rather than as part of a process of historical evolution' (p. 84). In the work of Touraine, that vague capacity of society to mobilize, transform itself, engender structures – perceived already by earlier authors – was pinned down much more concretely and relativized to the specific historical phase.

Another French contribution comes from a duo, Michel Crozier and Erhard Friedberg, sociologists of organizations, who come to grips with the interdependence of actors and systems (Crozier and Friedberg 1977). They realize that actors do not exist outside a system which determines their scope of freedom, but at the same time the system does not exist without the actors, who have produced it, support it and are solely empowered to change it. Like Touraine, they start with the rejection of the 'laws of history' (with their automatism, finalism, inevitability), and also of strong determinism, particularly of the materialist or technological sort (which conceives of the forms of human organization as fully shaped by the external context, the environment of the social system).

In its place they propose the image of social change as the continuous structuralization and restructuralization of the arena on which people perform actions in response to the problems and challenges they face. Social change is incremental; it emerges from their social games, negotiations, bargaining, conflicts and co-operation.

Collective activities of this sort are inherently creative because of the mechanism of 'collective learning', in which individual discoveries and innovations turn into shared social practices and become embedded in the system. In consequence, the traits of the system are changed, and even the transformation of the very mechanisms of transformation may ensue. There is no necessary, inevitable or 'natural' change; the social world is fundamentally undetermined, or at least 'underdetermined'; all change is the result of human inventiveness, creation and search. The recognition of such a human, contingent genealogy of all systems, even those which are apparently most rigid and immutable, allows for the critical perspective, a realistic appraisal of 'organizational freedom', and the ability to oppose and break with existing structural conditions. Such attitudes are among the prerequisites of what the authors call 'the learning society'. The discovery that collective learning is one of the fundamental mechanisms of social self-transformation is perhaps their crucial contribution to the ongoing search for agency.

Anthony Giddens and the idea of structuration

The British enter the debate most vigorously with the work of Anthony Giddens, elaborating for the last decade his 'theory of structuration' (Giddens 1979; 1981; 1984). He distances himself from all theories typical of the 'orthodox consensus' which assume reification of social wholes and social determination of actors (treating them as 'structural or cultural dopes'). Combining such critique of functionalisms and structuralisms with positive inspiration drawn from various brands of 'interpretative sociology', he goes so far as to deny the adequacy of the notion of structure itself. Putting the emphasis on the fluid, permanently changeable, fully contingent nature of social reality, whose only true ontological substratum lies in the actions and interactions of human subjects, he proposes to turn the static notion of structure into the dynamic category of 'structuration' as the description of collective human conduct. 'Our life passes in transformation' (Giddens 1979: 3) and its core content is the constant production and reproduction of society. Therefore, 'to study the structuration of a social system is to study the ways in which that system, via the application of generative rules and resources, and in the context of unintended outcomes, is produced and reproduced in interaction' (p. 66). The rules and resources that actors use are reshaped by the process of using them: 'the structural properties of social systems are both the medium and the outcome of the practices that constitute those systems' (p. 69). This is called the theorem of the 'duality of structure'.

The ultimate motor of 'structuration' is human actors (or agents), pluralities of individuals in their everyday behaviour. One of their core properties is 'knowledgeability', or reflectiveness: 'all social actors know a great deal about the conditions and consequences of what they do in their day-to-day lives' (Giddens 1984: 281). The fine-grained analysis of the 'practical consciousness' and 'discursive consciousness' of human actors goes far beyond earlier 'interpretative sociologies', but does not lead to one-sided absolutization. Some conditions are admitted as unacknowledged, and some consequences of action as unintended. Hence, even though history is seen as a contingent product of human agency, as made of 'events of which an individual is the perpetrator, in the sense that the individual could, at any phase in a given sequence of conduct, have acted differently' (p. 9), it does not mean that the product coincides with intentions: 'Human history is created by intentional activities but is not an intended project; it persistently eludes efforts to bring it under conscious direction' (p. 27).

Another aspect of human agents is their material (corporeal, bodily, biological) constitution, and consequently their inescapable embeddedness in time and space. 'Corporeality imposes strict limitations upon the capabilities of movement and perception of the human agent' (Giddens 1984: 111). The implications of this seemingly simple constatation are shown to be enormously complex, and rarely faced by sociologists.

With Giddens, agency is finally embodied in individual human beings. It is no longer the vague tendency of the system, nor the undefined drive of change-oriented collectivities, classes, movements, but the everyday conduct of ordinary people, often quite far from any reformist intentions, that is found to shape and reshape human societies. Undoubtedly, in the richness and depth of his detailed analyses of individual actors, Giddens goes further than any of the earlier authors in unravelling the mystery of agency.

Tom Burns and the Uppsala group: rule-systems theory

The opposite side of the agency – structure equation is taken up by Tom R. Burns and Helena Flam in their 'theory of rule systems' (Burns and Flam 1987). Even though they declare their intention of 'bridging of actor and structure levels' (p. 9), their focus is not on the actors who shape, but rather on the structures being shaped, which are conceived in normative terms as complex networks of rules. The normative orientation is already revealed in the first sentence of the volume: 'Human activity – in all of its extraordinary variety and originality – is organized and governed largely by socially determined rules and rule systems' (p. viii). One wonders – remembering that the authors work in Uppsala, Sweden – if there is some unwitting echo or conscious continuation of an important indigenous development in Swedish sociology sometimes known as the 'Uppsala School', namely the normative ontology of the social world worked out by Torgny Segerstedt (1966): 'Every kind of interaction and cooperation must presuppose common norms. It is because we have common norms and symbols with common meaning that we can make predictions' (Segerstedt 1966: 12).

The main thrust of rule-systems theory is the sophisticated analysis of social rules, which make the 'deep structures of human history' (Burns and Flam 1987: ix). They are seen as clustering into three kinds of 'modules': rule systems, rule regimes and grammars. Rule systems consist of 'sets of context-dependent and time-specific rules organized for structuring and regulating social transactions, for carrying out certain activities, performing specific tasks, or interacting in socially defined forms with others' (p. 13). Rule regimes are authoritative, backed by social sanctions and networks of power and control, and hence acquire an objective, external quality in human perception. They are close to what are normally called institutions (in the normative sense of this ambiguous category). At the individual level rule systems turn into 'generative grammars for social action' used by the actors 'to structure and regulate their transactions with one another in defined situations or spheres of activity' (p. 14).

This complex and multidimensional normative network is not treated as given, in traditional Durkheimian fashion, but rather as a product of human action: 'Social rule systems are human constructions' (Burns and Flam 1987: 30); 'human agents continually form and reform social rule systems' (p. 26). They do it in three ways: creating them, interpreting them and applying them. All these activities involve large margins of freedom and are 'underdetermined'; they are also the area of social conflicts and struggles, the specific 'politics' of rule-formation. Emerging from human actions, rule systems also impinge upon human actions. In full unison with Giddens, the authors speak of a 'dual relation': social rule systems

> organize and regulate social transactions, such as exchange or political competition, in terms of who is permitted to participate, what transactions are appropriate or legitimate, where and when may transactions be carried on, how are they to be carried out, and so forth. At the same time, transactional processes are essential to the formation and reformation of rule systems, as well as to their interpretation and implementation (*pp. 10–11*).

Thus 'human agents through their actions transform the very conditions of their actions' (p. 3). There is a hint, not developed further, that the key to this 'duality' may be found in the historical dimension of human reality: 'The systems which people follow currently have been produced and developed over long stretches of time. Through their transactions social groups and communities maintain and extend rule systems into the future' (p. 29). Burns and Flam add to the theory of agency a rich analysis of the normative structure, backed with a detailed scrutiny of selected empirical cases most relevant for contemporary society, such as economic markets, bureaucracy and technological complexes.

Margaret Archer and the elaborated theory of morphogenesis

Margaret S. Archer, another British participant, enters the debate about agency in 1982, in a sort of destructive mood, with a strong criticism of Giddens's 'structuration theory' (Archer 1985 [1982]). But almost immediately, she proceeds to the constructive phase, proposing her own version of the 'theory of morphogenesis', culminating with the important volume on *Culture and Agency* (1988), and apparently continuing the project beyond this point (Archer 1989). The main virtue of the morphogenetic perspective is found in the recognition that 'the unique feature distinguishing social Systems from organic or mechanical ones is their capacity to undergo radical restructuring' (Archer 1988: xxii). Such restructuring is ultimately due to human agency: 'structural patterning is inextricably grounded in practical interaction' (Archer 1985: 59). The central notion of *morphogenesis* 'refers to the complex interchanges [between structures and actions] that produce change in a System's given form, structure or state' (1985: xxii). To study such interchanges one must adopt the principle of 'analytical dualism' rather than conceptual 'duality'. The former means that action and structure are conceived as analytically separable, because 'the emergent properties which characterize socio-cultural systems imply discontinuity between initial interactions and their product, the complex system' (1985: 61). Contrary to that, the principle of dualism commits the fallacy of 'central conflation', 'the elision of the two elements [which] withdraws any autonomy or independence from one of them, if not from both' (1988: xiii).

There are two arguments in favour of analytic duality, and against dualism. One is methodological. Presenting action and structure as constitutive of one another does not lead to propositions about their dependence, precludes 'any examination of their interplay', and hence 'their influences upon one another cannot be unravelled' (1988: 13–14). The other, and more telling, argument is ontological: it is the case that action and structure are actually distinct because 'structural conditioning', 'social interaction' and consequent 'structural elaboration' occur at different moments in time. 'Subsequent interaction will be different from earlier action because conditioned by the structural consequences of that prior action' (1985: 61). More precisely, it means that 'structure logically predates the action(s) which transform it; and . . . structural elaboration logically post-dates those actions' (p. 72). With respect to culture, 'Cultural Elaboration is the future which is forged in the present, hammered out of past inheritance by current innovation' (1988: xxiv). Thus the principle of dualism engenders the second assumption typical of the theory of morphogenesis, namely the sequential, cyclical nature of action–structure interchanges.

In her latest contribution, Archer adds a new insight, namely that 'the self-same sequence by which agency brings about social transformation is simultaneously responsible for the systematic transforming of social agency itself . . . Agency leads to structural and cultural elaboration, but is itself elaborated in the process' (1989: 2). This opens up a new field of interest: the 'morphogenesis of agency'. In this context, the traits of the agency are spelled out – reflectiveness, purposiveness, promotiveness and innovativeness – with strong reservations about its exaggerated 'knowledgeability' or omniscience (p. 5). Two types of agency, 'corporate agents' and 'primary agents', are also distinguished, and different empirical sequences of their own morphogenesis (as well as their participation in morphogenesis) described. Thus, the third principle is added to the theory of morphogenesis. Crediting the concept to me (cf. Sztompka 1987), Archer names it 'double morphogenesis', and describes as a process 'in which the elaboration of both structure and agency are conjoint products of interaction. Structure is the conditioning medium and elaborated outcome of interaction: agency is shaped and reshapes structure whilst reshaping itself in the process' (Archer 1989: 33). Perhaps the most important message of Archer's theory is the grounding of action–structure dialectics in historical time.

The agential coefficient

From Buckley to Archer the debate on agency has come full circle. In the meantime, the theory of agency, focusing on the opposition of action and structure and attempting to bridge it has been elaborated and significantly enriched. In effect social reality has started to be perceived with a sort of agential coefficient. I propose to define this concept, summarizing the legacy of the theories of the agency, as the set of six ontological assumptions: (1) that society is a process and undergoes constant change; (2) that the change is mostly endogenous, taking the form of self-transformation; (3) that the ultimate motor of change is the agential power of human individuals and social collectivities; (4) that the direction, goals and speed of change are contestable among multiple agents, and become the area of conflicts and struggles; (5) that action occurs in the context of encountered structures, which it shapes in its turn, resulting in the dual quality of structures (as both shaping and shaped), and dual quality of actors (as both producers and products); and (6) that the interchange of action and structure occurs in time, by means of alternating phases of agential creativeness and structural determination.

The evolving theory of agency became recognized as the central area of sociological theorizing. It is acknowledged not only by its co-founders who claim that 'The problem of structure and agency has rightly come to be seen as the basic issue in modern social theory' (Archer 1988: ix), but also by more detached observers who are ready to admit that it 'promises to be a significant area of theoretical advance for some time to come' (Collins 1986: 1350).

14

The new historical sociology:
concreteness and contingency

The ascent of historical sociology

In the theories of agency, and particularly its more recent formulations, the recognition of time, the processual character and historical dimension of social reality, was already clearly emerging, though it was always a residual interest, a consideration marginal to the crucial relation of action and structure. This logic is reversed in historical sociology, which takes the opposition of continuity and change as its core problem, but by solving it arrives sooner or later at a quite sophisticated notion of agency. In this sense, there is a fundamental convergence of both lines of theoretical development, but the approaches are from opposite starting-points.

The story of the gradual ascendancy of historical sociology is both long and intricate (cf. Sztompka 1986). It is widely believed that sociology was born of history. Hence, the recent revival of historical interest among sociologists is sometimes considered as a return to the roots of the discipline. Nothing can be further from the truth. Historical sociology must be treated as a critical reaction to the traditional, highly peculiar uses of history typical of the founding fathers of sociological science. It is one thing to say that sociology was born of interest in historical events or processes, but quite another to say that sociology was born of the scientific study of history. The former is certainly true; as we have frequently emphasized, the European sociology of the nineteenth century was born as an attempt to comprehend and explain the great transition of traditional into modern society, with all the complex, accompanying processes of industrialization, urbanization, accumulation of capital, pauperization, proletarianization, emergence of new states and nations, ascendancy of new social classes etc. In this sense nineteenth-century European history provided the natural problematization for early sociological thought, and Comte's formula 'Savoir, pour prévoir, pour prévenir' set its goals and rationale.

But the historical subject-matter was not approached by means of a truly historical method; by reconstructing concrete events, carefully generalizing them, and obtaining no more than strictly delimited 'laws concerning history' (Mandelbaum 1948). Just the reverse: the universal, all-embracing and supposedly all-explaining 'laws of history' were stipulated a priori, and at most illustrated with random historical evidence gathered by means of what Comte labelled 'comparative method' (which again had not much to do with the concrete, historical, systematic comparison of societies). The evolutionist or developmental schemes of Comte, Spencer, Tonnies or early Durkheim were not derived from history, nor rooted in history, but rather imposed upon history (Nisbet 1969: 164–5). They also shared certain characteristic assumptions: they treated history mechanistically as an autonomous domain, a 'reality *sui generis*' from which human actors were strangely absent, and they treated the direction of history as predetermined, fatalistic, independent of human efforts. Such abstract formulae were the offspring of 'historiosophy' rather than historiography. Evolutionism and developmentalism did not in the least contribute to the emergence of a truly historical perspective. Just the opposite: instead of bringing sociology closer to history, it represented in fact the early form of ahistorism. We may call it, a little paradoxically, a 'historiosophical ahistorism'.

Even though dominant, this tendency was by no means exclusive. The nineteenth century may pride itself on producing also some exemplars of truly historical sociology, firmly rooted in rich historical materials, historically limited in validity and recognizing the role of human actors – individual and collective – as the ultimate creators of the changing social world. Such theories reject mechanistic and fatalistic assumptions, the reification of social processes, and restore man as a real historical subject. Three names among the early masters of sociology seem to represent this early, authentic historism: Karl Marx (at least in the earlier, historically focused period of his work), Alexis de Tocqueville (to the extent that he may be considered as a sociologist and not just a historian in the strict sense), and, most fully and unambiguously, Max Weber.

It is with the last that historical sociology came of age. All of Weber's immense scholarship is firmly rooted in vast historical knowledge, reaching from ancient civilizations to the birth of industrial capitalism. The application of a historical perspective led Weber to reject ahistorical, mechanistic 'laws of history' or developmental schemes, and to focus instead on concrete historical transitions, thresholds between epochs, eras and periods, and especially on the birth of capitalism in western Europe. It also implied the rejection of mechanistic or fatalistic interpretations of the historical process, and gave human agents, their motivations, intentions and actions, the crucial role in producing social, economic and political structures, even on the largest macroscale. A contemporary commentator has good reason to describe Weber as 'the most historically minded of the great sociologists' (Burke 1980: 20). The recent rebirth of historical sociology must be linked with the heritage of Marx, Tocqueville and particularly Weber, with their authentic historical work, rather than with the philosophical, a priori developmental schemes of Comte, Spencer, Tönnies or Durkheim.

Before such a rebirth occurred, sociology witnessed a long eclipse of the historical perspective. This was partly due to the second birth of sociological thought that had occurred in the United States at the turn of the century. American sociology had radically different roots from the European one. First of all, it was born in a different society, one poor in historical traditions, existing from its very beginning within a single socio-economic system of industrial capitalism, and thus unaware of the birth-pangs of transition from traditional to modern society, but at the same time exceptionally complex in its racial, ethnic and class composition, ridden with multiple cleavages, contradictions and conflicts, permeated with all brands of deviance and social pathology. The most pressing issue was, therefore, to ameliorate the present, existing order, rather than to establish a new social formation. American sociologists focused on the safeguarding of the smooth operation of the social system, eradicating crime and social disorganization, integrating local communities, improving the effectiveness of institutions, raising the productivity of labour and efficiency of managment. The solutions to such problems were sought in concrete empirical diagnoses, mainly at the micro-sociological level (Antonio and Piran 1978: 1–2).

These melioristic, presentist, empirical and micro-sociological concerns led American sociologists to different intellectual sources, to the tradition of psychology rather than historiosophy. The typical indigenous theoretical orientations of American sociology – pragmatism, social behaviourism, symbolic interactionism, and later exchange theory – were clearly inspired by a psychological orientation. If the questions relating to the operation of the whole society on the macro-scale had to be faced, Americans were ready to adopt the tradition of British functional anthropology of Malinowski and Radcliffe-Brown, who viewed society as a self-regulating, equilibrated, internally harmonious system (cf. Sztompka 1974). As early as the 1940s the school of structural functionalism was born and soon acquired a dominance in American sociology which it held for the next thirty years. Both the micro and the macro theoretical traditions typical of American sociology were thus abstracting from the historical dimension of social reality. Together with the narrow empiricism and pragmatic attitude of uncritical research workers, they were responsible for the ahistorical bias of American sociology. I shall refer to this brand of ahistorism, born and bred in the United States but spreading all over the world, as 'presentist ahistorism'.

Thus as an effect of the double genealogy of sociological science, European and American, an ahistorical orientation was to reign in the discipline for the major part of the twentieth century. The heritage of the first, European origins of sociology is to be found in historiosophical ahistorism – sociology above history – well represented by various brands of evolutionism, neo-evolutionism, theories of economic growth, models of modernization, or fatalistic and deterministic versions of neo-Marxism. The heritage of the second, American origins of sociology is to be found in presentist ahistorism – sociology without history, well represented by narrow empiricism, as well as by theories unabashedly ignoring the dimension of historical time.

In the epoch of reigning ahistorism, the historical perspective, though pushed to the margin, does not disappear completely. There are two bridges linking the tradition of Marx, Tocqueville and Weber with modern sociology. One is the rich stream of 'activist Marxism': the works of Gramsci, Lukács, the

Frankfurt School, the New Left etc. But this trend was mainly influential in philosophy and did not immediately affect the practice of sociology, at that time still programmatically anti-philosophical. Thus another intellectual phenomenon seems of greater importance. It is the case of those 'odd, if honored, grand older men of the discipline' (Skockpol 1984: 357), who occasionally take up the roles of historians, studying some limited, concrete fragment of the past, but, being trained as sociologists, are ready to apply to such studies their sociological, conceptual and theoretical frameworks. To give just a few examples: R. K. Merton traces the origins of experimental science in seventeenth-century England (1970); N. J. Smelser describes the evolution of the cotton industry in Britain at the threshold of the modern era (1959); S. N. Eisenstadt analyses the political systems of ancient, centralized empires (1963); S. M. Lipset reconstructs the historical geneaology of the American nation (1967). Even if exceptional, such works reach a wide audience and prepare the ground for the full renaissance of the historical perspective in sociology that comes about only in the 1970s and 1980s.

Even at the end of the 1950s strong criticism was already being directed against narrow empiricism and presentism. This may be called the first crisis of post-war sociology. Arguing for the necessity of theory, some authors formulate a straightforward demand for the restoration of the historical perspective. For C. Wright Mills, for example, it is a prerequisite for the true 'sociological imagination': 'Every social science – or better, every well considered social study – requires a historical scope of conception and a full use of historical material' (Mills 1959: 145). In the 1960s and 1970s the next challenge is directed against the functional 'grand theory', mainly on the ground that it implies a utopian, basically inadequate, image of society. Thus the second crisis of sociology ensues. The model of integration, consensus and stability is reshaped in the hands of conflict theorists into the model of conflict, coercion and change (Dahrendorf 1959; 1968; Rex 1969). The emphasis moves from the mechanistic self-regulation of the system towards the purposeful actions of individuals, groups, collectivities, social movements, social masses treated as the causal agencies, or at least the carriers of social change. The formula of sociology without history (or presentist ahistorism) is slowly undermined. Criticism extends as well to the formula of sociology above history, or historiosophical ahistorism. We have analysed in chapter 12 how the fatalistic, mechanistic, prophetic interpretation of Marxism is challenged by Popper (1950; 1964), and also how the metaphor of growth, underlying all evolutionist and neo-evolutionist theories and understood as progressive structural differentiation, is subjected to a devastating critique by Nisbet (1969; 1970) and Tilly (1984).

The new historism

On the background of these deep changes in contemporary sociology, the 'new historism' or 'historical sociology' emerges as a separate theoretical and methodological orientation. Even though in its revived form still pretty young, it has already generated significant contributions, both concrete and general. On the substantive, concrete side, one may point to those works which – following the path of Marx, Tocqueville and Weber, and later of Merton, Smelser, Eisenstadt and others – take up concrete time-bound and localized historical problems and subject them to generalizing, sociological analysis. The most common procedure is the inductive and comparative study of selected historical cases, seeking for the common mechanism of social processes. For example Barrington Moore (1966) traces the mechanisms of peasant rebellions and bourgeois revolutions in France, the United States, China and Japan, searching for the factors determining various scenarios of political development in the post-feudal area, democratic, fascist or communist. Charles Tilly studies the cases of social movements and collective protest in the 're-bellious century' of 1830–1930, particularly in France, England and Italy, building on that basis an original theory of collective action (Tilly et al. 1975, Tilly 1978). Theda Skockpol (1979) produces a comparative account of the French, Russian and Chinese revolutions, suggesting a common political mechanism operating in all cases. Michael Mann (1986) produces a comprehensive account of the sources and origins of power in human societies, from Neolithic times, through ancient Near East civilizations, the classical Mediterranean age, and medieval Europe, up to the industrial revolution in England, and carries this narrative on to the contemporary epoch, building a generalized model and theory of power on the basis of such extensive historical material. For our purposes, however, we have to focus on another legacy of historical sociology: general philosophical, metatheoretical and theoretical considerations throwing a new light on the very nature of social reality. I will discuss only those contributions which come from sociologists. The tendency towards reconciliation or integration of sociology and history originated also in theoretical history, especially in the French *Annales* School (e.g. Braudel 1980) and various branches of 'social history'. Historians of this orientation often arrive at an ontological image of society similar to that of the historical sociologists. An emphasis on the processual, constructed, historical nature of society is also found in several contemporary philosophers (e.g. Bhaskar 1986).

Norbert Elias and figurationist sociology

The birth of modern historical sociology as more than historically rooted research, but also as a distinct theoretical perspective on the social world, may be linked with the discovery and astonishing career of the long-ignored work of Norbert Elias. He is one of the first historical sociologists to mount a persistent attack on 'the retreat of sociologists into the present' (Elias 1987: 223), which was so typical of the 'orthodox consensus' at the level of theory, as well as their uncritical fact-finding at the level of empirical research. The antidote to that fallacy of abstracting from the diachronic and dynamic constitution of human society is found in the 'processual perspective', the recognition that 'the immediate present into which sociologists are retreating . . . constitutes just one small momentary phase within the vast stream of humanity's development, which, coming from the past, debouches into the present and thrusts ahead toward possible futures' (Elias 1987: 224). Societies are placed squarely in historical time: 'every present society has grown out of earlier societies and points beyond itself to a diversity of possible futures' (p. 226). This process is mostly unplanned, even though it houses shorter or longer episodes of planned, intentional social change. But there is no automatism or inevitable quality of change; the process is fully contingent, activated by human beings in their various complex interrelationships, interdependencies to which Elias gives the name 'figurations'. Their nodal points may be individual actors, but also groups and even states. Figurations form a 'flexible lattice-work of tensions' (Elias 1978: 130), 'a fluctuating tensile equilibrium, a balance of power moving to and from, inclining first to one side and then to the other' (1978: 131). Such webs or networks of interhuman relations with power as the main bond (linking people but also opposing them, generating their co-operation but also conflicts) are inherently fluid, unstable, undergoing all kinds of permutations. They are moving patterns or, if you will, patterns of movement, of longer or shorter duration. People in their 'figurations' make up the sole agency of historical change:

> Plans and actions, the emotional and rational impulses of individual people, constantly interweave in a friendly or hostile way. This basic tissue resulting from many single plans and actions of men can give rise to changes and patterns that no individual person has planned or created. From this interdependence of people arises an order sui generis, an order more compelling and stronger than the will and reason of the individual people composing it. It is this order of interweaving human impulses and strivings, this social order, which determines the course of historical change. (*Elias 1982: 230–1*)

On the other hand, once the figurations are established they feedback on the actions: 'individuals constitute historical figurations and are historically constituted by them' (Abrams 1982: 250). Thus, the dilemma of continuity and transformation is resolved in this 'immanent order of change' (Arnason 1987: 193), and as a by-product the notion of figurations bridges the action–structure gap. As was noticed by a contemporary commentator, 'Throughout his work runs a strong tendency to get beyond the customary polarities in thought, and to avoid any position identified with these polarities' (Goudsblom 1987: 332). In this sense Elias's project of historical sociology is synthetic *par excellence*.

Philip Abrams's project of 'historical sociology'

The most radical case for historical sociology was put forward in 1982 by Philip Abrams. He argues for the complete integration of sociology and history, and claims that the only serious way in which sociology can be done is historical. That is so for ontological reasons, because both sociologists and historians deal with the same 'maddeningly non-mechanical machine' (Abrams 1982: xiii), human society. To grasp it, both static and traditional developmental approaches, proposing 'laws and stages of evolution and development with a necessity of their own' (p. 8), are totally inadequate. 'In my understanding of history and sociology', he declares, 'there can be no relationship between them because, in terms of their fundamental preoccupations, history and sociology are the same thing. Both seek to understand the puzzle of human agency and both seek to do so in terms of the process of social structuring' (p. x).

The idea of a process helps to bridge both the traditional oppositions, of statics and dynamics, as well as of structure and action: 'The diachrony–synchrony distinction is absurd. Sociology must be concerned with eventuation, because that is how structuring happens' (Abrams 1982: x), and the 'sociology of process' provides 'an alternative to our tired and inadequate sociologies of action and system (p. xv), because 'process is the link between action and structure' (p. 3). Therefore 'society must be understood as a process constructed historically by individuals who are constructed historically by society' (p. 227). This process is endless, sequential and cumulative; at each stage the actions are undertaken under given conditions (possibilities) produced in the past, and in turn they reshape the circumstances for the future. This 'continuous process of construction is the focal concern of social analysis' (p. 16).

The process is made up of historical events: 'An event is a moment of becoming at which action and structure meet' (Abrams 1982: 192). The major turns of the process are effected by great events: 'The great events make decisive conjunctions of action and structure; they are transparent moments of structuring at which human agency encounters social possibility and can be seen clearly as simultaneously determined and determining' (p. 199).

The ultimate moving force of history is therefore the dialectics of human agency, and the course of history is set by the dialectics of structuring.

> The problem of agency is the problem of finding a way of accounting for human experience which requires simultaneously and in equal measure that history and society are made by constant and more or less purposeful individual action and that individual action, however purposeful is made by history and society. How do we, as active subjects make a world of objects which then, as it were, become subjects making us their objects? (*Abrams 1982: xiii*)

This is a core riddle setting the research programme for both sociology and history, as well as their offspring, historical sociology.

Charles Tilly: the meeting of sociology and history

A kind of personal synthesis of sociology and history is achieved by Charles Tilly, a prolific social historian and historical sociologist at the same time.

Apart from his rich substantive contributions, he makes some general programmatic statements about the historical nature of social reality and the significance of historical angle in sociological studies. The emphasis on the cumulative process is clearly there: 'As a phenomenon, history is the cumulative effect of past events on events of the present' (Tilly 1981: 12). Any current situation is not a necessary phase in a predetermined developmental sequence, but rather 'the outcome of a long, slow, historically specific process' (p. 39). At the same time, it provides a set of possibilities for the continuation of the process: 'Every structure or process constitutes a series of choice points. Outcomes at a given point in time constrain possible outcomes at later points in time' (1984: 14). The actual historical process is pluralistic and differentiated, combining various overlapping, conflicting complementary and parallel processes: 'There is no such thing as social change in general. Many large-scale processes of change exist; urbanization, industrialization, proletarianization, population growth, capitalization, bureaucratization all occur in definable, coherent ways. Social change does not' (1984: 33). Of course some processes may acquire leading importance in concrete historical periods, overshadowing the impact of others: 'Over the last few hundred years, the growth of national states and the development of capitalism in property and production have dominated the changes occurring in increasing parts of the world' (p. 49). But all this is contingent, and never inevitable.

Similarly, his image of society departs from any reified 'facticity'. Instead he adopts a sort of field theory, perceiving social reality not as a system but rather as a fluid, changing network of 'multiple social relationships, some quite localized, and some worldwide in scale' (Tilly 1984: 25). Thus the constitution of society and the flow of history are ultimately dependent on concrete human actions. Among those, Tilly chooses to focus on the everyday behaviour of ordinary people ('populist history' rather than 'elitist history') and particularly their collective actions, 'the ways that people act together in pursuit of shared interests' (1978: 5). These include, among others, 'contentious gatherings', collective violence, social movements and revolutions.

The message of Tilly's substantive and programmatic work is straightforward: sociology should become 'historically grounded' (1981: 12, 46), i.e. should look at societies 'comparatively over substantial blocks of space and time, in order to see whence we have come, where we are going, and what real alternatives to our present condition exist' (1984: 11). Such studies must be 'assuming that the time and place in which a structure or process appears makes a difference to its character, that the sequence in which similar events occur has a substantial impact on their outcomes' (p. 79).

Christopher Lloyd and 'structurism'

Rich explication of a position labelled as 'structurism' has been provided by Christopher Lloyd (1988). The intention that guides his work is clearly synthetic: 'The problem . . . is to bridge the subjective/objective and freedom/determinism gaps in order to show how people do indeed make their own history but also how particular circumstances, which are the result of people having made history in the past, condition their history-making' (Lloyd 1988: 301). The key to that puzzle is the processual nature of society: 'drawing a line between past and present seems to be entirely arbitrary and pointless. The "present" is always becoming the "past" and processes continually exist in both directions' (p. 20). Hence, 'social science must have as its basic aim the explanation of social transformation' (p. 10). This implies the necessity of historical perspective: 'Since structures are always changing they should always be studied in a historical mode' (p. 164).

Within the process, there is the mutual, dialectic interplay of structures and actions: 'Action is explainable by its structural and psychological imperatives and constraints, and structure and its history are explainable as the intended and unintended consequences of individual action and patterned mass behavior over time' (Lloyd 1988: 10). The moving force of this dialectics and the ensuing historical process is human agency, located 'within the conscious human agent, albeit an agent who always acts within a structural social, cultural, and geographical environment' (p. 192). Lloyd stresses: 'Individual and collective human action is the fundamental agent of history' (p. 37). 'Agential persons' are free within certain bounds of inherited choices, and they possess power to effect some, limited changes in the world. They do it both intentionally, and – more often – unintentionally, producing unintended and even unrecognized structural results.

Lloyd brings together these assumptions in the following account of his position:

> A structurist conception sees society as an ordered, independent but loosely integrated, constantly changing set of relations, rules, and roles that holds a collectivity of individual persons together. It transcends and has an existence independent of any individual but not all (or a significant proportion) of those individuals . . . In order to go on existing, it must be collectively reproduced by those individuals and it has a strong potential to be transformed into a different structure by their actions. (*pp. 16–17*).

The historical coefficient

As a result of the evolving emphasis on the historical dimension, social reality is perceived ever more often with a sort of 'historical coefficient'. I propose to use this name for a set of six ontological assumptions emerging as a common foundation of historical sociology.

1   It is assumed that social reality is not a steady state but, rather, a dynamic process. It occurs rather than exists, it consists of events rather than objects. Time is an immanent, internal factor of social life. What happens,

how it happens, why it happens, what results it brings about – all are taken to depend essentially on the time when it happens, the location in the processual sequence, the place in the rhythm of events characteristic for a given process. Not only the properties and traits of phenomena, but their regularities ('laws') are treated as time-dependent; in various phases of the process different mechanisms of events are held to obtain.

2   It is claimed that social change is a confluence of multiple processes with various vectors, partly overlapping, partly convergent and partly divergent, mutually supportive or destructive. The state of society is always a concrete cross-point of those differentiated, heterogeneous and multidirectional processes.

3   Society itself, undergoing change, is not perceived as an entity, object or system, but rather as a fluid network of relations, pervaded with tension as well as harmony, conflict as well as co-operation.

4   The sequence of events within each of the social processes is treated as cumulative. Each phase of the process is seen as an accumulated outcome, effect, crystallization, point of arrival of all preceding phases, and at the same time the germ, embedded potential, point of departure for the succeeding process. At each historical moment there opens up a determinate field of oportunities, possibilities, options for the future course of the process, significantly delimited by the whole past course of the process.

5   The social process is seen as constructed, created by human agents, individual or collective, through their actions. Behind every phase of the social process there are some people, collectivities, groups, social movements, associations etc. whose actions have brought it about. Every phase of the social process provides a pool of opportunities, resources, facilities – one is tenpted to say 'raw materials' – for the people taking up the construction of social reality.

6   It is recognized that people do not construct society 'as they please', but only in given structural conditions inherited from the past, i.e. constructed for them by their predecessors, in their turn similarly structurally constrained. It follows that there is a dialectics of actions and structures, in which actions are partly determined by earlier structures, and later structures are produced by earlier actions.

Of course any general acceptance of such a standpoint is still far away, and perhaps not easy to attain. But in the pluralist panorama of contemporary sociology, historical orientation is clearly in the ascendant. The scope and rapidity of this paradigmatic shift may be judged by comparing some opinions. In 1968 K. Erikson despaired: 'Sociology in the US continues to lack historical focus . . . Most of what passes for sociological research in this country is not informed by much in the way of a historical perspective' (Erikson 1971: 61). Only twelve years later K. Burke declared, 'Historical sociology is now a stream' (Burke 1980: 28). A year later C. Tilly noted: 'Some of America's best sociological talent is going into historical studies (Tilly 1981: 43), and in 1984 T. Skockpol proclaimed 'a golden period of historical sociology' and concluded: 'By now . . . a stream of historical sociology has deepened into a river and spread out into eddies running through all parts of the sociological enterprise' (1984: xii, 356).

In the image of social reality as endowed with 'historical coefficient', the old dichotomies of continuity and change, statics and dynamics, synchrony and diachrony, are finally overcome. The historical process is seen as agential accomplishment, the accumulated effect of productive and reproductive efforts of human actors, undertaken in the structural conditions shaped by earlier generations. As we have seen, the notion of human agency as the ultimate motor of the process, appears quite explicitly in the works of historical sociologists. Even though for them it is of residual interest, overshadowed by the riddle of stability and transformation, *de facto* their work also contributes to bridging the gap between action and structure.

The historical coefficient and the agential coefficient prove to be two complementary or even coextensive characterizations of social reality. The legacy of the theory of the agency converges with the inheritance of historical sociology in outlining the contours of the new vision of the social world.

15

Social becoming: the essence of historical change

Levels of social reality

In this chapter I wish to present an outline of my own theoretical approach, which I develop in more detail elsewhere (Sztompka 1991b). This is an attempt to synthesize and further elaborate the main ideas of theories of agency and modern historical sociology (see chapters 13 and 14 above).

Let us start by distinguishing two levels of social reality: the level of individualities and the level of totalities. The former is made up of people, as individuals or as members of concrete collectivities (groups, associations, communities, movements etc.). The latter is made up of abstract social wholes of a superindividual sort, representing social reality *sui generis* (societies, cultures, civilizations, socio-economic formations, social systems etc.). The social wholes are intepreted neither as mere congeries nor as metaphysical entities, but as structures; and social individuals are seen neither as passive objects nor fully autonomous subjects, but as bounded agents.

Now a second distinction may be added. It has to do with two modes of existence of social reality; the mode of potentialities and the mode of actualities. We refer to the former when speaking of inherent tendencies, germs or seeds of the future, capacities, abilities, 'powers' etc. We refer to the latter when speaking of processes, transformations, development, conduct, activities etc.

Both modes can be taken by each of the major components of the social world. Structures may be treated as potentialities actualizing themselves (unfolding) in operation; and agents as potentialities actualizing themselves (mobilizing) in action. Thus, by cross-cutting the two dichotomies (of levels and of modes), we arrive at four concepts making the cornerstones of our model: structures and agents, operations and actions.

Let us consider the relations between the cells of this fourfold structure (table 15.1). In the vertical dimension we postulate the complementary relations of emergence and autonomy. Structures are seen as emergent with respect to agents; even though they embrace agents, they possess their own, specific properties and regularities. They are inter-agential networks, not reducible to the sum of agents. But agents are also not reducible to their structural location; they possess some measure of autonomy, integrity, relative

Table 15.1

	Potentiality	*Actuality*
Totality	Structure	Operation
Individuality	Agent	Action

freedom to choose and decide. They are self-contained entities, with specific properties and regularities, and not only nodal points of structures.

Similarly, the operation of structures (functioning of society) must be treated as emergent with respect to actions taken by agents. Even though actions make the ultimate stuff of societal operation, the latter is not reducible to the former; combining numerous interrelated actions it acquires its own, specific momentum, pattern or sequential logic. It is more than the sum of actions. We defined structures as static emergents with respect to agents, even though without agents there would be no structures. In a parallel fashion, operation is a dynamic emergent with respect to actions, even though without actions there would be no operation. As Blau puts it: 'Although complex social systems have their foundation in simpler ones, they have their own dynamics with emergent properties' (1964: 20). Those properties may be analytically considered at their own level, in abstraction from the fact that the ultimate substratum of societal operation is made of social actions.

I would suggest three forms of such independent dynamics of structures. Thus one may observe a 'principle of inertia': it is usually more likely that the functioning will continue in the same fashion, rather than taking a radical turn (e.g. in the countries of 'real socialism', raising prices and taxes was for a long time a more typical response to economic shortages than switching from a planned to a market-oriented economy; changing leaders was much more common than replacing totalitarianism with democracy; building another coal mine was a standard investment decision, rather than turning to nuclear energy etc.). One may also observe a 'principle of momentum' (or continuation): when a certain phase or stage of operation is reached, it is likely to proceed to the next stage, rather than to stop or turn back. Schematically: if stage A is reached, then stage B is likely to follow (e.g. if a policy is adopted it tends to continue at least for some time; if investments are made in some area of economy, they engender further related investments; if disorganization appears in some domain of social life, it tends to widen and engulf other domains; if people's consumption needs are already satisfied to some extent it is hard to lower the level of need-satisfaction). Finally, there is also a 'principle of sequence': phases of the operation are patterned, and often cannot be omitted. There are routines of all sorts in social life, which have to be followed in regular sequence to be effective (e.g. the economy cannot be modernized without educating the labour force first; consumption patterns cannot be changed, without producing or importing new, original products).

These are only hypothetical illustrations, intended to show that emergent structures may be seen as unfolding in emergent fashion according to their own principles.

Conversely, actions are not mere embodiments of societal functioning fully embedded in the momentum of operation. They have some measure of autonomy, relative independence of the dynamic social context in which they participate. At least a part of what agents actually do may not fit the actual mode of social functioning; they may 'go against the current', act in anachronistic ways, or anticipate the future by exhibiting imagination, originality or innovativeness.

If we turn to the horizontal dimension of our fourfold table, the relation between agents and actions is quite intuitive. It is covered by the concept of 'mobilization'. Agents mobilize their potential capacities, abilities, needs, attitudes, dispositions in taking actions of various sorts. They eat when hungry, quarrel when angry, compose symphonies when talented, make revolutions when 'relatively deprived', wage wars when armed etc. Of course there are multiple factors which decide whether they actually do all this or abstain from action, keeping their potentialities latent. Some of the intermediate variables entering the causal nexus between agential potentialities and their manifestation in action will be discussed in the next chapter, when the model will be operationalized.

Much less obvious is the horizontal relation at the upper level, between structures and their functioning (operation). It will be grasped by the concept of 'unfolding'. Structures unfold in operation, discharge their inherent potentialities, tendencies, dispositions in functioning. For example, they are apt to break down and change when pervaded with contradictions, tensions or strains; conversely, they are likely to operate smoothly when internally homogeneous and harmonious. They are likely to produce stagnation when undifferentiated and centralized, whereas they are likely to develop when pluralistic and decentralized. Of course there are several intervening variables which decide whether the potentialities of structures will actually unfold or not. The tentative consideration of these has to be put off till later chapters. At the moment the simple examples given are intended only to prove the general point, that actualization of structures may be analytically conceived as separate from the actualization of agents, even though in reality both are intimately linked.

The middle level: agency and praxis

Having defined the level of structures (in their operation) and the level of agents (in their action) as distinct and separate, we must attempt now to bring them together, to conceptualize their linkage. This is a crucial move in the construction of our model. It is here, at the 'interface' (Archer 1988: xviii) between structures and agents, operations and actions, that the riddle of social becoming must be traced.

Several authors have pushed the search in this direction by emphasizing 'duality of structures' (and its logical corollary, duality of agents) or, more generally, 'analytical dualism' of social reality. For Giddens: 'duality of structure . . . expresses the mutual dependence of structure and agency' (1979: 69). Thus 'the constitution of agents and structures are not two independently given sets of phenomena, a dualism, but represent a duality. According to the notion of the duality of structure, the structural properties of social systems are both medium and outcome of the practices they recursively organize' (1984: 25). The 'duality of agents' could be proposed as a complementary principle, meaning that the properties of agents are both products of structures and resources for structure-building. A similar suggestion is made by Roy Bhaskar: 'If society is the condition of our agency, human agency is equally a condition for society, which, in its continuity, it continually reproduces and transforms. On this model, then, society is at once the ever-present condition and the continually reproduced outcome of human agency: this is the duality of structure' (1986: 123).

Margaret Archer challenges 'duality of structure' and opts for 'analytical dualism': 'the attempt to conceptualize how certain properties of the "parts" and certain properties of the "people" actually combine at the interface' (1988: xviii). She proposes to examine their interaction, their mutual interplay, rather than conflating them as 'tightly constitutive of one another' (p. xiii), because 'the whole point of analytical dualism is to be able to investigate the relations between them' (p. 141). I will not enter this debate because, utilizing the insights of both parties, I will propose a slightly different conceptualization, a third solution.

In the theory of 'social becoming', the levels of structure in operation and agents in actions will be treated neither as analytically separable nor mutually reducible. Instead the third, intermediate level will be postulated, and claimed to represent the only true substance of social reality, a specific social fabric. If we think of any empirical event or phenomenon in a society, anything that is actually happening, is it not always, without exception, a fusion of structures and agents, of operation and action? Show me an agent who is not enmeshed in some structure, a structure which exists apart from some individuals, an action which is not participating in societal operation, a societal operation not resolving into action. There are no structureless agents, and there are no agentless structures. But at the same time structures do not melt away in agents, and agents are not melted into structures.

I have always been struck by the wisdom of the sentence attributed to Charles H. Cooley: 'Self and society are twin-born' (in Fletcher 1971, vol. 2: 486), and by the earlier claim by Marx: 'Circumstances make men in the same measure that men make circumstances' (in McLellan 1971: 129). Why should we not take seriously the full implications of these insights? And the full implications are that there is no agential reality, nor structural reality *per se*. Neither is there any conceivable mode of real interaction between those two realities, between agents and structures, treated separately. Because in fact, they are fused together in one human-social world, one agential-cum-structural fabric of society. It is not the case that separate agents and structures interact producing some effects. Rather, the agential-structural reality in its internal, immanent unity appears in various permutations, various mixes of agential and structural ingredients, making up social events. The ultimate stuff, the real components of which society is made, is events, neither individual acts nor 'social facts', but their intimate, concrete fusions. Following our analogy, a similar solution may be offered to the 'mind–body' problem: the mind and body are completely fused in each person and in actions undertaken by human individuals. Human, individual reality consists of personal events (actions) in which various admixtures of those inseparable ingredients manifest themselves.

Let us think about this mediating, third level, placed between the level of totalities and the level of individualities, in terms of our distinction of two modes of existence: potentialities and actualities. Taking the hint from Marx, Gramsci and Lukács, we shall call the actual manifestations of the social fabric, the ongoing social events, by the term 'praxis'. Praxis is where operation and action meet; a dialectical synthesis of what is going on in a society and what people are doing. It represents the confluence of operating structures and acting agents, the combined product of the momentum of operation (at the level of totalities) and the course of actions undertaken by societal members (at the level of individualities). In other words, it is doubly conditioned (constrained and facilitated): from above, by the phase of functioning reached by wider society; and from below, by the conduct of individuals and their groups. But it is not reducible to either; with respect to both levels, of individualities and totalities, it is a new, emergent quality. In this way the concept of praxis is anchored vertically to two core concepts of our model referring to actualities: operation and action.

Now, remaining at this intermediate level, let us employ a sort of backward reasoning. If 'praxis' is the actuality, the manifestation of social fabric, then there must be something which is actualized, or manifested; the inherent potentiality for praxis, or, more precisely, a set of capacities, dispositions, tendencies immanent in the social fabric and allowing praxis to emerge. The concept of agency is proposed as correlative to praxis, located at the same level but referring to a different mode of existence, namely bearing upon the potentiality for praxis. I shall represent this phase of our reasoning in figure 15.1.

'Agency' so conceived is an attributive notion; it summarizes certain properties of the social fabric, this 'really real reality' of the social world. It is where structures (capacities for operation) and agents (capacities for action) meet; it is a synthetic product, a fusion of structural circumstances and agential endowment. As such, it is doubly conditioned: from above by the balance of constraints and limitations, but also by the resources and facilities provided by existing structures; and from below by the abilities, talents, skills, knowledge, attitudes of societal members and the organizational forms in which they are pooled together in collectivities, groups, social movements etc. But it is not

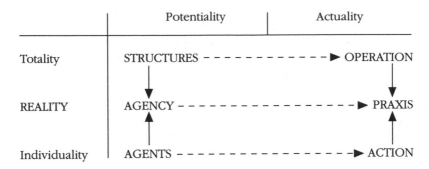

Figure 15.1   Dimensions and levels of a social process.

reducible to either; with respect to both levels (of totalities and individualities) it makes up a new, emergent quality.

So far we have anchored the concept of agency vertically, in two other core concepts of our model referring to potentialities: structures and agents. But it must also link itself horizontally, with the concept of praxis. As a potentiality, agency is actualized in praxis, manifested in social events. This horizontal link between agency and praxis will be covered by the term 'eventuation'. It is, again, a confluence of actualizations going on at other levels; a fusion of the unfolding of structures and the mobilization of agents. Thus it is conditioned from above and from below, but is not reducible to either of the processes, and represents a new, emergent quality. Like those constitutive processes, it is also contingent; eventuation is only possible, sometimes probable, but never necessary. Agency may be actualized in various measures; it may also remain latent or dormant.

Three sequences linking potentialities and actualities, namely structures-unfolding-in-operation, agents-mobilizing-in-action and the synthetic process of agency-eventuating-in-praxis, have been treated as linear, working in one direction only. We must correct this by recalling the ideas of 'duality of structure' and 'duality of agents'. Piaget focuses on the level of totalities, writing of 'the constant duality, or bipolarity, of always being simultaneously structuring and structured' (1971: 10). Plamenatz focuses on the level of individualities, saying of an agent: 'he is the product of his own activities . . . what he has done and its effects upon him' (1975: 76). As I read them, those formulations convey an important insight, concerning the feedbacks that must be included in the model. The first refers to the self-modifying propensity of structures; they are reshaped by their own operation. We may speak of the process of 'structure-building'. The second refers to the self-modifying propensity of agents; they are reshaped by their own action. We may speak of the 'moulding of agents'. I have referred to this process in a more concrete context as 'double morphogenesis' (Sztompka 1989: 127). Margaret Archer (1989) calls it the 'morphogenesis of the agency'.

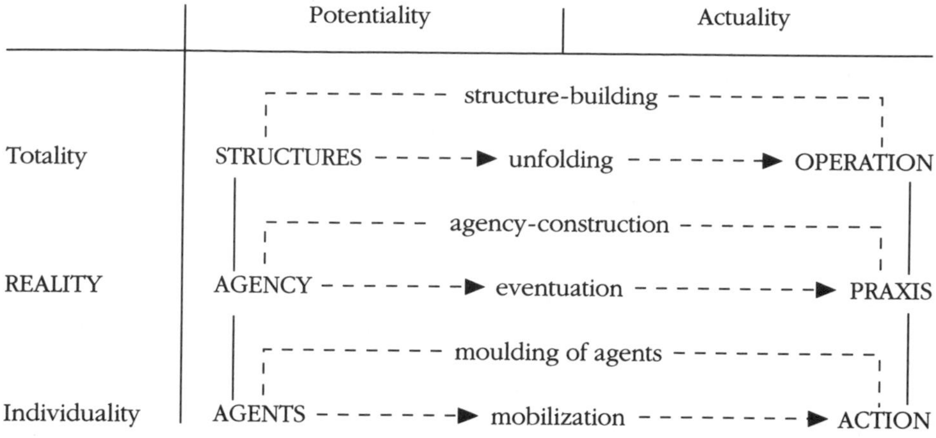

	Potentiality	Actuality

```
              r - - - - - - - - structure-building - - - - - - - - - ,
              ¦                                                       ¦
Totality      STRUCTURES - - - - -►  unfolding  - - - - - - ►  OPERATION
              ¦                                                       ¦
              ¦    r - - - - - - - - agency-construction - - - - - - - - -
              ¦    ¦                                                  ¦
REALITY       AGENCY - - - - - - ►  eventuation  - - - - - - - ►  PRAXIS
              ¦    ¦                                                  ¦
              ¦    ¦  r - - - - - - - - moulding of agents - - - - - - - - -,
              ¦    ¦  ¦                                                ¦
Individuality AGENTS - - - - - - ►  mobilization  - - - - - - - ►  ACTION
```

Figure 15.2 Agency and praxis in operation.

Applying the same idea, *mutatis mutandis*, to the mediating, third level of agential-structural reality, we may say that agency is significantly reshaped by praxis. We may speak of 'agency-construction'. To bring this point home, I shall allow those three feedbacks into our model, indicating them by reversed arrows. But the questions 'How can the potentialities be influenced by their own actualizations?' 'How does the self-generative mechanism really operate?' must be suspended. They have to await the moment when the dimension of time is introduced into the model. Then the misleading image of causation working backwards will disappear.

New categories of agency and praxis, as well as the addition of linking processes and feedbacks at all levels, have considerably enriched the model of social becoming. We may summarize the present stage of conceptual elaboration by means of an extended diagram (figure 15.2).

Environments: nature and consciousness

The model of social becoming, as constructed so far, hangs in the vacuum. Our next step must consist in supplying it with a wider context. Social becoming must be placed in the environment. I postulate two kinds of environments. The first is quite intuitive: it is nature. The second is less so: it is consciousness. Contrary to appearances there is a striking similarity between the two, as concerns their general status *vis-à-vis* human actions and societal operation. Because humans are natural corporeal beings, living in space and time, utilizing natural resources, affecting natural conditions etc., nature is an inescapable 'container' in which social life is flowing. People cannot exist outside it. Hence it is the first necessary environment of the social world. But humans are also thinking beings, utilizing symbols, communicating with others, formulating beliefs etc. They are always immersed in the milieu of ideas, their own, as well as those of their contemporaries and even their predecessors. Again people are not even conceivable outside that milieu. Hence consciousness can be treated as the second necessary environment of human society. In sum, the given, inevitable duality of the human constitution – as natural objects and conscious subjects at the same time – entails the duality of environments which surround human praxis.

Let us start from the more obvious side, from the natural environment. It appears in two guises: as the external natural conditions in which agents and structures act and operate, and as the internal constitutive traits of individuals, who are the ultimate substratum of society. The former may be illustrated by climate, topography, ecology, geology etc. These are clearly relevant to human actions; they are also relevant to the operation of structures. Some networks of interrelations are enabled, even enforced, and others precluded by natural conditions. Think of migration and trade routes, communication networks or settlement patterns in mountainous areas as opposed to the plains, emerging in valleys or along rivers, established on the coast or islands. Or think about the hierarchies of inequality of wealth or power typical for areas poor in resources, as opposed to those emerging in conditions of natural abundance. These are only random illustrations that come to mind. Nature affects society not only from without but also from within – via the biological constitution and genetic endowment of populations. Much of what goes on in a society depends on the mental skills, inborn talents, physical strength, endurance, health and fitness of each member as well as on the recurrence and distribution of those biological traits across various segments of the population. Even though, literally speaking, these influences operate from inside individuals, they may also be treated as environment in a more abstract sense, an environment with respect to what is irreducibly, specifically human in people and their societies.

In both forms, as external and internal influences, natural environment may appear as negative constraints (barriers, blockades) or positive enablements (facilitations, resources). To complicate matters even more, the relationship of nature to society must be seen as two-sided, reciprocal. Nature provides parametric conditions, but at the same time interactive conditions for human agency and praxis. It sets the field for the possible actualizations of the agency, but via praxis it can be shaped itself, and therefore the field can be modified. On the one hand it may be extended. This is what technology, civilization and, in general, 'humanized nature' is all about. Note that the 'internal environment', the inherited, biological or psychological endowment, can also be extended via action. This is what training, mental exercise, self-improvement and cultivation of fitness refer to. On the other hand, the feedback of praxis on the natural environment need not be positive or beneficial. It may also narrow the field of possibilities for the actualization of the agency. It is only recently that we have widely recognized the detrimental and even disastrous impact of human praxis on nature. Pollution, depletion of resources, shortages of energy, ecological destruction etc. are illustrations of this phenomenon as it affects the external, non-human environment, while the so-called 'civilizational illnesses', the deterioration of health, stamina or psychological well-being of populations show how the internal, hereditary constitution of individuals may also be adversely affected by their own actions.

Let us turn to the second type of environment, social conciousness or 'ideological milieu' in which social becoming operates. The immersion in consciousness must be treated as one of the distinguishing attributes of social systems. As Ian C. Jarvie puts it: 'The social world is peculiar in that its entities, processes and relations emerge from, and are constituted by, the actions of its members, and these in turn are predicated on the theories and pictures of it which they entertain from time to time' (1972: 10). Another formulation is given by Kenneth Boulding: 'Social systems are what I call "image-directed", that is, they are systems in which the knowledge of the systems themselves is a significant part of the system's own dynamics and in which, therefore, the knowledge about the system changes the system' (1964: 7).

Consciousness manifests itself at various levels of our model. Primarily it is of course the attribute of individual actors. I follow Giddens in attaching great importance to what he calls 'human knowledgeability': 'Human agents or actors . . . have, as an inherent aspect of what they do, the capacity to understand what they do while they do it' (1984: xxii). Therefore, 'To be a human being is to be a purposive agent, who both has reasons for his or her activities and is able, if asked, to elaborate discursively upon those reasons (including lying about them)' (p. 3). Elaborating some insights of Alfred Schutz, Giddens distinguishes two forms of consciousness – practical and discursive: 'Human actors are not only able to monitor their activities and those of others in the regularity of day-to-day conduct; they are also able to "monitor that monitoring" in discursive consciousness' (p. 29). This is undoubtedly a fundamental ontological fact, which must be taken into account in any picture of social reality. Consciousness, or awareness in this sense may be ascribed not only to actors, but to other kinds of agents: collective ones. We speak of 'group culture', 'idioculture', 'group ideology' (Ridgeway 1983: 252), having in mind the characteristic distribution of ideas in the group, the typical, dominant, widespread, average beliefs of group members. All this is pretty intuitive, but we have to turn towards more abstract conceptualization.

Moving from the bottom level to the top level of our model, we may consider consciousness in less individualistic terms, no longer as the content of human minds, but as superindividual relational networks binding ideas, beliefs, concepts in the comprehensive blocks of ideologies, doctrines, creeds, theories, traditions. These obviously endure longer than their individual carriers (people or groups who accept parts of them in their individual or collective consciousness), they are encoded, materialized and petrified in texts, and they serve as constraints or resources for individual thinking. They also have their own dynamics, and the principles of inertia, momentum and sequence proposed earlier seem to apply here as well. In this sense, consciousness is treated as Durkheimian 'collective representations', or 'social facts *sui generis*', or a Popperian 'Third World' (Popper 1982: 180).

From both sides consciousness impinges on the core ontological level of agency and praxis. The agential potentiality is significantly shaped both by what people in a given society actually think and believe (in their individual or collective consciousness), and what ideological structures (ideologies, creeds, traditions embedded in social consciousness) make them think and believe. The former may be treated as the internal environment of the agency, as it resides inside human heads. The latter may be treated as the external environment of the agency, as it has a sort of supra-individual existence, outside individual minds. Both, in their subtle and shifting mutual balance, delimit the field for the actualization of the agency; they provide constraints and facilitations by defining what sort of praxis is possible and what is impossible, which means are available and which precluded, which goals are feasible and which utopian. The limits put on the field by nature are hard, material. The limits imposed by consciousness may be treated as soft, ideological. This does not mean that the latter cannot exert extremely strong constraints on the agency. The history of totalitarian regimes, dogmatic despotisms, religious fundamentalisms etc. shows to what extent people may be enslaved by ruling doctrines and ideologies. The phenomenon variously described as 'captive mind' (Milosz 1953), 'thought control' (Koestler 1975), or 'third-dimensional power' (Lukes 1978), clearly refers to this kind of constraints. Praxis in turn, via a sort of feedback, crucially affects consciousness. It is in and through praxis that people acquire beliefs as well as test them, verify and falsify claims, confirm and reject their cherished ideas. It is in and through praxis, by proving their vacuity, ineffectiveness or anti-human effects, that ideological and doctrinal structures disintegrate and disappear, utopias are discredited and dogmas broken; even though it may take generations or ages, as the principle of inertia operates here with particular viciousness.

The fact that the operation of agency and praxis is immersed in the 'sea of consciousness' – the external and internal environment of thoughts, beliefs, ideas – has one more important implication. Consciousness not only exerts its own, proper impact on the agency and praxis, but mediates in the impact exerted by other environments, as well as in the very dialectics of agents and structures. People are not passive 'reactants', but they face reality with an active, anticipating attitude. They define, interpret, select the factors of their situations, and act on the basis of their perceptions and evaluations. As Merton puts it: 'we respond not only to the objective features of a situation, but also, and at times primarily, to the meaning that situation has for us' (1982b: 249). Consciousness, individual, collective and social, is a pool of resources (concepts, symbols, codes, frames etc.) for such interpretations. It may keep people blind to some constraints or opportunities, or open their eyes to them. It may cheat them, supplying inadequate intellectual tools for grasping reality, or serve the debunking of illusions by offering sharp critical notions. Thus natural conditions, in their constraining or enabling influence on the agency, are to a large extent mediated by the 'ideological milieu'. The agency has to be 'awakened' to natural threats or promises in order to eventuate in relevant praxis. Or it may remain dormant, ignore limitations and neglect opportunities as long as they are not perceived. By way of example, think of 'ecological awareness' as born only recently and moving large masses to counter-action against pollution, even though, objectively speaking, the world had been polluted much earlier, at least since the dawn of industrial era. Or think of the 'aerobic movement', the fitness craze appearing only when people recognized that physical exercise is beneficial, even though inaction and sedentary habits had been shortening their lives at least since the beginning of urban civilization.

It is not only the impact of the natural environment which is mediated by consciousness. The same mechanism is present also when any kinds of social structural conditions merge with agential endowment at the level of agency and praxis. Social structures do not constrain or enable people in any straightforward, immediate, mechanistic fashion, but only to the extent that people recognize them, define them as blocks or resources. For instance, as Tocqueville observed long ago, people may be exploited or deprived for ages and rebel only when egalitarian ideology is born with its concept of human rights, freedom, injustice etc. (1955). In a word, their revolutionary praxis emerges only if 'revolutionary awareness' is awakened. In a similar fashion, for many millennia women had been dominated by men, and only recently have they mobilized against their subjugation. The indispensable condition was the articulation of the 'feminist consciousness'. Structural blockades, barriers, obstacles evoke reactions and galvanize the agency only if they are defined as such. The same is true of structural chances, resources, facilities. The economic structures of the market or the political structures of democracy have proved their value in many parts of the world for a considerable time, but their full adoption in eastern Europe became possible only when a large degree of 'democratic consensus' emerged, with widespread agreement on the necessity for initiative, competition, pluralism, representation etc. Before the democratic opportunities could truly be utilized, they had to be acknowledged as opportunities.

Recognizing a crucial role of consciousness in the functioning of society, we must guard against one-sided absolutization. It would be an illusion to think that all that occurs in a society is intended and recognized by its members. Many authors have emphasized the important latent dimension of social life. There are structures, environmental conditions, even their own endowment, of which actors are unaware. And they are quite often unable to envisage the outcomes, especially long-range or indirect ones, of their own actions. This is stressed in Popper's account of 'situational logic'(1982: 117). For Merton it is the unintended and unrecognized consequences of purposive actions that are treated as the central concern of sociology: 'It is suggested that the distinctive intellectual contributions of the sociologist are found primarily in the study of unintended consequences (among which are latent functions) of social practices, as well as in the study of anticipated consequences (among which are manifest functions' (1968: 120). In similar vein Giddens observes: 'Human knowledgeability is always bounded. The flow of action continually produces consequences which are unintended by actors, and these unintended consequences also may form unacknowledged conditions of action in a feedback fashion' (1984: 27). These limitations of agents and actions are reflected at the intermediate level of our model, in the possible characteristics of agency and praxis, which sometimes must be seen as insulated from their external and internal environments of consciousness. Thus, one may postulate a spectrum of situations from 'blind agency' and 'spontanoues praxis' at one pole to 'self-aware agency' and 'rationally-controlled praxis' at the other. Along this scale all grades of influence that consciousness exerts on the functioning of society, may be ordered.

Enter time and history

In the model of social becoming, the factor of time is inevitably present from the very beginning. If we speak of the unfolding of structures in operation, or mobilization of agents for action, or eventuating agency through praxis, a time dimension is clearly assumed; all these processes can occur only in time. But so far the recognition given to time in our model is deficient on two counts. First it is only implicit; the temporal extension of processes is treated as self-evident and taken for granted. No systematic implications of temporality are yet drawn. Second, it is limited to what may be called the 'internal time' as opposed to 'external time'; the time of functioning as opposed to the time of transformation. The action of the agents, the operation of structures, and their synthetic fusion, the praxis of the agency, are not seen yet as producing any novelty, but rather as reproducing the same conditions. Thus the functioning of society is still static and not truly dynamic, covering only 'changes in', and ignoring 'changes of'. Therefore the model is still synchronic, and not truly diachronic. It is not static only in the most trivial sense that it recognizes some movement within social reality; but that is not seriously doubted by any student of society, irrespective of theoretical orientation. The acknowledgement of movement does not make the model dynamic. Something more is required. We have to overcome both deficiencies now, incorporating time into our model in a more explicit and less limited way.

In this we find good precedents. A strong emphasis on the factor of time is clearly visible in both lines of earlier theorizing that I am trying to synthesize in the theory of social becoming: the theory of the agency and historical sociclogy. They share the crucial insight that the linkage of the level of individualities and totalities is possible only if history is brought into the picture. Giddens calls for the 'incorporation of temporality into the understanding of human agency' (1979: 54), and in this connection introduces his core concepts of 'recursiveness' ('In and through their activities agents reproduce the conditions that makes these activities possible' (1984: 2)), and 'structuration' ('the ways in which the social system, via the application of generative rules and resources, and in the context of unintended outcomes, is produced and reproduced in interaction' (1979: 66)). This emphasis inevitably pushes the theory of the agency towards historical sociology: 'with the recovery of temporality as integral to social theory history and sociology become methodologically indistinguishable' (Giddens 1979: 8).

No wonder that in the first manifesto of historical sociology we find full support for 'the need to reconstitute the action and structure antinomy as a matter of process in time, to re-organise their investigations in terms of dialectics of structuring' (Abrams 1982: xvi). Abrams claims that 'the social world is essentially historical' (p. 3), and defines historical sociology as 'the attempt to understand the relationship of personal activity and experience on the one hand and social organisation on the other as something that is continuously constructed in time' (p. 16). Lloyd claims that 'human agency and social action relate dialectically to social structures over time' (1988: 11). He proposes to 'retain a temporal dimension as intrinsic to any study of society since structure, action, and behaviour are interrelated in a dynamic, transforming, manner' (p. 314), and specifies a sequence in which those three aspects appear: '(1) Given circumstances, which are enabling and disabling of action, (2) Conscious action that is historically significant, (3) The intended and unintended consequences of action, which turn into objective and seemingly unalterable conditions of action and thought' (p. 283).

Roughly similar phases in this sequence are carefully analysed by Archer under the labels of 'structural conditioning', 'structural interaction' and 'structural elaboration', making up the endless cycles of morphogenesis (1988: xxii). Already in 1986 she was 'taking time to link structure and agency' (Archer 1986), because 'without the proper incorporation of time the problem of structure and agency can never be satisfactorily resolved' (p. 2). She then made a crucial point, which seems self-evident, but only after it has been stated: 'structure and action operate over different time periods . . . structure logically predates the actions that transform it and structural elaboration logically post-dates those actions' (p. 22). Or in more poetic idiom: 'the future is forged in the present, hammered out of past inheritance by current innovation' (p. xxiv).

We can see that all conceptual components necessary to incorporate time, explicitly and fully, into our analysis are already there. We have only to express them in terms of our model. If we recognize that the model as elaborated so far depicts only one, single cycle of social becoming, we can approximate historical reality better by placing several replicas of the model side by side, along an axis of time. Each is seen as internally functioning (reproducing itself in 'internal time'), but also as extending its impact to the next one (producing it in 'external time'). The functioning of the earlier one is

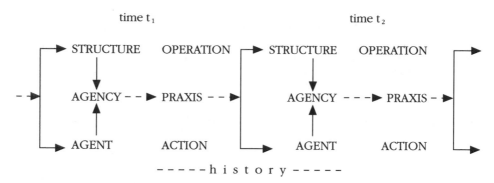

Figure 15.3   The flow of historical process.

seen as causally related to the functioning of the later one, transforming it in significant respects.

How is this causal nexus working? To put it simply: praxis at a certain time moulds the agency at a later time, which is actualized in changed praxis at a still later time, and this process continues unendingly. More concretely, the sequence can be dissected into a number of phases. Thus, ongoing social events, merging structural operation and agential action (or simply praxis) at any given time influence both structures (modifying or shaping new relational networks) and agents (modifying or shaping their immanent capacities) at the later time. As a result, modified or new agency emerges. The societal potentiality for praxis is changed. If and when the agency is actualized through eventuation, it is manifested in new praxis, itself expressing the fusion of the operation of new structures and actions of new agents. In turn, new praxis at a later time begins an analogical cycle, which via changed structures and agents, modified agency and its actualization, results in the emergence of further modified praxis. This sequence goes on endlessly, producing incessant cumulative transformations of society. It represents what we mean by human history, as opposed to the internal functioning of society.

Any existing state of society is therefore only a phase of a historical sequence, a product of past operation (accumulated historical tradition) and a precondition for future operation. Similarly, any social event (as a component of praxis) is in a sense a reflection of all previous history and a germ of future history. It is localized in the flow of historical time. Social becoming treated in the dimension of 'external time' or *longue durée* could be called making history. We shall represent this most complex historical dimension of social life in a schematic form (figure 15.3).

This image requires some comment. In this version of our model, to simplify the picture, we have included only the main lines of causation, indicated by arrows, and omitted internal causation relevant only to the functioning of society rather than its transformation. But one omission is made not only for didactic reasons. From now on we may erase the feedbacks, introduced

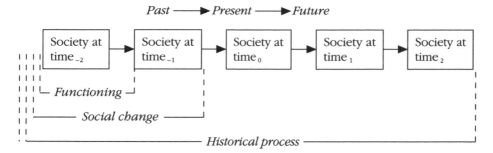

Past ——► *Present* ——► *Future*

Figure 15.4 Various time spans of social self-transformation.

tentatively earlier to express the important point that structures are reshaped in their operation, agents remoulded in their actions, and, in effect, agency reconstructed in its praxis. The backward arrows indicating feedbacks in the earlier scheme, can be straightened out now, when we recognize that the structures, agents and agency on which they feed back are different structures, agents and agency, namely, they exist later in time. It is true that operation feeds back on operating structures, actions feed back on acting agents, praxis feeds back on agency which it manifests – but no teleology is implied, because we speak of later structures, later agents and later agency, causally influenced by earlier operations, earlier actions and earlier praxis.

We must also not be misled by the didactic necessity of drawing the models representing societal functioning at various moments of time side by side. It does not mean that we are speaking of various societies interacting between them, or one influencing the other. In fact, these are not different societies, but different states, phases of functioning, of the same society. The sequence represents therefore the self-transformation of society between various moments in time, in and through its functioning at any moment in time.

The sequence of such self-transformation is continuous and endless. Therefore it is only for practical reasons that the scheme depicts only two consecutive phases; it could be extended in both directions, towards the future and towards the past. Changing the scale, and neglecting all internal details of social anatomy and physiology, the picture of social self-transformation through time could be represented as in figure 15.4.

As can be seen, the model now allows us to define precisely three concepts crucial for the understanding of social dynamics. 'Functioning' covers all that is happening in society at some moment in time. 'Social change' describes a single transformation of society from one, earlier state to the next, later state. 'Historical process' refers to the sequence of self-transformations that society undergoes in a long span of time. Accordingly we may enrich the earlier distinction of internal and external time by indicating two important varieties of the latter: the short-range time of social change, and the truly historical time of the *longue durée*.

Society does not exist in a vacuum, but rather in the double environment of nature and consciousness. Recognition of this fact will allow us to discover an additional important mechanism, through which the historical process functions. We have noted that both nature and consciousness enter into a mutual relationship with society, as shaping and shaped at the same time. Richer with the recognition of time, we may now disentangle this dialectic as well.

Let us start with nature. Praxis leaves an obvious imprint on nature, changing natural conditions (depleting forests, regulating rivers, ploughing land, pollluting air etc.), but also adding a whole new domain of transformed nature ('humanized nature', 'artificial nature') made of products and artefacts, technology and civilization (houses and roads, bridges and factories, gadgets and furniture etc.). This is a left-over from earlier praxis, which provides the conditions for later praxis. More precisely, it co-determines both the capacities of agents (what actions can be taken) and the potentialities of structures (what modes of structural operation are feasible), and in effect influences the synthetic quality of agency. The agency eventuates in changed praxis, which in turn reshapes the natural environment, and the cycle continues. One may say that the remnants of the earlier functioning of society are encoded in the natural environment and passed on to the next phases of functioning.

Quite a similar mechanism of continuity will appear when we turn to another environment of society, social consciousness. Ongoing praxis at any given time is reflected both in the ideas, beliefs, convictions held by agents (individuals or groups), and in the ideologies, creeds, doctrines acquiring more objectified, superindividual existence. Changed consciousness feeds back on the capacities of agents (redefining what actions are possible), and on the potentialities of structures (specifying what structural arrangements are feasible). In effect, the agency is significantly reshaped. In its actualization, it results in changed praxis at a later time, and this in turn brings about changes in consciousness. Once again the cycle repeats itself, and the process of incremental modifications of consciousness continues. Thus the heritage of the past phases of social functioning is encoded in social consciousness and transmitted to the future.

This mechanism, in which historical process involves the continuous re-modelling of environments (nature and consciousness) is supplementary with respect to the main one, which operates through reshaping structures and agents (and in effect their fusion, the agency).

Thus there are four causal loops that can be distinguished in the process of history-making: (1) via structural effects, (2) via agents' capacities, (3) via 'humanized' nature and (4) via modified consciousness. In all four cases praxis at a certain time leaves effects which outlast it and become an active, conditioning force for later praxis. The sum of such effects can be referred to as historical tradition, in the widest sense of this term (Shils 1981). In the course of the multi-stage, sequential process, the historical tradition has a tendency to accumulate. The accumulation is of course selective; some remnants of earlier periods are carried on and others vanish. Thus structures may disintegrate, agents may lose their already acquired capacities, artefacts may perish or become obsolete, ideas may be forgotten. This depends on a number of variables, some of which will be suggested in the next chapter. But there is always a core of tradition, which is transmitted from generation to generation, for long stretches of time. As a result, the process is endowed with considerable continuity and cumulativeness, and we witness the emergence of sequential patterns in history.

Most often, though not unexceptionally, the engendering of lasting effects by ongoing praxis, and the cumulation of these effects in transmitted tradition is unwitting; it operates without intention, purpose or even awareness. The effects are unintended and unrecognized by the members of a society, even though praxis itself is purposeful, intentional and often rational. As Giddens puts it: 'Human history is created by intentional activities but is not an intended project; it persistently eludes efforts to bring it under conscious direction' (1984: 27). Or in the more metaphorical language of Hollis: 'Actions have many consequences, which are systematic but initially unnoticed by everyone. They can be deemed the work of the Cunning of Reason if, when they surface, they are found to be the collective effects of individually rational decisions taken by role-players in the course of games' (1987: 205). In this case, if any pattern emerges in history it must be credited to the rule of the 'invisible hand'. But it cannot be denied that sometimes visible, and even all too visible, hands operate in history – dictators, tyrants, reformers, legislators, revolutionaries, prophets etc., who try to push the historical process along a preconceived path, in the intended direction, by means of planned transformations. Whether those attempts are successful or not, they present an alternative variety of history-making.

In both cases, however, the historical process is contingent and not predetermined or necessary. The residues of earlier praxis make up a field of possibilities (agential, structural, environmental) for later praxis. The field is always bounded but never optionless. There are always possible alternative paths of further process, starting at each phase of the process. Some are actualized in praxis, some are rejected; hence some historically present possibilities are used and others abandoned. Ultimately it depends on the decisions taken and choices made by the agents, who always 'could have acted otherwise'. If there is any necessity in history, it is a conditional necessity: if people decide to act, will it be in this or that way? The semblance of necessity appears only after the event, once decisions and choices have been made and action taken. Before that, the process is always open-ended. As Tilly puts it: 'a process constitutes a series of choice points. Outcomes at a given point in time constrain possible outcomes at later points in time' (1984: 14). In the long run, this contingent mechanism, produces all kinds of twisting, variable trajectories along which history moves. The mechanism described shows 'how people do indeed make their own history but also how particular circumstances, which are the result of people having made history in the past, condition that history-making' (Lloyd 1988: 301).

The becoming of social becoming

In our discussion so far we have built a multi-level model of social reality and endowed it with the double dynamics of internal functioning and self-transformations. Society is seen not only as built in a particular way but as having a particular mechanism of self-movement. Owing to the operation of that mechanism society is constantly changing. But is the mechanism itself immutable? Is it permanent and historically universal, or does historical relativization perhaps touch not only the parameters and variables of the model, but the very principles of its dynamics?

In a different language, this is a variant of the old question whether historical change means only a change of facts (states of society) or also a change of the regularities obtaining in a society (social laws) (Gewirth 1969). I opt for the latter solution (which may be called 'radical historism') and reject the notion of ahistorical, universal social laws (Sztompka 1984b). Translated into the terms of our model, this will mean that historical transformations embrace not only the agents, structures and agency, not only the actions, operations and praxis, not only the environments of nature and consciousness, but also the links among all those, the ways in which they combine producing social dynamics. In short, I will claim that, with the passage of time, the very principles of operation, the mode of functioning and change of human society, undergo significant transformations. The ultimate, most complex feedback loop is added to the model: it is not only the case that agency changes itself in the course of its own praxis, but also that social becoming changes its mode in the course of history. We enter here the domain of metadynamics. Poetically one may speak of the becoming of the very mechanism of becoming.

There are several hints in the literature showing that scholars have vaguely perceived this peculiarity of the social world. Marx and Engels had already spelled out the opposition between the 'kingdom of necessity' and the 'kingdom of freedom', or the 'prehistory' and 'true history' of human society, meaning by that a fundamental change of the principles of operation at the borderline dividing the class societies of the past from the expected classless society of the future. Contemporary Marxists speak of 'naturalistic history' as opposed to 'humanistic history', alluding to the growing role of human, rational intervention in modern epochs (Topolski 1978). Or think of Ward's opposition of genesis and telesis as two distinct principles of evolution, the latter involving purposefulness, awareness, and knowledge (Fletcher 1971, vol. 1: 479). A similar message is carried by other commonly counterposed pairs of concepts: market and plan, spontaneity and deliberation, the invisible hand and rational control, the cunning of reason and the realization of projects. They indicate not only a change of society, but metachange, the change of its most fundamental modes of changing.

Following the hints from earlier literature, I shall postulate that the mode of social becoming evolves in accordance with the kind of relationships linking society with its environments (nature and consciousness). The common denominator of the historical tendency embracing the mechanism of social becoming will be found in growing control over environments, in the sense of command over them and insulation from them. With respect to nature, this tendency is fairly obvious. The history of human civilization and technology is nothing but the gradual subjugation of natural resources to human needs and a growing protection of human society against natural threats. With respect to consciousness, the growth of human knowledge means, among other things, the evolving self-consciousness of social phenomena, regularities, mechanisms of social functioning and change, and the debunking of myths, illusions, 'false consciousness'. This allows for more anticipation, planning and purposeful shaping of social life. As the mechanism of social becoming grows less opaque to its own participants, it inevitably incorporates more human intervention.

As we know all too well, however, both tendencies produce not only beneficial effects, the improvement of social becoming, but also considerable side-effects or even counter-effects, distorting, endangering or even blocking societal functioning and change. Excessive conquest of nature has led to ecological disaster, pollution, depletion of natural resources etc. Excessive belief in reason, knowledge and planning of social life has led to human enslavement, poverty and even extermination under a variety of 'scientific' totalitarian projects. Thus the historical tendency seems to evolve towards a higher mark of control: recognition of the limitations of control, or in other words, self-control of the very aspirations to control.

The costs, dysfunctions, side-effects, long-range dangers of control over both kinds of environments, nature and consciousness, are perceived ever more clearly in modern society. Think of the eruption of ecological awareness, with its idea of harmony with nature and the imperative of bridling excessive ambitions to conquer it; or of the wave of anti-totalitarian, liberal-democratic awareness, with its idea of pluralism, tolerance, participation, spontaneity, and the renunciation of all attempts to impose preconceived, dogmatic blueprints on human history.

In terms of our model, these may be taken as indicators that the new mode of social becoming is slowly emerging, providing human society with more autonomy as well as more self-conscious, critical and realistic control over its own fate. It is like the next mutation on the eternal path from the fully objectified, blind existence of primitive people, through the naive megalomania of human power and reason, to the fully creative, wide awake existence of the expected future society, living in harmony with nature and reconciled with the limits of thought. This is the path of historical emancipation of human agency.

Our model of social becoming is now completed. We have analysed its complex internal constitution, provided it with the mode of internal functioning, placed it in historical time, endowed it with the mechanism of self-transformation, and even supplied it with the metamechanism through which its very principles of functioning and transformation undergo historical change.

Thus the most radical dynamic perspective has been applied; society appears as incessant, perpetual movement. We may start from any part of the model and see how it evolves in time. Whatever component we choose, it is seen as operating; any fact turns out to be an event; any agent resolves into actions; any state is only a phase of the ongoing process.

Part IV

Aspects of Social Becoming

16

Ideas as historical forces

Intangibles in history

Full recognition of the role of intangibles – beliefs, values, motivations, aspirations, attitudes – in the processes of social change became possible only when sociology moved from the historicist or developmentalist perspective towards an individualist orientation. In the former, holistic systems reigned, with their own irreducible properties and regularities, and people were treated as passive, dependent, fully moulded components. In order to elevate the ideal aspects to the role of determining factors, the historical processes could no longer be perceived as autonomous, independent of human actions, running at their own level somewhere above human heads. Instead, acting people had to be brought back into the core of sociological theory. This turn towards a position later described as methodological individualism was the achievement of Max Weber.

With Weberian 'humanist sociology', the social organisms or systems lose their central position in sociological theorizing, and the focus moves to agents and their actions. Sociology for Weber is the study of social actions, meaningful conduct directed towards others and oriented to their actual or expected responses. All complex social entities (economies, political systems, social organizations) are nothing but the accumulated, lasting outcomes of social actions, emerging in the course of human history. To explain them means to trace their roots in human actions; and, in turn, to explain actions (to understand them) is to unravel their meaning, the psychological motivations which impel people to action, as well as the cultural values, norms and rules which shape the form actions take. Thus, the ultimate explanatory factors are located in the realm of ideas, the categorical beliefs and normative rules that people hold. As Weber puts it himself: 'The magical and religious forces and the ideas of duty based upon them, have in the past always been among the most important formative influences on conduct' (Weber 1958).

From the residual or determined status given to ideas in typical evolutionist or developmentalist approaches, there is an about-turn to a perspective in which ideas are treated as central, independent factors. Weber himself referred to his own theory as 'the positive critique' of Marxian historical materialism in the sense that for him 'superstructure' rather than 'basis' (to use

Marxian terminology), or simply 'soft' belief systems rather than 'hard' economy or technology, become the active and effective forces of history. Some contemporary commentators claim that the major theme of Weber's entire work, 'Weber's Thesis', was the recognition of 'the function of ideology as an independent variable in social development' (Birnbaum 1953: 125).

The most conspicuous application of such an approach is to be found in Weber's interpretation of the origins of capitalism. This complex argument, put forward in 1904 in a classical essay, *The Protestant Ethic and the Spirit of Capitalism,* requires detailed scrutiny.

The spirit of capitalism

For Weber, like most of his nineteenth-century predecessors, the main goal was to understand modernity, the new, radically changed social world coming to maturation in western Europe and the US in the nineteenth century and expanding towards other regions of the globe. The central organizing principle of that modern system was capitalism, the rationalized, efficient, profit-seeking production of goods, based on private property and individual entrepreneurial efforts. In Weber's words, 'Capitalism is identical with the pursuit of profit, and forever renewed profit, by means of continuous, rational, capitalistic enterprise . . . the rational capitalistic organization of (formally) free labor' (Weber 1958: 17, 21). As it is put in a rather more extended description provided by a contemporary interpreter of Weber: 'The characteristics of rational capitalism itself are the entrepreneurial organization of capital, rational technology, free labor, unrestricted markets, and calculable law' (Collins 1980: 930).

Thus one of Weber's main concerns became: How was capitalism born and how did it succesfully survive? In other words he was seeking the explanation of the transition from traditional to capitalist society, and the continuing expansion of capitalism after its birth.

The logic of Weber's reasoning works backwards, in three steps. If capitalism, like all other structural wholes, is a result of human actions, then there must be some particular type of actions, carried out by some particular class of agents, exhibiting a particular kind of motivations, that are crucially involved in the origins of capitalism. Thus the first step involves the question: Who are the founders of capitalism? Weber responds: Both a new type of entrepreneurs and a new type of workers. The emergence of such new agents is a fundamental prerequisite for the origins of capitalism.

But what distinguishes this new type of entrepreneurs and workers? This question marks the second step in the argument. The answer is: A specific ethos or mentality, the 'spirit of capitalism'. This unique mixture of motivations and values includes:

> The profit motive i.e. treating acquisition, and in particular earning money, as the ultimate goal in life, no longer subordinate to the satisfaction of other needs. This offers a clear case of the displacement of goals, when

what is at most an instrument or means is turned into an autonomous end. The ascetic orientation, i.e. the avoidance of all spontaneous enjoyment and hedonistic consumption.
The idea of a calling, i.e. a duty defined as intense, disciplined, responsible, rational activity. This applies to the entrepreneurs, for whom organizational effort becomes an end in itself, and to the workers, who start to treat labour as an end in itself.

If the 'spirit of capitalism' permeating capitalist agents (entrepreneurs and workers) and engendering capitalist actions (organizing and labouring) is a prerequisite for the birth of capitalism, what is the origin of that 'spirit'? This is the third step in Weber's reasoning. The explanation cannot stop at the level of an ethos, but must search deeper for the sources of the ethos itself. It is here that Weber's most original (and contested) contribution comes.

The Protestant ethos

His point of departure is empirical. Namely, he observes a strikingly consistent correlation: at the period of early capitalism the crucial agents (business leaders, technically and commercially trained personnel, skilled workers) tend to be predominantly Protestant. In order to prove that such a correlation is not spurious, and that there is actual causation leading from the Protestant religious affiliation to involvement in pro-capitalist social roles, the conceivable common, independent causes of both phenomena must be checked. (1) Weber considers the possibility that both Protestantism and the spirit of capitalism may be due to a high level of cultural development, characteristic for certain countries and not for others. But comparative data show that the correlation holds equally well in highly developed and in less developed countries. (2) There is the possibility that in some regions particularly rich economic resources had already been accumulated in the period preceding the Reformation, and that these provided opportunities for subsequent capitalist development irrespective of religious loyalties. Again it turns out that in regions strikingly different in accumulated wealth the preponderance of Protestants in technical jobs and among the skilled labour force is constant. (3) Weber examines the hypothesis that the driving force of entrepreneurship and efficient labour may be a minority or marginal status in society rather than a particular religious affiliation. But the data show that business-oriented occupations are more common among Protestants, irrespective of their minority or majority status, or of their ruled or ruling position in a concrete country. Weber draws the conclusion that what is decisive for the particular role of Protestants in the generation of capitalism is the 'permanent intrinsic character of their religious beliefs, and not only in their temporary, external historico-political situations' (1958: 40).

But what is there in the content of the Protestant creed, that would produce motivations conducive for pro-capitalist activities? Weber notices that within Protestantism there is a variety of denominations, separate sects which seem to have had an unequally strong influence in the mobilizing of the capitalist ethos. The important differences have to do with their 'other-worldly' or 'this-worldly' orientation. The ascetic branches of Protestantism (Calvinism, Methodism, Baptism) are oriented toward this world, providing a combination of business acumen with religious piety. The former is expressed in the idea of a calling: the fulfilment of duty in worldly affairs as the highest form of moral activity. The latter is expressed in the idea of predestination: the achievement of grace and salvation in the other world as the result of fully sovereign and free decisions by God. In this unique mixture the ideological source of capitalism is to be found.

What is the motivational process stemming from these ideas? Weber postulates anxiety and existential uncertainty as common emotional conditions of the faithful. If God's verdicts are fully free and hence unpredictable, how can an individual know if he/she is chosen or condemned? There are no earthly means of influencing God's choices, because God is fully independent. On the other hand, God intervenes in this world, and to carry out his schemes and plans uses the elect, and obviously not the condemned. Therefore, if one is successful in intense, devoted, persistent worldly activity, this is the best available sign of being elect, the mark of grace and coming salvation. By the same token, if one is idle, wastes time in leisure, devotes oneself to consumption, this is a mark of damnation. Good, diligent work is not a means by which one can win salvation, but it serves as an earthly sign of God's grace. Successes, achievements in activity, particularly those measurable in objective, monetary terms, eliminate anxiety, restore confidence and, by the mechanism which modern sociologists call the 'self-fulfilling prophecy', bring about even more success ('Nothing succeeds like success' as the saying goes.) Thus, at the level of individual motivation, strong pressure for activism, be it entrepreneurship or labour, is originated. The external injection of ideology from the religious source is posited as indispensable for producing mobilization and effecting 'the first push' away from the traditional economy to the modern capitalist system. 'The religious valuation of restless, continuous, systematic work in a worldly calling, as the highest means to asceticism, and at the same time the surest and most evident proof of rebirth and genuine faith, must have been the most powerful conceivable lever for the expansion of that attitude toward life which we have here called the spirit of capitalism' (Weber 1958: 172).

Once this happens, the structure of social relationships becomes transformed. At first, this is in the negative sense, by the destroying of old structures. Solitude in the face of God and his verdicts and the purely individual test of grace found in worldly activity produce social atomization, the isolation of individuals and weakening of all traditional bonds and ties. The secret of pronounced individualism, self-reliance and individual competitiveness, so typical of a capitalist system, is found here in some basic orientations of Protestant religion. It can be contrasted with the more collectivist, community-oriented, solidarity-producing attitude of the Catholic Church. Weber approvingly quotes the point made by another contemporary author: 'The Catholic is quieter, having less of the acquisitive impulse; he prefers a life of the greatest possible security, even with a smaller income, to a life of risk and excitement, even though it may bring the chance of gaining honour and riches' (1958: 40).

Second, the transformation is also positive, by means of putting up new structures. Mobilized for activity and success, which are to serve as marks of salvation, individuals start to compare their achievements. Competition becomes a way of life. The accumulation of capital rather than consumption, reinvesting profits rather than using them, become the only rational strategies to safeguard success in the competitive entrepreneurial market. Similarly, diligent, efficient work becomes the only strategy to safeguard success in the competitive labour market. The system engenders sanctions which induce conformity. If an entrepreneur does not comply with this principle, the firm is eliminated. If a worker fails to comply, he/she loses a job. Maximalization of efficiency emerges as a tendency of the system. It provides it with internal dynamics and expansionist force.

At this moment the system starts to operate on its own, becomes self-reproductive without the necessity of continuing religious support. Even more so, it may eventually turn against religion as such, producing a strong secularizing tendency. 'The new persons shaped by the Protestant sects produce a new social order that not only captures its creators, but also the other actors in their economic vicinity. Once established, the new structure in turn transforms, educates, and selects new types of secular actors well adapted to the new order' (Hernes 1989: 156). A system which started as a historical accident in the north-west of Europe acquires momentum and expansionist strength to embrace large parts of the globe.

'Weber's Thesis' was written in polemical vein. It was mainly directed against Marxian historical materialism with its characteristic neglect of the ideal domain, which Marxism treated as a residual 'superstructure'. 'To speak . . . of a reflection of material conditions in the ideal superstructure would be patent nonsense' (Weber 1958: 75). But he could easily have been trapped in a one-sidedness of his own. Weber was aware of the danger. He recognized the biases and incompleteness of his proposed explanation and hastened to declare that his wish was not to 'substitute for a one-sided materialistic an equally one-sided spiritualistic causal interpretation of culture and of history' (p. 183).

Thus in his later work he introduced several corrections to the 'Thesis'. (1) In his extensive studies of ancient religions (1963), he showed that, depending on local, historical conditions, religion may have quite different or even opposite implications for social life. It is multifunctional phenomenon. For example in the case of China or India, their religious systems were found effectively to block rather than facilitate capitalist development. (2) In his *Theory of Social and Economic Organization* (1947), Weber extended his explanatory scheme beyond the realm of religion, including among independent variables other institutional and political factors: the development of centralized, bureaucratic states, the emergence of modern law, the idea of citizenship and individual rights etc. (3) The claims concerning Protestantism were limited. It was no longer seen as the ultimate cause but rather as a contributing factor, which at a certain point in the ongoing process of development towards capitalism, was able to liberate mass motivation for this-worldly activity (deliver it from other-worldly 'monasticism') and mobilize entrepreneurs and workers for intense efforts.

Innovational personality

'Weber's Thesis' and its central message – to look for important determinants of macro-historical processes in the micro-domain of human motivations, attitudes and values – has been very influential. Several modern theorists have attempted to elaborate and apply it to the conditions of highly developed capitalism. We shall focus on two, already classical examples of this theoretical trend.

Everett Hagen introduced the notion of innovative personality as the prerequisite for economic growth, spread of entrepreneurship and capital formation. He believes that there are distinct and opposite personality syndromes typical of traditional and modern society. In traditional society, its product, and the precondition for continuing operation, is the authoritarian personality. The innovational personality, a product and functional prerequisite of modern society, is directly opposite in all respects. The opposition may be represented as another polar dichotomy in table 16.1 (Hagen 1962):

Table 16.1   Authoritarian versus innovational personality

Trait	Authoritarian personality	Innovational personality
Attitude to reality	Compliance to patterns of life dictated by tradition and authorities and legitimated by their supposedly eternal nature and supernatural origins	Inquisitive and manipulative attitude to the world, in persistent search for its underlying regularities in order to influence and control the phenomena
Perception of individual role in the world	Submissiveness, obedience, conformity, avoidance of responsibility and the need for dependence	Taking personal responsibility for the bad sides of the world, coupled with the search for better solutions and attempts to introduce changes
Style of leadership	Rigidity, high expectations and strict demands directed to subordinates	Openness and tolerance to subordinates, encouraging their originality and innovativeness
Level of creativeness and innovativeness	Lack of creativeness and innovativeness	Creativeness, putting premium on originality and novelty, restless curiosity

Authoritarian personality is shaped by the conditions of stagnation, simple reproduction, self-perpetuating equilibrium, and, as its aggregated effect, brings about petrification of these conditions. Innovational personality is shaped by the conditions of modernity, and in turn helps to generate self-perpetuating changes and innovations which permanently revolutionize patterns of life, standards of living, values, techniques etc.

Like Weber, Hagen has to face the most difficult question of origins: how the modern innovational personality appears in the first place if clearly there is nothing within the traditional authoritarian syndrome which would generate it from the inside by means of an endogenous, immanent process. The first push away from tradition and towards modernity must be credited to some external factor, invoking exogenous causation. In Weber, it was the contingent factor of Protestant (Calvinist) religion. In Hagen, it is the historically specific circumstances which he labels 'status withdrawal'. This occurs when the established, predetermined, ascriptive statuses typical of traditional 'closed' society are undermined by emerging social mobility and 'opening' of class and stratification hierarchies. Such conditions appear on a massive scale with the breakdown of traditional order after great revolutions and the emergence of industrial, urban society. There are four typical cases of status withdrawal:

When a whole group (community, occupational category, aristocratic elite etc.) loses its earlier status, and consequently the same occurs to each of its members (e.g. traditional artisans replaced by factory workers, elite of elders replaced by elected representatives). A gap appears between the earlier and later status.

When a group is not regarded as highly as its members believe it deserves (e.g. a sort of relative deprivation experienced by members of ethnic groups, corporations, firms, inhabitants of local communities, sports teams etc., who feel that their groups are unjustifiably underestimated by the out-groups). The gap appears between the self-definition of status and the status actually enjoyed.

When there is a discrepancy or inconsistency between various dimensions of status (e.g. the prestige of a certain job, say that of the university professor, does not match the level of income or power, or when great power or income does not go together with high prestige etc.). A gap appears between the status a person (or an occupation) receives on one scale of stratification and the status as measured by another scale.

When the group is not (yet) accepted in the wider social setting, and its members share in its marginal status (e.g. ethnic minority groups, recent immigrants, *Gastarbeiter* etc.). A gap appears between a status aspired to and the one actually obtained.

All four situations, with their common denominator of a gap between actual and imagined statuses, remind one of Robert K. Merton's classical discussion of anomie (1938). No wonder Hagen becomes involved in reasoning analogous to Merton's. He claims that the structural inconsistency manifested by 'status withdrawal' brings about certain typical 'adaptations': from retreatism (resignation), through ritualistic adherence to received patterns, to innovation and rebellion against the situation perceived as unacceptable. Each of these adaptations occurs under specific concrete conditions. For Hagen the latter two (innovation and rebellion) are the most interesting, because they explain the emergence of the innovational personality. Here he puts forward a hypothesis which is perhaps the most dubious in his whole argumentation. The decisive factor, he believes, is the character of socialization (and especially the early child-rearing phase). In conditions of status withdrawal men, who are usually the more professionally involved, suffer more, and more readily give way to resignation or despair. Women, the crucial socializing agents, resent the patent weakness of their mates, and put strong emphasis on change, innovation, originality and creativeness in their child-rearing practices, in the hope of raising better-adapted offspring.

Achievement motivation

Another widely discussed theory focusing on psychological aspects of capitalist development was proposed by David McClelland (1967). He focused on the question whether there exists some common, universal personality syndrome, which could be found to precede any outburst of intensive economic development, whenever it occurs in history. His answer is in the affirmative: economic development always did and does result from a preceding spread of *achievement motivation* (need for achievement, or 'n Achievement' for short). Such motivation finds its best outlet in, and is particularly indispensable for, entrepreneurial activities. 'A society with a generally high level of n Achievement will produce more energetic entrepreneurs who, in turn, produce more rapid economic development' (McClelland 1967: 205).

The alternative personality syndromes, 'n Affiliation', or 'n Power' have opposite consequences. The spread of the affiliative needs prevents individual competitiveness, nonconformity, originality and innovativeness, eventually halting economic growth. Affiliative needs coupled with the need for power produce even more vicious totalitarian tendencies.

Achievement motivation, the universal precondition for economic expansion and growth, may appear in various historical epochs, and hence must be defined in relative terms. This is done by treating the standards of excellence, the measures or scales of achievement, as historically specific and variable, whereas the need for achieving the specific standard, whatever it is, is considered as universal and constant. As McClelland explicates it, achievement motivation is the striving for success by means of one's own efforts in situations involving an evaluation of one's performance in relation to some standard of excellence. Specifying it for the historical situation of expanding capitalism, 'n Achievement' comes down to a latent disposition to compete for a high standard of excellence rewarded in money, and for steady, ascending profit by accumulation rather than consumption.

There are several behavioural and attitudinal correlates of the achievement motivation, which result in the complex personality syndrome. On the behavioural side, achievement motivation is found to be linked with upward mobility, frequent travel, long hours of work, desire to accumulate capital, aspirations to educate the children, entrepreneurial activity. On the attitudinal side we see the innovative drive, high sense of responsibility, prospective planning of actions, preference for rational calculation, readiness for medium levels of risk.

How is this extremely important personality syndrome born and developed? The key is again in proper socialization, adequate child-rearing and training, which puts heavy emphasis on self-reliance, persistence in goal attainment, concern with excellence, esteem for hard work. McClelland urges sowing achievement motivation in order to harvest economic growth.

Of course, as with any sociological theory there are some doubts which may be raised against McClelland's account. One is the problem of 'who trains the trainers', or in other words what motivates parents or teachers to train their children or pupils for achievement rather than affiliation or power. Another is the question of explanatory completeness: is the postulated 'n Achievement' enough to explain economic expansion and growth? Or is it perhaps at most the necessary, but not sufficient condition? What about conducive historical circumstances, indispensable resources, opportunities of a more tangible (material, technical, political) sort? As one critic puts it: 'What happens in a situation where needs for achievement are plentiful but the outlets for its translation into enterpreneurship are absent or blocked?' (Chodak 1973: 180). Most likely we shall witness a grave crisis of aspirations and expectations or a widespread experience of acute relative deprivation. This may lead to passivism, apathy, or, under specific conditions, to the outbreak of revolutionary activism.

The predicament of the 'socialist mentality'

So far we have studied the positive role of ideas, ideologies, mental attitudes as causes or at least contributing factors of economic growth, expansion, progress. But under specific circustances, the same factors may play an opposite role, providing barriers and blocks to change. The dysfunctional significance of mental patterns in the processes of social change has been recently amply documented by events in eastern and central Europe, the revolutions of 1989, the breakdown of communism and its aftermath.

Many observers emphasize that one of the main obstacles, barriers, or 'frictions' (Etzioni 1991) in the transition from 'real socialism' to a democratic, market society is the widespread personality syndrome referred to as 'socialist mentality', 'socialist spirit', 'homo Sovieticus', or 'captive mind' (Milosz 1953).

This is the product of several decades of totalitarian or semi-totalitarian rule, which left a strong imprint on the motivations and attitudes of the population. There were two ways through which 'real socialism' shaped personality. First, there was the impress of socialist institutions, forms of organization, ideological structures. This was carried, via prolonged habituation, indoctrination, 'thought-control' (Koestler 1975) and imposition of a fake 'ideological reality' on human minds, to a point where it ultimately reached the domain of unreflexive motivations, subconsciousness, deep psychological codes. Second, there was a perhaps even stronger indirect mechanism of emerging 'adaptive reactions' or defence mechanisms that people developed as ways of coping with 'socialist' conditions. Those adaptive arrangements and mechanisms, having proved their effectiveness, became deeply rooted and petrified in popular consciousness.

Thus the domain of mass psychology shows surprising resistance to change and seems to outlast the organizational and institutional forms of 'real socialism' effectively destroyed by the democratic movements of the 1980s. The unfortunate legacy of 'real socialism' seems to be most lasting in the mental domain. I suppose that here resides the main mechanism through which communism is haunting post-communist societies from the grave. As a journalist puts it in metaphorical terms, the Berlin Wall may be down, but the 'wall in our heads' remains.

Let us analyse the anatomy of 'socialist mentality', taking the case of Poland. With allowance for some national variations, similar traits can be observed in other countries of the former socialist world.

A contemporary observer notes: 'The forty-five-year period of "building socialism" has transformed Polish society much more deeply than could be expected after witnessing the permanent resistance of the Poles to communist rule' (Mokrzycki 1991: 3). He adds: 'In Poland, apart from economic ruin and the grave psychological condition of society, the road to democracy is blocked in a sense by the very society, its deep, internal architecture' (p. 13). Another Polish sociologist warns against a similar danger: 'The basic problem which the reformers must recognize has to do with the fact that everyday actions of individuals will be modelled by habits developed in the course of social experiences radically different from those which should fill our new institutions' (Marody 1990: 167).

Empirical studies of social consciousness (values, preferences, tastes, consumption patterns etc.) have become the leading concern and a sort of trademark of Polish sociology. For four decades they have been supplying a host of data, adding up to a rather reliable picture of the 'Polish mind' under communist rule. Perhaps the most striking of all the numerous findings is that the 'Polish mind' appears to be split, torn apart by a sort of schizophrenia. The split seems to follow the public–private dichotomy. Quite different beliefs, motivations and attitudes seem to prevail with respect to the public world from those which apply in private life. From a long list of such antinomies (Marody 1987a and b), I shall pick out some illustrations.

1 People exhibit disparate attitudes to work. The negligence, inefficiency, absenteeism so typical of labour in the state-owned enterprises stands in surprising contrast with the discipline, care and diligence exhibited by those employed in the private sector, self-employed or working abroad.

2 There is a contrast between the area of work in general and personal life. The learned helplessness, reluctance to take decisions, delegation of responsibility, emphasis on security and egotistic benefits which dominate in public institutions, enterprises, administrative offices etc. contrast with the self-reliance, initiative, innovativeness, readiness for risk and altruism shown in relations with family or home.

3 In the physical environment, the neglect and disdain of state-owned or publicly shared property is sharply divergent from the almost excessive care and concern with private property. Compare the dirt, disorder and vandalism in the courtyards or staircases of big housing complexes, and the tidy, neat, meticulously cleaned interiors of the apartments. Similarly, a mere glance at the façade and surroundings is enough to distinguish the state-owned enterprise from a private workshop, the state-run store from a private grocery. A particularly sad expression of this schizoid split is in attitudes to property: stealing spare parts, materials or equipment from state-run enterprises is widely condoned and evokes no moral censure, while the theft of private goods is strongly condemned.

4 In the field of aspirations, ambitions and hopes, the bonus for passivism, conformism, submissiveness and mediocrity in public roles is clearly incongruent with the emphasis on success, self-realization and individual achievement in private life. The former leads to fatalism and a feeling of hopelessness in public affairs, wait-and-see attitudes and the 'free-rider syndrome'. People are reluctant to engage in public life, because they do not see any realistic way in which it could change anything, and at the same time they clearly perceive the risks and the price of activism. 'A fatalistic orientation . . . is thus a learned (and rational) response to a distant, capricious and unresponisve power imposed from without' (Thompson, Ellis and Wildavsky 1990, chapter 12: 3–4). The eminent Polish sociologist Stanislaw Ossowski called this the 'Lilliput syndrome'.

5 In politics, there is widespread distrust of public statements criticism of the mass media and scepticism about political appeals, accompanied by an immediate, naive readiness to believe rumours, gossip and prophecies transmitted through unofficial channels. The same people who say, 'TV lies', and 'In the press only the obituaries are true' are most responsive to, and ready to act on, the wildest myths if these are retailed by friends, neighbours or family members.

6 The authorities, both central and local, are perceived as alien and hostile; the government is seen as the arena of conspiracy, deceit and cynicism, or at least stupidity and inefficiency. At the same time private connections, networks and loyalties at work, among friends and at home are overestimated and idealized.

If this psychoanalysis of the 'socialist mind' is true (and each claim can be supported by considerable sociological evidence, not to speak of common-sense observations) a dismal picture appears. The pathological split in social consciousness cannot but become reflected in actual conduct. Again I select only a few illustrations from the rich sociological literature identifying typical patterns of action in communist societies.

1   Perhaps the most often mentioned is the dissociation of what people say and what they actually do, the striking difference between preaching and acting, their declarations and conduct. Classical examples refer to behaviour in the political domain, the common pattern of verbal opportunism, hypocrisy and cynicism. What is perhaps not recognized by outsiders is the fact that the same double standards of talk and action were often manifested by the authorities, and not only ordinary people. There was a strange, loose, nonchalant attitude to the enforcement of political declarations or ideologically motivated laws. Apparently the authorities also did not mean what they were saying or legislating. In fact this made life much more liveable, and allowed for much greater freedom and autonomy, than could be expected by looking at political declarations or laws. Is it an accident that the imposition of martial law in 1981, terrifying in the threats it spelled out, was by far the most benign case of the sort in recent history?

2   Special cases of this situation of double standards have been singled out by Polish sociologists for detailed scrutiny. One goes under the heading of fake or phoney actions (Lutynski 1990). This signifies puzzling ritualistic activities devoid of any intrinsic meaning or purpose at all. Their meaninglessness is clearly recognized by the actors, but also, paradoxically, by the authorities who expect or demand them. A classic case is the reports on the realization of production plans, almost invariably exaggerated and skewed. The bias aggregates as it passes through all levels of the centralized economy and produces entirely unrealistic economic statistics, which are taken afterwards as a basis for future plans. Likewise there were costly and burdensome electoral procedures, although the elected were in fact chosen and nominated in advance. The fact that everybody pretends to be serious and credible in these charades can only be explained by their 'extrinsic function' in affirming an opportunistic loyalty to the game everybody is playing, to its strange but autocratically imposed rules and principles.

3   Another variant of double standards is concerned not so much with actions as with speech. Sometimes it is called 'double talk', or more bluntly the 'structures of organized lying' (Ash 1990a: 18). It describes a dissociation between things said in public and in private. The context determines strikingly different forms and content: speaking (or writing) in public situations or in public roles, people use a specific syntax, vocabulary, phraseology, symbolism (what George Orwell called 'newspeak'). Speakers make dogmatic, uncritical, ideologically flavoured claims. Not many listeners take them seriously, and even the speakers turn to a completely different language and

defend opposite claims when they are no longer speaking in public. In private they are even able to distance themselves from their own conduct, to adopt a critical posture and ridicule their own words, almost as if there were two different games, completely separate and played under opposite rules.

4   A further pervasive behavioural pattern entailed by the opposition of the private and public spheres is the constant attempt to outwit or 'beat the system'. Sociologists have named this 'parasitic innovativeness' (Marody 1990). This may be a euphemism for downright cheating or fraud, but it may also take more subtle forms. One is the search for loopholes in legal regulations – an easy job considering the legislative chaos, antinomies, inconsistencies and excessively casuistic, detailed character of 'socialist law'. Another mechanism produces widespread 'institutionalized evasions' of rules, which are partly due to intentionally loose or inefficient enforcement. Finally there is constant vigilance to guard against expected irrational changes in the terms of trade (higher prices, taxes, duties), with the attempt to beat them by hoarding food or petroe, rushing to import or export goods, or opening businesses oriented to quick profit rather than long-term investment. The prevalence of such a 'grab-and-run' attitude shows that most people try to attain their private goals 'in spite of the system' rather than 'through the system'. It is interesting to note that such behaviour is often treated as praiseworthy, and those who are successful inspire wide esteem tainted with envy. The underlying, more or less conscious justification is based on the belief that it is a sort of equitable revenge on a system which is cheating the citizens, and a way to obtain some compensation for benefits unjustly lost.

5   The next characteristic behavioural pattern is a widespread reluctance to take responsible decisions, or a willingness to take them only in ways assuring unaccountability (on the phone, orally, without any records etc.), with a tendency to delegate responsibility (interminable 'passing the buck'), and at the same time to demand care, social security and other free benefits from the authorities. As this syndrome is normally typical for children, we may call it 'prolonged infantilism'. Its obverse side is the paternalistic posture often taken by the authorities. As Stefan Nowak observes, 'The belief that our socio-economic system should satisfy at least the minimum needs of all citizens seems to derive from four decades of socialist education. The perception of any deviance from this rule creates one of the strongest threats to the social legitimacy of the system' (1987: 11).

6   A final set of actions is prompted by what has been called 'disinterested envy'. Socialist ideology, with its emphasis on primitive egalitarianism well expressed by the slogan that 'all people have equal stomachs', implants a kind of instinct against unusual achievement, excessive profits, exceptional success, a fierce resentment of any sort of elite. Hence there appears a variety of actions taken to prevent others from reaching eminence, even if it is not occurring in the competitive context, and somebody's success does not diminish anyone else's chances. A famous joke describes the 'Polish inferno': sinners of all nationalities are boiling in huge pots on an open fire, each pot

guarded by armed devils. Only the pot marked 'Poland' is unguarded. Why? Because if anybody climbs out to escape, his compatriots will certainly pull him back in.

It might have been expected that once the institutional structures of 'real socialism' have been torn down, the 'socialist mind' will disappear as well. Unfortunately that is not the case. As one informed researcher testifies: 'What is striking when we analyse political attitudes in the 1990s is their surprising, truly structural similarity to the attitudes encountered and described in earlier periods' (Marody 1991: 166). By some vicious irony of history, the core opposition of the public and private spheres, together with most of its psychological and behavioural expressions, has outlived the communist system, and stands in the way of post-communist reforms. Let me enumerate some more spectacular symptoms of this surprising persistence.

In spite of constant reminders that 'we are at last in our own home', people seem not to care, and are reluctant to be involved in public actions. The continued passivism and political apathy are remarkable: in the first democratic elections after half a century, 38 per cent of the population chose not to vote, and in the local elections (even closer to 'our own home') 58 per cent were absent. Almost every second Pole did not think it worthwhile to cast his ballot for the first democratic president, and with a pluralistic spectrum of associations and political parties mushrooming during the year, more than 90 per cent of the population decided not to belong to any of them (*Gazeta Wyborcza*, 25 April 1991).

The government is still perceived as in opposition to society, as 'them' against 'us'. In free presidential elections Tadeusz Mazowiecki, a man of impeccable credentials and indisputable achievements, turned out to be 'tainted' by being in the government (as the first prime minister of post-communist Poland) and gained fewer votes than Stanislaw Tyminski, a populist demagogue arriving from Canada, completely unknown and precisely for that reason free of any association with the established authorities, which were still treated with suspicion.

People continue their game of 'beating the system', as if nothing has changed, as if the system were still alien, imposed, to be rejected. 'Parasitic innovativeness' flourishes in new forms made possible by privatization, the emerging capitalist market and the uncertainties of transitional laws. Masses of people are involved in all sorts of illicit trading, smuggling, tax and duty evasions. New, highly organized forms of such activities appear. To observers of the spreading entrepreneurial activities, it is amazing how large a part of them are still based on distrust, uncertainty of the future and traditional 'grab-and-run' tactics.

'Disinterested envy' is still very much around, and in fact has more opportunities of expression and more potential targets, as the number of those who have 'made it' (reached political office, become rich quickly, opened successful businesses, or attained public fame) is growing at considerable speed.

Resentment of this group easily resorts to old egalitarian modes of rhetoric. As an acute observer of the eastern European scene correctly notes: 'In most of these countries there is still widespread support for relatively egalitarian distribution of the wealth thus created and for a strong welfare state' (Ash 1990a: 21). The mood spreads to all kinds of elites, including the intellectuals (of course called the 'eggheads').

Among the majority who have not 'made it', or have even lost their earlier standard of living in the turmoil of revolutionary change (e.g. large segments of the working class, the peasantry, not to speak of more than a million unemployed – a phenomenon non-existent during the 'socialist' period), there is a growing nostalgia for the old arrangements of the paternalistic state accompanied by a clamour for compensation. There is the expectation that the government must provide for basic needs, free medical services, free education, jobs, pensions, social security and welfare benefits. Probably not so many would want to return to communism, but large masses dream of some 'third way', humanitarian capitalism, or (paraphrasing the old slogans about socialism) 'capitalism with a human face', or a 'Polish' road to capitalism.

These are only some of the moods and sentiments mysteriously resembling old ways of thinking and doing. They make up the persistent legacy of 'real socialism' haunting eastern European societies from the grave. Without overcoming this legacy, which may take at least a generation, the full success of post-communist transition will not be possible. This proves once again how powerful a factor in social change the ideas people hold may be.

17

Normative emergence: evasions and innovations

The normative core of social structure

Social life is regulated by rules. The order of norms, values, institutions regulating human conduct is considered as the central aspect of society by numerous scholars. In his classical formulation, Emile Durkheim conceived 'social facts' in unmistakably normative terms:

> When I carry out my obligations as brother, husband, or citizen, when I comply with contracts I perform duties which are defined externally to myself and my acts, in law and in custom. Even if they conform to my own sentiments and I feel their reality subjectively, this reality is still objective, for I did not create them, I merely received them through my education. . . . Here are the ways of acting, thinking and feeling that present the remarkable property of existing outside of individual consciousness. These types of conduct or thought are not only external to the individual but are, moreover, endowed with an imperative and coercive power, by virtue of which they impose themselves upon him, independent of his individual will. (*Durkheim 1972: 63–4*)

We find a similar normative emphasis in the idea of 'axionormative order' worked out by Florian Znaniecki. In his words: 'Social order in this view denotes simply axionormative order among phenomena called social . . . The social organization is founded on collectively recognized and supported norms, which regulate not only actions but experiences and representations of its members . . . All cultural phenomena are social since all are subjected to collectively sanctioned rules' (1971: 651–2). There was a strong concern with the normative foundations of social consensus and system equilibrium in the work of structural-functionalists (Parsons 1951). The 'dramaturgical school', and particularly Ervin Goffman, supplied a subtle analysis of the implicit normative framework of the social drama (Goffman 1963, 1967, 1971). Ethnomethodologists were digging ever deeper into the intricacies of the taken-for-granted normative assumptions underlying social life (Garfinkel 1967). More recently Tom Burns and his group (Burns and Flam 1987) have proposed a comprehensive theory of 'rule systems' and 'rule regimes'. These are just selected examples, but they prove that indeed 'The importance of social norms and their key position in social life have been widely recognized by social scientists' (Segerstedt 1966: 105). Perhaps it is no great exaggeration to claim with Harry Johnson that 'The concept of a norm is a central one in sociology' (1960: 8).

In this chapter we shall briefly examine two ways in which this crucial aspect of society may undergo changes: the process of institutionalized evasions and normative innovations.

Institutionalized evasions of rules

By normative change I understand the emergence, replacement or modification of components of the normative structure: norms, values, roles, institutions, institutional complexes. For the sake of simplicity, I shall speak of the change of norms, but all that will be said applies equally to other, more complex normative clusters. I shall focus on the way in which norms (or changed norms) emerge out of actions undertaken by various social agents. These may be ordinary people in their everyday behaviour, producing incremental change, or other agents undertaking normative reform, producing enacted change.

The change of norms presupposes a normative deviation as a sort of prelude. As Robert Bierstedt observes, 'some deviations from an old structure are almost certainly part of the process of creating a new one' (1981: 461), but deviations are not of a piece. This crucial category requires precise definition, and in the analysis that follows I shall draw heavily on the classical contributions of Robert Merton. He has suggested the following concept of a deviance: 'An adaptation is described as deviant (and not invidiously so) when behavior departs from what is required by cultural goals, or by institutional norms, or by both' (1959: 178). He observes that deviance should not be confused with merely idiosyncratic conduct; one must 'distinguish new forms of behavior that are well within the range of the institutionally prescribed or allowed and new forms that are outside this range. Following the useful terminology of Florence Kluckhohn, the first of these can be described as "variant" behavior and only the second as "deviant"' (p. 181). Similarly, the 'toleration' of variant behaviour, the scope of allowed concrete implementations of a general norm, is to be distinguished from 'factual permissiveness', the passive attitude of social audiences to behaviour regarded as deviant, and even more from what may be called 'institutionalized permissiveness', the prohibition against the negative sanctioning of deviant acts. The latter sense is adopted by Jacobsen, who defines permissiveness as 'the institutionalized social climate wherein a person can violate accepted norms in public without incurring sanctions' (1979: 223).

Merton distinguishes two major forms of deviance in the proper sense: nonconforming behaviour (or principled deviance) and aberrant behaviour (or expedient deviance). These differ in several important respects. (1) Nonconformity is public, while aberrant behaviour private: 'nonconformers announce their dissent publicly; they do not try to hide their departures from social norms. Political or religious dissenters insist on making their dissent known to as many as will look or listen; aberrant criminals seek to avoid the limelight of public scrutiny' (Merton 1982b: 72). (2) Nonconformity involves the withdrawal of legitimacy from current norms, while aberrant behaviour is accompanied by according legitimacy to norms: 'Nonconformers challenge the legitimacy of social norms they reject, or at least challenge their applicability to certain kinds of situations . . . Aberrants, in contrast, acknowledge the legitimacy of the norms they violate but consider such violation expedient or expressive of their state of mind' (p. 73). (3) Nonconformity is positive, constructive; aberrant behaviour is merely negativistic: 'nonconformers aim to change the norms they are denying in practice. They want to replace what they believe to be morally suspect norms with ones having a sound moral basis. Aberrants in contrast, try primarily to escape the sanctioning force of existing norms, without proposing substitutes for them' (p. 73).

Nonconforming and aberrant behaviour initiates two different paths of *normative morphogenesis*, with different stages and internal mechanisms. One may be called morphogenesis via normative innovation; the other, morphogenesis via norm evasion. Both are forms of social becoming. Let us take a closer look at each of them, starting with the second.

Morphogenesis via norm evasion starts from incidents of aberrant behaviour by individuals who find the norms too demanding for them, even though generally legitimate. As Jacobsen defines it: 'A norm evasion . . . is a special subtype of norm violations in that it is deliberate as well as devious' (1979: 220). For example, the thief does not question the legitimacy of the fifth commandment; he will certainly be outraged if something is stolen from him, and not surprised at all if caught and sentenced. In Merton's words, this case comes down to 'the gradual attenuation of legitimate, but by and large ineffectual, strivings and the increasing use of illegitimate, but more or less effective, expedients' (1968: 200). We certainly evade some norms all of the time, and some norms from time to time.

Some evasions of norms remain fully private, invisible, undetected, and therefore socially inconsequential. They do not initiate processes of social becoming, but when evasions are more widespread, undertaken by a plurality of individuals, public awareness is apt to be awakened. Their more and more frequent occurrence may become widely recognized, even though the culprits are not identified. When they do become identified, the examples of particularly skilful evaders may become the subject of public lore, often tainted with envy. As Merton observes: 'Those successful rogues – successful as this is measured by the criteria of their significant reference groups – become prototypes for others in their environment who, initially less vulnerable and less alienated, now no longer keep to the rules they once regarded as legitimate' (1964: 235). A good example is provided by private entrepreneurs in the countries of 'real socialism'; with their riches, conspicuous consumption, political connections, they are often taken as role-models, especially by the younger generation, even though everybody knows that to get anywhere they must have broken all sorts of laws regulating the planned economies.

The occurrence of common incentives to evasion among large collectivities of individuals, coupled with the widespread belief that 'everybody does it' and the tendency to imitate sucessful evaders, accounts for the patterning of evasions, their regular and repeatable character. For Robin Williams 'patterned evasion' signifies a situation 'where a publicly accepted norm is covertly violated on a large scale, with the tacit acceptance or even approval of the same society or group, at least as long as the violation is concealed' (1970: 419–0). Tax evasions, cheating in examinations, petty theft in business firms and avoidance of customs duties and currency controls provide familiar examples. A particularly interesting case typical for former socialist countries was the widespread theft of goods, raw materials, tools etc. from state-owned enterprises. Here the traditional moral inhibitions applying to private ownership apparently did not not work, because for many people 'state-owned' meant the same as 'nobody's'.

The occurrence of patterned evasions is the next step on the path of normative morphogenesis (but note that the norms are still accorded legitimacy). The most crucial phase comes when, as Merton puts it, 'A mounting frequency of deviant but "successful" behavior tends to lessen and, as an extreme potentiality, to eliminate the legitimacy of the institutional norms for others in the system' (1968: 234). It is only now that his concept of 'institutionalized evasions' fully applies:

> Evasions of institutional rules are themselves institutionalized when they are (1) patterned in fairy well-defined types; (2) adopted by substantial numbers of people rather than being scattered subterfuges independently and privately arrived at; (3) organized in the form of a fairly elaborate social machinery made up of tacitly cooperating participants, including those who are socially charged with implementing the rules; and (4) rarely punished and when they are, punished in largely symbolic forms that serve primarily to reafiirm the sanctity of the rules. (*Merton 1982b: 76*)

Institutionalization in this sense is more than the mere patterning, since it involves not only repetition or regularity of behaviour but the granting of a degree of legitimacy; widespread acceptance or even positive sanctioning to evasive behavior. This pattern evolves 'whenever the laws governing an organization have lagged behind the changing interests, values, and wants of the substantial part of the underlying population. For a time, the evasions make the law tolerable' (Merton 1963: ix). An excellent example of institutionalized evasions is provided by certain kinds of divorce procedures:

> to be effective evasions require an elaborate social machinery made up of tacitly cooperating clients, lawyers, judges, trained connivers and specialized creators of make-believe evidence of adultery; the evasive practices are widely known to depart from the letter and spirit of the law but . . . they are nevertheless

condoned by officers of the court charged with implementing the law; and finally, the evasions are rarely punished, and when they are, they provide largely ceremonial occasions for reaffirming the sanctity of the law. (*Merton 1963: ix–x*)

There are three more specific variants of institutionalized evasions. The first is 'norm erosion'. This occurs when evaded norms are long established and traditional in the normative structure, but no longer congruent with current realities. This is best illustrated by the slowly liberalizing sex mores, or the gradually weakening legal standards concerning pornography (the shifting line between 'soft' and 'hard' pornography, as well as constantly more permissive rules of acceptable nudity, typical of the so-called '*Playboy*' syndrome').

The second variant is 'norm resistance'. In contrast to the case of norm erosion, the norms being evaded are new, freshly introduced by enactment 'from above', and departing from established ways of conduct. 'The newly-imposed institutional demands are in fact evaded while the slowly-changing norms and sentiments continue to govern actual behavior' (Merton 1968: 372). A good example is the commonly encountered resistance to legal reforms running against shared customs, stereotypes, prejudices or strong moral convictions (as in the case of Prohibition, civil rights legislation, attempts to change marriage rules in African colonies, or collectivization of rural property in socialist countries).

A third modality involves 'norm substitution'. This occurs when an old norm remains in force but widespread evasion acquires tentative legitimacy through the scale and long tradition of its occurrence. As Jacobsen explains: 'Patterned evasions may acquire partial legitimacy by sheer longevity, and become a tradition by default. When this happens, the norm itself does not change, but the evasion gains a measure of legitimacy from "benign neglect"' (1979: 226). Thus prohibitions of smoking in public places are often ignored since 'no one seemed to object to it till now' (p. 226), but these become operative when violations are strongly objected to in public.

These successive types of institutionalized evasions lead to the final phase of a morphogenetic process: the introduction of new norms by the authorities, or their attaining, by evasion, the status of sanctioned norms, fully legitimized and embedded in a new normative structure. The old evasion becomes accepted and sanctioned as a new norm. For example, referring to the notoriously widespread evasions of obsolete divorce laws, Merton observes: 'should public testimony to these institutionalized evasions repeatedly occur, bringing out into the open the full extent of the gap between the principles of the law and the frequency of circumventory practices, this would also exert powerful pressure in its way for change of the law' (1963: ix). Similarly, notorious evasions of various proscriptions formerly imposed in eastern European countries on ownership of foreign currency (witnessed by the emergence of an extensive black market) has gradually led to the suspension of

obsolete and unrealistic laws, and then the enactment of new currency regulations, even more liberal than in some western countries (e.g. the removal
of limits to currency flow to and from abroad now obtaining in Poland). With
a normative reform of this sort, the situation changes completely: complying
with the old norm becomes an act of deviance (or at least anachronistic,
traditional or unusual conduct), whereas deviance in the old sense, becomes
an act of conformity. This closes a cycle of morphogenesis, and of course
opens a new one, as new norms will inevitably be evaded, at least by some
members of society, and the process of formulating, replacing and modifying
norms via normative evasions will start to operate again.

Normative innovations

The alternative mechanism of normative morphogenesis is the accumulation
of innovations. In this case the agents do not resort to expedient evasions of
norms they otherwise accept, but rather question the validity of the norms
themselves. The norm (routine, tradition, custom, law) is denied legitimacy
from the beginning, and rejective behaviour (nonconformity) is public, open
and sometimes even ostentatious. Sticking to Merton's terminology, the paradigmatic case of behaviour starting this process is called 'rebellion':

> This adaptation leads men outside the environing social structure to envisage
> and seek to bring into being a new, that is to say, a greatly modified social
> structure. It presupposes alienation from reigning goals and standards. These
> come to be regarded as purely arbitrary. And the arbitrary is precisely that
> which can neither exact allegiance nor possess legitimacy, for it might as well
> be otherwise. . . . Rebellion involves a genuine transvaluation, where the direct
> or vicarious experience of frustration leads to full denunciation of previously
> prized values. (*Merton 1968: 209–10*)

This concept has a very wide denotation: it applies to the innovator or
discoverer breaking through a received framework of prevailing technology
or dominant scientific paradigm; to the religious prophet or moral authority
dictating a new definition of goodness and justice; to the artist or writer
proposing a new style; to the enterpreneur reorganizing production or trade;
to the politician or ruler imposing new codifications of laws, and so on. In
each case it starts from some episode of human creativeness, originality or
dissent from existing traditions. By definition, such episodes must be exceptional, occurring only among a selected few, or at most a minority of societal
members. As the Loomises put it: 'The modes of nonconforming
adaptations . . . are in reality non-modal alternatives employed by the minority, which may in time supplant the conforming adaptations, and are likely to
do so to the degree that they are functionally superior for greater numbers of
the population than presently employed behavior patterns' (Loomis and Loomis
1961: 316).

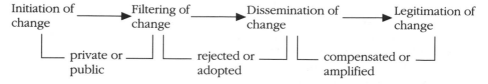

Figure 17.1   Sequential stages in the diffusion of innovations.

There is a considerable distance between the moment when some individual or a group of individuals conceives of an innovation, and the time when it becomes finally accepted and replaces earlier ways and modes of human conduct (cf. Coleman et al., 1966). The process can be broken into a sequence of four stages, as in figure 17.1.

At each stage we may observe full contingency; the process may continue or not, produce normative morphogenesis or become stopped in its tracks. There is some resemblance of this model to the notion of 'value-added' process in Smelser's account of collective behavior.

> Every stage in the value-added process . . . is a necessary condition for the appropriate and effective addition of value in the next stage. The sufficient condition for final production, moreover, is the combination of every necessary condition, according to a definite pattern. As the value-added process moves forward, it narrows progressively the range of possibilities of what the final product might become. (*Smelser 1962: 14*)

Thus, already at the first stage, the innovation may remain private, fully idiosyncratic, and attempts to publicize it may fail all along the line. Manuscripts remaining in drawers, prototypes of new machines left in cupboards, ideas dreamed about in private and not shared with others are examples of when innovations do not become public or widely known, and therefore cannot have any further social consequences. It is not by accident that one of the fundamental institutional rules included in the ethos of science demands the publication of discoveries, in print or at least orally, which Merton calls the norm of 'communism' or perhaps better 'communalism' of scientific results (1973: 273). The whole meaning and social significance of science would be lost without this prescription.

Visibility, however, is only a necessary, not a sufficient condition of success. Even when innovations become known, it does not mean that they are immediately socially consequential. The filtering of change involves various agents who may still block the innovation from spreading widely in society. Some of those agents may be non-specialized, taking up the filtering functions as a marginal activity (a conservative teacher suppressing all manifestations of individuality, traditionally oriented neighbours spreading gossip about the extravagant manners of a new tenant, a rigid manager forbidding any experiment with new production techniques). In modern societies, however, there are numerous specialized agents for whom the filtering of innovations (or 'gate-keeping') is not a marginal activity but their main *raison d'être*. Well-known examples would include censors, referees of articles or books, editorial boards, patent offices, qualifying committees etc. Of course this is not restricted to modern society. The infamous Inquisition and witch-hunts in medieval times were clearly the forerunners of ideological gate-keeping, much more vicious than most modern filtering mechanisms. Through the operation of various filtering or blocking mechanisms, normative innovations may be terminated at this early stage. By means of suppression, rigid and coercive social control, censorship, rejection, red tape, legislative obstruction etc., the normative innovation may be prevented from receiving consideration, recognition or initial acceptance in the wider community or society.

The main question of course concerns the nature of those criteria (or selectors) which stop some innovations from spreading out and allow others to get through. It may be suspected that a crucial selector, but one operating only in the long run, consists of the objective vested interests of the societal members. As Merton puts it: 'Some (unknown) degree of deviation from current norms is probably functional for the basic goals of all groups. A certain degree of "innovation", for example, may result in the formation of new institutionalized patterns of behavior which are more adaptive than the old in making for realization of primary goals' (1968: 236). In the short run, before that ultimate criterion affirms itself, the selection may be due to mystified images of vested interests shared by the people (false consciousness, ideology), or even more commonly, to the imposed particularistic interests of those in power (governments, strong pressure groups, dictators of fashions or styles, guardians of religious or ideological orthodoxy), able and resourceful enough to uphold the norms and values conducive to their well-being and suppress any threat from alternative norms and values.

Once the innovation succeeds in breaking through all filtering mechanisms and reaches wider society, the phase of dissemination begins. This may take various modalities.

1   There may be compensation, when the initial change triggers negative feedbacks tending to diminish the significance of normative innovation, render it inconsequential or eliminate it altogether by means of a counter-reform.

2   Another possibility is overcompensation, when the resistance mobilized against the normative innovation is so strong that the compensatory mechanisms overreact and 'spill over', not only preserving the *status quo* but ultimately changing the structure in the direction opposite to that intended. This is the backlash or 'boomerang effect' so common, for example, in the case of radical political reforms, many of which have their 'Thermidors'. 'The attempts to strengthen a given institutional structure may unleash forces that lead rather to its change; and the opposite may happen as well' (Baumgartner et al. 1976: 216).

3   A further possibility is the insulation of change, when the initial innovation does not evoke any further repercussions. It is preserved, but restricted to the area of normative structure where it was originally introduced, with no wider consequences for other segments of society. This is the case with local customs or regional dialects restricted to isolated communities.

4   There is the case of dispersion when the initial change leads to the haphazard transformation of a certain limited number of other components of the normative structure (some single norms and values, institutions, roles etc.). This leaves a chaotic imprint on the existing normative structure, modifying it at various points, but preserving the totality of the structure intact. Speaking metaphorically, it is change by patchwork. As an example, think of the numerous piecemeal reforms introduced in response to the crisis in the eastern European socialist economies, which did not touch the basic rules; or the multiplication of laws attempting to cope with emerging social problems in an unsystematic, opportunistic manner.

5   Finally we have the most important possibility, which may be called the amplification of change, based on the operation of positive feedbacks or 'second cybernetics' (Maruyama 1963). Here, the initial change triggers a chain of subsequent changes in the other components of the normative structure, leading to the multiplication of normative innovations, the enhanced significance and consequentiality of the original one, and in some cases the total transformation of the structure. This often happens in the area of technology, e.g. the consequences that the invention of the automobile, aeroplane and computer have had for the human way of life. The domain of politics provides other fitting illustrations: we recall what the birth of the independent trade union Solidarity did for the Polish political system, or what the introduction of relatively free and open media ('glasnost') did for Soviet society.

We may see that even at this stage the value-added process is not yet completed. The normative change may still be stopped, as occurs in cases of compensation and overcompensation. But once an innovation manages to stay, whether insulated in its original form or chaotically dispersed or amplified and spread across the normative structure, the crucial matter becomes its legitimation. To persist and influence society in the long run, the changed norms, values and institutions must acquire some measure of recognition, acceptance or even active support on the part of societal members. Otherwise their existence remains precarious. When newly established normative structures lack wider legitimacy and are backed only by coercion or threats of coercion from the ruling elites or dominant pressure groups, they generate the explosive potential for dissent, contestation, opposition and rebellion. Such normative innovations cannot last long, and their inevitable rejection is apt to generate a new cycle of normative change.

18

Great individuals as agents of change

History as a human product

Social change, including large-scale historical transformations, is the achievement of human actors, the result of their actions. There is nothing in social history that is not an effect, intended or unintended, of human efforts. 'That history is made by men and women is no longer denied except by some theologians and mystical metaphysicians' (Hook 1955: xi).

To say that people make history does not tell us much about who in fact makes it, whether all men and women or just some; whether all to the same extent or with different consequence; whether all in the same area or in different domains, in the same way, or by various roads. In brief, we ask:

Who makes history?
How much history do they make?
What history do they make?
How do they make it?

To approach these questions it is necessary to distinguish the contexts in which human actors operate, the degrees of influence that their actions may have on the course of social changes, the areas where their impact is to be felt, and the ways in which they leave their imprint.

In asking who makes history, we must be aware of the basic difference between individual actors (acting people) and collective agents (acting collectivities, task groups, social movements, associations, political parties, armies, governments etc.). We shall deal with collective agents and their potential for social change in chapter 19, focusing our attention now exclusively on individuals. Among individual actors, we notice three different types. One type consists of ordinary people in their normal, everyday activities. Most of what happens in a society consists of people working and resting, eating and sleeping, travelling and walking, talking and writing, laughing and quarrelling etc. The masses of ordinary people make up the ultimate stuff of which human society consists. But there are also exceptional actors. This second type consists of such individuals who, by virtue of special personal qualities (knowledge, competence, talents, skills, strength, cunning or even 'charisma') act as representatives of others, in their name or on their behalf (Dahrendorf 1979), or who manipulate or suppress others, even without their consent. This includes leaders, prophets, ideologues, patriarchs, statesmen, dictators, tyrants etc. The third type consists of those who occupy exceptional positions, which endow them with particular prerogatives (irrespective of exceptional personal qualities, which sometimes they may also possess, though often they do not). Their roles allow and even demand actions with consequences for other people, deciding their fate (in other words making binding decisions, and even exercising 'metapower'; shaping rules by which others are to abide). We have in mind rulers, legislators, managers, administrators, policemen etc.

This typology of actors can be cross-combined with another one, dealing with the characteristic modes of action. If we consider the form that actions can take, there seems to be a continuum. (1) At one pole we shall find everyday activities, with purely egotistic, private motivations and intentions. Unwittingly, in unintended and often unrecognized ways, each of them may have important side-effects affecting other people, or even more lasting social institutions; all of them, aggregated together, certainly have such far-reaching social consequences (e.g. using language, evading norms, inventing new tools). (2) Moving along the continuum we shall find actions taken in the wider context of collective behaviour, a sort of additive, poorly co-ordinated sum of individual actions, still devoid of common intent, but because of their massivenss and 'togethereness' able to produce immediate and important social consequences. Crowds, panics, hostile outbursts, riots illustrate this phenomenon. (3) Next in line come collective actions, also taken together with others, but now intended, purposeful, co-ordinated attempts to reach some common goal for the participants themselves or for the wider society (e.g. petitions, public manifestations, campaigns etc.). (4) A separate category is occupied by enterpreneurial activities, organizing, co-ordinating, mobilizing, educating, indoctrinating others in order to evoke action of the intended sort on their part. (5) Finally there are political actions, the exercise of power (or the struggle for power in order to exercise it later); ordering, manipulating, legislating, codifying (and also conspiring, campaigning, contesting elections etc.).

So much for the forms that actions may take. Now if we move to the content or target of actions taken by individual actors, one more typology can be added. Some actions are targeted directly on structures; they produce, or change, or support them. They make up the first category of our typology: the structure-building proper. This has several varieties. When new norms are imposed, original ideas devised, new interactions begun, new hierarchies of inequalities formed, we witness true morphogenesis. When norms are changed, ideas reformulated, interactional channels switched, opportunities redistributed, structural change obtains. When all that happens is that norms are enforced, ideas supported, lines of interaction sustained and inequalities petrified, these actions produce structural continuation. Structure-building in these various modes, does not exhaust all types of action. Another comprises those directed at other agents rather than structures. Here we shall find socializing, educating, indoctrinating, mobililizing, organizing, co-ordinating etc. By moulding, reshaping or enhancing agents' dispositions or capacities, such actions may also indirectly influence structures, contributing to social change. Finally, we encounter actions directed at the environment, targeted on objects, either nature, or already 'humanized nature', i.e. civilization. Labour is the paradigmatic example of this last category.

As we see, there are various guises in which 'people make history'. Hence, our second major question must be asked: How much history do they make? Is their contribution equal or varied? It is obvious that we have an extremely wide spectrum of cases, from actions of common people in their everyday routines to the extraordinary feats of great leaders. Understandably enough, the latter have been more salient, and accordingly have drawn much more attention from the beginning of the systematic study of social change. We shall follow this tradition. Therefore, without ignoring or denigrating the role of ordinary people, individually minuscule but in their aggregation decisive for the course of change, we shall focus on the role of great individuals, whose imprint on the shape of history has been incomparably larger and much more direct.

Clearly there are various scales and shades of 'greatness'. Even if we avoid moral evaluations and take into account only the measure of objective influence, the category will still be quite heterogeneous. Take the factor of time. At one pole we have those who have left, for good or ill, a lasting imprint on centuries of human history: Jesus and Buddha, Caesar and Napoleon, Stalin and Hitler, Copernicus and Edison. At the other pole there are those modern trend-setters, leaders of styles and fashions, fads and crazes, who may acquire a tremendous following and in some domains be able to change the life-patterns of large masses of people, but only temporarily, soon to be replaced by others: Elvis Presley and the Beatles, Madonna and Prince, Pierre Cardin and Gianni Versace. The scale of influence may also vary in space. There are those who have only a local following, or leave their imprint on limited communities or at most single countries, and there are those whose following or impact is truly global. Compare Pol Pot and Lenin, Pinochet and Hitler. Finally, the influence varies as to its subject. Here our third question comes in: What history do they make? At one pole there are leaders of action: generals, politicians, dictators. At the other, there are leaders of thought: prophets, sages, philosophers, scholars, intellectuals. And of course along all three axes, there is an extreme variety of concrete cases, differing in temporal extent, spatial scope and the area of influence.

Thus our last question has to be considered: How do they make history? Such an imprint is left either unwittingly or purposefully. Objective consequences and subjective intentions do not necessarily coincide. Copernicus certainly did not imagine that his astronomical discoveries would revolutionize scientific, religious and even common-sense thinking in the centuries to come. James Watt did not intend or anticipate the dramatic changes in the whole of human civilization which were to follow his invention of the steam engine. Niels Bohr did not envisage that his discoveries in the esoteric area of atomic particles would encourage the development of nuclear weapons, dramatically changing the military balance and political history of the world after the Second World War. These heroes of thought simply did not consider themselves as 'makers of history', even though their ideas resulted in vast historical changes. The heroes of action may also fall into this category. Alexander the Great may have been totally unaware that his victory over the Persians would save western civilization for the coming millennia. Christopher Columbus certainly did not dream that he was discovering the terrain of a future super-power, destined to dominate world history. They were just doing their job of fighting or sailing, ignorant of the fact that they were triggering processes of world-historical scale. Sometimes they were acting on sheer emotional or moral impulse – without any clear-cut goal at all. Rosa Parks, the black woman from Montgomery, Alabama, refusing to sit in the segregated part of a public bus, did not know that she was igniting the giant civil rights movement which was to change the face of America in the years to come.

On the other hand, of course, there are also those who consciously see themselves in great historical roles, with the ambition to change the world. Napoleon and Marx, Robespierre and Lenin, Gorbachev and Reagan are just some examples. In their case, the distinction of subjective intentions and objective consequences is still valid. Quite often, they do not coincide. The irony of history plays tricks on the most ambitious reformers and revolutionaries. Some produce lasting historical results, but different from, or even contrary to, what they intended. As Karl Popper observed, most revolutions produce consequences contrary to what was dreamed of by the revolutionaries. More generally: 'Even those [institutions and traditions] which arise as the result of conscious and intentional human actions are, as a rule, the indirect, the unintended and often the unwanted by-products of such actions' (Popper 1950: 286). The deeply moral, romantic and humanitarian concerns of Karl Marx degenerated into one of the most oppressive and inhuman political systems in world history. Here good intentions clearly escaped their creator and led to most vicious consequences. It may also be the other way round. In more recent history, all the evidence indicates that Mikhail Gorbachev, by initiating the policy of *glasnost* and *perestroika*, was trying to save the crumbling communist system rather than preside over its total collapse. His intentions, far from revolutionary, resulted in perhaps the deepest historical transformation of modern times. Thus his place in history books is guaranteed not so much by what he wanted to attain as by the objective role he played. It is only exceptionally that great leaders or politicians are able to achieve the historical goals that they set themselves. If they ever do, it is more likely in the case of small-scale piecemeal social reforms than with huge projects of global reconstruction (Popper 1964).

Competing theories

Systematic philosophical and sociological reflection on the role of great individuals in history has moved back and forth between two opposite orientations: heroic determinism and social determinism. Inevitably there has also arisen the middle-of-the-road position, trying to combine valuable insights from both the extreme doctrines. This will be called the evolutionary-adaptive approach.

The doctrine of heroic determinism is rooted in the more general assumptions of individualism and voluntarism. All there is in history, it assumes, is the effect of individual actions (individualism), and history is infinitely malleable, responsive to individual efforts (voluntarism). In other words, only individuals can influence history, and history is fully influenceable. Among individuals, it is claimed, it is the great individuals who make the most difference, who account for most historical change.

The classical formulation of this position appears in the work of the Scottish historian and philosopher Thomas Carlyle (1795–1881). He is quite emphatic: 'In all epochs of the world's history, we shall find the Great Man to have been the indispensable saviour of his epoch; the lightning without which the fuel never would have burnt. The History of the World . . . was the Biography of Great Men, (1963: 17). 'Universal history, the history of what man has accomplished in this world, is at bottom the History of the Great Men who have worked here' (p. 1). More specifically:

> They were the leaders of men, these great ones; the modellers, patterns, and in wide sense creators, of whatsoever the general mass of men contrive to do or to attain; all things that we see standing accomplished in the world are properly the outer material result, the practical realisation and embodiment, of Thoughts that dwelt in the Great Men sent into the world: the soul of the whole world's history, it may justly be considered, was the history of these. (*p. 1*)

The particular mark of greatness is the intellectual power to comprehend reality and the ability to act appropriately. There are exceptional individuals who 'are intuitively aware of the Divine Idea beneath appearances; and have an intimation of the significance of the universal processes going on behind the curtains of prosaic existence' (L. Young 1939: 81). The ultimate measure of greatness is in deeds. 'There is no question but that Carlyle puts a higher premium on the hero as a man of action than as a man of thought' (L. Young 1939: 84). The contribution of great individuals is reciprocated by the reactions of wider society. Carlyle believes that heroes evoke feelings of loyalty, reverence, obedience and worship from the masses of followers: 'We all love great men; love, venerate and bow down submissive before great men' (Carlyle 1963: 19). This provides the most important social bond: 'And what, therefore, is loyalty proper, the life-breath of all society, but an effluence of Hero-worship, submissive admiration for the truly great? Society is founded on Hero-worship' (p. 15). Carlyle provides us with meticulous analysis of several kinds of heroes: those who are identified with gods, those who are treated as only the representatives of gods (the prophets and the priests), then the poets, the writers, the rulers and artists: Mahomet, Dante, Shakespeare, Luther, Cromwell, Napoleon among others.

A similar stand, though even more radical, is taken by one of Carlyle's early followers, the historian Frederick Adams Wood. He focuses on just one category of heroes, the kings, and argues for their crucial importance to European history. The study of 386 sovereign monarchs led him to the conclusion that strong, mediocre and weak monarchs were ruling in strong, mediocre and weak periods in nations' histories in about 70 per cent of cases. Such a correlation was taken as proof that 'The work of the world has been initiated and directed by a few very great men' (1913, quoted in Hook 1955: 51). In an implicit way the doctrine of heroic determinism has become a canon of textbook historiography, with its focus on Caesars, Alexanders, Napoleons, Cromwells, Robespierres, Hitlers, Stalins and other icons.

The main challenge and difficulty for the proponents of the doctrine is the reference to the historical context, social circumstances, concrete situations in which great individuals act. Such consideration invariably shows that, irrespective of their personal greatness, they have always been constrained, limited in what they could achieve. Clearly, not everything can be done in human society, there are barriers to human will, even if it is the will of heroes. Thus at least in this constraining capacity, other factors, external to acting individuals, must be drawn into the analysis of history-making.

There is one way to counter this charge which is still open to dogmatic defenders of heroic determinism: to claim that the conditions which constrain heroes are merely the legacy of the great individuals living earlier, who have left the world shaped by their historical deeds. With this temporal corection, it is argued, the exclusive role of individuals seems confirmed. But such a 'genetic heroic determinism' comes dangerously close to infinite regress and tautological reasoning.

The doctrine of social determinism is founded on opposite assumptions and makes opposite claims. It is rooted in some version of 'historicism', emphasizing the predetermined course of history driven by immanent forces and insulated from the impact of human individuals, including the great heroes. Fatalism reigns, nothing can really be done about ongoing, necessary and irreversible changes, and the only effective actions are those which coincide with immanent historical tendencies, at most able to release them or speed them up. Thus individuals are fragments tossed on historical waves, either irrelevant or at best the carriers of historical processes, embodiments of history, its necessities, directions, and goals. It is the time that gives birth to great individuals.

Despite this, historical necessities can be consciousley recognized in various measures, perceived and anticipated more or less correctly. People are more or less perceptive, more or less sensitive to current tendencies, more or less imaginative in envisaging the future. In all these respects individuals differ. Those who are more successful in understanding the necessary tendencies of their time will attain higher stature as they adapt better and act more effectively. They become great individuals, their greatness lying in their higher ability to read and recognize historical necessities and to act accordingly, riding the crest of the historical wave.

There are two variants of such reasoning. One is idealistic, best represented by Hegel, for whom 'The History of the World is nothing but the development of the Idea of Freedom' (1956: 456). The necessary unfolding of the Spirit is reflected in historical events. Great people are able to embody the Spirit better, to fall in step with the necessary course of history. They are 'Thinking men who had an insight into the requirements of the times: what was ripe for development' (quoted in Hook 1955: 63).

Another variant is materialistic and is best represented by the so-called 'historical materialism' proposed by Marx in his late period, and elaborated by a number of orthodox Marxists (Kautsky, Plekhanov, Stalin). For them – as we have shown in chapter 11 – the 'iron' necessities of historical development are rooted in economy and the emergence of classes with their conflicting interests. Great individuals are those who are able to grasp and represent class interests most adequately. Then they may become the 'handmaidens' of history, taking the the lead of the mass movements embodying class interests.

The main difficulty for the proponents of social determinism is the observation that some great individuals undoubtedly do change the course and speed of history. What would happen if they were not present on the historical stage? Would European history be the same if a stray bullet had hit Napoleon on the bridge at Lodi at the start of his career? Would world history have run the same course if Lenin had been arrested on his train journey from Switzerland to Russia and been unable to lead the October Revolution? Would the collapse of communism have occurred in fateful 1989 if Gorbachev had not dismantled the entrenched Soviet Empire? There are innumerable counterfactual questions like these which can validly be asked. If one makes the mental experiment, the answers must be negative: no, history would not have been the same without those great individuals. They do make a difference.

There is one defensive strategy open to the dogmatic social determinists. Great persons are the products of historical times, they may say; such individuals simply meet the needs of the epoch. Those needs are defined as necessary and have to be met by somebody, but there is no inevitability in the ascendancy of any concrete individual to a historical role. Concrete individuals are replaceable; if one were absent, another would appear to fulfil the same ultimately necessary historical role. What of those numerous cases when clearly great leaders were missing, did not appear despite pressing historical need? There seems to be nothing wrong with this argument except that there is no conceivable way it could be tested; it is empirically vacuous, since any possible evidence will fit. Thus the defence has a suspiciously *ad hoc* flavour.

It was ridiculed by Carlyle: 'The Time call forth? Alas, we have known Times call loudly enough for their great man; but not find him when they called! He was not there; Providence had not sent him; the Time, calling its loudest, had to go down to confusion and wreck because he would not come when called' (1963: 16).

In view of the inherent weaknesses of both approaches, though they also convey some important insights, the synthetic, middle-of-the-road position seems the most reasonable. It may be called 'adaptive-evolutionary' because it invokes the ideas of random mutation and natural selection. The approach, perhaps best articulated by the students of genius in science, Alfred Kroeber (1952) and Robert Merton (1973: 366–70), can be generalized and extended to other areas besides the sociology of science. Its chief asset is the allowance it makes for the important causal role of both great individuals and the social context, in mutual interaction. The argument is rooted in two principles. The principle of variation asserts the random factor of eminence (talent, skills, resourcefulness, genius) appearing in some proportion in every population. There is always some pool of outstanding individuals resulting from a kind of genetic accident. As H. Poincaré (1854–1912) put it long ago: 'The greatest bit of chance is the birth of a great man' (quoted in Hook 1955: 228). Even Carlyle recognized the undetermined appearance of genius, interpreted in his case as a gift of God: 'The most precious gift that Heaven can give to the Earth: a man of "genius" as we call it; the Soul of a Man actually sent down from the skies with God's message to us' (1963: 56).

Then the second principle starts to operate, the principle of selection. Eminent people must hit a 'ripe soil' for their ideas, innovations, actions. They must meet some existing and independently evolved social demand in the needs, expectations, aspirations of the population. If they do, their eminence is recognized, and compensated, among other rewards, by their increased capacity to influence and lead other people, and in this manner to effect social change and change the course of history. They are influential because they are followed by others. In this case they not only fulfil the verdicts of history but can really shape history, as long as they can persuade or coerce others to follow. On the other hand, if their message misses the demand of the times, no persuasion or coercion will do. They will be ignored or defeated, abandoned and forgotten. No historical consequences will follow from their actions, and they will play no historical role if they do not fit the social circumstances. There is no greatness in human society except socio-individual greatness, the happy coincidence of social and individual factors.

If one accepts this theoretical position, there are two more specific problems which have to be addressed: (1) How does this interplay of social and individual factors operate in the process of acquiring greatness, becoming the hero? (2) How is this interplay of social and individual factors manifested in being a hero, in the process of social change and history being influenced by the great individual?

Becoming a hero

People are born with certain talents, and some find a supportive socializing milieu which opens out and develops those talents, but the crucial moment comes later, when society recognizes or ignores their claim to eminence. To become a leader one must have followers. To become a prophet there must be believers. To become a famous writer there must be readers. To become a great pianist, the audiences have to be there. To count in society, one's greatness must be public and not private. It is here that the selective social mechanisms operate, elevating some individuals to the status of heroes and refusing this status to most others.

There are four proofs which indicate the importance of this social aspect of greatness.

1   There are numerous cases of outstanding individuals (innovators, artists, researchers, writers) acquiring recognition and influence only posthumously or, even worse, having their achievements credited to later authors. Such men and women clearly did not fit their times, the social conditions were not ripe for their impact, the necessary receptiveness for their ideas was not there, they anticipated a future epoch which had not yet come. The examples are numerous. In science those whose true influence came only after their death include Galileo, Cavendish, Gauss, Galois, Fleck and many others. In painting, there are the famous cases of Van Gogh, Toulouse-Lautrec and Modigliani, dying in poverty and unknown to their contemporaries only to be acclaimed and honoured decades later, and in music the similar fate of Mussorgski and Bartók.

2   The second argument is in a sense the reverse. It shows how the ripe social context not only acknowledges achievement but encourages and evokes it. The best instances come from science, where we find the widely reported phenomenon of multiple independent discoveries (Merton 1973: 343–82) appearing in clusters in periods when the scientific communities were somehow ready for the breakthroughs in specific fields. There are the famous examples of calculus (Newton and Leibniz), nitrogen (Rutherford and Scheele), the telegraph (Henry, Morse, Steinheil, Wheatstone, Cooke), photography (Daguerre, Niepce, Talbot), the planet Neptune (Adams and Leverrier), the phonograph (Cros and Edison). The scope of such 'multiples' seems to grow as we enter the epoch of modern science. Not many years ago an important breakthrough in the physics of superconductors was reported almost simultaneously by more than twenty scholars working independently. Commenting on such cases G. and J. Lenski say: 'Though not denying the ability of the individuals involved [we] suggest that few of those who have contributed most to the advance of knowledge were indispensable' (1974: 93). Rather, it was the overall condition of an academic discipline as a whole which became ripe for certain types of discoveries or inventions. One possible mechanism responsible for this may be, to put it metaphorically, a sort of a spotlight on

certain areas of research where any important results are immediately reported, becoming public, recognized and bringing fame to their authors. The context preselects those who are to become great.

3   The next proof is to be found in the historical fact that there are whole epochs of flourishing creativity, innovativeness, originality, sometimes called 'golden ages'. Greece in the fifth century BC, Maya civilization, the Italian Renaissance in the fifteenth century and the French Renaissance in the sixteenth may serve as illustrations. Why there and then? It is contrary to any known principles of nature to assume that so many more people of genius were born in those times and countries. The only explanation is a social context conducive to the flowering of human achievement.

4   The final argument concerns the notoriously unequal representation of great individuals between the sexes, races and ethnic communities. In the case of gender: in the public life of most known societies, the political leaders, monarchs, presidents and military heroes have been predominantly, if not exclusively, male. The indicators of scholarly and artistic fame are also heavily skewed towards men. If one looks at the lists of Nobel prizewinners, the acme of recognition, there are eighty-six men and only seven women in literature, ninety-seven men and only four women in chemistry. Again no available evidence could support the claim of some inborn, genetic superiority of men in respect of creativeness or innovativeness. The only explanation is ingrained social prejudice and discrimination with unequal access to the resources necessary for achievement (training, facilities, available time etc.), and unequally distributed attention to cases of actual achievement (access to publication, opinion-making gate-keepers, public notice etc.). Similar illustrations can easily be found for racial or ethnic minorities too. Here negative social selection is clearly at work, denying to members of certain gender categories, racial and ethnic groups the equitable recognition of their achievements and preventing them from entering the pantheon of heroes.

In the process of social selection differing criteria of eminence are taken into account. These provide the accepted justifications of unique, extraordinary social standing, or in other words legitimations of greatness. Such legitimating factors become institutionalized, turn into norms and rules for deciding who should be granted recognition. The bases of legitimacy vary greatly, depending on the area of achievement.

In the realm of religion, politics and warfare, which breed most of the heroes of historical stature, the earliest and most general criterion was personal charisma. As Edward Shils defines it,

> Charisma is the quality which is imputed to persons, actions, roles, institutions, symbols, and material objects because of the presumed connection with 'ultimate', 'fundamental', 'vital', order-determining powers. This presumed connection with the ultimately 'serious' elements in the universe and in human life is seen as a quality or a state of being, manifested in the bearing or demeanor and

in the actions of individual persons; it is also seen as inhering in certain roles and collectivities. (*Shils 1968: 386*)

This quality is believed to be of supernatural origins, a sign of divine grace, election or calling, a pre-designation for extraordinary deeds by the endowment of unusual talents and powers. Charisma may be subjectively, intensely experienced by its carriers, giving them a feeling of unique might, tenacity and calling. It may also be perceived by others who recognize it or ascribe it to some persons. Both self-ascription and social ascription of charisma are mutually reinforcing, and only together give birth to truly charismatic persons. As defined by Shils, 'Those persons who possess an intense subjective feeling of their own charismatic quality and who have it imputed to them by others, we will call charismatic persons' (1968: 386). If the latter is lacking, we witness at most the usurpation of charisma without any social consequences. If the former is lacking, we have a case of feigned, socially invented charisma, elevating mediocrities to fame and influence.

The notion of charisma, present since antiquity in religious contexts, was taken up and theoretically elaborated by Max Weber. He treated it as one of the three foundations of legitimate power or influence that some people may have over others in the political, military, religious and intellectual area (the alternative bases of legitimacy being legal-rational and traditional). Charismatic authority was found in creative, innovative, resourceful personalities – leaders, prophets, warriors, sages – recognized as such by their willing followers or subjects. It was seen as endowed with the strongest dynamic potential, necessarily entailing social change. For Weber 'charismatic authority is of necessity revolutionary' (Shils 1968: 387). Whereas traditional authorities and legal-rational authorities have a proclivity to routine conduct or conformist actions (implementing established life-ways or following normative principles, in which they find justification of their status), charismatic authorities, drawing their legitimacy from forces above and away from existing social institutions, are unconstrained in their struggle to leave their personal imprint on the historical process. They are ready to break the established order and to create a new order in its place. 'Charismatic persons, and those who are responsive to charismatic persons, aspire to larger transformations. They seek to break the structures of routine actions and to replace them with structures of inspired actions which are "infused" with those qualities or states of mind generated by immediate and intensive contact with the "ultimate" – with the powers which guide and determine human life' (Shils 1968: 387).

Charismatic persons develop characteristic styles of action and personality traits, which help to strenthen their image as envoys of God, incarnations of fate, harbingers of history, Fuehrers of the people etc.:

They are highly demanding and autocratic, dictating courses of action for their followers and punishing insubordination.
They keep their distance from followers, disciples and lieutenants, and

emphasize it by various props (highly formal dress or uniform, special forms of address, high platforms for speeches, huge audience rooms or offices).
They undertake extraordinary actions intended to prove their special powers (miracles performed by the saints, Mao swimming the Yangtze River).
They are highly dogmatic, fanatically devoted to the realization of projects they put forward and intolerant of criticism.
They effectively insulate themselves from unfavourable turns in public opinion, by establishing a circle of fanatical supporters, worshippers and sycophants who engender the 'group-think' phenomenon (conviction of invulnerability, omnipotence, sagacity and righteousness).

The significance of charismatic legitimation for authority is greatest in periods of social crisis, when established ways of life, rules and laws are undermined, ruling elites discredited and traditions rejected. Then the only acceptable source of authority must be sought outside the existing order. This is precisely the case with charisma, by definition springing from supernatural sources. In such periods there is also heightened sensitivity and receptiveness to charisma on the part of the masses. This is because charismatic leaders meet at least three psychological needs which become pressing in conditions of crisis:

The need for security, which finds an outlet in a paternal figure taking matters into his hands. This was perceived by Carlyle, who asserted that the most important service of kings is to 'command over us, to furnish us with constant practical teaching, to tell us for the day and hour what we are to do' (1963: 257).
The tendency to seek vicarious compensation for personal failure, inadequacy, poverty by emotional identification with a great hero, taking pride in his deeds – which a contemporary social psychologist calls 'heroization *per procura*' (Marody 1987b: 92).
The urge to avoid responsibility and personal commitment in highly uncertain ('anomic') conditions, by delegating it to a strong leader. This is emphasized by Erich Fromm, who finds in this attitude one of the psychosocial causes of fascism (Fromm 1941).

In more stable conditions, other, internal bases of authority become more important: the legal-rational, resting in an established hierarchy of offices rather than the traits of their individual incumbents, or the traditional, founded on the ancient and continuous customs of the community. The significance of agents invested with these sorts of authority for implementing radical changes will naturally be smaller than those endowed with charisma. We have dwelt at considerable length on the issue of charisma because, in the political arena, this is the trait most often ascribed to the 'makers of history', those most significant agents of social change about whom we learn from history books. In fields other than politics and religion, different criteria of eminence may be encountered. In science, knowledge is institutionalized as the fundamental criterion, both in the sense of competence (erudition, expertise) and of creativeness (innovativess). The ethos of science recognizes those who have mastered existing knowledge and also enriched it. In the arts, perfection of execution and originality (ingenuity) of form and content are decisive. In technology, efficiency and usefulness (applicability) become marks of excellence.

Being a hero

Irrespective of the ways through which one attains the status of hero, and irrespective of the legitimating criteria applied, the moment such a person is socially recognized, vast opportunties to initiate and influence social change become open. But before a potentially powerful and influential person can actually leave an imprint on the historical process, other conditions must be satisfied.

1 The social (political, economic) situation must be such that single decisions can be decisive for the future course of processes. This happens when the field of historical alternatives is relatively vast, and each of the possible scenarios is 'underdetermined', not prejudged by the earlier stages of the process. 'The existence of possible alternatives of development in a historic situation is the presupposition of significant heroic action' (Hook 1955: 114). At such 'bifurcation points', minor factors acquire disproportionately significant consequences, and the history of the world hangs on trivial details. Among those minor factors, 'tipping the scales', so to say, single decisions, choices taken by the individual person may acquire great weight, pushing processes in a direction which cannot easily be reversed. Such conditions occur in periods of social destabilization, disorganization, pre-revolutionary turmoil, post-war breakdowns etc. 'During a period of wars and revolutions, the fate of peoples seems to hang visibly on what one person, perhaps a few, decide' (Hook 1955: 3). To have a chance of a truly historical role, a great individual must be in such a historical period, living in an exceptional time. In this sense heroes are bred by heroic ages.

2 An eminent individual must actually be in a position to take crucial decisions in an authoritative manner – in other words, must actually exercise the prerogatives of power or influence when the opportunity of historically consequential action opens itself. The greatest commander will not do much if he is arrested; the most eminent politician will not do much if he is deposed. We may say that, in order to play a historical role, a great individual must not only live at the right time, but also be in the right place. In this sense heroes are bred by heroic locations.

3 Truly historical change occurs only if large numbers of people are involved. No person can change history single-handedly. To be historically

effective, a great individual must be able to move other people to action, to mobilize them or to coerce them, to lead them by example, to frighten them by force of character, to convince them by ideas, to arouse them by emotions – in brief, to pull or to push them from routine and stagnation. Great numbers must be at hand when the historically important decision is taken; there must exist a potentially available pool of obedient or enthusiastic followers. The commander must have an army, the revolutionary leader an angry crowd, the prophet believers expecting good news, the president obedient, law-abiding citizens. Thus an ultimate prerequisite for exercising a heroic role, for implementing significant social change, is the existence of rich human resources ripe for mobilization.

Affecting history

By various routes, in various measures, for good or ill, great individuals effect social changes and transform historical processes. It is chiefly for that reason that they are later socially defined as 'great'.

Their historical role takes two forms. Sidney Hook distinguishes between 'eventful individuals' and 'event-making individuals'. The former are great in virtue of what they actually do. Not themselves necessarily of any extraordinary level of wisdom, imagination or moral integrity, they 'stumble upon greatness', being present at the right place and time and taking the right decisions. They make proper use of opportunities that presented themselves, and historical consequences follow, rightly credited to their deeds. 'The eventful man is a creature of events in that by happy or unhappy conjunction of circumstances he finds himself in a position where action or abstention from action is decisive in a great issue' (Hook 1955: 163). Quite oten such people are initially unaware of the historical significance of their actions.

The opposite case is that of 'event-making individuals'. These are great in virtue of who they were. They represent extraordinary qualities of mind and heart: intelligence, clear vision, strong convictions, persistence in following their goals, leadership skills. It is among such individuals that charismatic heroes are recruited; they feel elected themselves, and others recognize their charisma. The unique style of their actions lies not only in using opportunities as they come, but in actually creating opportunities. 'The event-making man . . . finds a fork in the historical road, but he also helps, so to speak, to create it. He increases the odds of success for the alternative he chooses by virtue of the extraordinary qualities he brings to bear to realize it' (Hook 1955: 157).

There are numerous traps on the road to historical greatness. Quite often attempts to change history fail, even in the hands of individuals of the highest stature. Our earlier discussion indicates a number of possible blunders preventing the success of potential heroes or leading to the downfall of those who had attained recognition earlier. (1) First, there is the common failure to define the field of possibilities adequately; to see historical alternatives when they are really present, to avoid wishful thinking and the invention of historical alternatives, when in fact they are absent. (2) There is the common tendency to think in terms of dichotomies, of the 'either/or' sort, ignoring the complexity of social situations as well as the multitude of their possible developments. (3) There is the common inability to estimate correctly the likelihood, as well as the intrinsic costs, of each available course of action, and to spot those 'windows of opportunity' which make it possible to achieve most at the lowest price. (4) There is the notorious disregard of the possible unintended consequences, by-products, side-effects of the decision being taken, especially if they seem distant in time. (5) There is the pervasive inability to predict mass reactions to decisions being considered, overestimating or underestimating the potential of popular mobilization, misreading the public mood, misinterpreting popular goals and aspirations. (6) Perhaps the final trap is the most dangerous: it is to ignore the limitations of human mastery over social and historical circumstances, and to cast oneself in the role of omnipotent God.

Those who manage to overcome these difficulties and to avoid these traps, fully deserve to be called 'great individuals'.

19

Social movements as forces of change

Social movements among agents of change

The embodiments of human agency are manifold. Social change is brought about by various agents, but among them there is one which, at least in the modern era, becomes particularly salient. Any time we switch on the news on TV, it is there. We see crowds in city squares protesting against oppressive government, the grim faces of British coalminers on strike, American young-sters picketing a nuclear plant, students fighting the riot police on the streets of Seoul, Muslims attacking Christians or vice versa, Serbs fighting Bosnians and Bosnians fighting Serbs, black Africans rallying against apartheid, women picketing abortion clinics and French peasants blocking highways. All these are social movements, perhaps the most potent forces of social change in our society.

Many authors notice this particular role of social movements. They see them as 'one of the chief ways through which modern societies are remade' (Blumer 1951: 154); 'creators of social change' (Killian 1964: 426); 'historical actors' (Touraine 1977: 298); 'transforming agents of political life' or 'carriers of historical projects' (Eyerman and Jamison 1991: 26). Some authors go so far as to claim that 'mass-based movements and the conflict they generate are *primary* agents of social change' (Adamson and Borgos 1984: 12).

How do social movements fit among other agents of social change? Let us approach this question starting with the distinction of various ways in which agentially driven social change may originate. Taking the first criterion, some changes may originate 'from below', in the activities undertaken by large masses of ordinary people, with varying degrees of 'togetherness'; other changes may originate 'from above', in the activities of powerful elites (rulers, governments, managers, administrators etc.) able to impose their preferences on other members of society. Taking the second criterion, some changes may be intended, willed by the agents, effected as the realization of their pre-conceived projects; other changes may emerge as unintended side-effects, by-products of actions aimed at entirely different goals.

Cross-cutting these two criteria (locus of agency and intentionality of agency), we arrive at a fourfold typology: (1) Latent change originating 'from below' (e.g. people acting in everyday life, making choices, taking decisions for their

Table 19.1   The typology of change

		Locus of agency	
		From below	*From above*
Intentionality of agency	Latent	1	2
	Manifest	4	3

own private goals, unwittingly produce economic changes, demographic trends, shifts of customs, lifestyles etc.). The accumulated and combined effects of dispersed individual actions result in secular trends which can be grasped on the macro-scale, in abstraction from the mass of actions that generate them. Sometimes such long-range trends, shifts and drifts are referred to as social movements (or 'general social movements', as opposed to particular social movements). We find this usage unjustifiable, as there are better, widely used terms, like trends, tendencies, currents, macroprocesses, signifying the phenomenon in question. We intend to reserve the term 'social movement' for a specific embodiment of agency. (2) Latent change originating 'from above' (e.g. actions taken by governments unwittingly produce side-effects, or even boomerang effects – changes opposite to those intended). (3) Manifest change originating 'from above' (e.g. successful implementation of plans, enactment of reforms by governmental, administrative or managerial bodies). (4) Manifest change originating 'from below' (e.g. enforcement of political reform by mobilized masses). These distinctions may be summarized by means of table 19.1

The last category (4) describes the situation in which people get together and organize themselves to some degree, in order to produce envisaged change in their society. Depending on the degree of organization, the spectrum will run from spontaneous and diffuse crowds and riots, through social movements, to interest groups, lobbies and highly bureaucratized political parties fighting *for* power (political parties *in* power will already belong to a different category of our typology, together with rulers and governments, as agents imposing changes 'from above').

Social movements defined

The adequate definition of social movements must differentiate this phenomenon both from other categories of agents (1, 2 and 3) and from other inhabitants of the same category (4). Thus it must comprise the following constitutive components:

(1) A collectivity of people acting together.
(2) The shared goal of collective action is some change in their society, defined by participants in similar ways.

(3) The collectivity is relatively diffuse, with a low level of formal organization.
(4) The actions have a relatively high degree of spontaneity, taking non-
institutionalized, unconventional forms.

To sum up: by social movements we mean loosely organized collectivities
acting together in a non-institutionalized manner in order to produce change
in their society.

The same emphases are to be found in numerous definitions proposed in
the literature. In some of the classical formulations social movements are
understood as

> 'Collective enterprises to establish a new order of life' (Blumer 1951: 199)
> 'Collective enterprises to effect changes in the social order' (Lang and Lang
> 1961: 507)
> 'Collective efforts to modify norms and values' (Smelser 1962: 3)
> 'Collectivity acting with some continuity to promote or resist change in
> society or group of which it is a part' (Turner and Killian 1972: 246)
> 'Collective efforts to control change, or to alter the direction of change'
> (Lauer 1976: xiv).

Contemporary authors give more extended characterizations of social movements as

> 'The expression of a preference for change among members of a society',
> or specifically 'Collective attempts to express grievances and discontent
> and/or to promote or resist change' (Zald and Berger 1978: 828, 841)
> 'More-or-less organized forms of collective action aimed at social change',
> or more precisely 'Groups of individuals gathered with the common pur-
> pose of expressing subjectively felt discontent in a public way and chang-
> ing the perceived social and political bases of that discontent' (Eyerman
> and Jamison 1991: 43–4)
> 'Unconventional group attempts to produce or prevent change', or in more
> detail 'Unconventional groups that have varying degrees of formal organi-
> zation and that attempt to produce or prevent radical or reformist type of
> 2change' (Wood and Jackson 1982: 3).

Finally in a more contextual, descriptive fashion, movements are referred to
as

> 'Specific kind of concerted-action groups; they last longer and are more
> integrated than mobs, masses and crowds, and yet are not organized like
> political clubs and other associations' (Rudolph Heberle in Banks 1972: 8).
> 'A sustained series of interactions between national powerholders and

persons successfully claiming to speak on behalf of a constituency lacking formal representation, in the course of which those persons make publicly-visible demands for changes in the distribution or exercise of power, and back those demands with public demonstrations of support' (Tilly 1979b: 12)

Perhaps the most common and most emphasized facet of all definitions is the intimate link between social movements and social change. As Wood and Jackson observe, 'Change is a basic defining characteristic of social movements . . . Social movements are closely related to social change' (1982: 6). This point, though seemingly obvious, requires three elucidations.

1   Social change as the goal of a movement may mean different things. The aim may be positive, to introduce something which is not there (a new government or political regime, new customs, lows or institutions) or negative, to halt, prevent or reverse changes resulting either from processes un-related to social movements (e.g. deterioration of the natural environment, decline of fertility rates, growth of crime), or from the activities of other competing movements (e.g. anti-abortion legislation passed under pressure from the pro-life movement, and vigorously opposed by the pro-choice movement).

2   Social movements may have various causal status with respect to change. On the one hand, they may be treated as ultimate causes of change, i.e. as conditions necessary and sufficient to bring it about. The problem with this position is that usually, in order to be successful, social movements must occur in conducive social circumstances, encounter a favourable 'opportunity structure', or (to put it metaphorically) 'ride the crest' of other social forces. They are effective only if complemented by other factors. Their active pres-ence is rarely, if ever, a full, complete cause of change. Usually they figure only as a necessary or supplementary, but probably never as a sufficient condition of social change.

On the other hand, social movements may be treated merely as effects, epiphenomena, or symptoms accompanying processes unfolding by their own thrust and momentum (e.g. accompanying the progress of modernization, urbanization, the emergence of mass society or sudden economic crisis). To put it metaphorically, in this perspective they are like a fever reflecting deeper changes in the social organism. The problem with this position is that as a matter of empirical fact many social movements do contribute to social change, modify its course, direction and speed – not to speak of some which actually do initiate and effect change.

The most reasonable approach strikes the golden mean. It considers social movements as mediators in the causal chain of social praxis. They are seen as both the products of earlier social changes and the producers (or at least co-producers) of further social transformations. Movements appear here as vehicles, carriers, transmitters of ongoing change, rather than either its ultimate cause or merely a surface manifestation. They do not arise in a vacuum, but at some historical juncture join the social process and attempt to affect its course. Tom Burns grasps this intermediate status of social movements, writing of them as 'social actors, groups, organizations and movements as bearers as well as makers and reformers of rule systems . . . They are the bearers of social structure in the form of acquired rule systems, and at the same time, they produce, reproduce and transform rule systems through their actions and transactions' (Burns et al. 1985: iv). A similar point is made by Dieter Rucht: 'Social movements are at the same time products and producers of societal patterns. Though they act within a historically created and relatively stable frame, they also actively participate in changing political discourses, power constellations, and cultural symbols' (1988: 306). Let us use a simple diagram:

Preceding social processes → Social movements → Succeeding social processes

---

The ongoing flow of social change

3   The third elucidation concerns the area where the change brought about by a social movement actually occurs. Normally social change effected by a movement is taken as located in the wider society, external to the movement itself. It looks as if the movement was acting on society from without, but it should not be forgotten that any social movement makes up a part of the very society undergoing change, includes some (and sometimes quite a massive) segment of its members and embraces some (and sometimes quite a large) area of its functioning. Therefore it is in fact internal to society, acting on society from within. It is a case of society changing society. A considerable part of the changes produced by the movement are changes in the movement itself (of its membership, ideology, rules, institutions, forms of organization etc.), and even the external changes, in the wider society (of its laws, political regimes, culture) brought about by the movement feed back on its own members and structures, change the environment of their actions, as well as the endowment of the actors (their motivations, attitudes, accepted ideologies etc.). Social movements are peculiar in this intimate mutual link between external and internal changes: they change society, changing themselves in the process, and they change themselves (mobilize, organize) in order to change society more effectively. Changes *in* the movement and changes *by* the movement go hand in hand, making mutually interlinked, concurrent processes. This unique trait of social movements justifies the claim of Gary Marx and James Wood that 'social movements are more dynamic than most other social forms' (1975: 394). They are social change *par excellence.*

Social movements and modernity

Most probably social movements are historically universal phenomena. People in all human societies must have had reasons to combine and fight for their collective goals, and against those who stood in the way of attaining them. Historians describe rebellions, uprisings, eruptions of discontent as far back as antiquity, strong religious movements in the Middle Ages, powerful peasant revolts in 1381 and 1525, the Reformation, and cultural, ethnic and national movements since the Renaissance. Huge social movements contributed to the birth of modernity at the time of the great bourgeois revolutions, English, French, American. During all that time the strategies and tactics of the movements, their 'repertoires of contention' (Tilly 1979a) have been evolving, but most observers agree that it is only in mature modern societies that the 'era of social movements' has really begun. It is only in the nineteenth and twentieth centuries that social movements have become so numerous, so massive, so salient and so consequential for the course of change. Contemporary observers offer confirmation: 'Highly modernized societies have a tendency to become "movement societies"' (Neidhardt and Rucht 1991: 449). 'Social movements are a central part of what we mean by modernity. [They] are a defining characteristic of modern politics and modern society' (Eyerman and Jamison 1991: 53). 'Social movements are linked to deeply rooted structural changes that have been identified as modernization breakthroughs in the spheres of "system" and "life world"' (Rucht 1988: 324).

There are several reasons for the particular salience and significance of social movements in the modern period, some of them already identified in the characterizations of modernity provided by the classical nineteenth-century authors.

1   The first may be called 'Durkheim's Theme', the sheer physical congestion of large masses of people in a limited area, which occurs with urbanization and industrialization and produces a great 'moral density' of population. This makes for better opportunities for contact and interaction, for elaborating common points of view, articulating shared ideologies and recruiting supporters. In short, the chances for mobilization of social movements are significantly raised. Would the socialist movement have been possible without the factory system, with thousands of workers in direct, personal contact? Is it an accident that university campuses, with their concentrated masses of students, have been the breeding ground for contestations of all sorts?

2   The next typical feature of modernity, which we may call 'Tönnies's Theme', is the atomization and isolation of individuals in the impersonal *Gesellschaft* or, to use more modern idiom, the 'lonely crowd' (Riesman 1961). The experience of alienation, solitude and uprootedness evokes a craving for community, solidarity and 'togetherness'. Membership of social movements provides a substitute satisfaction of these universal human needs. In this way

modern mass society supplies a rich pool of potential members, ready to be recruited and mobilized.

3   The 'Marxian Theme' notes the unprecedented growth of social inequalities, with steep hierarchies of wealth, power and prestige, accompanying the modern capitalist economy. This produces a widespread experience and perception of exploitation, oppression, injustice and deprivation generating group hostilities and conflicts. People whose vested interests are endangered are ready to fight against those who endanger them. The 'structural conduciveness' (Smelser 1962) for the appearance of social movements is more pronounced than ever before.

4   The 'Weberian Theme' concerns the democratic transformation of the political system, opening the field for collective action for large masses of people. The expression of dissent, articulation of vested interests and activism in their defence become the legitimate right and, even more, the expected duty of the responsible citizen. 'The political opportunity structure' (Tarrow 1985) for the appearance of social movements is radically transformed.

5   A feature which may be called 'Saint-Simon's and Comte's Theme' is the modern emphasis on the conquest, control, domination and manipulation of reality, initially of nature but eventually also of human society. The belief that social change and progress depend on human action, that society may be shaped by its members to their own benefit, is an important ideological prerequisite for activism, and hence for the mobilization of social movements. Voluntarism feeds social movements, fatalism kills them.

6   Modern society has experienced a general cultural and educational upgrading. Participation in social movements demands some degree of awareness, imagination, moral sensitivity and concern with public issues, with the ability to generalize from personal or local experience. All these are positively correlated with the level of education. The educational revolution which accompanies the spread of capitalism and democracy extends the pool of potential members of social movements.

7   The final feature is the emergence and spread of the mass media (Molotch 1979). These are powerful instruments for articulating, shaping and unifying beliefs, formulating and disseminating ideological messages, moulding 'public opinion'. They extend the horizon of citizens beyond their personal world towards the experiences of other groups, classes and nations socially or geographically remote. Two consequences follow. (a) This opening-up produces the important 'demonstration effect', i.e. the chance to compare one's own life with the lives of other societies. The perception of unjustified disadvantage and the accompanying feeling of 'relative deprivation' provide a conducive psychological background for social movements. (b) It is also through the mass media that people learn about the political creeds, attitudes and grievances of others. This allows them to estimate the extent of the common plight, to break out of their 'pluralistic ignorance' or the mistaken, paralysing belief that one is alone in misery and discontent. Instead it generates solidarity, loyalty and consensus extending far beyond the immediate social

circle. This feeling of common cause and supra-local solidarity is another socio-psychological precondition for the emergence of social movements.

Types of social movements

Social movements come in all shapes and sizes, they present a tremendous variety of forms. To get some bearings in this heterogeneous class of phenomena a typology is needed. This may be constructed by means of several criteria.

1 Social movements differ in the scope of intended change. Some are relatively limited in purposes, aiming to modify some aspect of society without touching its core institutional structure. They want change *in* rather than change *of*. We call these reform movements. Examples are: pro- and anti-abortion movements demanding appropriate changes in legislation, movements for animal rights demanding bans on experimentation, movements demanding speed limits on German autobahns. Other movements attempt deeper changes, reaching the foundations of the social organization. Because of the central, strategic location of the institutions they attack, the changes, if effected, spread far beyond the immediate target and produce transformations *of* society rather then merely changes *in* society. We call these radical movements. Examples are the civil rights movement in the US, the anti-apartheid movement in South Africa and national liberation movements in colonial countries. In the extreme case, when the intended changes embrace all core aspects of the social structure (political, economic and cultural) and are aimed at achieving a total transformation of society in the direction of some preconceived image of an 'alternative society' or 'social utopia', we speak of revolutionary movements such as the millenarian, fascist and communist movements.

Another formulation of the same typology is given by Neil Smelser, who distinguishes between 'norm-oriented' and 'value-oriented' movements. 'The norm-oriented movement is action mobilized in the name of generalized belief [shared ideology] envisioning a reconstitution of norms ... The value-oriented movement is collective action mobilized in the name of a generalized belief envisioning a reconstitution of values' (Smelser 1962: 9). Values, in Smelser's sense provide fundamental guidelines of conduct, they define and regulate the proper ends of human endeavour, e.g. justice, knowledge, democracy, freedom. Norms are the proper means to be selected in the pursuit of these ends e.g. discipline, decency, learning, labouring. 'Norms, then, are more specific than general values, for they specify certain regulatory principles which are necessary if these values are to be realized' (p. 27).

2 Social movements differ in the quality of intended change. Some emphasize innovations, strive to introduce new institutions, new laws, new forms of

life, new beliefs. In brief, they want to shape society to a pattern which has never been found before. Their orientation is to the future. They propose changes directed forward, and put the emphasis on novelty. We may call them progressive movements. Examples are republican, socialist and women's liberation movements. Other movements turn to the past. They seek to restore institutions, laws, ways of life and beliefs which were already established in the past but later eroded or abandoned in the course of history. The changes they propose are directed backward, and the emphasis is put on tradition. We may call them conservative or 'retroactive' movements. Examples are the ecological movement and fundamentalist religious movements, the 'Moral Majority' in the US calling for a return to family values, royalist movements advocating the return of dynastic rule, ethnic revivals in eastern and central Europe following the collapse of communism. The distinction between progressive and conservative movements may be aligned with the common political distinction of left and the right. Left-wing movements most often assume a progressive orientation, right-wing movements are usually conservative.

3   Social movements differ with respect to the targets of intended change. Some focus on a change of social structures, others on changing individuals. Structure-directed movements take two forms. (a) Sociopolitical movements (or, as Charles Tilly calls them, 'national social movements') attempt changes in politics, economics, class and stratificational hierarchies. 'By national social movement I mean a sustained challenge to state authorities in the name of a population that has little formal power with respect to the state' (Tilly 1985: 1). (b) 'Sociocultural movements' address more intangible aspects of social life, promoting changes in beliefs, creeds, values, norms, symbols, everyday life-patterns, for example the beatniks, hippies and punks. The movements targeted on individuals rather than structures, also take two forms. (a) Sacred, mystical or religious movements strive for the conversion or redemption of their members and the general revival of religious spirit. Examples include revivalist movements in the Middle Ages, Islamic fundamentalist movements, the evangelization movement proclaimed by Pope John Paul II. (b) The secular variant seeks the personal, moral or physical well-being of members, as with fitness movements and self-improvement fads.

In structure-directed movements there is an implicit assumption that modified structures will provide a new socializing environment for individuals and remould their personalities accordingly. Similarly, in the personality-oriented movements, there is an implicit assumption that improved people will eventually shape better social arrangements. Thus there is usually some awareness of the link between changes effected at the structural and individual levels. But priorities differ: some movements find a key to change in modifying structures, others in modifying people.

Combining the criterion of a target with the criterion of scope David Aberle proposed a fourfold classification of social movements: transformative movements, aimed at total change in structures; reformative movements, aimed at partial change in structures; redemptive movements, aimed at total change in individual members; and alternative movements, aimed at partial change in individual members (Aberle 1966).

4   Social movements differ with respect to the 'vector' of intended change. As I have already mentioned, for most movements the 'vector' is positive: such movements attempt to introduce some change, to make a difference. There are also occasions when movements are mobilized to prevent change; the 'vector' is then negative. A typical case occurs when a movement is mobilized in response to negatively evaluated changes brought in the wake of general social trends, as their outcomes or unintended side-effects. Numerous anti-modernity movements belong to this category, e.g. those defending native cultures, fighting globalization, reviving ethnic or national particularisms, asserting fundamentalist religious creeds. In a sense, ecological movements belong here too, as they are evoked by the environmental destruction, pollution and depletion of resources resulting from the excesses of industrialism. There are movements mobilized to stop or reverse some concrete legislation or governmental decision, for example the anti-bussing movement in the US, which opposes the enforced method of racial integration of schools (Useem 1980), or the 'self-defence' movement of Polish peasants against high interest rates and expensive credit. Another special case is the countermovement mobilized in response to the emergence and expansion of a competing movement. Movements sometimes appear as symmetrically coupled: left and right, anti-Semitism and Zionism, pro-life and pro-choice, atheism and fundamentalism, democratic reformers and hard-liners.

5   Social movements differ with respect to the underlying strategy or 'logic' of their action (Rucht 1988). Some follow 'instrumental' logic; these strive to obtain political power, and by means of that to enforce intended changes in the laws, institutions and organization of society. Their primary aim is political control. When successful, such movements turn into pressure groups or political parties, enter parliaments and governments. The Green Party in Germany and the victorious Solidarity movement in Poland provide recent illustrations. Other movements follow 'expressive' logic; these strive to affirm identity, to gain acceptance for their values or ways of life, to achieve autonomy, equal rights, cultural and political emancipation for their members or wider constituencies. The civil rights, ethnic, feminist and gay rights movements are prime examples. Is it an accident that one of the most powerful movements of recent decades, the woman's liberation movement, has never aspired to the status of a political party or to parliamentary representation? 'I argue that the women's movement follows primarily an expressive logic, whereas the environmental movement tends toward an instrumental logic' (Rucht 1988: 319).

6   Differing types of movements are found to dominate in different historical epochs. This enables us to distinguish two comprehensive types most relevant for modern history. The movements dominating the early phases of modernity were focused on economic interests, their members generally recruited from single social classes, organized in rigid, centralized fashion. The trade union, labour and farmers' movements are classical examples. These are called 'old social movements'. With the development of modernity they gradually become obsolete. In recent decades the most developed capitalist societies, entering the phase of late modernity or even, as some authors claim, post-modernity, witness the emergence of another type of social movement. These are appropriately labelled 'new social movements' (Touraine 1981; Offe 1985). Prototypical cases include the ecological, peace and feminist movements. Three traits give them unique qualities. (a) They focus on new issues, new interests, new fronts of social conflict. In reaction to the invasion by politics, economics, technology and bureaucracy of all domains of human existence, their main concern is with quality of life, group identity, expanded life-space, the championing of 'civil society', and in general with post-material, non-economic, 'soft' values. 'In contrast to the old labor movement, the new social movements have not primarily articulated economic demands but have been more concerned with cultural issues dealing with questions of individual autonomy and with issues related to new, invisible risks affecting people in more or less similar ways, irrespective of their social positions' (Kriesi 1989: 1079). (b) Their constituencies are not correlated with any specific classes but rather cut across traditional class divisions, representing issues of vital concern to members of different classes. In class terms, the only mark of their composition is the over-representation of the higher-educated strata and middle classes, due perhaps to their higher sensitivity and awareness and greater discretionary resources of free time, money, and energy (Kriesi 1989: 1085–9). (c) New social movements are usually decentralized, taking the form of extended and relatively loose networks rather than hierarchical, rigid organizations.

7   If one looks at the concrete society at the concrete historical moment, there will always appear a complex and heterogeneous array of social movements representing the different types discussed above. On this intricate social stage some phenomena stand out. First of all we shall notice movements and countermovements linked in a 'loosely coupled conflict' of mutually stimulating and reinforcing quality (Zald and Useem 1982: 1). To be more exact: 'movements of any visibility and impact create conditions for the mobilization of countermovements. By advocating change, by attacking the established interests, by mobilizing symbols and raising costs to others, they create grievances and provide opportunities for organizational enterpreneurs to define countermovement goals and issues' (Zald and Useem 1982: 1). The countermovement develops a peculiar, distorted mirror image of the movement it opposes: 'the countermovement gains its impetus and grows from showing

the harmful effects of the movement . . . It chooses its tactics in response to the structure and tactics of the movement' (Zalad and Useem 1982: 2). The appearance of strong countermovements usually leads to the dogmatization, rigidity and inflexibility of the movement's structure, strongly enforced loyalty, tight integration in the organizational forms and the oligarchization (bureaucratization) of authority.

Some clusters of related movements will become visible. McCarthy and Zald speak of 'social movement industries' (SMI) as the more inclusive systems covering movements of similar or identical goals, defending common sets of preferences (1976: 1219). For example, the working-class movement embraced spontaneous outbursts (of the Luddist type), trade unions, socialist organizations etc.

Finally, the overall picture of social movement activity will differ from one society to another. Garner and Zald define the most inclusive whole within which social movements operate as the 'social movement sector' (SMS): 'it is the configuration of social movements, the structure of antagonistic, competing and cooperating movements which in turn is part of a larger structure of action (political action, in a very broad sense) that may include parties, state bureaucracies, the media, pressure groups, churches, and a variety of other organizational factors in a society' (Garner and Zald 1981: 1–2). The unique character of the SMS gives a specific flavour or tone to the operation of each constituent movement. It also determines the overall level of activism in a given society. One may conceive of a synthetic measure of societal activism and passivism related to the scope and vitality of the whole SMS. A society which wants to take a full advantage of its own creative potential, which wishes to form and reform itself to the benefit of its members, has to allow, even to encourage, the free operation of social movements, resulting in a rich and varied SMS. This is the 'active society' (Etzioni 1968a). Societies which suppress, block or eliminate social movements destroy their own mechanism of self-improvement and self-transcendence. With a narrow or non-existent SMS they become the 'passive societies' of ignorant, indifferent and impotent people, who are given no chance to care for the fate of their society and consequently cease caring altogether. Their only historical prospect is stagnation and decay.

Internal dynamics of social movements

Social movements arise at some moment, develop, pass through distinguishable phases, decay and terminate. This internal, emergent quality of social movements was already emphasized by the classic author in the field, Herbert Blumer: 'a movement has to be constructed and has to carve out a career in what is practically always an opposed, resistant or at least indifferent world' (1957: 147). The 'career' of the movement may be brief or prolonged.

Between the initiation and termination there are constant changes and processes going on within the movement. These embrace the members as well as the constituent organizations, institutions and normative systems. We shall deal with this internal dynamics of social movements first, and then address the issue of external dynamics, i.e. the impact of social movements on the wider society within which they operate. These are two sides of a closely interrelated process which we call the 'double morphogenesis' of social movements (Sztompka 1987).

In the internal dynamics of the movement, we propose to distinguish four major stages: origins, mobilization, structural elaboration, and termination.

1   All social movements originate in some historically specific conditions. They emerge within a historically given structure. In general, the pre-existent structure may be said to constitute a pool of resources and facilities for the movement. Thus the ideal pre-existent structure normally serves as a treasury of ideas from which the movement shapes its creed, ideology, definition of goals, identification of enemies and allies, vision of the future. These are never pure inventions. Rather, the ideological horizon of a given society, cultural area or historical epoch is always pre-established. The movement articulates these encountered, traditional views, selects from them, changes emphases, arranges them into coherent systems, and of course on this basis adds innovations, but never produces its ideological system from scratch. Seeming novelty is never absolute; at most it is partial. This was already observed long ago with respect to revolutionary movements, which were found to borrow rather than invent their slogans and battle cries as well as their images of the better world. For example, some hints in this direction given by Marx were later developed into a whole 'theory of revolutionary retrospection' by a Polish Marxist of the early period, K. Kelles-Krauz: 'The ideals by which the whole reformist movement wishes to replace the existing social norms are always similar to norms from the more or less distant past . . . The source of the ideal of the future, like the source of any idea, has to be in the past – in a certain social form that has become antiquated' (Kelles-Krauz 1962). For instance, if we look at the whole symbolic and ideological sphere of the Solidarity movement in Poland, it could not be comprehended without reference to the long tradition of Polish Catholicism.

Turning to the next area of pre-existent structure, the normative structure, it is found to play a different role. It often serves as the negative frame of reference, something to be opposed or rejected, the target for the movement. The norms, values, institutions, roles of the established normative order are criticized, ridiculed, challenged. Some movements focus on norms, treating them as inefficient, inadequate or improper means to otherwise accepted ends. Others challenge values as well, as unjust, wrong, misconceived. As a rule, a certain sequence seems to obtain. Smelser argues that it is only when 'norm-oriented' movements are strongly opposed by countermovements, blocked by authorities, suppressed or endangered, that the escalation of goals and qualitative change of demands occurs, leading to the appearance of 'value-oriented' movements (Smelser 1962: 330–5). Again, Solidarity in Poland and other liberating movements in eastern Europe provide perfect illustrations of this effect, when a constant radicalization of demands could be observed resulting in considerable part from the stubborn resistance of entrenched political elites. The most violent, bloody and tragic revolutionary outburst came precisely in the country where the tyranny, repression and governmental control were most rigid, in Romania.

The pre-existent interactive (organizational) structure has other functions. It produces the field of constraints as well as facilitations for the movement. The communication networks established among members of a society or some segment of the population prior to the start of a movement play a crucial role in the process of recruitment and mobilization. Freeman discusses 'the key role of preexisting communication networks as the fertile soil in which new movements can sprout' (1973; 1983b). She illustrates it with the case of women's liberation movement. Similarly, the networks of interlinked associations or communities based on common religious or ethnic loyalties (clubs, churches, ethnic groups, patriotic societies etc.) are helpful in speeding up the mobilization and recruitment to social movements once the occasion arises. In the case of the civil rights movement in the US, it is often observed that 'among Blacks – the dense network of segregated colleges, women's clubs, newspapers, union locals, and small businesses, provided the organizational infrastructure of the movement. The black church provided many of its organizers, its music and rhetoric, and much of its resilient spirit' (Adamson and Borgos 1984: 129). A similar role of the Catholic Church, as well as earlier informal circles and associations of oppositional character (e.g. the Committee for the Defence of Workers, KOR), was clearly visible during the early days of the Solidarity movement in Poland in the 1980s. An equally important role is played by the existing channels of political expression, or as it is sometimes called, the 'political opportunity structure' (available associations, self-governing bodies, local administrative centres, co-optable political elites etc.). As Zald and Useem point out, 'political structures vary in the extent to which they provide movement opportunities' (1982: 15).

Finally, we come to the last area, the pre-existent, structure of social inequalities, the established hierarchies of wealth, power and prestige. Here the pre-existent economic and power inequalities with resulting contradictions and conflicts among segments of population (classes, strata, interest groups etc.) are often taken to be the prime motivating factor for the mobilization of movements. The hierarchical differentiation of vested interests is seen to produce tensions and strains, grievances and deprivations in the population, motivating people to join movements of protest or reform. Those deprived of opportunities, life-chances, access to valued goods and resources, provide a ready clientele for social movements; they are easily recruited and mobilized to action aimed at structural redistribution of privileges and gratifications (Dahrendorf 1959; Oberschall 1973).

Conducive structural conditions and structural strains (Smelser 1962) are necessary but not sufficient to generate a movement. In the next phase the process has to move to the area of social consciousness. 'Successful collective action proceeds from a significant transformation in the collective consciousness of the actors involved' (McAdam et al. 1988: 713). People affected by the structural strains must develop some awareness of their plight, some definition of the factors or agents responsible for their condition, some vision of a possible better situation and some project of escape from here to there. They must articulate and share an ideology or, as Smelser calls it, a 'generalized belief' (1962: 79). This has recently been called the 'frame alignment processes', through which a variety of 'frames' or world views present in society are mobilized by activists to legitimate the movement's goals and actions (Snow et al.: 1986). Once objective strains and tensions are coupled with common ideological awareness, the situation is ripe for the initiation of the movevement.

Then, most often, some relatively insignificant event plays the role of a precipitating factor, actually starting the 'career' of the movement. Such an event provides a focus for widely experienced grievances, raises the level of awareness, creates an exemplar of heroic contestation, provokes open expression of supportive opinions and unravels the wide reach of oppositional consensus (breaking up 'pluralistic ignorance', when nobody is certain how many others share one's grievances and how many are actually ready to join in action). It also tests the resolve of the authorities, or the lack thereof. In the case of Rosa Parks refusing to take a seat in the segregated part of a bus, the conflict growing out of one small incident developed into the most powerful social movement in American history, the civil rights movement. In another case, an elderly worker, Anna Walentynowicz, was fired from the Lenin Shipyard at Gdansk in 1980 for political reasons. The workers rose in her defence, and within days the largest political movement in recent European history, Solidarity, was well on its way.

2   The precipitating event closes the first stage in the movement's career, that of origins, and initiates the phase of mobilization. The first wave of recruitment involves those who are most affected by the conditions against which the movement arises, those who possess the most acute awareness and sensitivity to the issues central to the movement and those who are most committed intellectually, emotionally, morally and politically to the movement's causes. Such people join out of conviction, treating the movement as an instrument for attaining intended social changes. Once the movement starts on its way, grows and achieves successes, the second wave of recruitment follows. This brings the members who seek community and meaning in life. Participation in successful collective action offers that. The 'Bandwagon effect' operates not only in elections but also in recruitment to social movements. There is also a fringe of cynical opportunists who join in the hope of

tangible benefits, e.g. lucrative positions when the movement wins. In this second wave, people join out of convenience rather than conviction.

No wonder that such varied motivations produce different kinds of bonds, keeping members within the movement. Several layers of participation may be observed, from core activists, through followers, fellow-travellers to 'free riders', who sympathize with the movement at a distance, hoping that its victory will bring them benefits as well. This onion-like composition becomes particularly evident when a movement runs into trouble, is firmly suppressed or defeated. Then the outer layers get out first, abandoning the cause while core activists persevere, sometimes to revitalize the movement at a later time.

Recruitment is not enough; members must be mobilized for collective action. Here the study of social movements almost invariably proves the great significance of charismatic leaders: Jesus Christ, Buddha, Muhammad, Martin Luther King, Lech Walesa, Vaclav Havel and many of smaller, yet still exceptional stature. They get a grip on their followers, inspire them with enthusiasm and provoke them to heroic actions. By taking extraordinary actions themselves, they confirm their leadership position. In this way the first step is taken to the emergence of internal differentiation, organization and hierarchical structure in the movement. In the 1970s an influential school emerged under the name of Resource Mobilization Perspective which took the phase of recruitment and mobilization as one of its foci (McCarthy and Zald 1976; Oberschall 1973; Gamson 1975; Tilly 1978). By mobilization they mean 'the processes by which a discontented group assembles and invests resources for the pursuit of group goals' (Oberschall 1973: 28). In this process a particular role is played by mobilizers or 'movement entrepreneurs', skilled organizers and leaders, who sometimes turn into a sort of professionals ready to take organizing and managerial roles in various kinds of movements. 'Grievances and discontent may be defined, created, and manipulated by issue entrepreneurs and organizations' (McCarthy and Zald 1976: 1215).

3   This opens the next major stage in the movement's development: the structural elaboration. This proceeds along the path from an aggregate of mobilized individuals to a fully-fledged movement organization.

(a)   We can distinguish four sub-processes of internal morphogenesis. To begin with, one may observe the gradual emergence (articulation) of new ideas, beliefs, creeds, 'a common vocabulary of hope and protest' (Rudé 1964: 75). With time, some movements develop their own, peculiar *Weltanschauung*.

(b)   Then, there is the emergence (institutionalization) of new norms and values – regulating the internal functioning of the movement and providing criteria for the critique of external conditions on which the movement targets itself. This is the focus of Turner's theory of the 'emergent norm' (Turner and

Killian 1972). It is worth noticing that the internal norms and values of the movement may refer to its internal operation, behaviour toward co-members, bonds of loyalty or comradeship etc.; but they may also specify certain ways of dealing with opponents, of carrying out external structural changes. The latter make up the 'repertoires of contention' (Tilly 1985) or tactics of struggle which define what is permitted, preferred, prescribed or proscribed in dealings with the movement's opponents and enemies. In the internal normative structure of the movement, one may thus distinguish 'the ethos of solidarity' and 'the ethos of struggle'.

(c) The next sub-process is the emergence (patterning) of a new internal organizational structure: novel interactions, relationships, bonds, ties, loyalties, commitments among members. What Zurcher and Snow say of commitment may be applied *mutatis mutandis* to any of the other interpersonal links obtaining in the movement: 'it is an emergent and interactional phenomenon that must be developed by the movement itself' (1981: 463). The ultimate effect of internal structure-building in this area is the appearance of a fully formed 'social movement organization' (SMO), defined as 'a complex, or formal organization which identifies its goals with the preferences of a social movement or a countermovement and attempts to implement those goals' (McCarthy and Zald 1976: 1218). For example, the civil rights movement in the US comprised several organizational forms: the Congress of Racial Equality, the National Association for the Advancement of Colored People, Southern Christian Leadership Conference, the Student Non-Violent Coordinating Committee etc. Similarly the movement known under the name of Solidarity includes Citizens' Committees, Fighting Solidarity, the Independent Association of Students, Rural Solidarity etc.

(d) Finally among the sub-processes, there is the emergence (crystallization) of new opportunity structures, new hierarchies of dependence, domination, leadership, influence and power within the movement. The movement's membership base is always internally stratified; there are various levels of participation, commitment, responsibility. The optimum effect is certainly 'the alignment of individual interests and movement goals' (Zurcher and Snow 1981: 472), when participation in the movement satisfies members' needs and aspirations while at the same time contributing to the social changes sought by the movement.

Two typical sequences of these morphogenetic processes can be singled out, depending on the movement's origins. When the movement arises in a 'volcanic', spontaneous fashion ('from below') as a sort of eruption of long-accumulated grievances and discontents, it normally begins at the interactive level. Common participation in the outbursts of collective behaviour (riots, manifestations, crowds etc.) breeds bonds, loyalties, commitments, and in effect produces some rudimentary organizational structure. Then comes ideology, sometimes infused into the movement from without, sometimes borrowed from earlier doctrine, sometimes articulated by charismatic leaders.

Next the normative system slowly evolves when the ethos of solidarity and the ethos of struggle emerge. Finally, the internal divisions between leaders, followers, rank-and-file, sympathizers, fellow-travellers and 'free riders' become crystallized in the opportunity structure.

The alternative sequence is to be observed when the movement arises as the result of manipulation, conspiracy, organizational enterpreneurship ('from above'). This is the case which is at the centre of attention for the Resource Mobilization School. Here the beginning of the movement is normally marked by indoctrination spreading out a suggestive vision of the future as well as a radical critique of the present, and indicating persons or groups blocking the way from here to there. Then comes the institutionalization of the new normative order entailed by the ideology. This is enacted by the movement's organizers and backed by the sanctions they administer. On this basis, the new actual patterns of interaction and more permanent relatioships slowly appear among the movement's members. Finally, the differentiation of opportunities within the movement (variable access to various resources controlled by the movement) becomes crystallized, with clear-cut divisions between leadership elite and rank-and-file, members and public, participants and sympathizers.

Of course in concrete empirical situations both sequences may overlap, and processes may mutually enforce each other. For example, in the case of the class-based, grass-roots movements of social protest in the US, 'The glue which cemented the ranks of these movements was a commitment to certain programmatic goals [ideal and normative structure in terms of INIO scheme], and equally important, an engagement in mass action – in boycotts, cooperatives, sit-ins, strikes' (Adamson and Borgos 1984: 14).

The various sub-processes or phases in the internal morphogenesis of the movement do not necessarily proceed harmoniously. Often one may observe the overgrowth of some at the expense of others, giving rise to various forms of pathology and producing internally crippled movements. Thus too strong an emphasis on the articulation of the ideal structure produces utopianism and various brands of dogmatism or fundamentalism. Too much concern with the institutionalization of the normative structure leads to overregulation, and paradoxically often breeds anomie. Heavy stress on personal bonds, private loyalties, intimate and intense interactions among the movement's members easily degenerates into factionalism, nepotism and particularistic criteria of acceptance to higher positions. The differentiation of opportunities, vested interests or life-chances among members often leads to oligarchization and displacement of goals, when the leadership puts the preservation of the movement itself over and above the realization of its initial programme. McCarthy and Zald see this danger clearly: 'SMO's operate much like any other organization, and consequently, once formed they operate as though organizational survival were the primary goal. Only if survival is assumed can other goals be pursued' (1976: 1226).

Needless to add, the pathological developments described above seriously impair the external effectiveness of the movement in producing change, making it crippled in yet another way. On the other hand, a harmonious internal morphogenesis raises the structure-building potential: 'As mobilization advances, as the unit commands more resources, and as more of the available total resources are used jointly rather than individually, the unit increases its ability to act collectively' (Etzioni 1968b: 243).

4   A brief comment about the last stage in the movement's career: its termination. There are two possibilities. One is optimistic: the movement wins and therefore loses its *raison d'être*, demobilizing and dissolving. The other is pessimistic: the movement does not win but is suppressed and defeated, or it exhausts its potential of enthusiasm and gradually decays without achieving victory. But the situation may be more ambivalent. Sometimes, the complete success of the movement may pre-empt its goals, lead to its quick dissolution and provoke a backlash of counterforces. The achievements of the movement may be lost if there is no longer any force to guard them. This is what some movement leaders refer to as 'a crisis of victory' (Adamson and Borgos 1984: 4). In other cases, failure may help to spot and define weaknesses in earlier efforts, identify the truly committed supporters, eliminate opportunists, regroup forces, put enemies in the spotlight, and in effect allow a reshaping of the movement's tactics leading to its revival in new forms. This may be called 'victory in defeat' (Sztompka 1988). This is what happened with the suppressed Solidarity movement in Poland in the late 1980s, leading to its ultimate victory in 1989.

External dynamics of social movements

Now we have to turn to the other side of 'double morphogenesis', namely the impact of the social movement on wider society, and particularly its role in producing structural transformations. We shall look at the social movement as if it were a 'black box', forgetting about the complex internal functioning and developments described above, and focus exclusively on what it does to the external society in which it operates.

From this perspective, the crucial property of the movement is its effectiveness in introducing structural transformations. This may be called its 'morphogenetic potential'. Judging the effectiveness of the movement in introducing structural changes requires relativization. The effect on external structures may be evaluated as relative to the movement's proclaimed goals, or in comparison to concrete, objectively given historical chances. Piven and Cloward succinctly remind us: 'What was won must be judged by what was possible' (1979: xiii). Similarly, the manifest effects of the movement, of which its members are fully aware, must be distinguished from possible latent functions (unintended and unrecognized side-effects). Finally short-range effects must be distinguished from long-range effects which will manifest themselves only in the future.

Thus the balance of consequences of the social movement is always complex and ambivalent. What is a success in terms of one relativization, may well prove to be failure in terms of another, and vice versa. For example, a defeated, crushed, destroyed oppositional movement may leave lasting structural effects, preparing the way for its ultimate victory. As Oberschall puts it: 'A movement may be ruthlessly suppressed and yet many of the changes it had sought might still be brought about at a later time, for confrontation is a warning signal to the ruling groups that they had better change course or else face even more explosive upheavals in the future' (Oberschall 1973: 344). For example, it may be shown that in spite of the initial demise of the Solidarity movement with the imposition of martial law it succeeded in infusing the system with the 'logic of reform', enlarged the scope of participation in political life, transformed the balance of forces in political elites and left a strong imprint on the collective consciousness (Sztompka 1988). All that prepared the victory of Solidarity eight years later. On the other hand, a movement apparently realizing all of its proclaimed goals may prove to be a failure compared to the pool of abandoned historical possibilities, to what was objectively attainable under given circumstances. Here, it is usually many years later that such earlier possibilities are unravelled. Further, the effects judged as a movement's successes may entail unintended and unrecognized (latent) costs outweighing the benefits. Finally, immediate gains may well be lost in view of long-range developments.

The morphogenetic potential of the movement may manifest itself in the disruptive (destructive) and creative (constructive) modes. Normally, in order to introduce structural innovations, the movement has to break down or at least weaken existing structures. Only later can constructive efforts start. Some movements stop short of the truly creative potential, exercising only a disruptive, destabilizing influence. Movements devoid of creative potential are in a sense crippled; a fully-fledged movement has to exhibit the twin potentials, destructive and constructive, to be historically consequential.

Structure-transforming potential, both disruptive and constructive, may take various forms depending on the aspect (level, dimension) of social structure at which it is aimed. We may distinguish four forms of morphogenetic potential. An ideological potential of the movement may be conceived as the measure of its impact on the ideal structure; the degree to which the movement's creed, *Weltanschauung*, vision of the present, image of the future, definitions of enemies and allies etc. spread out in a society. For example, the significant ideological role of the civil rights movement in the US is stressed by Coser: 'the shock of recognition, the jolt to conscience, occurred only when the Negroes, through by-and-large nonviolent action in the South and through increasingly violent demonstrations and even riots in the North, brought the problem forcibly to the attention of white public opinion and the white power structure' (1967: 86). In the case of Poland, the Solidarity movement, suppressed and delegalized by martial law in 1981, developed extensive underground publishing and educational activities, revealing to the masses various 'white spots' of Polish history, the true dimensions of Stalinist crimes, abuses of state bureaucracy, irrationality of economic policies etc. This prepared the ground for eventual electoral victory and the demise of the communist government in June 1989.

The 'reform potential' of the movement will mean the measure of impact on the normative structure, expressed in introducing new values, ways of life, rules of conduct, role-models among the wider population. Movements able to do that achieve what Burns and Buckley have called 'meta-power' or 'relational control' (Burns and Buckley 1976: 215); they institute a new framework of rules for the social game. This ability is rightly considered to be most essential: 'Major struggles in human history and contemporary society revolve around the formation and reformation of major rule systems, the core institutions of society' (Burns 1985: v).

Then, there is the reorganizational potential, understood as the measure of impact on the patterns and channels of social interaction (social organization), the establishing of new social ties, formation of new groups, creation of communication networks, forming of inter-group coalitions etc. This process is clearly visible in the transition from the monolithic, centralized, autocratic systems of eastern Europe to pluralistic, democratic, market-oriented societies. During the 'autumn of nations' in 1989, we witnessed the mushrooming of innumerable associations, voluntary groups, political parties, unions filling out the 'sociological vacuum' so characteristic of totalitarian regimes.

Finally we may distinguish redistributional potential as the measure of the movement's impact on the opportunity structure; the extent to which the movement is able to raise benefits, privileges, gratifications for its members, followers, adherents or sympathizers, and by the same token to take them from the movement's opponents or enemies. The disbanding of the 'nomenklatura' system in the post-communist societies of eastern Europe is a recent telling example. The redistribution of 'life-chances' among the population is the final effect of the movement's structure-building activity, and access to power proves especially crucial for preserving the benefits achieved and controlling the distribution of resources and goods in the future. As Tarrow remarks: 'In the absence of changes in the structure of political power, the advantages gained and legitimate access accorded during cycles of protest are always reversible' (1985: 53). This explains why the issue of power is so central for all reform-oriented or revolutionary movements attempting redistribution on the largest scale.

Only if all four domains of the social structure are effectively attacked can the social movement attain its full dynamic potential. I would save the term 'revolutionary movement' for this limiting case. In actual reality, movements are often crippled, one-sidedly focusing on a single area of structural change. For example, some succeed solely in spreading myths, utopias, wishful thinking and empty ideologies with no counterpart in other dimensions of the social structure. Speaking of peasant rebellions, Wolf stresses that this is far from sufficient for success: 'such a myth often can and does move peasants to action, but it provides only a common vision, not an organizational framework of action. Such myths unite peasants, they do not organize them' (1969: 108). Other movements may focus on spreading new patterns of interaction, new ways of life, which *per se* is also not enough for sigificant and lasting structural change. The examples of beatniks, hippies, punks, skinheads and similar counter-cultural movements easily come to mind.

If we turn to revolutionary movements – many-sided in the character of their targets and most comprehensive in the scope of their structural impact – two typical, alternative sequences of external morphogenesis may be observed. One originates 'from below'; it starts with a new ideology, from which new norms and values are gradually derived; then their implementation produces actual new patterns of interaction and organization; these finally entail new networks of vested interests. This is the spontaneous morphogenetic process. An alternative sequence proceeds in the reverse order. It starts with the redistribution of resources, opportunities, life-chances 'from above', by decree of the movement which has seized power; then the exercise of new opportunities leads to new patterns of interaction via facts rather than via rules; it is only their gradual crystallization and patterning which results in new norms and values; finally new ideas, beliefs and creeds emerge as justifications or rationalizations of new structural arrangements in other spheres. This is the cycle of enacted morphogenetic process.

Now we have to bring our observations about the internal and external dynamics of social movements together. The 'double morphogenesis' of social movements should not be taken to imply the sequence of phases or stages in which the internal morphogenesis (emergence of the movement's internal structure) would precede in time the external morphogenesis (emergence or transformation of wider social structures under the impact of the movement). We should not be misled into thinking that the movement first crystallizes itself in order to acquire morphogenetic potential, and only later is able to employ it for structural reform. This assumption of a linear time-sequence must be rejected, and the categories of 'before' and 'after' abandoned.

The social movement produces or influences changes in a society not only when it is completely, finally structured itself, but rather all the time from its beginning, during its own internal morphogenesis. Similarly the changes in a society going on outside the movement proper feedback on its development not only when they are completed, but all the time during their gradual build-up, constantly modifying the movement's career, its momentum, speed and direction. As Lauer aptly observes: 'When we deal with a social movement, we are dealing with two processes that intersect and interact with each other – the process of the movement itself and the processes of the larger society within which the movement is operative' (1976: xiv). Two interrelated processes of structural emergence, internal and external proceed concurrently.

The becoming of the movement and the becoming of new social structures are mutually and intimately interlinked, stimulating or arresting each other. There is a constant mutual interplay of partial internal morphogenesis with partial external morphogenesis.

The state of social movement theories

Let me close this chapter with some metatheoretical assesment of the contemporary state of social movement theories, current tendencies and prospects for the future.

The sociology of social movements, like any other subfield of sociology, is intimately related to general theories of society. This link is mutual. First, any research on social movements has to assume, more or less openly, some general image of society. Second, the results attained by the study of social movements add plausibility to certain general images of society and undermine others. In other words, different general theories of society entail different views of social movements, and conversely different general theories acquire different measures of corroboration from the ongoing research on social movements.

Take some examples. The developmentalist ('historicist') theory, which depicts a historical process as endowed with a specific logic, meaning or form, and as progressing in predetermined fashion according to some 'iron laws' of history, must treat social movements merely as symptoms, epiphenomena of ongoing social changes. They appear like a fever in moments of social crises, breakdown or revolutionary breakthroughs. But the real causes of change lie elsewhere, in the realm of historical necessity. The post-developmentalist theory' focusing on the creative role of human agency and asserting the contingent, open-ended nature of historical process, will treat social movements in a completely different fashion: as agents, creators, constructors, crucial actors in a historical process.

Let us consider the orthodox version of historical materialism in comparison with the modern theory of 'new social movements'. On the face of it, the difference lies mostly in the kind of social collectivities picked out for consideration: homogeneous economic classes versus heterogeneous special interest groups, cutting across traditional class divisions. In fact the opposition of the two approaches runs much deeper. In Marxist theory, social movements, rooted in class interests, are mere demiurges of history, vehicles, carriers, executors of necessary developmental tendencies. At most they may release or speed up historical processes, but they cannot cause them. They are evoked with the force of inevitability by universal historical patterns, emerge at predetermined moments to fulfil their revolutionary mission and then leave the social stage.

In the modern theory of social movements, they become the true causal agents of social change, and not merely emanations of an autonomous historical process. They produce, construct, create, and do not merely execute transformations and revolutions. They self-consciously write the script of history, rather than playing out prescribed roles. Therefore they do not automatically appear when needed, but have to be actively recruited and mobilized. They fight not for some preordained, final end of history, which can at most be accelerated, but for specific causes to be consciously selected.

Let us take another pair of opposite general theories. Within the system theory of society (e.g. orthodox 'structural-functionalism'), social movements cannot but appear as disturbances, pathologies, deviant manifestations of disorder or social disorganization, to be countered or compensated by the equilibrating mechanisms of the system. On the other hand, within the modern rational choice approach, social movements would figure as normal means for attaining political ends, as specific forms of political action taken by collectivities of people striving for their goals, when they have no routine, institutional opportunities for interest-representation.

To generalize from these examples and simplify the picture, we may say that there are two traditionally opposite models of society, which are correlated with two opposite approaches to the study of social movements. The first model emphasizes the mobilization of actors: social movements appear from below, when the volume of grievances, discontent and frustration of human populations exceeds a certain threshold (Gurr 1970). One variety of this model carries a sort of volcanic image (Aya 1979): social movements are seen as a spontaneous outburst of collective behaviour which only later acquires leadership, organization, ideology (movements just happen). Another variety carries an enterpeneurial or conspirational image: a social movement is treated as a purposeful collective action, recruited, mobilized and controlled by leaders and ideologues (conspirators, 'movement enterpreneurs' etc.) in an attempt to reach specific goals (in this model, social movements are shaped) (Tilly 1978).

The second, opposite model emphasizes the structural context, facilitating or constraining the emergence of social movements; in short, movements break out when conditions, circumstances, situations are conducive. One variety of this model is rooted in the metaphor of the safety-lid: movement-potential (present in some measure in every society, and treated as constant) is released from above, when the constraints, blockages and controls at the level of political system are weakened (Skockpol 1979). Another variety emphasizes access to resources: movements are evoked by the opening of new means and opportunities, facilitating collective action (McCarthy and Zald 1976; Jenkins 1983). Most often the character of the political system (and particularly the scope of 'political opportunity structures' (Tarrow 1985), in both the sense of constraints and of facilitations, is indicated as the core, decisive factor.

The recent period has produced a strong thrust towards theoretical synthesis, overcoming the opposition of action-oriented and structure-oriented theories. The clear reflection of such a synthesizing tendency is to be found in current theories of social movements. Representatives of the field interviewed in the mid-1980s by Aldon Morris and Cedric Herring are unanimous: 'All of the theorists we interviewed on both sides of this theoretical divide maintain that both social psychological and structural variables are crucial to understanding social movements although they differ over how they should be combined into a comprehensive theory. The issue is whether it is possible to erase this bipolarity and combine the two approaches' (Morris and Herring 1985: 72). This mood continues. It is not long since Dieter Rucht declared: 'An important task for further research would be not simply to confront macro and micro-structural analysis in isolation . . . but rather to erect conceptual bridges' (1988: 325). Several scholars are making concrete efforts to move in this direction. Let me mention four examples.

Bert Klandermans argues that the strong structural (organizational) bias of the fashionable resource-mobilization theory of social movements leads to the neglect of the individual, social-psychological dimension. This, he believes, has to be redressed by combining a new, modified social-psychological theory (stressing rational action, mobilization of consensus and mobilization for action) with a properly curbed resource-mobilization approach. The author proclaims: 'The theory formulated in this paper aims at a break with both the traditional social-psychological approaches to social movements and the neglect of social-psychological analyses by resource mobilization theory' (Klandermans 1984, 596–7).

Myra Ferree and Frederick Miller make a similar attempt to enrich the resource-mobilization perspective by elaborating the missing subjective level. They focus on two psychological processes crucial for reform-oriented or revolutionary movements. One is system attribution (in most cases politicization), i.e. directing discontent and putting the blame on institutional structures rather than persons (rulers). Another is evoking the commitment of participants i.e. shaping the motivations conducive to recruitment and action. In their view, an improved psychological perspective has to be restored into structural-organizational theories to make them more adequate. 'Incorporating cognitive social psychological assumptions in place of incentive terminology in the resource mobilization framework should help clarify both the relationship between movements and the wider society and the processes of development and growth movement organizations undergo' (Ferree and Miller 1985: 55).

Even more striking is the attempt to 'bridge the gap between collective behavior and resource mobilization' proposed by one of the leading exponents of the collective behaviour approach, Ralph Turner. He recognizes the cognitive gains reached within the resource-mobilization perspective, and argues against treating it as an unreconcilable alternative to the more traditional approach of Park, Blumer, Smelser and himself. He admits that resource-mobilization theory adds crucial insights to three questions unresolved within the orthodox theory of collective behaviour. One is the question of 'extra-institutionality': why people depart from established institutional ways. Another is 'translating feelings into action': why people convert extra-institutional dispositions into actions. The third is the puzzle of 'acting collectively': why people get together to express their feelings and drives. Thus, both schools of theory 'can be articulated, to produce a more complete and balanced theory of social movements incorporating the most essential contributions from each' (Turner 1987: 1).

The effort at compromise comes also from the opposite side of the theoretical divide. The very founders of the resource-mobilization perspective, Doug McAdam, John McCarthy and Mayer Zald, reviewing the field of social movements, have hardly started on their way before issuing a manifesto of reconciliation: 'Only by combining the broad conceptual foci of the newer and older approaches can we hope to produce a full understanding of movement dynamics' (1988: 695). Their thrust is concentrated on rejecting one-sided explanations, whether 'from above', invoking structures, or 'from below', invoking actions, and explicating the links between macro-structural conditions (political, economic, organizational) and the micro-dynamics of evolving movements. 'The point is we can no more build social movements from the individual up than down from some broad societal process. We believe the real action takes place at a third level, intermediate between the individual and the broad macro contexts in which they are embedded' (p. 709).

This trend towards synthesis and reconciliation seems right and proper. Sociological wisdom is not reserved for one theory or school. The tremendous complexity of the phenomenon of social movements demands multiple sources of enlightenment, and can be adequately explained only by a plurality of theories, or ultimately by a multidimensional theory. 'Efforts to establish a relation between the approaches may enable us to get a more complete idea of the social regularities behind the emergence, existence and impacts of social movements' (Neidhardt and Rucht 1991: 443).

Such efforts may also provide an important testing ground or 'strategic research site' (Merton 1973: 371) for the general theory of society attempting the synthesis of 'two sociologies', the individualistic sociology of actions and the holistic sociology of structures. First of all, social movements embody the characteristic two-sidedness of social reality; the dialectics of individuals and social wholes. McAdam, McCarthy and Zald observe that 'The real action in social movements takes place at some level intermediate between the macro and micro' (McAdam et al. 1988: 729). Oberschall believes that the processes occurring in social movements are 'providing a link between the micro- and macroaspects of [sociological] theory' (1973: 21). Zurcher and Snow aptly point out: 'Nowhere is the reciprocity between the individual and social structure more conceptually and empirically obvious than in the operation of social movements.' Hence: 'the social movement milieu is an excellent stage upon which to observe how social factors influence and are influenced by actors'(pp. 447, 475). Thus, social movements represent an intermediate form in the anatomy of social reality.

Second, social movements represent also an intermediate stage in the dynamic emergence of the social fabric. Thus they allow us to grasp social reality as it comes to birth. This intermediate quality of social movements means, on the one hand, that they take part in the shaping, constructing, reforming of external society. They are some of the most important agents of structural change and structure-building. As Touraine puts it, 'social movements belong to the processes by which a society produces its organization on the basis of its system of historical action and via class conflicts and political transactions' (Touraine 1977: 298). Studying social movements allows us to grasp wider social structures in the process of their emergence or transformation.

Third, social movements also have an intermediate quality in another sense: in their internal constitution they are something between mere congeries of acting individuals and fully-fledged, crystallized social wholes: 'movements are neither fully collective behavior nor incipient interest groups . . . Rather, they contain essential elements of both' (Freeman 1973: 793). Thus studying social movements allows us to grasp the intermediate phase of internal structure-building, to see how the internal structures of the movement emerge and change. Killian sums up this point: 'the study of social movements is not the study of stable groups or established institutions, but of groups and institutions in the process of becoming' (1964: 427). A similar point is made by Rucht: 'Social movements do not form stable and clearly definable social entities. They experience cycles of expansion and contraction, and their aims and strategies may change as well' (1988: 313).

Thus social movements appear as crucial components of the socio-individual field in the process of constant self-transformation. Their study provides strong corroboration for the theory of social becoming.

20

Revolutions: the peak of social change

Revolution as a form of change

Revolutions are the most spectacular manifestations of social change. They mark fundamental ruptures in the historical process, reshape human society from within and remould the people. They leave nothing as it was before; they close epochs and open new ones. At the moment of revolution, societies experience the peak of their agency, the outburst of the potential for self-transformation. In the wake of revolutions, societies and their members seem to be revitalized, almost born anew. In this sense revolutions are the signs of social health.

Compared to other forms of social change, revolutions are distinguished by five traits. (1) They bring about changes of the vastest scope, touching all levels and dimensions of society: economy, polity, culture, social organization, everyday life, human personalities. (2) In all these areas the changes are radical, fundamental, reaching the core of societal constitution and functioning. (3) The changes are exceptionally rapid, happening as suddenly as outbursts of dynamics in the slow flow of historical process. (4) For all these reasons revolutions are also the most salient displays of change; the times are exceptional, and hence especially memorable. (5) They evoke particular emotional and intellectual reactions from their participants and witnesses: an eruption of mass mobilization; enthusiasm, excitement, elation, exhilaration, optimism and hope; a feeling of might and omnipotence; the joy of activism and regained meaning of life; rocketing aspirations and utopian visions of the immediate future.

The occurrence of revolutions worthy of the name is not uniformly spread across history. Most of them seem to be linked with the modern or recent period. The revolutions known as 'great' – the English (1640), American (1776) and French (1789) – gave birth to the epoch of modernity. The Russian (1917) and Chinese (1949) revolutions began the period of communism, and the anti-communist revolutions in eastern and central Europe (1989) brought it to a close. Thus great revolutions seem to be intimately related to modernity, and with the ascent of modernity their significance seems to be growing. The 'rebellious century' is the name given by some historians to the period from 1830 to 1930 (Tilly et al. 1975). Among sociologists 'there is a considerable consensus that, if any century deserves the title of the "century of revolution", it is the present one' (Taylor 1984: 4). Perhaps together with 'progress' and 'science', 'revolution' makes up a trio of concepts embodying the meaning of our time.

The idea of revolution: a glimpse of its history

Like most social concepts, 'revolution' lives a double life, appearing in two guises. First, it belongs to societal discourse, pervading common sense. Here it evolves into a complex image, strongly imbued with valuations and emotional commitments, which may be called the 'myth of revolution'. Second, it belongs to sociological discourse, appearing in scientific reasoning. Here it evolves into a complex theoretical construct, engendering explanatory hypotheses. It is normally called a 'theory of revolution'. Both levels of discourse, societal and sociological, are components of social consciousness. As such they enter into a two-sided, dialectical relationship with social life: they reflect actual conditions, human actions, forms of social organizations and institutions; and they also reflexively feed back on social life. The myth of revolution and the theory of revolution are therefore both the mental reconstructions of their time and significant causal factors in themselves.

They are mutually interdependent, too, and the second dialectical relationship operates not so much *between* the two levels, but this time *within* the level of social consciousness, between societal and sociological discourse. As we know all too well, sociological theory is often only slightly more sophisticated common sense. The theory of revolution draws heavily on the myth of revolution; with some inevitable time-lag, it explicates and systematizes what ordinary people think about revolution. But it also acquires some autonomy, going beyond common sense. This is possible because theory, inspired as it is by common sense, may develop its own momentum, start to live its own life and follow its own logic of elaboration. It is also because a single theory is not isolated but links with other theories, falls under the impact of a wider 'theoretical movement' and reflects the premises of a dominant theoretical approach or orientation. Going beyond common sense, the theory of revolution may then feed back reflexively on the myth of revolution, become an important factor in reshaping the widespread image of revolution and hence, indirectly, influence the probabilities and forms of revolutionary action.

The concept of revolution in its modern sense is relatively young. The term had already appeared in the fourteenth century, but with a much more general, and different, meaning. At that time it signified merely circular movement, turning around. Nicolaus Copernicus titled his famous volume 'On the Revolutions of Celestial Bodies' (1543), and in the language of astronomy or technology we still refer to motions along a circular trajectory or rotations of a wheel as revolutions. In the seventeenth century the term was appropriated by political philosophy. It came to mean the cyclical change of rulers or whole political elites in the emerging states.

It is only in the eighteenth century, with the great French Revolution (1789) as the archetype, that the modern concept of revolution took shape. It came to be used for the description of similar epochal breakthroughs, the fundamental reshaping of society by society. The nineteenth century, with its unmatched dynamism and optimism of expanding modernity (industry, urbanism, capitalism), was also the golden era for the idea of revolution, which pervaded everyday thinking as well as political and social theory. Society was seen as undergoing necessary progressive change, guided by reason or history, always for the better, towards some ideal future order. Revolutions were treated as inevitable, crucial thresholds on this road, moments of galvanizing and accelerating rational and beneficial processes. With the work of Karl Marx the concept of revolution took a peculiar twist, entering the domain of ideology as a powerful tool of the anti-capitalist critique and the foundation of the alternative communist project.

The myth of revolution starts to crumble and break down in the twentieth century, the era of decaying modernity. Progress gives way to crisis as the leitmotif of the epoch. The myth of revolution is undermined by the convoluted and tragic experience of actual revolutions. Two questions cannot but arise in common consciousness. (1) Why is it that revolutions never end in what was dreamed of by the revolutionaries. By some irony of history, they often end in its opposite, resulting in more injustice, inequality, exploitation, oppression and repression? (2) Why is reason so often replaced by violence, sheer coercion, thoughtless destruction? Why are the Promethean revolutionaries so typically displaced by aggressive, irrational and terrorist mobs? Revolution is still perceived as a fundamental break in social continuity, brought about by human masses in a violent and sudden manner, but it is no longer seen as an embodiment of some ultimate logic of history, or as necessarily progressive or ultimately reasonable. The common metaphors of volcanic eruption, prairie fire or earthquake suggest that revolutions are viewed as disasters rather than as redemptions or salvations of mankind. Most people no longer dream of revolutions but fear them. In this ideological climate, historians and sociologists start to question the glorious or heroic images of past revolutions, and a wave of 'revisionist' accounts appears.

The modern concept of revolution

The modern concept of revolution derives from two intellectual traditions: historiosophical and sociological. The historiosophical concept of revolution signifies a radical breach of continuity, a fundamental disruption, a 'cataclysmic break' (Brinton 1965: 237) in the course of history. The focus rests on the overall pattern of a historical process, and revolutions mark the qualitative thresholds in this pattern. Most often this assumes some version of developmentalist thinking. The typical example is Karl Marx's vision of the sequence of socio-economic formations, where 'social revolutions' signify qualitative leaps to a higher phase of development.

The Sociological concept of revolution refers to mass movements using or threatening coercion and violence against rulers in order to enforce basic and lasting changes in their societies. The focus moves from the overall pattern, necessary direction and ultimate outcomes towards the causal agents, mechanism and alternative scenarios of social processes, the means that people use to shape and reshape history. Revolution is treated as the strongest manifestation of human creativeness, expressed in collective action at critical junctures of the historical process. This means a more voluntaristic point of view, with the emphasis on agency and contingency. Such a concept is typical of recent post-developmentalist theories of social change, which abandon the idea that history is prearranged according to some constant pattern or 'logic'.

The reflection of both traditions, historiosophical and sociological, is to be found in current definitions of revolution. We shall order them into three groups. The first group includes definitions emphasizing fundamental, wide-ranging transformation of society (with the paradigmatic case of 'great' revolutions clearly in mind). The focus is on the scope and depth of change. In this sense 'revolution' is an antonym of 'reform'. Thus, we find a revolution defined as 'sudden, radical changes in the political, social and economic structure of society' (Bullock and Stallybras 1977: 542), or 'a sweeping sudden change in the societal structure, or in some important feature of it' (Fairchild 1966: 259). This meaning is also characteristic of common metaphorical usage, when we speak of technological, scientific or moral revolution, and revolutions in fashion or art.

The second group includes definitions emphasizing violence and struggle, as well as the speed of change. The focus is on the techniques of change. In this sense 'revolution' is an antonym of 'evolution'. Thus numerous authors define revolution as:

'attempts to realise changes in the constitution of societies by force' (C. Johnson 1968: 1)
'fundamental sociopolitical change accomplished through violence' (Gurr 1970: 4)
'drastic, sudden substitution of one group in charge of the running of a territorial political entity by another group hitherto not running the government' (Brinton 1965: 4)
'the seizure (or attempted seizure) of control over governmental apparatus – understood as the principal concentrated means of coercion, taxation and administration in society – by one class, group, or (more likely) coalition, from another' (Aya 1979: 44).

Perhaps the most useful are the definitions of the third group, combining both aspects of revolutions in a synthetic formulation. Thus revolutions are understood as:

'rapid, fundamental, and violent domestic change in the dominant values and myths of a society, in its political institutions, social structure, leadership, and government activities and policies' (Huntington 1968: 264)
'rapid, basic transformations of a society's state and class structures ... accompanied and in part carried through by class-based revolts from below' (Skockpol 1979: 4)
'the seizure of state power through violent means by the leaders of a mass movement, where that power is subsequently used to initiate major processes of social reform' (Giddens 1989: 605).

To sum up, there seems to exist a consensus on basic, constitutive components of the phenomenon. (1) Revolutions refer to fundamental, comprehensive, multidimensional changes, touching the very core of the social order. In this sense, fragmentary reforms of laws, administration, replacement of governments etc. do not count as revolutions. (2) Revolutions involve large masses of people mobilized and acting within a revolutionary movement. The most characteristic cases involve peasant revolts (Jenkins 1982) and urban uprisings. In this sense, even the deepest, most fundamental changes, if imposed by rulers 'from above' (e.g. Meiji reforms in Japan, Ataturk's reforms in Turkey, Nasser's reforms in Egypt, Gorbachev's *perestroika*), will not count as revolutions. Similarly, even fundamental changes, if brought about by spontaneous social trends, cannot be referred to as revolutions (except in the loose, metaphorical usage when we speak of technological or scientific revolution). (3) Most authors seem to believe that revolutions necessarily involve violence and coercion.

This is the only contestable point, in view of the historical evidence of principally non-violent but surprisingly effective and far-reaching 'revolutionary' movements, like Ghandism in India, or recent social movements in eastern and central Europe, enforcing the collapse of communism (e.g. the 'peaceful revolution' of Polish Solidarity, or the 'velvet revolution' in Czechoslovakia). Contemporary observers do not hesitate to call the latter cases by the name of revolution. Let us consider the view of an eminent British historian: 'The revolutions of 1989 have been real revolutions: popular revolts before which armed governments, one after another, have collapsed; the recovery by nations of lost liberty' (Trevor-Roper 1989: 14). One may argue that, even though in the case of anti-communist revolutions (with the sad exception of Romania) actual violence was almost absent, the potential threat of violence was clearly implied by the massiveness of mobilization and the level of commitment or emotional arousal of the masses. It was under the pressure of such a persistent threat of force that the communist authorities finally abdicated.

To complete our definitional account of revolution, we have to list other concepts which are used to refer to the outbreaks of collective behaviour or collective action, different from revolutions. By *coup d'état* or 'palace revolution' we mean the sudden, extra-legal replacement of rulers, government or personnel of political institutions without any modification of political regime, economic organization or cultural system. By 'rebellion', 'insurrection' or 'uprising', we mean episodes of massive violent activism directed against the internal rulers or external conquerors which result in minor concessions or reforms rather than revolutionary transformation. By 'mutiny', we mean refusal of obedience by subordinate groups not accompanied by any positive vision of required change. By *putsch*, we mean the forced take-over of government by the army, or segments of the army, or a group of officers commanding sufficient support from the army. By 'civil war', we mean armed conflict between segments of the same society, motivated most often by religious or ethnic enmities and aimed at the annihilation or suppression of opponents. By 'war of independence', we mean the struggle of dependent, colonized or conquered societies against external powers. Finally by 'riot', 'turmoil' and 'social unrest', we mean spontaneous, dispersed expressions of discontent, grievances, frustrations lacking specific focus and not aspiring to any definite change. As we see, collective behaviour and collective actions take multiple forms, but revolutions clearly stand out among them. All such phenomena may in concrete historical situations accompany revolutions, precede or follow them, but they are not the same as revolutions (Tilly 1978: 198).

The course of revolution

Historically known revolutions are extremely varied. Let us consider some famous cases: the English (1640), American (1776), French (1789), Russian (1917), Mexican (1919), Chinese (1949), Cuban (1959), Philippine (1985), eastern and central European (1989). Is there anything they have in common? Is it possible to generalize inductively from such dispersed events, and unravel their typical course?

The earliest sociological accounts of revolution took up such an inductive strategy, attempting to 'establish certain uniformities of description' (Brinton 1965: 254). These came to be known as 'natural histories of revolutions' (Edwards 1927; Brinton 1965). The typical sequence is taken to consist of ten stages.

1   It is argued that all revolutions are preceded by a typical condition called a 'revolutionary prodrome' (Brinton 1965: 27): the intensification of discontent, grievances, disorders and conflicts due to economic or fiscal crisis. These are experienced most painfully by the social classes on the rise, rather than those which are already the most wretched and oppressed. 'The

strongest feelings seem generated in the bosoms of men – and women – who have made money, or at least who have enough to live on, and who contemplate bitterly the imperfections of a socially privileged aristocracy' (Brinton 1965: 251).

2   At the next stage, there occurs the 'transfer of allegiance of the intellectuals' (Edwards 1927): the spread of critical, reform-oriented disputes, various forms of agitation, proliferation of philosophical or political pamphlets and doctrines directed against the old regime. Take the case of the French Revolution and 'call the roll – Voltaire, Rousseau, Diderot, Raynal, d'Holbach, Volney, Helvétius, d'Alembert, Condorcet, Bernardin de St. Pierre, Beaumarchais – rebels all, men leveling their wit against Church and State' (Brinton 1965: 44). A state of social consciousness which may be called 'revolutionary spirit' begins to spread out.

3   Next comes the attempt by the regime to deflect the growing threat by partial reforms (e.g. the initiatives of Louis XVI in France, the Stolypin reforms in Russia), but these are read as belated and forced, signs of weakness, undermining the legitimacy of the old regime even more.

4   The growing inability of the state to govern efficiently results in a 'paralysis of the state' (Goldstone 1982: 190). This at last gives the revolutionaries the opportunity to seize power.

5   The old regime collapses and there is a 'revolutionary honeymoon', a period of euphoria after victory.

6   Internal divisions start to appear among the victorious revolutionaries. There are conservatives attempting to minimize change, radicals who want to push forward and moderates looking for gradual reform.

7   The moderate reformers dominate, attempting to preserve some continuity with the past by using the organizations and administrative personnel left by the earlier regime. This cannot meet the heightened aspirations, hopes and dreams of the masses, and post-revolutionary malaise sets in.

8   Radicals and extremists are able to exploit the widespread frustration, mobilize the masses and replace the moderates.

9   The stage of 'terror' begins when radicals attempt to enforce order and wipe out all traces of the old regime. The ensuing social turmoil provides the opportunity for strong dictators or military leaders to seize power.

10   Eventually some balance is restored with the final stage, the 'Thermidor', or 'convalescence from the fever of revolution' (Brinton 1965: 205), when 'the excesses of the radicals are condemned, and the emphasis shifts from political change to economic progress within a framework of stable institutions' (Goldstone 1982: 192).

Such an account of a revolution exhibits some important aspects of the phenomenon. It tells us something about *how* revolutions happen, but it does not answer the most important question: *why* they happen. The latter is the domain of the theories, rather than mere 'natural histories', of revolutions. Any theory worthy of the name must consist of at least three types of component:

(1) it has to suggest a general image or conceptual model of the phenomenon; (2) it must select certain factors or variables as primary determinants, causes or mechanisms of a revolution; (3) it must entail a set of testable hypotheses about the interdependences among variables, and in particular the origins, course and outcomes of revolutions.

The models of revolution

The most general classification of the theories of revolution can be based on the assumed image or model. Some theories emphasize the agency, the mobilization of actors; other theories put the stress on the structural context, the conditions in which revolutions occur. Thus, within the earlier type we find the most traditional, 'volcanic model' of revolution. Revolutions break out from below, spontaneously, as the result of accumulated tensions, grievances, discontents passing a certain threshold. They are carried out by the masses of desperate people, each of whom cannot continue living as before. There is the image of 'the periodic eruption of social-psychological tensions that boil up in human groups like lava under the earth's crust or steam in a geyser' (Aya 1979: 49).

A similar emphasis on agency is taken by the different, 'conspirational model'. Revolution is still seen as primarily somebody's creation, but this time the agents are not the masses themselves, but rather outside agitators pushing the masses to revolutionary action. The masses fall prey to the manipulation, propaganda and ideology by which professional revolutionaries (or their elite groupings) instigate people to action. Revolutions appear as 'the work of subversives who, with a sinister genius for cajolery and coercion, provoke otherwise disinterested masses to violence' (Aya 1979: 49). In this perspective revolutions do not break out but result from a plot. 'The school of plot regards revolutions as a forced and artificial growth, its seeds carefully planted in soil worked over and fertilized by the gardeners – revolutionists, mysteriously brought to maturity by these same gardeners against the forces of nature' (Brinton 1965: 86).

The second type of theories focuses on the structural context. These assume that in every society there is always a large pool of discontent, but only under certain conducive structural conditions will it result in a revolution. Revolutions are not made but released. One variety of such reasoning is represented by the 'safety-lid model'. Revolutions erupt only when there is a breakdown of governmental control, a relaxation of repressive measures, a collapse of the state. 'Revolutionary situations have developed due to the emergence of politico-military crises of state and class domination. And only because of the possibilities thus created have revolutionary leaderships and rebellious masses contributed to the accomplishment of revolutionary transformations' (Skockpol 1979: 17).

Another variety of this approach may be called the 'open-treasury model'.

Revolutions erupt only when new resources and opportunities emerge. Among them, crucial importance is attached to 'political opportunity structures', the framework of laws, rights and freedoms opening the chances for collective action. Other opportunities have to do with the ecological proximity of large masses of people in urban and industrial settings. Finally some authors hold that the social disorganization and imbalance (system disequilibrium) produced by rapid social change creates conducive structural opportunities for revolutionary mobilization.

Agency-focused and structure-focused models of revolution differ in what they take for granted and what they consider as problematic. Each seems to grasp a part of the truth. Perhaps future theorizing will take a more eclectic, multidimensional turn, attempting to integrate all sides of the most complex phenomenon of revolution into one coherent model. Let us take a closer look at some theories of revolution, which may provide the material for such a future synthesis.

Major theories of revolution

I propose to illustrate four major 'schools' in the theory of revolution – behavioural, psychological, structural and political – by the work of their most famous representatives. Of necessity the discussion will be highly selective, and sketchy (for more thorough treatment cf. Taylor 1984).

1 The first modern theory of revolution was proposed in 1925 by Pitirim Sorokin (1967). He based his conclusions primarily on the experience of the Russian revolution of 1917, in which he participated and played some political role. His theory may be treated as an example of the behavioural approach as he focuses on 'the revolutionary perversion of the behavior of individuals' (p. 367), and searches for the causes of such perversion in the domain of basic human needs or instincts. 'The performance of the grandiose tragedies, dramas and comedies of revolutions on the historical stage is determined chiefly by the repressed inborn reflexes' (p. 383). Revolution is marked by fundamental changes in typical human behaviour. 'The conventional garment of civilized behavior is speedily cast off and instead of a socius we are left face to face with a beast let loose' (p. 372). Sorokin traces and documents such changes in six areas: 'the transformation of speech-reactions', 'the perversion of the reactions of ownership', 'the perversion of sexual reactions', 'the perversion of the labor reactions', 'the perversion of the reactions of authority and subordination', and 'the perversion of religious, moral, esthetic and other acquired forms of conduct' (pp. 41–169). These multiple perversions 'break the conditional reflexes, do away with obedience, discipline, order and civilized forms of behavior and turn human beings into wild hordes of mad people' (p. 376).

Then the author asks the crucial theoretical question: 'Why?' and puts forward two main causal hypotheses. The first refers to the driving force behind the revolutionary masses. 'The immediate cause of revolution is always the growth of "repression" of the main instincts of the majority of society, and the impossibility of obtaining for those instincts the necessary minimum of satisfaction (p. 367). 'Either an exceedingly strong "repression" of the most important instincts, or a repression of a great number of them, is indispensable to produce a revolutionary outburst . . . Further, it is necessary that the "repression" should spread, if not over the large majority, at least over a considerable part of society' (p. 369). Among the main insticts Sorokin lists: desire for food, individual security, collective self-preservation of a group, basic comforts (housing, clothing, necessary temperature), the sex reflex, ownership, self-expression and individual identity. Restrictions on freedom of communication, speech and action, monotony of experience and suppression of creativeness are singled out as additional contributing conditions. The author points out that repressions and restrictions acquire different motivating force depending on the comparative framework of 'what one used to have before' and of 'what the others have' (p. 369), i.e. relative to the accustomed or the standard level of satisfaction.

The second hypothesis refers to the reaction of the established power elites. 'It is also necessary that those social groups which defend the existing order should lack the means for the suppression of subversive attempts' (p. 370). Otherwise, if they possess sufficient coercive power, revolutions will end at most as crushed riots. 'Pre-revolutionary epochs literally strike the observer by the incapacity of the authorities and the degeneracy of the ruling privileged classes: they appear equally incapable of carrying out the ordinary functions of power, to say nothing of opposing revolution by force' (p. 399).

Two hypotheses specifying necessary conditions of revolution together define the sufficient condition. If both conditions – pressure from below and weakness from above – coincide, the revolution becomes inevitable.

Revolutions, however, do not redress the predicaments of suppressed instincts. Just the reverse: post-revolutionary chaos increases the difficulty in satisfying basic needs. People start to crave for order and stability. At the same time revolutionary fervour is exhausted as the 'reserve-fund of energy in the human organism' is limited. In effect, counter-revolution is likely to begin, and it has a good chance of victory. 'The population resembles an inert mass, ready to be molded. It presents favorable material for the activity of any "repressers"' (p. 410). The day of despots and tyrants comes. Such is the ironic conclusion of all revolutions.

2   The psychological theories leave the realm of behavioural reflexes or basic instincts and move into the realm of more complex motivational and attitudinal orientations. Such theories are closest to common sense. No wonder they have acquired great popularity and become the most elaborated of all approaches. Perhaps the most influential of them was proposed by James Davies (1962) and Ted Gurr (1970) under the name 'relative deprivation

theory'. Revolutions are caused by a painful mental syndrome spreading among the population, aggravated by being widely shared and motivating a collective struggle to alleviate it. 'Misery breeds revolt', or more precisely, misery of which people are aware and which they define as injustice pushes people to rebellion.

The concept of relative deprivation was introduced by W. G. Runciman. In his account, 'The magnitude of relative deprivation is the extent of the difference between the desired situation and that of the person desiring it (as he sees it) . . . The degree of a relative deprivation is the intensity with which it is felt' (Runciman 1966: 10). More precisely, in the formulation of Ted Gurr it refers to a perceived discrepancy between value expectations (goods and conditions of life to which people believe they are rightfully entitled) and value capabilities (goods and conditions they actually expect to attain or maintain, given the social means available to them) (Gurr 1970: 24).

The crucial point is that people feel they are entitled to certain standards of achievement. Even if they are extremely impoverished in the absolute sense but accept it as due to their fate or providence or predetermined social status, no revolutionary ferment will arise. It is only when they start to question the actual conditions, to define what they *should* properly have and to perceive the difference between what they should have and what they actually can have that relative deprivation is born. This experience is closely related to the perception of injustice, stemming from the comparison between what people actually have and what others, similar to them, have already achieved. The feeling of injustice is born in the condition of 'social inflexibilities that differentially restrict a group from attaining conditions enjoyed by other groups' (Gurr 1970: 129). The theme of deprivation (relative to justified aspirations), plus the theme of injustice (relative to what others already enjoy), pervades social consciousness in the period immediatley preceding revolution. 'What is needed is the consciousness of poverty and the consciousness of oppression, and the conviction that poverty and oppression are not the natural order of this world. It is curious that in this case experience alone, no matter how painful, does not suffice' (Kapuscinski 1985: 86). It is necessary to define it and perceive it as painful. 'Revolutions cannot do without the word "justice" and the sentiments it arouses' (Brinton 1965: 35).

How does this mental syndrome arise? What is its etiology? If the dimension of time is adduced, one may distinguish three historical developments leading to the emergence of acute relative deprivation reaching the revolutionary level. The first route is called aspirational deprivation. The curve of achievement remains more or less constant, but at some moment the curve of justified aspirations rises considerably. It may happen because of an influx of new ideologies (value systems, religious or political creeds) setting new standards of what people deserve and should justifiably expect. Or there is the 'demonstration effect' of standards of living enjoyed by other societies or by some privileged groups in one's own society. As a result, even though nothing changes as far as actual life conditions are concerned, the expected

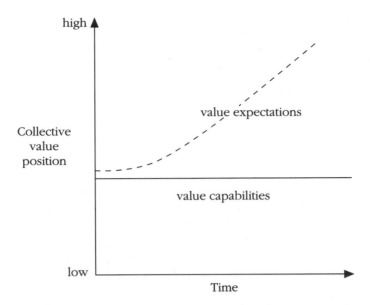

Figure 20.1   Aspirational deprivation (*source*: Gurr 1970: 51). Reproduced by permission of Princeton University Press.

standards are raised and this change, which is of an exclusively psychological sort, makes the deprivation unbearable. People 'are angered because they feel they have no means for attaining new or intensified expectations' (Gurr 1970: 50). The 'revolution of rising expectations' may ensue (figure 20.1).

The symmetrical opposite of aspirational deprivation is called decremental deprivation. In this case the aspirations remain more or less constant, but suddenly there is a drop in realistically attainable standards of living. This may happen because of economic or fiscal crisis, a decline in the efficiency of the state in providing for public security, the narrowing down of political opportunities for participation with the turn towards an autocratic or dictatorial regime. The gap between what people still consider their due and what they actually can have becomes unbearable. 'Men are likely to be more intensely angered when they lose what they have than when they lose hope of attaining what they do not yet have' (Gurr 1970: 50). The 'revolution of withdrawn benefits', as this case may be called, is perhaps even more common in history, than the 'revolutions of rising aspirations' (figure 20.2).

The third case, known as 'progressive deprivation', is analysed by James Davies (1962) and represented by the so-called J-curve (figure 20.3). It combines the mechanisms exhibited by the two previous cases. Aspirations and achievements rise in parallel for a considerable time, marking a period of prosperity and progress in actual life conditions accompanied by a related expansion of hopes and dreams for the future. Then the curves suddenly part, with aspirations continuing to rise while actual achievements are blocked

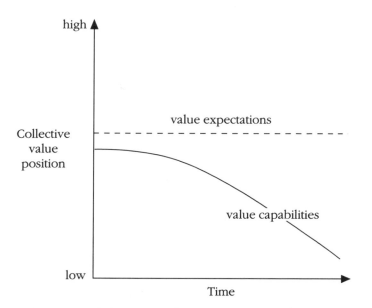

Figure 20.2 Decremental deprivation (*source*: Gurr 1970: 47). Reproduced by permission of Princeton University Press.

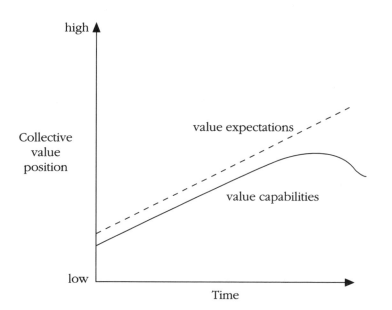

Figure 20.3 Progressive deprivation (*source*: Gurr 1970: 53). Reproduced by permission of Princeton University Press.

or even reversed (because of natural disasters, war, economic breakdown etc.). This produces an ever-widening, unbearable gap. 'The crucial factor is the vague or specific fear that ground gained over a long period of time will be quickly lost' (Davies 1962: 8). The 'revolution of frustrated progress', as it may be called, will ensue. As Davies explains,

> Revolutions are most likely to occur when a prolonged period of objective economic and social development is followed by a short period of sharp reversal. The all-important effect on the minds of people in a particular society is to produce, during the former period, an expectation of continued ability to satisfy needs – which continue to rise – and then, during the latter, a mental state of anxiety and frustration when manifest reality breaks away from anticipated reality. (*Davies 1962: 6; 1971*)

Of all theories of revolution, the theory of relative deprivation generates the greatest amount of specific testable hypotheses. Gurr (1970: 360–7) lists almost 100 and provides tentative corroboration by means of numerous illustrations and statistical as well as historical evidence. The main charge raised against relative deprivation theory is its psychological bias and the neglect of structural variables. 'The stress upon individual-level psychological processes took no account of the macro-structural context: revolutions were portrayed as a manifestation of uncontrollable frustration and aggression or cognitive dissonance rather than as arising from structure inequalities in wealth, power and status between different groups in societies' (Taylor 1984: 91).

3   The alternative theories of revolution focus their attention on the macro-structural level, with the neglect of psychological factors. For the so-called 'structural theories' revolutions are outcomes of structural strains and tensions, and primarily the specific configurations of relations between citizens and the state. The causes of revolutions are to be sought at the specifically social level, in the context of class and group relations (national and international) rather than in the heads of citizens, their mentalities or attitudes. The leading contemporary exponent of the school, Theda Skockpol, calls for a 'structural perspective, to emphasize objective relationships and conflicts among variously situated groups and nations, rather than the interests, outlooks or ideologies of particular actors in revolutions' (1979: 291). She quotes Eric Hobsbawm as saying that 'the evident importance of the actors in the drama . . . does not mean that they are also dramatist, producer, and stage-designer' (p. 18).

On the basis of thorough historical evidence, Theda Skockpol compares the French, Russian and Chinese revolutions, producing a generalized structural account of their causes as well as their course and outcomes. They follow a three-stage pattern. (1) There are structural breakdowns and crises, political and economic, within the old regime. 'Caught in cross-pressures between domestic class structures and international exigencies, the autocracies and their centralized administrations and armies broke apart, opening the

way for social-revolutionary transformations sparheaded by revolts from below'
(Skockpol 1979: 47). (2) The crisis of the regimes opens the opportunities for
mass revolts of the peasantry and/or urban workers. The breakdown of the
old regime is a necessary but not sufficient coindition for a revolution. 'Peasant revolts have been the crucial insurrectionary ingredient in virtually all
actual (i.e. successful) social revolutions to date' (pp. 112–13). But they could
occur only in the conditions of earlier political breakdown. 'It was the
breakdown of the concerted repressive capacity of a previously unified and
centralized state that finally created conditions directly or ultimately favorable
to widespread and irreversible peasant revolts against landlords' (p. 117). (3)
The main theme of the revolution during the third stage is also political: it is
the reconsolidation, reorganization and reintegration of the state and administration by the new political elite coming to power after the succesful overthrow of the old regime. 'The revolutions were fully consummated only once
new state organizations – administrations and armies, coordinated by execu-
tives who governed in the name of revolutionary symbols – were built up
amidst the conflicts of the revolutionary situations' (p. 163). Typical for
Skockpol's theory is the emphasis on political and international factors. 'Both
the occurrence of revolutionary situations in the first place and the nature of
the New Regimes that emerged from the revolutionary conflicts depended
fundamentally upon the structures of state organizations and their partially
autonomous and dynamic relationships to domestic class and political forces,
as well as their positions in relation to other states abroad' (p. 284). She
predicts: 'in future revolutions, as in those of the past, the realm of the state
is likely to be central' (p. 293).

Structural theory is again charged with one-sidedness and neglect of
psychological, individual aspects. It clearly focuses on the structural preconditions and structural effects, neglecting the whole complex process occurring
in between, when masses of mobilized people organized by leaders actually
conduct the revolution. 'Skockpol forgets that human beings thinking and
acting (however haphazardly) are the mediating link between structural conditions and social outcomes. Structural conditions, moreover, do not dictate
absolutely what humans do; they merely place certain limits on human action
or define a certain range of possibilities' (Himmelstein and Kimmel 1981:
1153). The message critics derive from the analysis of structural theories is the
same as we submitted earlier: the call for a synthetic, multidimensional position. 'Skockpol treats structural analysis and voluntarist analysis as mutually
exclusive opposites, rather than as two necessary elements of a complete
sociological explanation' (Himmelstein and Kimmel 1981: 1154).

4   Political theories of revolution adopt an even more limited perspective.
They treat revolutions as inherently political phenomena emerging from
processes occurring exclusively in the political domain. They are seen as
resulting from 'shifting power balances and struggles for hegemony between
contenders for control of the state' (Aya 1979: 49). A good example of such

a focus is provided by the theory of Charles Tilly (1978). The author believes that revolutions are not extraordinary, exeptional, deviant phenomena, but rather – to paraphrase the famous formula of Clausewitz – they are just 'the continuation of politics by other means', i.e. varieties of the normal political process in which various groups attempt to realize their goals by winning power. Revolutions are the extreme forms of contention for political control (hence 'the contention model' of revolution). They occur only when the contenders are able to mobilize the massive resources necessary to wrest power from the old regime (Goldstone 1982: 193). The wider context in which revolutions must be conceptually located is called the 'polity model'. It is a set of interrelated components including among others: 'Government: an organization which controls the principal concentrated means of coercion within the population. Contender: any group, which, during some specified period, applies pooled resources to influence the government. Contenders include challengers and members of the polity. A member is any contender which has routine, low-cost access to resources controlled by the government; a challenger is any other contender' (Tilly 1978: 52). Needless to say, it is among the challengers without institutionalized, legitimate ways to realize their interests that revolutionary mobilization occurs. By mobilization Tilly means an increase in resources under the collective control of the challengers or an increase in the degree of collective control (p. 54). Mobilization is a prerequisite of collective action in pursuit of common ends. Revolution is a special form of collective action distinguished by particular preconditions ('revolutionary situation'), and particular ends ('revolutionary outcomes'). The most important trait of revolutionary situation is 'multiple sovereignty' or, in other words, 'multiplication of polities'. 'A revolutionary situation begins when a government previously under the control of a single, sovereign polity becomes the object of effective, competing, mutually exclusive claims on the part of two or more distinct polities. It ends when a single sovereign polity regains control over the government' (p. 191). Here the population is confronted with at least two power centres with incompatible demands: the former government and the contending government. There are four varieties of this situation. (1) As with conquest, when one sovereign polity attempts to subordinate another sovereign polity. (2) When a subordinate polity (e.g. a state under the control of a federal government, or a colony subjected to foreign power) asserts sovereinty. The archetype of this is an anti-colonial or national uprising. (3) When challengers mobilize and acquire control over fragments of the government apparatus. (4) When the polity is fragmented into two or more blocks, each of which acquires partial control over the government (pp. 191–2). Revolution breaks out when a sufficient proportion of citizens transfers allegiance and loyalty to the alternative power centre. The revolution wins when the transfer of power actually occurs, and one set of power-holders is replaced by another. 'Great revolutions are extreme in both regards: extensive splits between alternative polities, large-scale displacement of existing members' (p. 195).

Several hypotheses are put forward concerning the causes of revolutions. They are ordered in two groups: the causes of revolutionary situations, and the causes of revolutionary outcomes. Multiple sovereignty, the crux of the revolutionary situation, arises when:

1   There appear sufficiently visible challengers (political opposition, dissidents) advancing claims to control over the government (revolutionary leadership emerges and ideology is articulated). At this stage, a particularly important role is played by charismatic leaders and intellectuals.

2   They acquire support, both in words and (primarily) in actions and the commitment of resources, from a significant segment of the population (the masses are mobilized). This happens either when the government fails to meet the usual demands of the population, or when it increases its demands on the population. 'An increase in taxes is the clearest example, but military conscription, the commandeering of land, crops, or farm animals, and the imposition of corvées have all played an historical role on the incitement of opposition' (Tilly 1978: 205).

3   The government is unable or unwilling to suppress the challengers (the power-holders lose control over the instruments of violence). One typical case is involvement in external war, another is international pressure to forgo extreme forms of violence against the challengers, even if they are available.

The extent of the transfer of power, the crux of revolutionary outcomes, depends on:

1   The size and rigidity of the split between power-holders and challengers. When the split takes the form of a simple, mutually exclusive alternative, it necessitates the unambiguous commitment of the population to one side or the other and prevents co-optation of former power-holders to the post-revolutionary government. The transfer is therefore complete.

2   The scope of coalitions between members of the polity and challengers prior to and during the revolution. The less of them, the more complete the post-revolutionary transfer of power. On the other hand, without them the revolution may fail, and no transfer at all may result.

3   The control of the means of violence by the challengers. 'No transfer of power at all is likely in a revolutionary situation if the government retains complete control of the military' (Tilly 1978: 214). To win, revolutionaries must obtain coercive resources: weapons and the support of some segments of the police or the army. This is why the loyalty of the army is such a crucial factor in most revolutions, and most revolutions win when the army switches sides and joins the challengers.

Tilly suggests a typical, 'idealized revolutionary sequence' as consisting of seven stages. (1) There is the gradual emergence of challengers and articulation of their claims to power. (2) There follows a mobilization of supporters accepting those claims. (3) Attempts of the government at repressive, forced demobilization fail. (4) Challengers and their coalitions succeed in establishing partial control over some segment of the governemnt (a region, a division, a part of personnel). (5) They struggle to expand such control. (6) The challengers win, are defeated or are co-opted by entering a ruling coalition with the former power-holders. (7) The single, sovereign governmental control over the population is re-established (1978: 216–17). It is only at this stage that further structural transformations of society can occur (economic, cultural, legal, moral) and if they do, we are apt to speak of 'great' revolutions.

One of the weaknesses of the theory advanced by Tilly is its insufficient specificity. Stan Taylor points out that the author does not tell us why some governments are able to co-opt, compensate, threaten or appease potential challengers, incorporating them into the routine, institutionalized political process, while others are unable to do so, and face the onset of a revolutionary situation. 'Tilly did not try to account for why, in some cases, groups should be accepted by the polity while in others they should be rejected' (1984: 146). Similarly, the author fails to explain why in some cases the army remains loyal, and in others defects to the revolutionary side, thus deciding the revolutionary outcome. Unfortunately the weakness of insufficient specificity is non-specific for Tilly's theory; it is shared by the 'political process theory' with all other theories of revolution, and perhaps with most other sociological theories as well.

Defined ignorance in the study of revolutions

In spite of their various weaknesses and one-sided biases, various theories of revolution add important insights and a considerable amount of plausible knowledge to our understanding of this most complex, macro-historical phenomenon. One of their contributions is also in sharpening our sensitivity to the vast remaining lacunae of wisdom, the puzzles and question marks concerning revolutions. In other words, they extend the area of defined, or 'specified ignorance' (Merton 1968: 363, 471): things we do not know, but know that we should know in order to comprehend the phenomenon of revolutions. At the close of this chapter I propose to discuss five puzzles or paradoxes facing future theorizing in this domain.

1   The first concerns the outbreak of revolutions. Various theories give us hints of the numerous factors and forces, determinants and co-determinants, necessary and sufficient conditions, facilitating and restraining circumstances, conducive and hindering situations, on which the outbreak depends. Some refer to human behaviour; some to motivations, intentions, emotions and ideas; some to the societal and cultural context; some to economic interests;

some to political opportunities. Clearly, it is only when all (or selected ones) of these factors appear in certain unique combinations (or alternative configurations) that revolutions actually occur. What is this unique explosive mix, the specific revolutionary conjecture, or revolutionary syndrome, that must appear at the given time and place if revolution is to break out? We do not know.

2   The second puzzle concerns revolutionary mobilization. How is it that masses of people suddenly overcome the barrier of apathy, passivism, inertia, obedience, and decide to fight for their interests and ideals? What explains the explosion of commitment, participation, activism and defiance that we observe at the outset of revolutions? Is it simply the result of skilful manipulation by revolutionary leaders? Or does it signify that some threshold of unbearable frustrations has been passed, which leads to spontanous action? How can such a threshold be determined, when the fact is that sometimes people are able to endure incomparably more oppression and deprivation than at other times? We do not know.

3   The next puzzle concerns the revolutionary heritage. What is the impact of earlier revolutions (whether succesful or failed) on later revolutions? Do revolutions occur as singular episodes, with their own, unique causality each time emerging anew? Or do revolutions follow cycles, form long-range historical sequences, where earlier revolutionary attempts, victories or failures, weigh heavily on the course of later attempts? Where can a common causality be found underlying the whole series of revolutionary outbreaks? We do not know.

4   The fourth puzzle, or rather paradox, concerns the results of revolution. Revolutions, especially when succesful, engender heroic myths; their accomplishments are exaggerated, the costs ignored. But from some historical perspective the side-effects, the human price, the boomerang effects, become unravelled, tempering the early euphoria. Quite soon the heroic myth of the Russian Revolution was crushed by the evidence of misery, oppression, savagery and death that it brought about. The final collapse of communism at the end of the twentieth century provided the ultimate proof that the project it attempted to implement was entirely misconceived from the outset. Then there is the heroic myth of the great French Revolution crumbling under the evidence provided by recent 'revisionist' historiography (Sullivan 1989; Shama 1989), and recently ironically referred to as 'so glorious, yet so savage' (*Newsweek*, 3 April 1989, p. 45). Why is it so often the case that revolutions produce something so utterly different from what was dreamed of by the revolutionaries? Why is it that the momentum of the revolution so often 'demolishes so ruthlessly that in the end it may annihilate the ideals that called it into being' (Kapuscinski 1985: 86)? Is this vicious logic inescapable? We do not know.

5   The final puzzle or paradox is that of predictability. Most observers agree that none of the historically known revolutions has ever been predicted. Crane Brinton comments: 'The actual revolution is always a surprise'

(1965: 66). Ryszard Kapuscinski reflects on the Iranian revolution: 'A coup or a palace takeover may be planned, but a revolution never. Its outbreak, the hour of that outbreak, takes everyone, even those who have been striving for it, unawares. Everyone stands amazed at the spontaneity that appears suddenly and destroys everything in its path' (1985: 86). In the late 1980s students of revolution had to admit another predictive failure. Jean Kirkpatrick expressed the mood of bafflement in the face of the anti-communist revolution of 1989: 'what a fantastic surprise the collapse of communism was. I believe there has been no greater surprise in modern history – and we should admit it – than the speed and the totality with which communist regimes fell in Eastern Europe and in the socialist fatherland itself – the Soviet Union' (1992: 7). Why is it the case? One intepretation of the predictive failure may refer to epistemological limitations: the complexity of historical events of that scale, the lack of sufficient initial information, the lack of rigorous, mathematical models etc. All that of course can potentially be improved. Some authors proclaim such an epistemological optimism. 'There is little ground for belief that anyone today has enough knowledge and skill to apply formal methods of diagnosis to a contemporary society and say, in this case revolution will or will not occur shortly' (Brinton 1965: 250).

> The study of revolutions remains much like the study of earthquakes. When one occurs, scholars try to make sense of the myriad of data that have been collected, and build theories to account for the next one. Gradually, we gain a fuller understanding of them, and the conditions behind them; but the next one that occurs still surprises us. Our knowledge of revolutions, like that of earthquakes, is still limited. We can detail the patterns of those that have occurred, and we can list some of the conditions conducive to them; but better understanding of exactly when they are likely to occur still lies in the future. (*Goldstone 1982: 205*)

But one may suggest more fundamental ontological reasons for unpredictability. Perhaps in this area prediction is not just hard but impossible in principle. (1) Because revolutionary events depend on actions taken by multitudes of individuals, they occur as aggregated effects of myriads of individual decisions. Each of these decisions is taken by individuals placed in unique biographical and social situations, and each human individual happens to be at least marginally erratic, capricious, underdetermined in what he/she decides to do. Thus on the aggregated, macro-scale, the condition described in the natural sciences as 'chaos' seems to prevail, preventing any specific prediction. (2) Prediction is hard because the mobilization and co-ordination of revolutionary actions demand strong leaders, and the appearance of such leaders of sufficient talent, stature and charisma is to a large extent a secret of genetics. (3) Because the phenomenon of revolution incorporates multiple processes (growth of discontent and grievances, mobilization of the masses, reactions of the entrenched elites, pressures of external powers, to name but a few), though each of these may be regular, theoretically accountable and to some extent even predictable, in their concrete, unique combination, cross-cutting at a certain historical moment, these processes produce irreducible novelty, emergent phenomena not explainable or predictable by any partial theories. (4) In the case of revolutionary social changes the circular logic of reflexivity and self-destroying prophecy is particularly vicious. If the theory *were* predictive, the prediction of revolution would certainly be acted upon by the defenders of the old regime, who at that moment would still have enough force to paralyse the revolution and prevent its victory, thus falsifying the prediction by their actions. Hence the paradox: the theory of revolution is impossible because if it provides predictions, they are bound to be falsified by events; if it does not provide predictions, it is not a theory at all. In this area, perhaps, interpretations after the event, a better conceptual organization of complex historical experience and some improved orientation in the chaos of events is the most that we should expect from so-called 'theories of revolution'. That in itself would be a great intellectual feat.

Bibliography

This bibliography occasionally acknowledges some works which form part of the background to this book but are not specifically cited in the text.

Aberle, David 1966. *Peyote Religion Among the Navaho.* Chicago: Aldine

Abrams, Philip 1982. *Historical Sociology.* Ithaca: Cornell University Press

Adam, Barbara 1988. 'Social versus natural time, a traditional distinction re-examined', in: Young, and Schuller, pp. 198–226

Adam, Barbara 1990. *Time and Social Theory.* Cambridge: Polity Press

Adamson, M. and Borgos, S. 1984. *This Mighty Dream: Social Protest Movements in the United States.* Boston: Routledge & Kegan Paul

Addis, Laird 1968. 'Historicism and historical laws of development', *Inquiry*, 11 (1968), pp. 155–74

Addis, Laird 1969. 'The individual and the Marxist philosophy of history', in: M. Brodbeck (ed.), *Readings in the Philosophy of the Social Sciences*, pp. 317–35, New York: Macmillan

Alexander, Jeffrey C. 1982. *The Antinomies of Classical Thought: Marx and Durkheim* (vol. 2 of *Theoretical Logic in Sociology*). Berkeley: University of California Press

Alexander, Jeffrey C. (ed.) 1985. *Neo-functionalism.* London: Sage

Alexander, Jeffrey C. 1988a. 'Durkheim's problem and differentiation theory today', in: Alexander 1988b, pp. 49–77

Alexander, Jeffrey C. 1988b. *Action and Its Environments.* New York: Columbia University Press

Alexander, Jeffrey C. 1988c. 'The new theoretical movement', in: Neil J. Smelser (ed.), *Handbook of Sociology*, pp. 77–102, Newbury Park: Sage

Alexander, Jeffrey C. 1990. 'Between progress and apocalypse: social theory and the dream of reason in the twentieth century', in: J. Alexander and P. Sztompka (eds), *Rethinking Progress*, pp. 15–38, London: Unwin Hyman

Alexander, Jeffrey C. 1992. 'Post-modernization theory'. Uppsala: SCASSS (mimeo)

Alexander, Jeffrey C. and Colomy, Paul (eds) 1988. *Differentiation Theory and Social Change: Historical and Comparative Approaches.* New York: Columbia University Press

Antonio, R. J and Piran, P. 1978. 'Historicity and the poverty of empiricism'. Uppsala: IXth World Congress of Sociology (mimeo)

Appelbaum, Richard P. 1970. *Theories of Social Change*. Chicago: Markham

Apter, David 1968. *Some Conceptual Approaches to the Study of Modernization*. Englewood Cliffs: Prentice Hall

Archer, Margaret S. 1985. 'Structuration versus morphogenesis', in: S. N. Eisenstadt and H. J. Helle (eds), *Macro-Sociological Theory*, vol. 1, pp. 58–88, London: Sage

Archer, Margaret S. 1986. 'Taking time to link structure and agency'. New Delhi: XIth World Congress of Sociology (mimeo)

Archer, Margaret S. 1988. *Culture and Agency*. Cambridge: Cambridge University Press

Archer, Margaret S. 1989. '*The morphogenesis of social agency*'. Uppsala: SCASSS (mimeo)

Arnason, Johann 1987. 'Figurational sociology as a counter-paradigm', *Theory, Culture and Society*, 4, 2–3, pp. 429–56

Aron, Raymond 1961. *Introduction to the Philosophy of History*. London: Weidenfeld and Nicolson

Aron, Raymond 1968. *Main Currents in Sociological Thought*, vol. I. Garden City: Doubleday Anchor

Aron, Raymond 1969. *Progress and Disillusion: The Dialectics of Modern Society*. New York: Mentor Books

Ash, T. Garton 1990a. 'Eastern Europe: the year of truth', *New York Review of Books*, 15 February, pp. 17–22

Ash, T. Garton 1990b. *We The People: The Revolution of 89*. Cambridge: Granta Books

Avineri, Shlomo 1968. *The Social and Political Thought of Karl Marx*. Cambridge: Cambridge University Press

Aya, Rod 1979. 'Theories of revolution reconsidered', *Theory and Society*, 8, 1, pp. 39–99

Back, Kurt W. 1971. 'Biological models of social change', *American Sociological Review*, 36 (August), pp. 660–7

Banaszczyk, Tadeusz 1989. *Studia o przedstawieniach zbiorowych czasu i przestrzeni w durkheimowskiej szkole socjologicznej* (Studies on the collective representations of time and space in the Durkheimian sociological school). Wroclaw: Ossolineum

Banks, Joseph A. 1972. *The Sociology of Social Movements*. London: Macmillan

Bauman, Zygmunt 1989a. *Modernity and The Holocaust*. Cambridge: Polity Press

Bauman, Zygmunt 1989b. 'Sociological responses to postmodernity', in: C. Mongardini and M. L. Maniscalco (eds), *Moderno e Postmoderno*, pp. 127–52, Rome: Bulzoni

Bauman, Zygmunt 1991. *Modernity and Ambivalence*. Cambridge: Polity Press

Baumgartner, Tom, Buckley, W., Burns, T. R. and Schuster, P. 1976 'Metapower and the structuring of social hierarchies', in: T. R. Burns and W. Buckley (eds), *Power and Control*, pp. 215–88, Beverly Hills: Sage

Bell, Daniel 1974. *The Coming of the Post-industrial Society*. London: Heinemann

Bell, Wendell and Mau, J. A. (eds) 1971. *The Sociology of the Future*. New York: Russell Sage Foundation

Bellah, Robert 1968. *Habits of the Heart*. Berkeley: University of California Press

Bendix, R. 1964. *Nation Building and Citizenship*. New York: Wiley

Berlin, Isaiah 1966. 'The concept of scientific history', in: W. H. Dray (ed.), *Philosophical Analysis and History*, pp. 5–53, New York: Harper & Row

Bernstein, Richard, J. 1972. *Praxis and Action*. London: Duckworth

Bhaskar, Roy 1986. *Scientific Realism and Human Emancipation*. London: Verso

Bierstedt, Robert 1981. *American Sociological Theory: A Critical History*. New York: Academic Press

Birnbaum, Norman 1953. 'Conflicting interpretations of the rise of capitalism: Marx and Weber', *British Journal of Sociology*, 4 (June), pp. 125–41

Black, Cyril E. (ed.) 1976. *Comparative Modernization*. New York: Free Press

Blau, Peter M. 1964. *Exchange and Power in Social Life*. New York, Wiley

Blumer, Herbert 1951. 'Collective behavior', in: A. McClung Lee (ed.), *Principles of Sociology*, New York: Random House

Blumer, Herbert 1957. 'Collective behavior', in: J. B. Gittler, *Review of Sociology: Analysis of a Decade*, pp. 127–58, New York: Wiley

Bock, K. 1978. 'Theories of progress, development and evolution', in: T. Bottomore and R. Nisbet (eds), *A History of Sociological Analysis*, pp. 39–80, New York: Basic Books

Boudon, Raymond 1981. *The Logic of Social Action*. London: Routledge

Boudon, Raymond 1986. *Theories of Social Change: A Critical Appraisal*. Cambridge: Polity Press

Boudon, Raymond and Bourricaud, F. (eds) 1989. *A Critical Dictionary of Sociology*. Chicago: University of Chicago Press

Boulding, Kenneth E. 1964. 'The place of the image in the dynamics of society', in: G. K. Zollschan and W. Hirsch (eds), *Explorations in Social Change*, pp. 5–16, Boston: Houghton Mifflin

Boulding, Kenneth E. 1967. 'The learning process in the dynamics of total societies', in: S. Z. Klausner (ed.), *The Study of Total Societies*, pp. 98–113, New York: Praeger

Braudel, Fernand 1972. 'History and the social sciences', in: P. Burke (ed.), *Economy and Society in Early Modern Europe*, pp. 11–42, London: Routledge & Kegan Paul

Braudel, Fernand 1980. *On History*. London: Weidenfeld and Nicolson

Breed, Warren 1971. *The Self-Guiding Society*. New York: Free Press

Brinton, Crane 1965 [1938]. *Anatomy of Revolution*. New York: Harper & Row (Vintage Books)

Brzezinski, Zbigniew 1970. *Between Two Ages: America's Role in the Technetronic Era*. New York: Viking Press

Buckley, Walter 1967. *Sociology and Modern Systems Theory*. Englewood Cliffs: Prentice Hall

Bukharin, N. I. 1929. Imperialism and World Economy. New York: International Publishers

Bullock, Alan and Stallybras, Oliver (eds) 1977. *The Fontana Dictionary of Modern Thought*. London: Fontana/Collins

Burke, P. 1980. *Sociology and History*. London: Allen & Unwin

Burns, Tom R., Baumgartner, T. and Deville, P. 1985. *Man, Decisions, Society: The Theory of Actor-System Dynamics for Social Scientists*. New York: Gordon and Breach

Burns, Tom, R. and Buckley W. 1976. *Power and Control*. London: Sage

Burns, Tom R. and Dietz, Thomas 1991. 'Institutional dynamics: an evolutionary perspective'. Buenos Aires: Internatioanl Political Science Association (mimeo)

Burns, Tom R. and Dietz, Thomas 1992. 'Cultural evolution: social rule systems, selection, and human agency', *International Sociology*, 7, 3, pp. 259–83

Burns, Tom R. and Flam, H. 1987. *The Shaping of Social Organization*. Beverly Hills: Sage

Cannadine, David 1985. 'The context, performance and meaning of ritual: the British monarchy and the "invention of tradiion", *c.* 1820–1977', in: Hobsbawm and Ranger, pp. 101–64

Cardoso, Fernando 1973. 'Associated dependent development: theoretical and practical implications', in: Alfred Stepan (ed.), *Authoritarian Brazil: Origins, Policies and Futures*, New Haven: Yale University Press

Cardoso, Fernando and Faletto, E. 1969. *Dependency and Development in Latin America*. Berkeley: California University Press

Carlyle, Thomas 1963. *On Heroes, Hero-Worship and the Heroic in History*. London: Oxford University Press

Chazel, François 1988. 'Sociology: from structuralist determinism to methodological individualism', in: J. Howorth and G. Ross (eds), *Contemporary France: A Review of Interdisciplinary Studies*, vol. 2, pp. 187–202, London: Pinter

Chirot, Daniel 1977. *Social Change in the Twentieth Century*. New York: Harcourt Brace Jovanovich

Chodak, Szymon 1973. *Societal Development*. New York: Oxford University Press

Cohen, E., Lissak, M. and Almagor, U. (eds) 1985. *Comparative Social Dynamics; Essays in Honor of S. N. Eisenstadt*. Boulder: Westview Press

Coleman, J., Katz, E. and Menzel, H. 1966. *Medical Innovation: A Diffusion Study*. New York: Bobbs-Merril

Collins, Randall 1980. 'Weber's last theory of capitalism: a systematization', *American Sociological Review*, 45 (December), pp. 925–42

Collins, Randall 1986. 'Is 1980's sociology in the doldrums?' *American Journal of Sociology*, 91, pp. 1336–55

Collins, R. 1988. *Theoretical Sociology*. San Diego: Harcourt Brace Jovanovich

Coser, Lewis A. 1967. *Continuities in the Study of Social Conflict*. New York: Free Press

Coser, Lewis A. and Coser Rose 1990. 'Time perspective and social structure', in: Hassard, pp. 191–202

Crozier, Michel and Friedberg, Erhard 1977. *L'Acteur et le système*. Paris: Editions du Seuil

Dahrendorf, Ralf 1959. *Class and Class Conflict in Industrial Society*. Stanford: Stanford University Press

Dahrendorf, Ralf 1964. 'Recent changes in the class structures of European societies', *Daedalus*, 93, 1

Dahrendorf, Ralf 1968. *Essays in the Theory of Society*. Stanford: Stanford University Press

Dahrendorf, Ralf 1979. *Life Chances*. Chicago: University of Chicago Press

Dahrendorf, Ralf 1980. 'On representative activities', in: T. F. Gieryn (ed.), *Science and Social Structure: A Festschrift for Robert K. Merton*, pp. 15–27, New York: New York Academy of Sciences

Dahrendorf, Ralf 1990. *Reflections on the Revolution in Europe*. London: Chatto & Windus

Darwin, Charles 1964 [1859]. *On the Origin of Species*. New York: Mentor Books

Davies, James C. 1962. 'Toward a theory of revolution', *American Sociological Review*, 27, pp. 5–19

Davies, James C. 1971. *When Men Revolt and Why*. New York: Free Press

Davis, Kingsley and Moore, Wilbert E. 1945. 'Some principles of stratification', *American Sociological Review*, 10, 2, pp. 242–9

Dietz, T. and Burns, T. 1992. 'Human agency and evolutionary dynamics of culture', *Acta Sociologica*, 35, pp. 187–200

Dunn, John 1972. *Modern Revolutions: An Introduction to the Analysis of a Political Phenomenon*. Cambridge: Cambridge University Press

Durkheim, Emile 1915. *The Elementary Forms of Religious Life*, tr. J. W. Swain. London: Allen & Unwin

Durkheim, Emile 1964 [1893]. *The Division of Labor in Society*. New York: Free Press

Durkheim, Emile 1972. *Selected Writings*, ed. A. Giddens. Cambridge: Cambridge University Press

Edwards, L. P. 1927. *The Natural History of Revolution*. Chicago: University of Chicago Press

Eisenstadt, Shmuel N. 1963. *The Political Systems of Empires*. Glencoe: Free Press

Eisenstadt, Shmuel N. 1966a [1964], 'Breakdowns of modernization', in: William J. Goode (ed.), *The Dynamics of Modern Society*, pp. 434–48, New York: Basic Books

Eisenstadt, Shmuel N. 1966b. *Modernization: Protest and Change*. Englewood Cliffs: Prentice Hall

Eisenstadt, Shmuel N. 1973. *Tradition, Change and Modernity*. New York: Wiley

Eisenstadt, Shmuel N. 1974. 'Studies of modernization and sociological theory', *History and Theory*, 13, pp. 225–52

Eisenstadt, Shmuel N. 1978. *Revolution and the Transformation of Societies*. New York: Free Press

Eisenstadt, Shmuel N. 1980. 'Cultural orientations, institutional entrepreneurs, and social change: comparative analysis of traditional civilizations', *American Journal of Sociology*, 85, 4, pp. 840–69

Eisenstadt, Shmuel N. 1983. 'Development, modernization and dynamics of civilization', *Cultures et Développement*, 15, 2, pp. 217–52

Eisenstadt, Shmuel N. 1992a. 'A reappraisal of theories of social change and modernization', in: Haferkamp and Smelser (eds), pp. 412–30

Eisenstadt, Shmuel N. 1992b. 'The breakdown of communist regimes and the vicissitudes of modernity', *Daedalus* (Spring 1992), pp. 21–41

Eliade, Mircea 1959. *Cosmos and History*. New York: Harper & Row

Elias, Norbert 1978. *What is Sociology?* London: Hutchinson

Elias, Norbert 1982. *The Civilizing Process*, vols 1 and 2. Oxford: Basil Blackwell

Elias, Norbert 1986. '*Technik und Zivilisation*'. Hamburg: German Sociological Association (mimeo)

Elias, Norbert 1987. 'The retreat of sociologists into the present', *Theory, Culture and Society*, 4, 2–3, pp. 223–48

Erikson, K. T. 1971. 'Sociology and the historical perspective', in Bell and Mau

Etzioni, Amitai 1968a. *The Active Society*, New York: Free Press

Etzioni, Amitai 1968b. 'Mobilization as a macrosociological conception', *British Journal of Sociology*, 19, 3, pp. 243–53

Etzioni, Amitai 1991. 'A socio-economic perspective on friction'. Washington: IAREP/SASE Conference (mimeo)

Etzioni-Halevy, Eva 1981. *Social Change: The Advent and Maturation of Modern Society*. London: Routledge & Kegan Paul

Evans-Pritchard, E. E. 1963 [1940]. *The Nuer*. London: Oxford University Press

Eyerman, Ron 1992. 'Modernity and social movements', in: Haferkamp and Smelser (eds), pp. 37–54

Eyerman, Ron and Jamison, Andrew 1991. *Social Movements: A Cognitive Approach*. Cambridge: Polity Press

Fairchild, Henry P. 1966. *Dictionary of Sociology and Related Sciences*. Totowa, NJ: Littlefield, Adams

Farley, John E. 1990. *Sociology*. Englewood Cliffs: Prentice Hall

Feldman, Arnold S. and Moore, Wilbert E. 1962. 'Industrialization and industrialism: convergence and differentiation', *Transactions of the Fifth World Congress of Sociolology*, Washington, DC, ISA

Femia, J. 1987 [1981]. *Gramsci's Political Thought*. Oxford: Clarendon Press

Ferree, Myra Marx and Miller, Frederick D. 1985. 'Mobilization and meaning: toward an integration of social psychological and resource perspectives on social movements', *Sociological Inquiry*, 1, pp. 38–59

Fletcher, Ronald 1971. *The Making of Sociology*, vols 1–3. New York: Charles Scribner's Sons

Frankel, Boris 1987. *The Post-industrial Utopians*. Cambridge: Polity Press

Freeman, Jo 1973. 'The origins of the women's liberation movement', *American Journal of Sociology*, 78, 4, pp. 792–811

Freeman, Jo 1983a. 'A model for analyzing the strategic options of social movement organizations', in: J. Freeman (ed.), *Social Movements in the Sixties and Seventies*, pp. 193–210, New York: Longman

Freeman, Jo 1983b. 'On the origins of social movements', in: J. Freeman (ed.), *Social Movements of the Sixties and Seventies*, pp. 8–30, New York: Longman

Fromm, Erich 1941. *Escape from Freedom*. New York: Holt

Fromm, Erich 1963 [1956]. *The Sane Society*. London: Routledge & Kegan Paul

Fromm, Erich 1966 [1951]. *Marx's Concept of Man*. New York: Ungar

Fromm, E. 1979. *To Have or to Be?* London: Sphere Books, Abacus Edition

Fukuyama, Francis 1989. 'The end of history?' *The National Interest* (Summer), pp. 3–18

Fukuyama, Francis 1992. *The End of History and the Last Man*. New York: Free Press

Gamson, W. A. 1975. *Strategy of Social Protest*. Homewood, IL: Dorsey Press

Garfinkel, Howard 1967. *Studies in Ethnomethodology*. Glencoe: Free Press

Garner, Roberta and Zald, M. N. 1981. 'Social movement sectors and systemic constraint: toward a structural analysis of social movements'. Ann Arbor: Center for Research on Social Organization (Working Paper no. 238) (mimeo)

Gella, Aleksander 1966. *Ewolucjonizm a początki socjologii* (Evolutionism and the beginnings of sociology). Wrocław: Ossolineum

Gewirth, Allan 1969 [1954]. 'Can men change laws of social science?' in: L. I. Krimerman (ed.), *The Nature and Scope of Social Science: A Critical Anthology*, pp. 217–27, New York: Appleton

Giddens, Anthony 1971. *Capitalism and Modern Social Theory*. Cambridge: Cambridge University Press

Giddens, Anthony 1979. *Central Problems in Social Theory*. London: Macmillan

Giddens, Anthony 1981. *A Contemporary Critique of Historical Materialism*. London: Macmillan

Giddens, Anthony 1984. *The Constitution of Society*. Cambridge: Polity Press

Giddens, Anthony 1985. *The Nation-State and Violence*. Cambridge: Polity Press

Giddens, Anthony 1989. *Sociology*. Cambridge: Polity Press

Giddens, Anthony 1990. *The Consequences of Modernity*. Cambridge: Polity Press

Giddens, Anthony 1991. *Introduction to Sociology*. New York: Norton

Goffman, Erving 1963. *Behavior in Public Places*. New York: Free Press

Goffman, Erving 1967. *Interaction Ritual*. Garden City: Doubleday

Goffman, Erving 1971. *Relations in Public*. New York: Harper & Row

Goldstone, Jack A. 1982. 'The comparative and historical study of revolutions', *Annual Review of Sociology*, 8, pp. 187–207

Goldthorpe, John 1971. 'Theories of industrial society: reflections on the recrudescence of historicism and the future of futurology', *Archives européennes de sociologie*, 12, pp. 263–88

Goody, J. 1968. 'Time: social organization', in: *International Encyclopedia of the Social Sciences*, vol. 16, pp. 30–42, New York: Macmillan

Goudsblom, Johan 1987. 'The sociology of Norbert Elias: its resonance and significance', *Theory, Culture and Society*, 4, 2–3, pp. 323–38

Gramsci, Antonio 1971. *Selections From the Prison Notebooks*. New York: International Publishers

Gramsci, Antonio 1972. *The Modern Prince and Other Writings*. New York: International Publishers

Granovetter, Mark 1978. 'Threshold models of collective behavior', *American Journal of Sociology*, 83, 6, pp. 1420–43

Granovetter, Mark 1979. 'The idea of "advancement" in theories of social evolution and development', *American Journal of Sociology*, 85, 3, pp. 489–515

Gunder Frank, André 1969. *Latin America: Underdevelopment of Revolution*. New York: Monthly Review Press

Gurr, Ted 1970. *Why Men Rebel*. Princeton: Princeton University Press

Gurvitch, Georges 1963. 'Social structure and the multiplicity of times', in: Tiryakian, pp. 171–84

Gurvitch, Georges 1964. *The Spectrum of Social Time*. Dordrecht: Reidel

Gurvitch, Georges 1990. 'Varieties of social-time', in: Hassard, pp. 67–76

Gusfield, Joseph R. 1966. 'Tradition and modernity: misplaced polarities in the study of social change', *American Journal of Sociology*, 72 (January), pp. 351–62

Habermas, Jurgen 1983. 'A reconstruction of historical materialism', in: T. Bottomore and P. Goode (eds), *Readings in Marxist Sociology*, pp. 212–18, Oxford: Clarendon Press

Habermas, Jurgen 1987. *Philosophical Discourse of Modernity*, Cambridge: Polity Press

Haferkamp, H. and Smelser, N. J. 1992a. 'Introduction', in: Haferkamp and Smelser (eds), pp. 1–11

Haferkamp, H. and Smelser, N. J. (eds) 1992b. *Social Change and Modernity*. Berkeley: University of California Press

Hagen, Everett 1962. *On the Theory of Social Change*. Homewood, IL: Dorsey Press

Hagerstrand, Torsten 1988. 'Time and culture', in: G. Kirsch, P. Nijkamp and K. Zimmerman, *The Formulation of Time Preferences in a Multidisciplinary Perspective*, pp. 33–42, Aldershot: Gower

Hamelink, C. J. 1983. *Cultural Autonomy in Global Communications*. New York: Longman

Hannerz, Ulf 1987. 'The world in creolisation', *Africa*, 57, 4, pp. 546–59

Hannerz, Ulf 1989a. 'Notes on the global ecumene', *Public Culture*, 1, 2, pp. 66–75

Hannerz, Ulf 1989b. 'Scenarios for peripheral cultures'. Binghamton: State University of New York (mimeo)

Harre, R. and Secord P. F. 1972. *The Explanation of Social Behaviour*. Oxford: Basil Blackwell

Harris, Marvin 1968. *The Rise of Anthropological Theory*. New York: Columbia University Press

Hassard, John (ed.) 1990. *The Sociology of Time*. London: Macmillan

Hawley, Amos H. 1978. 'Cumulative change in theory and in history', *American Sociological Review*, 43, 6, pp. 787–96

Hegel, Georg W. F. 1956 [1837]. *The Philosophy of History*. New York: Dover

Heraclitus 1979 [fifth century BC]. *Heraclitus on the Universe*. Cambridge: Cambridge University Press

Hernes, Gudmund 1976. 'Structural change in social processes', *American Journal of Sociology*, 82, 3, pp. 513–47

Hernes, Gudmund 1989. 'The logic of The Protestant Ethic', *Rationality and Society*, 1, 1, pp. 123–62

Himmelstein, Jerome L. and Kimmel, Michael S. 1981. 'Review essay: States and revolutions: the implications of Skockpol's structural model', *American Journal of Sociology*, 86, 5, pp. 1145–54

Hobsbawm, Eric 1983a. 'The idea of progress in Marx's thought', in: T. Bottomore and P. Goode (eds), *Readings in Marxist Sociology*, pp. 208–12, Oxford: Clarendon Press

Hobsbawm, Eric 1983b. 'Mass-producing traditions: Europe, 1870–1914', in: Hobsbawm and Ranger, pp. 263–307

Hobsbawm, Eric and Ranger, Terence 1985 [1983]. *The Invention of Tradition*. Cambridge: Cambridge University Press

Hobson, J. A. 1902. *Imperialism: A Study*. New York: Pott

Hollis, Martin 1987. *Cunning of Reason*. Cambridge: Cambridge University Press

Holton, Robert 1990. 'Problems of crisis and normalcy in the contemporary world', in: J. Alexander and P. Sztompka (eds), *Rethinking Progress*, pp. 39–52, Boston: Unwin Hyman

Homans, George C. 1971. 'Bringing men back in', in: H. Turk and R. L. Simpson (eds), *Institutions and Social Exchange*, pp. 102–16, Indianapolis: Bobbs-Merrill

Hook, Sidney 1955 [1943]. *The Hero in History*. Boston: Beacon Press

Huntington, Samuel P. 1968. *Political Order in Changing Societies*. New Haven: Yale University Press

Huntington, Samuel P. 1976. 'The change to change: modernization, development and politics', in: Black, pp. 25–61

Inkeles, Alex 1976. 'A model of the modern man: theoretical and methodological issues', in: Black, pp. 320–48

Inkeles, Alex and Smith, D. H. 1974. *Becoming Modern*. Cambridge, MA: Harvard University Press

Israel, Joachim 1971. *Alienation*. Boston: Allyn and Bacon

Jacobsen, Chinoch 1979. 'Permissiveness and norm evasions: definitions, relationships and implications', *Sociology* (May), pp. 219–33

Jahoda, Marie 1988. 'Time: a social psychological perspective', in: Young and Schuller, pp. 154–71

Jarvie, I. C. 1972. *Concepts and Society*. London: Routledge & Kegan Paul

Jenkins, J. Craig 1982. 'Why do peasants rebel? Structural and historical theories of modern peasant rebellions', *American Journal of Sociology*, 88, 3, pp. 487–514

Jenkins, J. Craig 1983. 'Resource mobilization theory and the study of social movements', *Annual Review of Sociology*, 9, pp. 527–53

Johnson, Chalmers 1964. *Revolution and the Social System*. Stanford: Hoover Institution Studies

Johnson, Chalmers 1968. *Revolutionary Change*. London: University of London Press

Johnson, Harry M. 1960. *Sociology*. New York: Harcourt Brace Jovanovich

Kaplan, David and Manners, Robert A. 1972. *Culture Theory*. Englewood Cliffs: Prentice Hall

Kapuscinski, Ryszard 1985. 'Revolution', *The New Yorker*, 11 March, pp. 86–101

Kelles-Krauz, Kazimierz 1962 [1896]. *Pisma Wybrane (Collected works)*. Warsaw: Ksiazka i Wiedza

Kerr, C., Dunlop, J. T., Harbison, F., Harbison H. and Myers, C. A. 1960. *Industrialism and Industrial Man*. Cambridge, MA: Harvard University Press

Killian, L. M. 1964. 'Social movements', in: R. E. L. Faris (ed.), *Handbook of Modern Sociology*, Chicago: Rand McNally

Kimmel, Michael S. 1990. *Revolution: A Sociological Interpretation*. Cambridge: Polity Press

Kirkpatrick, Jean J. 1992. 'After communism, what?' *Problems of Communism*, 41 (January–April), pp. 1–7

Klandermans, Bert 1984. 'Mobilization and participation: social-psychological expansions of resource mobilization theory', *American Sociological Review*, 49, pp. 583–600

Koestler, Arthur 1975 [1940]. *Darkness at Noon*. New York: Bantam Books

Kornhauser, William 1968. 'Mass society', in: *International Encyclopedia of the Social Sciences*, vol. 10, pp. 58–64, New York: Macmillan

Kotkin, Joel and Kishimoto, Yoriko 1988. *The Third Century: America's Resurgence in the Asian Era*. New York: Crown

Kriesi, Hanspeter 1989. 'New social movements and the new class in the Netherlands', *American Journal of Sociology*, 94, 5, pp. 1078–116

Kroeber, Alfred 1952. *The Nature of Culture*. Chicago: University of Chicago Press

Kuhn, Thomas S. 1970 [1962]. *The Structure of Scientific Revolutions*. Chicago: University of Chicago Press

Kumar, Krisham 1978. *Prophecy and Progress: The Sociology of Industrial and Post-industrial Society*. Harmondsworth: Penguin

Kumar, Krishan 1988. *The Rise of Modern Society: Aspects of the Social and Political Development of the West*. Oxford: Basil Blackwell

Lackey, Pat N. 1987. *Invitation to Talcott Parsons' Theory*. Houston: Cap and Gown Press

Lang, K. and Lang, G. 1961. *Collective Dynamics*. New York: Crowell

Langton, John 1979. 'Darwinism and the behavioral theory of sociocultural evolution: an analysis', *American Journal of Sociology*, 85, 2, pp. 288–309

Lasch, Christopher 1991. *The Truly and Only Heaven*. New York: Norton

Lauer, Robert H. 1971. 'The scientific legitimation of fallacy: neutralizing social change theory', *American Sociological Review*, 36 (October), pp. 881–9

Lauer, Robert H. (ed.) 1976. *Social Movements and Social Change*. Carbondale: Southern Illinois University Press

Lenin, Vladimir I. 1939 [1917]. *Imperialism. The Highest Stage of Capitalism*. New York: International Publishers

Lenski, Gerhard E. 1966. *Power and Privilege*. New York: McGraw Hill

Lenski, Gerhard E. 1975. 'Social structure in evolutionary perspective', in: P. M. Blau (ed.), *Approaches to the Study of Social Structure*, pp. 135–53, New York: Free Press

Lenski, Gerhard 1976. 'History and social change', *American Journal of Sociology*, 82, 3, pp. 548–64

Lenski, Gerhard E. and Lenski, J. 1974. *Human Societies: An Introduction to Macrosociology*. New York: McGraw Hill

Lerner, Daniel 1958. *The Passing of Traditional Society*. Glencoe: Free Press

Levy, Marion J. 1952. *The Structure of Society*. Princeton: Princeton University Press

Levy, Marion J. 1966. *Modernization and the Structure of Societies*. Princeton: Princeton University Press

Lewis, J. David and Weigart, Andrew J. 1990. 'The structures and meanings of social-time', in: Hassard, pp. 77–104

Lipset, Seymour M. 1967. *The First New Nation*. New York: Basic Books

Lloyd, Christopher 1988 [1986]. *Explanation in Social History*. Oxford: Basil Blackwell

Loomis, C. P. and Loomis, Z. K. 1961. *Modern Social Theories*. Princeton: Van Nostrand

Lopreato, Joseph 1984. *Human Nature and Biocultural Evolution*. Boston: Allen & Unwin

Lukács, Gyorgy 1971. *History and Class Consciousness*. Cambridge MA: MIT Press

Lukács, Gyorgy 1982–4. *Wprowadzenie do ontologii bytu spolecznego (Introduction to the ontology of the social object)*, vols 1–5. Warsaw: PWN (Polish Scientific Publishers)

Lukes, Steven 1974. *Power: A Radical View*. London: Macmillan

Lukes, Steven 1978. 'Power and authority', in: T. B. Bottomore and R. Nisbet (eds), *A History of Sociological Analysis*, pp. 633–76, New York: Basic Books

Lukes, Steven 1985. *Marxism and Morality*. Oxford: Clarendon Press

Lutynski, Jan 1990. *Nauka i polskie problemy (Science and Polish problems)*. Warsaw: PIW

Lyotard, Jean-François 1984. *The Post-Modern Condition*. Minneapolis: University of Minnesota Press

Lyotard, Jean-François 1988. *Peregrinations: Law, Form, Event*. New York: Columbia University Press

McAdam, Doug, McCarthy J. D. and Zald, M. N. 1988. 'Social movements', in: Neil J. Smelser (ed.), *Handbook of Sociology*, pp. 695–738, Newbury Park: Sage

McCarthy, John D. and Zald, Mayer N. 1976. 'Resource mobilization and social movements: a partial theory', *American Journal of Sociology*, 82, 6, pp. 1212–41

Macionis, John J. 1987. *Sociology*. Englewood Cliffs: Prentice Hall

McClelland, David 1967 [1961]. *The Achieving Society*. New York: Free Press

McLellan, David 1971. *The Thought of Karl Marx*. New York: Harper & Row

McLuhan, Marshall 1964. *Understanding Media: The Extensions of Man*. New York: Signet Books

McMurtry, J. 1978. *The Structure of Marx's World-View*. Princeton: Princeton University Press

Magee, Bryan 1973. *Karl Popper*. New York: Viking Press

Maier, Joseph 1964. 'Cyclical theories', in: W. J. Cahnman and A. Boskoff (eds), *Sociology and History: Theory and Research*, pp. 41–62, New York: Free Press

Mandelbaum, Maurice 1948. 'A critique of philosophies of history', *Journal of Philosophy*, 45, pp. 365–78

Mandelbaum, Maurice 1957. 'Societal laws', *British Journal for the Philosophy of Science*, 8, 3, pp. 211–24

Mann, Michael 1986. *The Sources of Social Power*, vol. 1. Cambridge: Cambridge University Press

Marcuse, Herbert 1964. *One Dimensional Man*. Boston: Beacon Press

Marody, Miroslawa 1987a. 'Antynomie spolecznej swiadomosci' (Antinomies of social consciousness), *Odra*, 1, pp. 4–9

Marody, Miroslawa 1987b. 'Antynomie zbiorowej podswiadomosci' (Antinomies of collective subconsciousness), *Studia Socjologiczne*, 2, pp. 89–99

Marody, Miroslawa 1990. 'Dylematy postaw politycznych i orientacji swiatopogladowych' (Dilemmas of political attitudes and orientations), in: J. J. Wiatr (ed.), *Wartosci a przemiany ladu gospodarczego i politycznego: Polska 1980–1990*, pp. 157–74, Warsaw: Wydawnictwo UW

Martindale, Don 1960. *The Nature and Types of Sociological Theory*. Boston: Houghton Mifflin

Maruyama, Mogoroh 1963. 'The second cybernetics: deviation-amplifying mutual causal processes', *General Systems*, 8, pp. 233–41

Marx, G. T. and Wood, J. L. 1975. 'Strands of theory and research in collective behavior', *Annual Review of Sociology*, 1, pp. 363–428

Marx, Karl 1953. *Grundrisse der Kritik der politichen Ökonomie* (Outlines of the Critique of Political Economy). Berlin: Akademie Verlag

Marx, Karl 1954. *Capital*, vols 1–3. Moscow: Progress Publishers

Marx, Karl 1955. *Przyczynek do krytyki ekonomii politycznej* (Contribution to the critique of political economy). Warsaw: Ksiazka i Wiedza

Marx, Karl 1971. *The Grundrisse*, ed. and tr. D. McLellan. New York: Harper & Row

Marx, Karl and Engels F. 1960. *Dziela* (Works). Warsaw: Ksiazka i Wiedza

Marx, Karl and Engels F. 1968. *Selected Works*. Moscow: Progress Publishers

Marx, Karl and Engels F. 1975. *O materializmie historycznym* (On historical materialism). Warsaw: Ksiazka i Wiedza

Marx, Karl and Engels, F. 1985 [1848]. *The Communist Manifesto*. New York: Pathfinder Press

Mazlish, Bruce 1966. *The Riddle of History*. New York: Minerva Press

Merton, Robert K. 1938. 'Social structure and anomie', *American Sociological Review*, 3, pp. 672–82

Merton, Robert K. 1959. 'Social Conformity, Deviation and Opportunity-Structure', *American Sociological Review*, 24, 2, pp. 177–89

Merton, Robert K. 1963. 'Foreword', in: H. J. O'Gorman (ed.), *Lawyers and Matrimonial Cases*, pp. vii–xiv, Glencoe: Free Press

Merton, Robert K. 1964. 'Anomie, anomia, and social interaction: contexts of deviant behavior', in: M. Clinard (ed.), *Anomie and Deviant Behavior: Discussion and Critique*, pp. 213–42, New York: Free Press

Merton, Robert K. 1965. *On the Shoulders of Giants*. New York: Harcourt, Brace & World

Merton, Robert K. 1968. *Social Theory and Social Structure*. New York: Free Press

Merton, Robert K. 1970 [1938]. *Science, Technology and Society in Seventeenth-Century England*. New York: Howard Fertig

Merton, Robert K. 1973. *The Sociology of Science*. Chicago: University of Chicago Press

Merton, Robert K. 1975. 'Thematic analysis in science: notes on Holton's concept', *Science*, 188, 25 April, pp. 335–8

Merton, Robert K. 1976 [1936]. 'The unanticipated consequences of social action', in: R. K. Merton, *Sociological Ambivalence*, pp. 145–55, New York: Free Press

Merton, Robert K. 1982a. 'Progress in science? A shapeless cloud of a question', Philadelphia: Temple University (mimeo)

Merton, Robert K. 1982b. *Social Research and Practicing Professions*, Cambridge: Abt Books

Merton, Robert K. 1982c. 'Socially expected durations: a temporal component of social structure'. San Francisco: American Sociological Association (mimeo)

Merton, Robert K. 1984. 'Socially expected durations: a case study of concept formation in sociology', in: W. W. Powell and R. Robbins (eds), *Conflict and Consensus: A Festschrift for Lewis Coser*, pp. 262–83, New York: Free Press

Merton, Robert K. and Kendall, Patricia L. 1944. 'The boomerang response', *Channels*, 21, 7, pp. 1–7

Mills, C. Wright 1959. *Sociological Imagination*. New York: Oxford University Press

Milosz, Czeslaw 1953. *The Captive Mind*. New York: Knopf

Mishan, Edward J. 1977. *The Economic Growth Debate: An Assessment*. London: Allen & Unwin

Mokrzycki, Edmund 1991. 'Dziedzictwo realnego socjalizmu a demokracja zachodnia' (The legacy of real socialism and western democracy). Warsaw: IFIS PAN (mimeo)

Molotch, Harvey 1979. 'Media and movements', in: M. Zald and J. D. McCarthy (eds), *The Dynamics of Social Movements*, pp. 71–93, Cambridge, MA: Winthrop

Moore, Barrington 1966. *Social Origins of Dictatorship and Democracy*, Boston: Beacon Press

Moore, Wilbert E. 1963a. *Man, Time and Society*. New York: Wiley

Moore, Wilbert E. 1963b. *Social Change*. Englewood Cliffs: Prentice Hall

Moore, Wilbert E. 1963c. 'The temporal structure of organizations', in: Tiryakian (ed.), pp. 161–9

Morris, Aldon and Herring C. 1985. 'Theory and research in social movements: a critical review'. Ann Arbor: University of Ann Arbor (mimeo)

Mumford, Lewis 1964 [1934]. *Technics and Civilization*. New York: Harcourt, Brace & World

Naisbitt, John and Aburdene, Patricia 1990. *Megatrends 2000: The New Directions for the 1990's*. New York: William Morrow

Neidhardt, Friedhelm and Rucht, Dieter 1991. 'The analysis of social movements: the state of the art and some perspectives for further research', in: D. Rucht (ed.), *Research on Social Movements*, pp. 421–64, Frankfurt: Campus Verlag

Nettl, J. P. and Roberston, R. 1968. *International Systems and the Modernization of Societies*. London: Faber and Faber

Nisbet, Robert 1969. *Social Change and History*. New York: Oxford University Press

Nisbet, Robert A. 1970. 'Developmentalism: a critical analysis', in: J. C. McKinney and E. A. Tiryakian (eds), *Theoretical Sociology*, pp. 167–204, New York: Appleton-Century-Crofts

Nisbet, Robert 1980. *History of the Idea of Progress*. New York: Basic Books

Novotny, Helga 1988. 'From the future to the extended present', in: G. Kirsch, P. Nijkam and K. Zimmerman (eds), *The Formulation of Time Preferences in a Multidisciplinary Perspective*, pp. 17–31, Aldershot: Gower

Nowak, Stefan 1987. 'Spoleczenstwo polskie drugiej polowy lat 80-tych' (Polish society in the second part of the 1980s). Warsaw: Polskie Towarzystwo Socjologiczne (mimeo)

Oberschall, Anthony 1973. *Social Conflict and Social Movements*. Englewood Cliffs: Prentice Hall

Oberschall, Anthony 1978. 'Theories of social conflict', *Annual Review of Sociology*, 4, pp. 291–315

O'Connell, James 1976. 'The concept of modernization', in: Black, pp. 13–24

Offe, Claus 1985. 'New social movements: challenging the boundaries of institutional politics', *Social Research*, 52, 4, pp. 817–68

Ollman, Bertell 1975. *Alienation: Marx's Conception of Man in Capitalist Society*. Cambridge: Cambridge University Press

Parsons, Talcott 1951. *Toward a General Theory of Action*. New York: Harper & Row

Parsons, Talcott 1964 [1951]. *The Social System*. Glencoe: Free Press

Parsons, Talcott 1966. *Societies: Evolutionary and Comparative Perspectives*. Englewood Cliffs: Prentice Hall

Parsons, Talcott 1970. 'Some considerations on the theory of social change', in: S. N. Eisenstadt (ed.), *Readings in Social Evolution and Development*, pp. 95–139, Oxford: Pergamon Press

Parsons, Talcott 1971. *The System of Modern Societies*. Englewood Cliffs: Prentice Hall

Persell, Caroline Hodges 1987. *Understanding Society*. New York: Harper & Row

Piaget, Jean 1971. *Structuralism*. New York: Harper & Row

Piven, F. F. and Cloward R. A. 1979. *Poor People's Movements*. New York: Vintage Books

Plamenatz, John 1975. *Karl Marx's Philosophy of Man*. Oxford: Clarendon Press

Plamenatz, John 1986 [1963]. *Man and Society*, vol. 2. Harlow: Longman

Popper, Karl R. 1950 [1945]. *The Open Society and Its Enemies*, vols 1 and 2, Princeton: Princeton University Press

Popper, Karl R. 1964 [1957]. *The Poverty of Historicism*. New York: Harper & Row

Popper, Karl R. 1968. 'Postscript: after twenty years', to *Logic of Scientific Discovery*, second rev. edn, New York: Harper & Row

Popper, Karl R. 1982. *Unended Quest: An Intellectual Autobiography*. London: Fontana/Collins

Prebisch, K. 1950. *The Economic Development of Latin America and Its Problems*. New York: UN Publications

Quadagno, Jill S. 1979. 'Paradigms in evolutionary theory: the sociobiological model of natural selection', *American Sociological Review*, 44 (February), pp. 100–9

Rex, John 1969. *Key Issues in Sociological Theory*. London: Routledge & Kegan Paul

Ridgeway, Cecilia L. 1983. *The Dynamics of Small Groups*. New York: St Martin's Press

Riesman, David 1961. *The Lonely Crowd*. New Haven: Yale University Press.

Ritzer, George, Kammeyer, Kenneth C. and Yetman, Norman R. 1987. *Sociology: Experiencing a Changing Society*. Boston: Allyn and Bacon

Robertson, Roland 1992. 'Globality, global culture, and images of world order', in: Haferkamp and Smelser (eds), pp. 395–411

Rostow, Walt W. 1960. *The Stages of Economic Growth: A Non-Communist Manifesto*. London: Cambridge University Press

Roy, William G. 1984. 'Class conflict and social change in historical perspective', *Annual Review of Sociology*, 10, pp. 483–506

Rubinstein, David 1981. *Marx and Wittgenstein*. London: Routledge & Kegan Paul

Rucht, Dieter 1988. 'Themes, logics, and arenas of social movements: a structural approach', in: L. Kriesberg (series Ed.), *International Social Movement Research*, vol. 1, pp. 305–28, Syracuse: JAI Press

Rudé, G. 1964. *The Crowd in History*. New York: Wiley

Rueschemeyer, Dietrich 1986. *Power and the Division of Labour*. Stanford: Standford University Press

Runciman, W. G. 1966. *Relative Deprivation and Social Justice*. Berkeley: California University Press

Sahlins, Marshall 1960. 'Evolution: specific and general', in: Sahlins and Service, pp. 12–44.

Sahlins, Marshall and Service E. (eds) 1960. *Evolution and Culture*. Ann Arbor: University of Michigan Press

Schafer, Wolf 1991. 'Global history: conceptual feasibility and environmental reality'. Stony Brook: SUNY (mimeo)

Segerstedt, Torgny T. 1966. *The Nature of Social Reality*. Stockholm: Svenska Bokforlaget

Shama, Simon 1989. *Citizens: A Chronicle of the French Revolution*. New York: Knopf

Shils, Edward 1968. 'Charisma', *The International Encyclopaedia of the Social Sciences*, vol. 2, pp. 386–90, New York: Macmillan

Shils, Edward 1981. *Tradition*. Chicago: University of Chicago Press

Skockpol, Theda 1977. 'Wallerstein's world capitalist system: a theoretical and historical critique', *American Journal of Sociology*, 82, 5, pp. 1075–90

Skockpol, Theda 1979. *States and Social Revolutions*. Cambridge: Cambridge University Press

Skockpol, Theda (ed.) 1984. *Vision and Method in Historical Sociology*. Cambridge: Cambridge University Press

Smelser, Neil J. 1959. *Social Change in the Industrial Revolution*. London: Routledge & Kegan Paul

Smelser, Neil J. 1962. *Theory of Collective Behavior*. New York: Free Press

Smelser, Neil J. 1968. *Essays in Sociological Explanation*. Englewood Cliffs: Prentice Hall

Smelser, Neil J. 1973 [1967]. 'Processes of social change', in: N. J. Smelser (ed.), *Sociology: An Introduction*, pp. 709–62, New York: Wiley

Smelser, Neil J. 1992. 'External and internal factors in theories of social change', in: Haferkamp and Smelser (eds), pp. 369–94

Smith, Anthony D. 1973. *The Concept of Social Change: A Critique of the Functionalist Theory of Social Change*. London: Routledge & Kegan Paul

Smith, Anthony D. 1976. *Social Change: Social Theory and Historical Process*. London: Longman

Snow, D. A., Burke R. E, Worden, S. K. and Benford, R. D. 1986. 'Frame alignment processes, micromobilization, and movement participation', *American Sociological Review*, 51, pp. 464–81

Sorokin, Pitirim A. 1937. *Social and Cultural Dynamics*, vols. 1–4. New York: American Book Company

Sorokin, Pitirim A. 1963. 'Reply to my critics', in: P. J. Allen (ed.), *Pitirim A. Sorokin in Review*, Durham NC: Duke University Press

Sorokin, Pitirim A. 1966. *Sociological Theories of Today*. New York: Harper & Row

Sorokin, Pitirim 1967 [1925]. *The Sociology of Revolution*. New York: Howard Fertig

Sorokin, Pitirim and Merton Robert K. 1937. 'Social time. A methodological and functional analysis', *American Journal of Sociology*, 42, 5, pp. 615–29

Spencer, Herbert 1893. *Principles of Sociology*, vols 1–3. London: Williams and Norgate

Spencer, Herbert 1972. *On Social Evolution*. Chicago: University of Chicago Press

Spengler, Oswald 1939 [1918]. *The Decline of the West*. New York: Knopf

Steward, Julian H. 1979 [1955]. *Theory of Culture Change*. Urbana: University of Illinois Press

Strasser, Hermann and Randall, Susan C. 1981. *An Introduction to Theories of Social Change*. London: Routledge & Kegan Paul

Sullivan, S. 1989. 'Refining the revolution', *Newsweek*, 20 February

Swingewood, Allan 1975. *Marx and Modern Social Theory*. London: Macmillan

Szacki, Jerzy 1980. *Spotkania z Utopia (Encounters with Utopia)*. Warsaw: Iskry

Szalai, Alexander (ed.) 1972. *The Use of Time*. Paris: Mouton

Sztompka, Piotr 1974. *System and Function*. New York: Academic Press

Sztompka, Piotr 1979. *Sociological Dilemmas*. New York: Academic Press

Sztompka, Piotr 1981. 'The dialectics of spontaneity and planning in sociological theory', in: Ulf Himmelstrand (ed.), *Spontaneity and Planning in Social Development*, pp. 15–28, Beverly Hills: Sage

Sztompka, Piotr 1983. 'Social development: the dialectics of theory and action', *Reports on Philosophy*, 7, pp. 79–98

Sztompka, Piotr 1984a. 'The global crisis and the reflexiveness of the social system', *International Journal of Comparative Sociology*, 25, 1–2, pp. 45–58

Sztompka, Piotr 1984b. 'On the change of social laws', *Reports on Philosophy*, 8, pp. 33–40

Sztompka, Piotr 1986. 'The renaissance of historical orientation in sociology', *International Sociology*, 1, 3, pp. 321–37

Sztompka, Piotr 1987. 'Social movements: structures in statu nascendi', *The Polish Sociological Bulletin*, 2, pp. 5–26 (reprinted in: *Revue internationale de sociologie*, 2 (1989), pp. 124–55

Sztompka, Piotr 1988 [1984]. 'The social functions of defeat', in: L. Kriesberg and B. Misztal (eds), *Research in Social Movements, Conflicts and Change*, vol. 10, pp. 183–92, Greenwich, Conn.: JAI Press

Sztompka, Piotr 1989. 'Social movements: structures *in statu nascendi*', *Revue Internationale de Sociologie*, 2, pp. 124–55

Sztompka, Piotr 1990. 'Agency and progress; the idea of progress and changing theories of change', in: J. Alexander and P. Sztompka (eds), *Rethinking Progress*, pp. 247–63, London: Unwin Hyman

Sztompka, Piotr 1991a. 'The intangibles and imponderables of the transition to democracy', *Studies in Comparative Communism*, 24, 3, pp. 295–311

Sztompka, Piotr 1991b. *Society in Action: The Theory of Social Becoming*. Cambridge: Polity Press and Chicago: University of Chicago Press

Sztompka, Piotr 1992. 'Dilemmas of the great transition'. Cambridge, MA: Harvard Center for European Studies (Working Paper Series, no. 19)

Tarkowska, Elzbieta 1987. *Czas w spoleczenstwie* (Time in society). Wroclaw: Ossolineum

Tarrow, Sidney 1985. 'Struggling to reform: social movements and policy change during cycles of protest'. Ithaca: Cornell University: Center for International Studies (Occasional Paper no. 15)

Taylor, Stan 1984. *Social Science and Revolutions*. London: Macmillan

Thompson, M., Ellis, R, and Wildavsky, A. 1989. *Cultural Theory*. Berkeley: California University Press

Tilly, Charles 1978. *From Mobilization to Revolution*. Reading, MA: Addison-Wesley

Tilly, Charles 1979a. 'Repertoires of contention in America and Britain, 1750–1830', in: M. Zald and J. D. McCarthy (eds), *The Dynamics of Social Movements*, pp. 126–55, Cambridge, MA: Winthrop

Tilly, Charles 1979b. 'Social movements and national politics'. Ann Arbor: Center for Research on Social Organization (Working Paper no. 197) (mimeo)

Tilly, Charles 1981. *As Sociology Meets History*. New York: Academic Press

Tilly, Charles 1984. *Big Structures, Large Processes, Huge Comparisons*. New York: Russell Sage Foundation

Tilly, Charles 1985. 'Social movements, old and new' New York: Center for Studies of Social Change, NSSR (Working Paper no. 20) (mimeo)

Tilly, Charles, Tilly, L. and Tilly, R. 1975. *The Rebellious Century (1830–1930)*. Cambridge, MA: Harvard University Press

Tipps, Dean C. 1976. 'Modernization theory and the comparative study of Societies: a critical perspective', in: Black, pp. 62–88

Tiryakian, Edward A. (ed.) 1963. *Sociological Theory, Values and Sociocultural Change: Essays in Honor of Pitirim Sorokin*. New York: Free Press

Tiryakian, Edward A. 1985a. 'The changing centers of modernity', in: E. Cohen, M. Lissak and U. Almagor (eds), *Comparative Social Dynamics*, pp. 131–47, Boulder: Westview Press

Tiryakian, Edward A. 1985b. 'From Durkheim to Managua: revolutions as religious revivals'. Savannah: Society for the Scientific Study of Religion (mimeo)

Tiryakian, Edward A. 1985c. 'On the significance of de-differentiation', in: Shmuel N. Eisenstadt and H. J. Helle (eds), *Macro-sociological Theory*, pp. 118–34, Beverly Hills: Sage

Tiryakian, Edward A. 1991. 'Modernisation: exhumetur in pace', *International Sociology*, 6, 2, pp. 165–80

Tiryakian, Edward A. 1992. 'Dialectics of modernity: reenchantment and de-differentiation as processes', in: Haferkamp and Smelser (eds.), pp. 78–96

Tocqueville, Alexis de 1945. *Democracy in America*, vols 1 and 2. New York: Knopf

Tocqueville, Alexis de 1955 [1856]. *The Old Regime and the French Revolution*. New York: Doubleday Anchor

Toffler, Alvin 1970. *Future Shock*. London: Bodley Head

Toffler, Alvin 1975. *The Eco-Spasm Report*. New York: Bantam Books

Tominaga, Ken'ichi 1985. 'Typology in the methodological approach to the study of social change', in: S. N. Eisenstadt and H. J. Helle, *Macro-Sociological Theory (Perspectives on Sociological Theory*, vol. 1), pp. 168–96, London: Sage

Topolski, Jerzy 1974. 'Aktywistyczna koncepcja procesu dziejowego' (Activist conception of historical process), in: J. Kmita (ed.), *Metodologiczne implikacje epistemologii marksistowskiej*, pp. 309–24, Warsaw: PWN (Polish Scientific Publishers)

Topolski, Jerzy 1978. *Rozumienie historii* (Understanding history). Warsaw: PIW (Polish Editorial Institute)

Topolski, Jerzy 1990. *Wolnosc i przymus w tworzeniu historii* (Freedom and coercion in the making of history). Warsaw: Panstwowy Instytut Wydawniczy

Touraine, Alain 1974. *The Post-industrial Society*. London: Wildwood

Touraine, Alain 1977. *The Self-production of Society*. Chicago: University of Chicago Press

Touraine, Alain 1981. *The Voice and the Eye*. Cambridge: Cambridge University Press

Touraine, Alain 1984. *Le Retour de l'acteur*. Paris: Fayard

Touraine, Alain 1985. 'Social movements and social change', in: Orlando Fals Borda (ed.), *The Challenge of Social Change*, pp. 77–92, London: Sage

Toynbee, Arnold 1934–61. *Study of History*, 12 vol. London: Oxford University Press

Toynbee, Arnold 1948. *Civilization on Trial*. New York: Oxford University Press

Toynbee, Arnold J. 1963. 'Sorokin's philosophy of history', in: P. J. Allen (ed.), *Pitirim A. Sorokin in Review*, pp. 67–94, Durham NC: Duke University Press

Trevor-Roper, Hugh 1985. 'The invention of tradition: the Highland tradition of Scotland', in: Hobsbawm and Ranger, pp. 15–41

Trevor-Roper, H. 1989. 'Europe's new order', *The Independent Magazine*, 30 December, pp. 14–15

Tucker, D. F. B. 1980. *Marxism and Individualism*. Oxford: Basil Blackwell

Turner, Ralph H. 1987. 'Social movement theory: bridging the gap between collective behavior and resource mobilization'. Los Angeles: UCLA (mimeo)

Turner, R. and Killian, L. M. 1972 [1957]. *Collective Behavior*. Englewood Cliffs: Prentice Hall

Useem, Bert 1980. 'Solidarity model, breakdown model, and the Boston anti-busing movement', *American Sociological Review*, 45 (June), pp. 357–69

Vico, Giambattista 1961 [1725]. *The New Science of Giambattista Vico*. New York: Doubleday Anchor

Wallerstein, Immanuel 1974. *The Modern World-System I.* New York: Academic Press

Wallerstein, Immanuel 1980. *The Modern World-System II.* New York: Academic Press

Wallerstein, Immanuel 1983 [1979]. *The Capitalist World-Economy.* Cambridge: Cambridge University Press

Wallerstein, Immanuel 1989. *The Modern World-System III.* San Diego: Academic Press

Wallerstein, Immanuel 1991. *Unthinking Social Science: The Limits of Nineteenth-Century Paradigms.* Cambridge: Polity Press

Weber, Max 1947. *The Theory of Social and Economic Organization.* London: Routledge & Kegan Paul

Weber, Max 1954 [1922]. *Max Weber on Law, Economy and Society,* ed. M. Rheinstein. Cambridge: Cambridge University Press

Weber, Max 1958 [1920–21]. *The Protestant Ethic and the Spirit of Capitalism.* New York: Charles Scribner's Sons

Weber, Max 1963. *The Sociology of Religion.* Boston: Houghton

Weber, Max 1985. *Selections in Translation,* ed. W. G. Runciman. Cambridge: Cambridge University Press.

Weinberg, Ian 1976. 'The problem of convergence of industrial societies: a critical look at the state of a theory', in: Black, pp. 353–67

White, Leslie 1949. *The Science of Culture.* New York: Grove

White, Leslie 1959. *The Evolution of Culture.* New York: McGraw Hill

Whitehead, Alfred N. 1925. *Science and the Modern World.* New York: Macmillan

Williams, Robin M., Jr 1970 [1951]. *American Society.* New York: Knopf

Wolf, E. R. 1969. *Peasant Wars of the Twentieth Century.* New York: Harper & Row

Wood, Frederick A. 1913. *The Influence of Monarchs.* New York

Wood, James L. and Jackson, M. 1982. *Social Movements: Development, Participation and Dynamics.* Belmont: Wadsworth

Worsley, Peter 1984. *The Three Worlds: Culture and World Development.* London: Weidenfeld and Nicolson

Young, Louise M. 1939. *Thomas Carlyle and the Art of History.* Philadelphia: University of Pennsylvania Press

Young, Michael 1988. *The Metronomic Society: Natural Rhythms and Human Timetables.* Cambridge, MA: Harvard University Press

Young, M. and Schuller, T. (eds) 1988. *The Rhythms of Society.* London: Routledge

Zald, Mayer N. and Berger, M. A. 1978. 'Social movements in organizations: coup d'état, insurgency, and mass movements', *American Journal of Sociology,* 83, 4, pp. 823–61

Zald, M., and Useem, B. 1982. 'Movements and countermovements: losely coupled conflict'. Ann Arbor: CRSO Working Paper no. 276 (mimeo)

Zeitlin, Irving M. 1981. 'Karl Marx: aspects of his social thought and their contemporary relevance', in: B. Rhea, (ed.), *The Future of the Sociological Classics*, pp. 1–15, London: Allen & Unwin

Zerubavel, Eviatar 1981. *Hidden Rhythms: Schedules and Calendars in Social Life*. Chicago: University of Chicago Press

Zerubavel, Eviatar 1990. 'Private-time and public-time', in: Hassard, pp. 168–77

Znaniecki, Florian 1971. *Nauki o kulturze (The sciences of culture)*. Warsaw: Polish Scientific Publishers

Zollschan, George K. and Hirsch, Walter (eds) 1964. *Explorations in Social Change*. Boston: Houghton Mifflin

Zurcher, L. A. and Snow D. A. 1981. 'Collective behavior: social movements', in: M. Rosenberg and R. H. Turner (eds), *Social Psychology: Sociological Perspectives*, pp. 447–82, New York: Basic Books

Index

abandoned historical possibilities, 293

Abrams, P., 207–8, 225

achievement motivation, 242–3 *see also* innovational personality, modern personality

action, 214–15;
  in Marx's theory, 164, 165–6

active society, 39, 194, 285

Adam, B., 13, 41, 42, 43, 44, 49, 52

adaptive upgrading, 120–1, 134

agency, 22, 37–8, 127, 128, 138, 176, 208, 210, 217, 301, 308;
  concept of, 217–18
  embodiments of, 191–3
  theories of, 193–200

agential coefficient, 200 *see also* historical coefficient

ahistorism, 204;
  historiosophical, 204
  presentist, 204

Alexander, J. C., 33, 78, 123, 124, 130, 137

alienation, 78, 167–8, 279;
  of labour, 167

amplification of change, 258

analytical dualism, 199 *see also* duality of structure

anomie, 79, 241

anti-globalism, 95

anti-traditionalism, 67

Archer, M., 199–200, 216, 218, 225

authoritarian personality, 241

axionormative order, 250

bifurcation points in history, 271 *see also* field of possibilities

boomerang effect, 20, 140, 257 *see also* self-destroying prophecy, unintended consequences

Buckley, W., 17, 193–4

Burns, T., 101, 126, 127, 128, 197–9, 250, 278, 294

capitalism, 70–1, 72, 90, 170, 236, 280;
  spirit of, 236–7
  see also world-system theory

Carlyle, T., 263–4, 266

charisma, 268–9

charismatic authority, 269

charismatic person, 269

civilizations, 145–9

class antagonism, 161, 171

class conflict, 161, 171

class consciousness, 171 *see also* social class (for itself), social consciousness

class contradiction, 161, 170

collective action, 60, 194, 195;
  forms of, 306, 316
  see also social movement

Collins, R., 70, 73, 201, 236

Comte, A., 3, 8, 26, 32, 70, 101–2

convergence theory, 13, 134–5

counterfactual questions, 265

countermovements, 283–5

counter-revolution, 310

creativeness, 148, 164, 166, 168, 194, 196, 304

creolization of culture, 94 *see also* globalization

crisis, 34, 303

culture mentality, 151